Self-Organising Multi-Agent Systems
Algorithmic Foundations of Cyber-Anarcho-Socialism

Self-Organising Multi-Agent Systems
Algorithmic Foundations of Cyber-Anarcho-Socialism

JEREMY PITT

Imperial College London, UK

NEW JERSEY · LONDON · SINGAPORE · BEIJING · SHANGHAI · HONG KONG · TAIPEI · CHENNAI · TOKYO

Published by

World Scientific Publishing Europe Ltd.
57 Shelton Street, Covent Garden, London WC2H 9HE
Head office: 5 Toh Tuck Link, Singapore 596224
USA office: 27 Warren Street, Suite 401-402, Hackensack, NJ 07601

Library of Congress Control Number: 2021943336

British Library Cataloguing-in-Publication Data
A catalogue record for this book is available from the British Library.

SELF-ORGANISING MULTI-AGENT SYSTEMS
Algorithmic Foundations of Cyber-Anarcho-Socialism

Copyright © 2022 by World Scientific Publishing Europe Ltd.

All rights reserved. This book, or parts thereof, may not be reproduced in any form or by any means, electronic or mechanical, including photocopying, recording or any information storage and retrieval system now known or to be invented, without written permission from the Publisher.

For photocopying of material in this volume, please pay a copying fee through the Copyright Clearance Center, Inc., 222 Rosewood Drive, Danvers, MA 01923, USA. In this case permission to photocopy is not required from the publisher.

ISBN 978-1-80061-042-2 (hardcover)
ISBN 978-1-80061-043-9 (ebook for institutions)
ISBN 978-1-80061-044-6 (ebook for individuals)

For any available supplementary material, please visit
https://www.worldscientific.com/worldscibooks/10.1142/Q0307#t=suppl

Desk Editors: Balasubramanian Shanmugam/Michael Beale/Shi Ying Koe

Typeset by Stallion Press
Email: enquiries@stallionpress.com

For Sophie and Stephanie

ANDY: Look at that. An ordinary spoon. I'd never noticed it before ... It just sits in a drawer. Out of the drawer ... Into the peas ... Stir the custard ... Into the wash, out o' the wash ... Up on the hooks with all the other spoons ... And all the time, just waiting for the fatal day when it'd drastically alter the course of a man's life.

Life is Sweet (Dir. Mike Leigh, 1990)

Preface

The primary difficulty with writing a Preface to your book is the pressure to produce a text that is, or at least tries to be: (a) witty, (b) profound, (c) grateful, (d) all three, or (e) other. Obviously I have had to go for (e).

This book has been long in the making, strange in the writing, and grown in the telling. Long in the making, because it pretty much started with being admonished as an undergraduate for writing self-modifying code and 30 years later being appointed to a Chair for more or less doing precisely that. I first started working on multi-agent systems in the mid-1990s, so more than 20 years ago; some work that has made it into this book was done as part of the EU ALFEBIITE project 2000–2004; and the first paper that I published which referred to self-organisation was in about 2008, so still more than 10 years ago.

Strange in the writing, because it has been bookended by the first and second London lockdowns as a result of the COVID-19 pandemic.

Although I had proposed and taught an M.Eng. Master's course on Self-Organising Multi-Agent Systems (SOMAS) in the Autumn Term of 2019, and had intended to write a supporting textbook, I only really got the time and space in the aftermath of the first wave of the COVID-19 pandemic and during my own convalescence from it. For the support and encouragement during that "unprecedented" (drink! drink! drink!) period, I remain deeply grateful to my Personal Physician and my Lockdown Buddy, and only mildly resentful towards the Lockdown Cat, who either regards my laptop as competition for prime sleep estate, or thinks that I still need help with the typing (and if the latter, some might argue he's kind of got a point...). Anyway, he is still there trying to "help" me even as I am (trying) to finish this.

And finally, grown in the telling, because, well, this is research, and the knowledge we have has increased while the book was being written, the wicked social problems we face in the Digital Society have become increasingly complex, and my opinions on some of the subjects broached herein have become increasingly sharp. It is to be hoped that some of this insight is expressed coherently and intelligibly in the concluding section of each chapter. These can be pretty much summarised as (spoiler alert):

- If you set up a strategic interaction where selfishness is the rational choice, you will see selfishness; if you layer a meta-game on top to make cooperation the rational choice, you will see cooperation;
- Values and preferences are not an infallible, unquestionable and timeless product of votes;
- If somebody says to you: "there is no completely fair way of doing it", tell them "yes there is";
- Legitimate governance is only possible with the active and revocable consent of the governed; and
- We (as a species) evolved the capacity to engage in politics because it provided us with the means to solve collective action problems and live together (better) at scale.

All the same, just because I have given all the ending(s) away in the free preview, doesn't mean you *don't* have to buy the book. Publishing house and an aged cat to support on my frugal pension, and all that.

This is the end result. Perhaps it is not so often that a book starts with its own critique, but in the best spirit of Flawed Masterpieces, it is the product of a career into which I have poured heart and soul, and dragged quite a fair few friends and colleagues along with me. But, if all political careers end in failure, perhaps all academic careers can only reach way-points on the route to imperfection, because there is no terminating state; so by my own admission the current volume is by no means perfect (although if the tech companies can have 'generations', the publishers got there first with 'editions', so maybe this is just JeremyBook (first generation)).

However, if this were a football match between UndeniablyFlawed City and RedeemingFeatures United, RedeemingFeatures United would stage a come back from 3-0 down at half-time to pull off a scarcely credible 4-3 victory, despite conceding a first-minute own goal to PersonalityCrisis, conceding twice more in the first half to SpreadTooThin and ObviousBias, and playing most of the book with only ten men, after Prolog, who was shown a yellow card for a bad infinite loop in Chapter 1, got a straight red in Chapter 4 for a shocking two-footed lunge on the assignment operator.

What is meant by this? Just that it started off as textbook, as stated, but it's not sure if it wants to be a textbook, a research monograph, or a memoir in the finest spirit of *Surely You're Joking, Mr Feynman*. Maybe it is all three; maybe it is none of them. But it certainly covers a lot of ground, and so the risk of treating some subjects too slightly, and some aspects not at all, and by half-time (or the end of Chapter 5) it is probably pretty clear where I am going with this, and whose side I am going to be on. However, in the fullness of chapters, it is to be hoped that the inter-disciplinarity and unconventionality will have persuaded you to share the joy in pottering among and marvelling at so many extraordinary ideas and results from game theory, social choice theory, psychology, philosophy and political science, and their formalisation in algorithms; that Qu-Prolog, having seemingly done nothing except simulate The Cat since Chapter 1 scores a late equaliser with SimDemopolis, and that a goalmouth scramble sees a last minute winner, because Democracy By Design wasn't just fascinating and great fun to do, *it is really important to the 'real world', too.*

Speaking of which, there are two bits of serendipity which are worth mentioning. The first is that in 2010 I got called to do jury service. I took a book with me: *Governing the Commons*, by Elinor Ostrom. An ordinary book, I'd never really noticed it before: on the shelf, off the shelf, back up on the shelf with all the other books. And all the time, just waiting for the fatal day when it'd drastically alter the course of a man's life. Because I spent most of the two weeks studying the principles in the book and implementing them in the prototype for the system described in Chapter 6. One judge even appointed me foreperson of the jury because he'd seen me taking copious notes; I guess he thought it was about the case, but actually it was Prolog predicates that I was going to code up that night. Ahem. Hopefully I have redeemed myself in the eyes of Justice with Chapter 7; but no jury service, no Chapter 6; no Chapter 6, no book.

The second is the 'Brexit' referendum on the UK's withdrawal from the European Union. If that referendum had gone in favour of 'remain', it is unlikely that Chapter 10 would have been written, and certainly not in this style. No lost referendum, no Chapter 10; no Chapter 10, no book. But, on the whole, I would rather the UK would have stayed in the European Union and foregone having to write the final chapter.

And still on the subject of the 'real world', it should perhaps be noted that the second section of each chapter starts with a motivating example based on an experience that presumably we can all relate to: sharing a common space such as an office or a house. It should be stressed that in these examples, any similarity to actual persons or actual events, is purely coincidental; even the one in Chapter 6, where they have all signed their names, and especially the one in Chapter 7, which in no way refers to anyone who used to wear his academic gown on Commemoration Day only for local bragging rather than institutional respect. Then he would swank about the department, swank about the common room, and swank about the campus; no wonder everywhere he went people would say: "Gee, what a swanker". Actually, the Ministry of Culinary Affairs of Chapter 10 is (perhaps surprisingly) fictitious, but the legislation on which it is based on is all too depressingly real.

There are many people to thank who were directly or indirectly responsible for my work in general or this book in particular. First and foremost, I am deeply grateful to Abe Mamdani and Jim Cunningham, for showing me how to do "this stuff", and how you could be successful at doing "this stuff" and still be a nice person. It remains a cause of considerable sadness that Abe is no longer with us.

My wildly peripatetic career has occupied nine offices in three buildings in two departments, all covered by a circle with a radius of less than 100 metres. But this means that I enjoyed the benefits of working with some influential scientists and engineers from both Computing and Electrical Engineering: Igor Aleksander, Keith Clark, Sue Eisenbach, Chris Hankin, Bob Kowalski, Kin Leung, Jeff Magee, Patrick Purcell, Marek Sergot, Richard Syms and Bob Spence. From outside Imperial College, the ideas in this book took shape, and were sharpened by inter-disciplinary collaborations with Andrew Jones (philosophy), Andrzej Nowak (psychology), Josiah Ober (political science) and Katina Michael (humanity). Much of the last four chapters is due to joint work with or inspired by them, and their insight into social processes. I am also grateful, for various and many kindnesses and collaborations, to Makoto Amamiya, Jon Bing, Cristiano Castelfranchi, John Henry Clippinger, Simon Dobson, Steve McArthur, Christian Müller-Schloer, Mihaela Ulieru and Pallapa Venkataram. My thanks also to Peter Robinson for development and support of Qu-Prolog, which has been quite the revelation.

I am grateful for belonging to some 'communities' and the collective action they produced. Firstly, there is the research partnership that worked on a series of EU Coordination Actions that ran from about 2008 to 2016, including Emma Hart (thanks for all the parkrun/coffee/Guardian Quiz combos), Ben Paechter and Jennifer Willies at Edinburgh Napier University, Callum Egan for continually making me look good on video (no small challenge), and Giacomo Cabri, Gusz Eiben and Alois Ferscha at partner institutes. Secondly, there is the Editorial Board of *IEEE Technology & Society Magazine*, Roba Abbas, Terri Bookman, Katina Michael, Kristina Milanovic and Christine Perakslis; in particular Terri who somehow manages to do a serious job and be completely hilarious at the same time, and Katina whose generosity of spirit is seemingly boundless and from which so many of us benefit so richly. Thirdly, there is my involvement as a Trustee with the Association for Information Technology Trust (AITT), and here I have enjoyed and benefitted from working with Igor Aleksander, Catherine Griffiths, Frank Land and Carsten Sørensen.

I am equally grateful to a number of friendships and research partnerships which have inspired and/or sustained me over the years, especially Stephen Cranefield, Joao Cunha, Marcello D'Agostino (the Godfather), Yiannis Demiris (Dude! you know why), T. Iwao-San, Peter Lewis, Maite López-Sánchez, Steve Marsh (thanks for the eponymous deck), Ana Paiva (I agree, Abe would be delighted) and Jan-Philipp Steghöfer. I have also benefitted from working with a number of extremely talented Research Fellows and PostDocs (or they were at the time), including Dídac Busquets, Patricia Charlton, Victoria Lush, Régis Riveret, Magda Roszczynska-Kurasinska and Agnieszka Rychwalska.

I have also had the profound good fortune to have worked with a particular group of outstanding and remarkable young (or they were when they started) people otherwise labelled as 'my' Ph.D. students. Unfortunately, only some of the work of some of them has found its way into the book, so it would be unfair to identify some when I am so grateful to them all, as it is everybody's work that contributes to a group and a research programme. However, my thoughts inevitably turn to the families of Petar Goulev and Brendan Neville; I am sure they are both deeply missed. I travelled a lot with Brendan, and he implemented the first version of PreSage (PreSage-2 is described in Chapter 1) and developed the trust framework presented in Chapter 8. He was a valued friend as much as a trusted colleague.

For the production of the book, I am grateful to Lance Sucharov, my Publisher at World Scientific Publishing, for giving me a third go; and Michael Beale, the Production Editor, for his considerable patience and help in hauling the manuscript over the line. I would also like to thank Rajesh Babu for his LaTeX assistance and Balasubramanian Shanmugam for the smooth project management. Some chapters are partially based on previously published material and thanks to the Association for Computing Machinery (ACM), the British Computer Society (BCS), the Institute of Electrical and Electronics Engineers (IEEE) and Springer Publishers for permission to re-produce. The original sources are referenced in the text. Particular thanks to IEEE President Ray Liu of the University of Maryland.

Some of the work in Chapter 9 was developed while being supported by Leverhulme Trust Research Fellowship (RF-2016-451) and a University of Otago William Evans Visiting Fellowship, hosted by

Stephen Cranefield, for which many thanks (and for the accommodation at Abbey College). Some of the work in Chapter 10 was developed while on sabbatical at Florida Atlantic University and Edinburgh Napier University, and many thanks also to my hosts at those institutions, Andrzej Nowak and Emma Hart.

I would additionally like to thank many friends and colleagues who helped, read and/or commented on the text, including Alexander Artikis, Rui Cardoso, Stephen Cranefield, Peter Lewis, Maite Lopez-Sanchez, Steve Marsh, Kristina Milanovic, Simon Powers and Julia Schaumeier (there is still insufficient confectionery). Any residual imperfections are mine alone. Thanks are also due to Dan Goodman for inspiring the subtitle; to all the students who took the SOMAS course in 2019 and gave me useful feedback (especially those who participated in the EdTech Workshop); and to all those students who took the course during the weirdness of Autumn 2020. Thanks to Ezgi Ozyilkan for commentary and Noé Guisset for text corrections, and particular thanks to Asimina Mertzani for suggesting the Hands-Up Protocol on Teams that let me know that I wasn't just sitting with my back to The Cat talking to a pane of glass.

Everyone needs some release away from work, and here I would like to thank everyone at Hittenhope for the elite football and Brentford for the ... football; West Middlesex golf club and those with whom I played *golf'*; Rebecca Burton, my Pilates instructor (slash Guardian Angel); Salie Lewie of the Alan Winner Academy for the Tai Chi Chuan, Qi Gong, and welcoming of paradox; and parkrun for, well, runs in various parks all over the planet and for demonstrating one of Andrzej's theories.

And finally, my deepest gratitude of all goes to the whole family: my parents Jan and Mike, Jennifer, Sophie and Stephanie (and OK, OK, Doogle, a bit). But truly I must have done something right in a past life to have been so generously rewarded in this one.

Jeremy Pitt
London, 2021

About the Author

Jeremy Pitt is Professor of Intelligent and Self-Organising Systems in the Department of Electrical and Electronic Engineering at Imperial College London. He received a B.Sc. in Computer Science from the University of Manchester and a Ph.D. in Computing from Imperial College (University of London). He has been teaching and researching on Artificial Intelligence and Human–Computer Interaction for over 30 years, where his research programme has used computational logic to specify algorithmic models of social processes, with applications in cyber-physical and socio-technical systems, especially for sustainable, fair and legitimate self-governance. He has collaborated on research projects extensively in Europe as well as in India and New Zealand, and has held visiting professorial positions in Italy, Japan and Poland. He has published more than 200 articles in journals, conferences and workshops, and this work has received several Best Paper awards. He is a trustee of the AITT (Association for Information Technology Trust), a Fellow of the BCS (British Computer Society) and of the IET (Institution of Engineering and Technology), and in 2018 was appointed as Editor-in-Chief of *IEEE Technology and Society Magazine*.

Contents

Preface   vii

About the Author   xv

Part I: Foundations   1

Chapter 1.   Multi-Agent Systems   3
- 1.1   Introduction   3
- 1.2   Example: The SmartHouse   6
  - 1.2.1   Community Energy Systems   6
  - 1.2.2   Three Contextual Issues   8
- 1.3   Open Systems and Agent Societies   10
  - 1.3.1   Open Systems   10
  - 1.3.2   Open Societies and Agent Societies   13
- 1.4   Methodology: Sociologically-Inspired Computing   14
- 1.5   Autonomous Agents and Multi-Agent Systems . . .   16
  - 1.5.1   Autonomous Agents   17
  - 1.5.2   Multi-Agent Systems   22
- 1.6   Agent Communication   23
  - 1.6.1   The Contract-Net Protocol   23
  - 1.6.2   Standardisation and FIPA ACL   25
  - 1.6.3   Institutionalised Power   26
- 1.7   Specification of Agent Societies   28
  - 1.7.1   Norm-Governed MAS (NG-MAS)   28

	1.7.2	Dynamic NG-MAS	29
	1.7.3	Event Calculus	32
1.8		Simulation and Animation	35
1.9		Summary	39

Chapter 2. Self-Organising Systems — 41

2.1		Introduction	41
2.2		Example: Same As It Ever Was	43
2.3		Emergence	45
	2.3.1	Swarms	45
	2.3.2	Cellular Automata	46
	2.3.3	Self-Organisation	48
	2.3.4	Planned Emergence	50
2.4		The Self and The Organisation	51
	2.4.1	The Self	52
	2.4.2	The Organisation	53
2.5		The Dimensions of Self-Organisation	56
	2.5.1	An Analytic Framework for Self-Organisation	56
	2.5.2	The General Setting for Self-Organisation	56
2.6		The Mechanics of Change	59
	2.6.1	Parameter Modification	60
	2.6.2	Policy Modification	62
2.7		Summary	66

Part II: Strategic Interaction — 69

Chapter 3. Game Theory — 71

3.1		Introduction	71
3.2		Example: The Kitchen Stand-Off	73
3.3		Game Theory: Terminology and Representation	74
	3.3.1	Utility and Preferences	74
	3.3.2	Games: Matrix Form and Extensive Form	76
3.4		Solution Concepts	78
	3.4.1	Dominant Strategy	78
	3.4.2	Nash Equilibrium Strategy	78

	3.4.3	Pareto Optimal Strategy	79
	3.4.4	Social Welfare Maximisation	80
	3.4.5	The Kitchen Stand-Off, Revisited	81
	3.4.6	The Hawk–Dove Game, aka Chicken	83
3.5	The Prisoners' Dilemma		85
	3.5.1	Analysing the Prisoners' Dilemma	85
	3.5.2	The Iterated Prisoners' Dilemma	87
	3.5.3	A Slight Digression on Rationality	89
3.6	Other 2-Player Games		90
	3.6.1	(Pure) Coordination Game	90
	3.6.2	Battle of the Sexes	91
	3.6.3	Stag Hunt Game	91
	3.6.4	Ultimatum Game	93
	3.6.5	Focal Point Games	93
3.7	Beyond 2-Player Games		94
	3.7.1	n-Player Games	94
	3.7.2	Coalitions and the Shapley Value	96
	3.7.3	Evolutionary Game Theory	96
3.8	Summary		97

Chapter 4. Social Choice Theory — 101

4.1	Introduction		101
4.2	Example: The Big Breakfast Menu Variations		102
4.3	The Vocabulary of Social Choice Theory		103
	4.3.1	Basics	104
	4.3.2	Aggregation Rules	104
	4.3.3	Some 'Nice' Properties	106
	4.3.4	The Condorcet Winner and Condorcet Loser	108
	4.3.5	Example: Skulduggery in the Roman Senate	110
4.4	Voting Procedures		112
	4.4.1	Running Example	112
	4.4.2	Procedures	112
	4.4.3	The D'Hondt Method	116
4.5	Paradox Abounds		117
	4.5.1	Condorcet's Paradoxes	117
	4.5.2	Yet More Paradoxical Results	119
	4.5.3	Arrow's Impossibility Theorem	120

		4.5.4	Gibbard–Satterthwaite Theorem 121
		4.5.5	Comparison of Voting Methods 122
	4.6	A Voting Protocol 123
		4.6.1	Actions and Fluents 124
		4.6.2	Institutionalised Powers 124
		4.6.3	Permission and Obligation 126
		4.6.4	Implementation Route 128
	4.7	Summary and Conclusions 128

Chapter 5. Alternative Dispute Resolution — 131

5.1 Introduction 131
5.2 Example: The Missing Sausage Quarrel 133
5.3 Alternative Dispute Resolution 134
5.4 Test Domain 136
  5.4.1 Mass-Participation Content Creations 136
  5.4.2 Colored Trails 138
  5.4.3 Coloured Trials 139
  5.4.4 Experimental Parameters in Coloured Trials 141
5.5 Error Toleration: Access Control 141
  5.5.1 Basics of Access Control 142
  5.5.2 Fluents, Actions and Institutionalised Power 143
  5.5.3 Permission and Obligation 145
  5.5.4 Sanction 146
5.6 Error Retrospection: Regulatory Compliance 148
  5.6.1 Token Surrender 148
  5.6.2 Location Movement 149
  5.6.3 Communication: Token Exchange 150
  5.6.4 Outcome 152
5.7 Error Recovery: Alternative Dispute Resolution . . . 152
  5.7.1 Informal Specification 152
  5.7.2 Phase I: Initiation 154
  5.7.3 Phase II: ADR Method Selection 155
  5.7.4 Phase III: Execution 158
5.8 Summary 159

Chapter 6. Ostrom Institution Theory — 163

6.1 Introduction 163

6.2	Example: The Common-Pool Refrigerator		165
6.3	Collective Action		167
	6.3.1	Three Types of Collective Action	167
	6.3.2	Common-Pool Resource Management	169
	6.3.3	Linear Public Good Games	170
6.4	Self-Governing (Ostrom) Institutions		172
	6.4.1	Collective Action: Analytically and Empirically	173
	6.4.2	Self-Governing Institutions	174
	6.4.3	Institutional Analysis and Development	177
6.5	Self-Organising Electronic Institutions		179
	6.5.1	Structural and Functional Specification	179
	6.5.2	Procedural Specification	182
	6.5.3	Self-Governing Institutions and Sustainable MAS	183
6.6	Boundaries and Congruence		184
	6.6.1	Experimental Setting	185
	6.6.2	Specification Space	186
	6.6.3	Policy Specification	187
	6.6.4	Experimental Results	189
6.7	Dignity, Polycentricity and Self-Amendment		190
	6.7.1	Principle 7 and the Zone of Dignity	191
	6.7.2	Principle 8 and Polycentricity	193
	6.7.3	The Paradox of Self-Amendment	197
6.8	Summary		199

Part III: Social Interaction 203

Chapter 7. Computational Justice 205

7.1	Introduction		205
7.2	Example: The Biscuit Distribution Dilemma		207
7.3	Justice and Fairness: A Brief Overview		209
	7.3.1	A Brief Review of Distributive Justice	210
	7.3.2	Fairness	212
	7.3.3	Rescher's Theory of Distributive Justice	215
7.4	Distributive Justice		217
	7.4.1	Satisfaction and Compliance	218

	7.4.2	Representing Legitimate Claims	219
	7.4.3	Computing a Resource Allocation	219
	7.4.4	Self-Organising the Weights	221
	7.4.5	Some Experimental Results	223
7.5	Retributive Justice		226
	7.5.1	Experimental Setting	227
	7.5.2	Policy Specification	229
	7.5.3	Experimental Results	231
7.6	Procedural Justice		232
	7.6.1	Participation Principle	234
	7.6.2	Transparency Principle and Balancing Principle	238
	7.6.3	Procedural Justice: On Reflection	240
7.7	A General Framework		241
7.8	Summary		242

Chapter 8. Artificial Social Construction — 245

8.1	Introduction		245
8.2	Example: The Cheese-and-Wine Controversy		247
8.3	Trust		248
	8.3.1	Making Decisions Under Uncertainty	249
	8.3.2	A Socio-Cognitive Trust Framework	251
	8.3.3	Trust in a Producer–Consumer Scenario	253
8.4	Forgiveness		253
	8.4.1	Trust Breakdowns	254
	8.4.2	A Forgiveness Framework	255
	8.4.3	Forgiveness in Computer-Mediated Communication	258
8.5	Electronic Social Capital		259
	8.5.1	Favours	259
	8.5.2	Social Capital	260
	8.5.3	A Social Capital Framework	261
	8.5.4	The Unscrupulous Diners' Dilemma	264
8.6	Values		265
	8.6.1	Depreciating Values	265
	8.6.2	Reinventing Values	268
8.7	Artificial Social Constructionism		271
8.8	Summary		272

Chapter 9. Knowledge Aggregation	275
9.1 Introduction	275
9.2 Example: The Kitchen Aggravation	277
9.3 Judgement Aggregation	279
9.3.1 The Condorcet Jury Theorem	279
9.3.2 The Doctrinal Paradox	281
9.4 Opinion Formation	284
9.4.1 Hegselmann–Krause Model	285
9.4.2 Ramirez-Cano–Pitt Model	285
9.5 Social Networks	286
9.5.1 Networks: Some Definitions and Metrics	287
9.5.2 Ring and All-to-All Networks	289
9.5.3 Random Graphs (Erdös–Rényi) Networks	291
9.5.4 Small-World (Watts–Strogatz) Networks	292
9.5.5 Scale-Free (Barabási–Albert) Networks	293
9.6 A Framework for Interactional Justice	295
9.6.1 Individual Self-Assessment	295
9.6.2 Collective Assessment	297
9.6.3 Implementation	298
9.7 Experiments with Interactional Justice	300
9.7.1 Economy of Scarcity	301
9.7.2 'Clique' Detection and Protection	302
9.7.3 Network Variations	305
9.8 Summary	307
Chapter 10. Algorithmic Self-Governance	311
10.1 Introduction	311
10.2 Example: The Ministry of Culinary Affairs	313
10.3 Knowledge Management	315
10.3.1 Knowledge Management in Classical Athens	315
10.3.2 Facts, Policies and Values	317
10.4 Relevant Expertise Aggregation	320
10.5 The Tolerance of Dissent	322

10.6	Basic Democracy and Demopolis		324
	10.6.1	Basic Democracy	325
	10.6.2	Demopolis	327
	10.6.3	SimDemopolis	328
10.7	Experiments with SimDemopolis		330
	10.7.1	Civic Participation	330
	10.7.2	Legislation	336
	10.7.3	Entrenchment	338
10.8	Algorithmic Comparative Politics		341
10.9	Summary: Why This Stuff Matters		344

Bibliography   347

Index   369

PART I

Foundations

Chapter 1

Multi-Agent Systems

1.1 Introduction

The transition to the Digital Society envisaged by the Digital Transformation involves the increasing use of digital tools and technologies both in the reconfiguration of business processes, organisational structures and commercial transactions, and in the recasting of social processes, physical infrastructure and relational interactions. This is having a profound impact on the nature of ownership (e.g. possession of goods being replaced by subscription to services), the sense of belonging to communities, and citizens' access to infrastructure for physical resources such as water, energy and transport, and social resources such as health, education and governance. Consequently, more of our lives, interactions and decisions are either mediated through technology, or delegated to technology altogether, and our social problems have to be solved through, or with, or by technology.

In this context, there is a challenge to engineer ever more complex socio-technical and cyber-physical systems to support and enhance this full spectrum of human activities. A *socio-technical system* is one which recognises the importance of interactions between people and technology in system design: the technology with which we are concerned is a computational intelligence, as manifested by a software agent, 'smart' device, robot and so on. A *cyber-physical system* is one in which control of a physical process or device is managed by software: overall operation of the system is dependent on interaction between physical and software components.

Increasingly, there is cross-over between the two system approaches, as demonstrated by medical monitoring, e.g. Health 4.0

(Lopes *et al.*, 2019) industrial process control, e.g. Industry 4.0 (Fakhar Manesh *et al.*, 2020) and virtual organisations (Cevenini, 2003); energy generation and distribution, e.g. SmartGrids (Liu *et al.*, 2016) and Community Energy Systems (Prasad Koirala *et al.*, 2016); and transportation, e.g. autonomous vehicles, from driverless cars (Mitchell Waldrop, 2015) to drones (-as-a-service (Alwateer and Seng, 2020)).

The key common feature here is *interaction*, whether it is interaction purely between software artefacts, or between a software artefact and a person, or human–human interaction mediated by software artefacts (*cf.* (Prouskas and Pitt, 2004)). All these interactions relate to a critical requirement to solve some problem of coordination or *collective action*.

A collective action problem is a situation where a group of individuals need to make common cause in order to achieve a shared objective. It would generally be more beneficial for the group both as a whole and as individuals if they cooperated, but due to conflicting or competing individual preferences or behaviours, they may often fail to do so.

This is the critical question addressed by this book: how to design and implement socio-technical and cyber-physical systems such that their 'individuals' (human or computational intelligences) can solve *collective action problems at scale*? The transition to the Digital Society will not automatically produce some harmonious utopia: there will still be existing problems (e.g. how to achieve an equitable distribution of scarce resources), and there will be new problems (e.g. how to implement checks and balances on political authority in digital systems), and there will be planetary-scale problems, e.g. how to deal with anthropogenic climate change.

In answering this question, the two primary technologies we will apply are those of *multi-agent systems* and *self-organising systems*. A multi-agent system is a distributed computing paradigm in which a system is composed of many interacting, intelligent (software) *agents*, i.e. autonomous components each encapsulating some degree of computational intelligence (Wooldridge, 2009). A self-organising system, for our purposes here, is another distributed computing paradigm involving the *purposeful* formation of structures or procedures to achieve a certain task (note that self-organisation occurs in many social, physical, chemical and biological systems, and is not always purposeful). We are particularly concerned with the definition of procedures which we will call *conventional rules*: these are rules that, as opposed to physical laws (like gravity), are made up, mutually agreed and modified as necessary by the agents themselves.

These two technologies provide the computational foundations for the specification and implementation of systems of autonomous components interacting in the context of such conventional rules, i.e. self-organising multi-agent systems. We will use these technologies firstly, to analyse and develop solutions to *strategic* interactions involving problems of action selection, preference selection and dispute resolution; and secondly to analyse and develop solutions to *social* interactions involving problems such as achieving fairness, managing knowledge and legitimately maintaining order.

Accordingly, this book is (like Gaul, for those who know *Asterix*) divided into three parts: Part I focuses on the two technologies, Multi-Agent Systems and Self-Organising Systems; Part II focuses on strategic interaction, studying Game Theory, Social Choice Theory, Dispute Resolution, and (Ostrom) Institution Theory; and Part III focuses on social interaction, studying Justice, Social Construction, Knowledge Aggregation and Self-Governance. (The fourth part, like Gaul, is not quite an indomitable village but all that has happened while the book was being written).

This first chapter then introduces the basic elements of multi-agent systems. It begins in Sec. 1.2 with an example, based on a 'Smart'House situated in a Community Energy System. This house will also provide the setting for a running example which will subsequently appear in the second section of every chapter of this book. Here it will be used to give a motivating example of cyber-physical and socio-technical systems, and highlight some of the critical generic problems affecting strategic and social interactions in this context.

After the example, the chapter will move on to the technical exposition of some key topics in multi-agent system design, specification and programming. Section 1.3 considers a conceptual perspective from the viewpoint of *open systems* (with a slight digression on open societies). From this, Sec. 1.4 takes a methodological perspective, as part of our approach to developing 'technical' systems is to analyse social systems and formalise properties of human society and social interactions in *agent societies*. Since implementation is the end-point of the methodology, a practical perspective offers a simple definition of an autonomous (intelligent) agent and multi-agent system from an implementation point of view in Sec. 1.5.

This definition entails communication between autonomous agents in a multi-agent system, which is also fairly critical for a study of "interaction", so in Sec. 1.6, agent communication is studied, with an emphasis on the formalisation of *institutionalised power* (Jones and Sergot, 1996): the capability of designated agents to perform actions of particular significance in specific contexts. Institutionalised power is used in Sec. 1.7 in the specification of multi-agent systems in the *Event Calculus* (EC) (Kowalski and Sergot, 1986). The EC is a logical calculus used for reasoning about events and the effect of events, and a version is included in the implementation of PreSage-2. PreSage-2 is a multi-agent simulator and animator, presented in Sec. 1.8, as an exemplar of the kind of tool that can be used to explore the behaviour of intelligent agents interacting in *open agent societies*. The chapter concludes in Sec. 1.9 with a brief discussion of system lifetime and a pointer to self-organisation.

1.2 Example: The SmartHouse

In this section, we illustrate the spectrum of cyber-physical and sociotechnical systems (and their cross-over), using the idea of a SmartHouse as part of a Community Energy System. This scenario is also used to highlight some confounding features that motivate a solution based on self-organising and multi-agent systems, rather than a 'traditional' software engineering development model.

1.2.1 *Community Energy Systems*

Responding to a need to address anthropogenic climate change through the use of fewer fossil fuels and less of each of them, or in search of more environment-friendly generation than nuclear power stations, a community energy system is a type of SmartGrid. In a 'traditional' community energy system, there is a central generator serving a set of consumers (e.g. households). In future, community energy systems may be decentralised with both the generation and the decision-making pushed to the edges, i.e. the households themselves (an excellent example is provided by the small town of Schönau in Germany).

In the conception of a decentralised community energy system, there are a group of geographically co-located residences. Each residence, or SmartHouse, will have installed its own renewable energy source, for example roof-mounted photovoltaic cells, or a small wind turbine. This is the source of energy generation. The house has the usual variety of domestic appliances requiring energy consumption. There may be some form of energy storage, through advances in battery technology or even an electric vehicle (which as a 'distributed battery' could act as both energy storage and energy consumer). The generation and consumption of energy is monitored through a 'Smart'Meter (see Fig. 1.1).

The problem then is distribution: the connection between generation and consumption. If the energy generated and stored by a SmartHouse were always equal to the energy consumed, then the balance would eliminate the problem. However, renewable energy sources tend to be stochastic: sometimes too much energy is generated, in which case, it needs to be stored somewhere (if the home-battery is full, and following the power systems maxim "don't waste wind"); and at other times not enough is generated, in which case the shortfall will have to be covered from somewhere (if the home-battery is empty).

One solution is to team up with other SmartHouses in an aggregated SmartVillage, or Community Energy System, and form a common-pool resource (Pitt *et al.*, 2014a). In a SmartVillage, each SmartHouse *provisions* the energy that it generates to the common pool, and *appropriates* the energy that it consumes from the

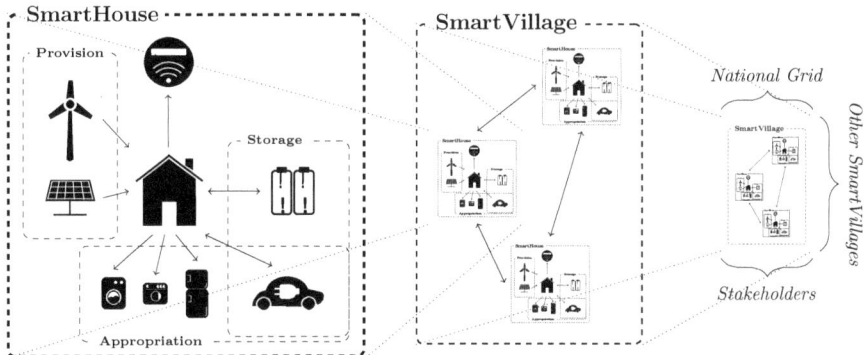

Fig. 1.1. From SmartHouse to System of (Community Energy) Systems

same pool. In other words, this changes the focus of energy distribution from the demand side (the consumers determine the demand, and the generators have to supply it) to the supply side: i.e. the generators make a certain amount of energy available, and the consumers have to determine who gets to use it.

Nevertheless, even a SmartVillage cannot be guaranteed to be entirely self-contained in an equal balance of energy supply and demand, on diurnal, seasonal or annual scales. In other words, the prospect remains that either too much or too little energy will be generated, and so the SmartVillage is faced with the same problem, just on a larger scale. In fact, we have a hierarchical system of systems, as even aggregations of villages need to establish policies — i.e. mutually agreed sets of conventional rules — for the satisfactory operation of the system: atomically, globally and on every level in between. This means that the range, scale and type of problems to be addressed, for example in energy distribution, are further complicated by three contextual issues of polycentricity, entanglement and 'wickedness'.

1.2.2 Three Contextual Issues

Polycentric systems (Ostrom, V., 1972; Ostrom, E., 2010) are defined as those with multiple centres of autonomous decision-making. In a community energy system, there are many different stakeholders; not just the obvious prosumers (occupants of the SmartHouses), but also service providers (equipment, installation, maintenance), ombudsman for dispute resolution, system administrators (for the grid and the computer network), app entrepreneurs (providing apps for the SmartMeter), policy advisors, regulators and citizens' pressure groups (e.g. for a Green New Deal). All of these separate entities have some sort of stake in the common-pool resource, have an interest in its maintenance, and are trying to extract something from it, each according to their own interests and priorities.

Therefore, this is a distributed multi-criteria sub-optimisation problem. Furthermore, it is possible to identify at least four 'layers' in relation to the management and problem-solving of the whole system, with interaction between autonomous components occurring at every layer; behaviours and decisions taken at one layer can also have an impact on adjacent layers:

- Delegated — humans out of the loop: Operation is controlled by 'smart' automation, which works without (or with limited) user awareness; e.g. regulation of refrigerator compressor cycles for load-balancing and voltage control;
- Programmable — humans on the loop: Operational requirements are specified by users, and automation resolves the constraints; e.g. programmable appliances such as dishwashers: the user specifies constraints (completion time, cost), and delegates to the appliances the task of negotiating a schedule;
- Interactive — humans in the loop: Automation indicates active intervention is required by humans; e.g. using a SmartMeter to initiate pre-emptive action for overload prevention; and
- Attentive — humans are the loop: A human participant may occupy multiple different stakeholder roles besides producer and consumer in a community energy system, e.g. being called upon to consider investment decisions, interactions with third parties, resolution of internal disputes, and so on.

Moreover, each layer presents its components with a governance, coordination or collective action problem, requiring a group of autonomous actors (i.e. agents) to self-organise. For example, one refrigerator may be programmed (or learn) to not switch off its compressor, while the others do, thereby getting the benefits of refrigeration and load-balancing, i.e. it *free rides* in a *public goods game* — until every refrigerator behaves similarly. The programmable appliances also face a coordination dilemma: if they operate sequentially, they can be better off than if they operate simultaneously, but they need to agree on a procedure, and on the rules about that procedure, to define the sequence. At the interactive level, SmartMeters could support computer-mediated human–human interactions to resolve collective action problems like overload protection and blackout prevention. Finally, at the attentive level, the human participants face governance issues that have characterised the management of common-pool resources (CPRs) throughout history, defining conventional rules to regulate access to and investment in a CPR.

However, as well as each layer having to address its own problems, the layers are also *entangled*. A solution at one layer may have unexpected repercussions at another layer. Each SmartVillage is itself a system of systems (or at least a system with these entangled layers) as well as a system in a system of systems as depicted in Fig. 1.1.

A wicked problem is defined as a social problem whose complexity and continually changing requirements are such that there is not necessarily an obvious terminating condition, or even a consistent set of criteria by which to evaluate such a condition if it even existed. The kinds of wicked problems facing community energy systems include sustainability, emergency response, and governance (especially establishing and maintaining legitimate, stable and 'good' governance).

It will be noted that for each of these social problems, there is no end state. Considering sustainability, it can be asserted "X has been sustained"; and it can be claimed that "S is sustainable"; but neither guarantees that "X will be sustained (indefinitely)". One of the problems of sustainability is that everything appears to be all right, until suddenly it isn't, perhaps because a tipping point has been reached (Gladwell, 2000). (The old joke: man falls out of the window of a 20-storey building: as he passes the 10th floor, he says "all OK so far".) Reaching a tipping point may require dealing with an unexpected emergency or potentially catastrophic situation, for which the system may not even have been designed. As for 'good' governance, this will be addressed in Chapter 10.

To address these issues, we first consider the implications of viewing a community energy system, and by extension other cyber-physical and socio-technical systems, as an *open system* (Hewitt, 1986). Then, since we are identifying a wicked problem as a type of *social* problem, we consider the features of a 'society' that might be the source of solutions.

1.3 Open Systems and Agent Societies

1.3.1 *Open Systems*

Open systems, as defined in Hewitt (1986), comprise autonomous components of heterogenous provenance interacting asynchronously, in parallel and peer-to-peer. These "autonomous components" are, of course, agents. Interaction implies that it is reasonable to assume that there is a common language, and a specification of correct behaviour and interfaces that facilitate interoperation; on the other hand, autonomy and heterogeneity imply that it is not reasonable to assume that the agents share a common objective, nor to assume that there is a centralised agent-controller that is directing or determining the actions of all other agents; and not to assume either that their behaviour will necessarily comply with the specification.

Hewitt compiles a list of the fundamental characteristics of open systems, including asynchrony, concurrency, decentralisation, inconsistency, continuity and arm's-length relationships. These are all also features of the SmartVillage scenario. We can extend this with a list of what might be called 'non-functional hazards', i.e. problems that are a product of being an open system, and not simply the problem that the open system is trying to solve. These are co-dependence, mutability, partiality, expectation of error, self-determination, economy of scarcity, endogenous resources and no full disclosure. We briefly discuss each of these hazards in turn.

Co-dependence and *competition*: Each agent is reliant on other agents for successful accomplishment of its own goals, but those other agents may themselves be unreliable, for example, if the agents are competing for the same (scarce) resources.

Trust: The environment, network topology and constituent agents can vary rapidly and unpredictably. Therefore, each agent will frequently be exposed to 'first encounter' problems, i.e. how to interact in a situation or with an agent that has not been previously encountered; and to 'nth encounter' problems, how to interact in a situation for which knowledge of previous encounters can be leveraged.

Partiality and *uncertainty of knowledge*: Because interactions are asynchronous, in parallel, and peer-to-peer, this implies that there is no single source of 'true' knowledge. Therefore, each agent only has a partial (and possibly subjective) knowledge of the overall system and some of its other agents; furthermore the union of these knowledge bases may be inconsistent (this does not mean that it is necessary to 'give up' logic for open systems (Kowalski, 1988)).

Expectation of error: Actuality (what is the case) and ideality (what ought to be the case) do not necessarily coincide. In other words, an agent may fail to comply with behaviour specified by some codification of systemic rules (or due process). There are, however, a variety of potential causes, for example by accident, convenience, necessity or malice. It may also be that the rule is inefficient or even wrong. It is necessary to distinguish between these causes in order to recover from them through the enforcement of corrective action, which can range from forgiveness or punishment to modification of the rules.

Economy of scarcity with *indivisible goods*: In an economy of scarcity, there are insufficient resources for every agent to get everything that they wanted, but each agent has to get all that they wanted because a fraction is useless. In such circumstances, we distinguish between 'satisfy', 'suffice' and 'satisfice': satisfy means to meet someone's wants fully, and suffice means to meet someone's needs adequately. To satisfice means to get a 'good enough' or 'least bad' solution when the optimal solution is not available (Simon, 1956). However, given enough time, it may be sufficient to satisfice (i.e. to give an agent all of what they want some of the time, when some of what they want all of the time is no help, and all of what they want all of the time is not an option).

Endogeneous resources: In a system where all the resources are provided by the appropriators themselves, as in a sensor network or a micro-grid, all tasks such as determining the resource allocation method, computing the resource allocation itself, and monitoring the resource appropriation must be 'paid for' from the very same resources. If too much resources are expended on these activities, it might leave nothing for 'real' jobs (both Pitt and Schaumeier (2012) and Balke *et al.* (2013)) report how the costs of needless and/or excessive monitoring deplete resources in this way).

No full disclosure: Hewitt referred to this as *arm's length relationships*, but the essential problem is that agents are autonomous and internal states cannot be checked for compliance (with conventional rules). Moreover, incoming ('new-to-the-system') agents might not have all the information required for 'appropriate' behaviour, or for reliable investment decisions (e.g. contributing to a common pool).

Self-determination: There is no central (software) controller, and decision-making may be too fast, frequent or complex for intervention by a (human) operator. Therefore, the agents have to solve the problem for which the system has been developed, cope with the three contextual issues above, and resolve any of these hazards *by and between themselves*. There is no guarantee that this will be done 'perfectly'.

However, the benefit of an 'open systems' perspective is that it offers a prescriptive (i.e. rule-based) approach to establishing the information-processing foundations of decision-making and action-taking in organisations. In particular, Hewitt proposes *due process* as the central activity for generating sound, relevant and reliable information (in an organisational rather than judicial context). He notes also that: due process provides a record of decision-making processes, which can be referenced later, e.g. for purposes of accountability (*cf.* Cranefield *et al.*, 2018); due process is supposed to be reflective (see Pitt *et al.*, 2020a); and logical reasoning takes places within due process.

Our approach will also take a prescriptive, logic-based approach to reinforcing the information-processing foundations of action-taking and decision-making in institutions, and of institutions themselves, using a language and reasoning beyond (but building on) the micro-theories of Hewitt. Additionally, this approach will provide the logical and computational foundations for activities beyond due process, and develop algorithmic approaches to justice, social construction, knowledge management, governance and reflection.

1.3.2 *Open Societies and Agent Societies*

It is tempting to try to unify the 'open' in *open system* with the 'open' in *open society*, with the ultimate goal of creating open societies of agents, or open agent societies.

Open society was the term used by Karl Popper to describe a socio-political system founded on individual freedom and rights, scientific innovation, a market economy (with appropriate constraints on the concentration of economic power), and the rule of law (i.e. appropriate constraints on the concentration of state power). Popper was rejecting the political philosophies of, among others, Plato and Marx, arguing that the belief in a universal truth and the quest for an ideal social order paved the way for totalitarianism. Instead, he advocated dealing with social problems through piecemeal reform, akin to applying the scientific method to eliminate false theories, bringing about systemic improvement through proven gradual increments rather than unprovable radical leaps.

This temptation[1] remains fascinating and there are a number of loose connections that can be identified in various chapters of this book, but it remains a challenge for the future. Nevertheless, an underlying contention of this book is that if we can create societies of agents, where the agent societies exhibit the problem-solving capability of human-societies, then we can design, specify and implement socio-technical and cyber-physical systems which have similar problem-solving capabilities. To be fully systematic about this, we need a methodology for transforming observations and theories about human society into algorithmic models.

1.4 Methodology: Sociologically-Inspired Computing

One approach to addressing these issues is to observe how similar problems have been resolved in natural (biological or social) systems, and formalise such solutions in an appropriate calculus suitable for engineering a computational solution to be used in an artificial system or computer model.

This has, in fact, been the approach of the synthetic method underlying research in artificial societies and artificial life (Steels and Brooks, 1994). The main steps involve generalising some observed phenomena to produce a theory, from which an artificial system can be constructed and used to test predicted claims. The outcome of applying the synthetic method is to engineer an artificial system, and the resulting animation, experiment or performance serves to support or refute the theory.

Several other attempts to apply ideas from the social sciences to the design of computational systems (see, e.g. Edmonds *et al.*, 2005) have followed a similar pattern. Furthermore, researchers in biologically-inspired computing, notably those concerned with artificial immune systems (Andrews *et al.*, 2010) have developed a comparable approach. However, in Jones *et al.* (2013), another variation of

---

[1]Which has not been entirely resisted, and not altogether successfully, see Pitt *et al.* (2001), Pitt (2005) and Pitt and Artikis (2015).

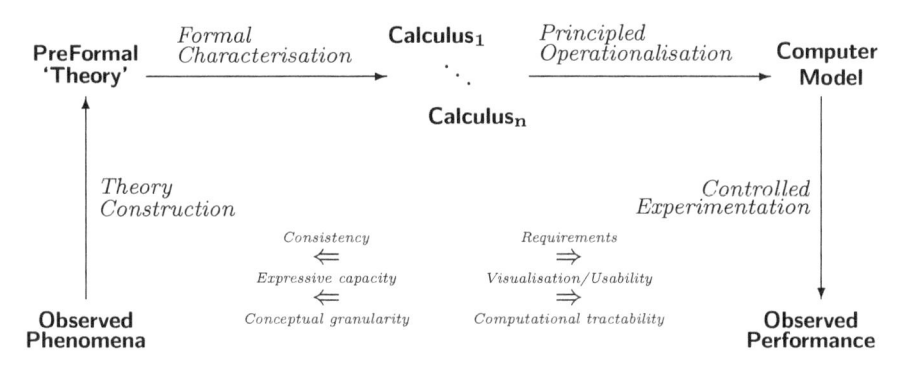

```
                Formal           Calculus₁      Principled
PreFormal    Characterisation                Operationalisation     Computer
 'Theory'    ─────────────────▶      ⋱      ──────────────────▶      Model
                                  Calculusₙ


       Theory                                              Controlled
    Construction                                         Experimentation
                         Consistency           Requirements
                             ⇐                     ⇒
                      Expressive capacity   Visualisation/Usability
                             ⇐                     ⇒
   Observed           Conceptual granularity  Computational tractability    Observed
  Phenomena                                                               Performance
```

Fig. 1.2. Methodology for Sociologically-Inspired Computing

the synthetic method was proposed. In this approach, a distinction was made between the social sciences source and engineering artificial societies. The transition from theory to artificial system was no longer direct and included the application of an intermediate step. In addition, the results of observed performance were not used to justify or refute the source theory, but were instead used to adjust the formalisms underpinning the artificial system.

This methodology, called *sociologically-inspired computing*,[2] is illustrated in Fig. 1.2. The first step is to formulate a theory by defining, for example in natural language, the terms and principles that are used to denote or describe the observed social phenomena. The second step of formal characterisation leads from the (predominantly) informal representations of the source theory, to formal representations, expressed in a formal language or 'calculus' of some kind (where by 'calculus' it is meant any system of calculation or computation based on symbolic manipulation). The final step is systematic, controlled experimentation with a computational model of an artificial system derived from the formal representation.

---

[2]The term 'sociologically-inspired' was chosen as a parallel to 'biologically-inspired', although it is not, perhaps, such a good term. We take inspiration not just from sociology, but from across the social and natural sciences, and indeed have formalised theories from linguistics, philosophy, law, psychology, cognitive science, physiology, economics and political science in our search for computable solutions to engineering problems.

As explained in Jones *et al.* (2013), there are (at least) two types of formal representations. Firstly, there are those representations that aim to provide an analysis of conceptual structure, identifying the fundamental elements of which complex concepts are composed, and articulating the principles governing their composition and interrelations. Crucially, these representations, being used for a conceptual characterisation of the theory, are *theory-facing* and constrained primarily by considerations of expressive capacity, and not those of computational tractability. Secondly, there are those representations that are more suitable to the development of software models and simulations: this is the basis of a computational framework for the original theory.

However, the key points to note about these representations are that they should be informed and guided by the conceptual characterisations of a theory-facing representation, but they may well involve some degree of simplification, or approximation, and there may be some abstractions that can be tolerated in a theory-facing representation, but not in an *implementation-facing* one. It is expected, though, that the designer should be fully aware of how the conceptual characterisation is being approximated, or how the computational framework is being enriched (i.e. it is not a matter of 'theory hacking' in a preferred formalism).

The final step of principled operationalisation is concerned with moving from the computational framework to a model of the artificial system, with algorithmic intelligence of the components embedded in identifiable functions and processes. This step may also be selective or approximate, but it too is principled, in that it is conducted knowing which selections and approximations have been made, and why.

1.5 Autonomous Agents and Multi-Agent Systems

There are many introductory texts explaining autonomous agents and multi-agent systems: see, for example, Wooldridge (2009) and Russell and Norvig (2016). The purpose of this section is not to compete with those works or condense them into two pages. Rather, it is to give an intuition of the agent/multi-agent design abstraction, a route to implementation, and an understanding of why agents/multi-agent systems are generally the target computer model of the sociologically-inspired computing methodology.

1.5.1 *Autonomous Agents*

At the highest level of abstraction, we identify three principal characteristics of an autonomous agent: ownership, intelligence and asynchrony.

In terms of *ownership*, perhaps in contrast to the "X-as-a-service" software model of cloud computing, we propose that an agent is owned or represents a human person or organisation, and has responsibility for undertaking some task that has been delegated to it. This means that agent-based systems are more than embedded systems, are actually *situated* systems, and actions in the digital society can have consequences in the analogue world. Some of these consequences may be legal, but may be covered by different legal codes (for example, under UK law, a bid in an auction house establishes a verbal contract and the bidder is legally obliged to pay for the lot if the bid wins; however, placing a bet is unenforceable and a bookmaker is not obliged to honour a winning bet).

In terms of *intelligence*, we propose that an agent would ideally possess a sufficiently 'large' number of internal states to avoid being a predictable (deterministic) state machine. For example, Garry Kasparov, World Chess Champion from 1985 to 2000, had claimed that no computer would ever beat him; yet, when he lost to IBM's Deep Blue in 1996–1997, he attributed creativity, intelligence and strategic intention to the machine. (There is a caveat to increasing machine intelligence, which is the creation of digital dependence: see Robbins (2019).)

Asynchrony implies that input can arrive from either other agents or the environment in which they are situated at any time, and impact ongoing processes or activities. This has three ramifications: firstly, information that is known to be needed may not be available; secondly, unanticipated information may become available; and thirdly, the rate of computation has to be tailored to the rate of arrival of any information. (A planning system that replans after every new input may never make any progress if the arrival rate is faster than the computation; a planning system that computes to completion but ignores any incoming information may find its plans rendered redundant by that information.)

What these three characteristics mean is that at the very lowest level of abstraction, an agent is an embedded software process, which encapsulates some notion of state, and communicates with others by message passing. There are many *agent architectures* whose implementation can demonstrate the three principle characteristics, including the *BDI* agent architecture (Rao and Georgeff, 1998), the *teleo-reactive* agent architecture (Krasnogor Nilsson, 1994), the *HAMMER cognitive architecture* for robots (Demiris and Khadhouri, 2006) and the *MAPE-K* control loop from Autonomic Computing (Huebscher and McCann, 2008). We review each of these in turn, with a basic Qu-Prolog agent as a starting point.

Qu-Prolog[3] is a multi-threaded Prolog which provides high-level communication between threads, and was primarily intended as a prototyping language for developing interactive theorem provers. However, the two features of multi-threading and rapid-prototyping provide effective support for experimenting with multiple interacting processes, which are communicating symbols and performing symbolic reasoning. A basic Qu-Prolog agent can then be implemented as a message-processing control loop (see the code snippet in Fig. 1.3),

```
...
thread_fork( Name, launch(Name) ),
...

launch( Name ) :-
    thread_handle( Handle ),
    register(Name) ->> oracle:delphi,
    registered <<- _,
    make_agent_profile( Name, Handle ),
    agent_event_loop.

agent_event_loop :-
    Msg <<- From,
    process_message_a( Msg, From ),
    agent_event_loop.
```

Fig. 1.3. Agent-Thread Control Loop

---

[3] http://staff.itee.uq.edu.au/pjr/HomePages/QuPrologHome.html.

which waits until the agent receives a message, processes it, and repeats (until it receives a self-terminate message).

When a new agent-thread is forked, it is given a unique identifier, `Name`, and a goal, `launch`. Qu-Prolog creates a handle, which is a Prolog term of the form `X:Y@Z`, where `X` is thread name, `Y` is the identifier registered with the inter-process communication server used by Qu-Prolog (Pedro), and `Z` is the IP-address of the machine on which the Qu-Prolog process is running. The operators `->>` and `<<-` send and receive messages, so it can communicate with other agents. One of these is a designated name-server thread called `oracle` registered with Pedro as `delphi` (the IP address does not need to be specified if it is the same machine). A separate name-space is created for that agent, giving it control over its own state. A digital 'environment' accessed through a global name-space is a simple 'embedding' which completes the three characteristics specified earlier.

A more sophisticated agent architecture is the *BDI agent* architecture. This stems from the *Intentional Stance*, proposed by Dennett (1987) (as mentioned in passing in Sec. 1.4). The idea behind the intentional stance was that an object could be perceived as a rational agent by ascribing to it beliefs, representing its informational state, and desires (or goals), representing its motivational state. With a bit of reasoning, one could then infer that object's intentions, representing its deliberative state. This gives the reasoner predictive leverage over the object, i.e. if one can predict an object's behaviour, one can take advantage of it.

If this intentional stance is instead considered as a *design* stance, then this serves as a design template for a rational agent, and there are many useful implementations and variations. The BDI agent is a good (if unintentional) exemplar of the methodology of Sec. 1.4, where modal logic is used as the calculus for formal characterisation of Dennett's (pre-formal) theory, and a computer model is implemented as an operationalisation of this characterisation.

A 'standard' computer model of a BDI agent (Rao and Georgeff, 1998) consists of one control loop, two interfaces (sensors and actuators), three 'stores' (belief store (B), goal store (D) and intention store (I)), and four functions (belief revision, option generation, filter, and action selection).[4] The control loop can be specified as follows:

$$B \leftarrow B_0; D \leftarrow D_0; \quad \%\text{initialisation}$$
while *true* **do**
$\quad \gamma \leftarrow \text{get\_next\_percept};$
$\quad B \leftarrow \text{belief\_revision}(B, \gamma);$
$\quad D \leftarrow \text{option\_generation}(B, I);$
$\quad I \leftarrow \text{filter}(B, D, I);$
$\quad \alpha \leftarrow \text{action\_selection}(I);$
$\quad \text{actuate}(\alpha);$

Here, the *belief revision* function updates the belief store based on the agent's current beliefs and a new perception. The *option generation* function updates the goal store based on updated beliefs and current intentions. Option generation can be seen as a kind of planning, and so the goal store is a set of plans, where each plan is a sequence of actions. The *filter* function updates the intention store based on updated beliefs, goals and current intentions. Effectively, this function implements a *commitment strategy*, for example filtering out plans whose goals it is considered impossible to achieve. The *action selection* function selects one plan from the intention store, takes the first action from that plan, and executes (actuates) it. The effect of actions has to be perceived, and the cycle repeats.

A *teleo-reactive* program (or agent) was defined by Nilsson (1994) as a program whose actions are directed towards achieving goals (the teleo- part) and in a way that is appropriate to the current perceived state of the environment (the -reactive part). A possible

---

[4]Way back when I was seriously trying to program BDI agents, I started playing the RPG computer game *Baldur's Gate*. This game provided a sort of rudimentary BDI engine that enabled the player to program behaviour by specifying rules of the form "IF beliefs AND goals THEN action-sequence". I never got beyond the second level of the game because I spent more time trying to program the non-player characters to stop re-enacting the Battle of the Somme at every opportunity. I did manage to program the player character to just stand there doing nothing while his mates got turned into chutney by some psychopathic goblins, which did make me think (a) I've got a day-job to do this kind of stuff, and (b) finally there's a character I can really identify with...

implementation defines a set of reactive rules that continuously sense the environment and trigger actions whose execution eventually leads the system to satisfy a goal.

For example, the behaviour of a certain animal can be defined by the following teleo-reactive program:

$detectFood \rightarrow eat.$

$hungry \rightarrow whine.$

$detectKeyboard \wedge needAttention \rightarrow sitOnKeyboard.$

$detectPerson \rightarrow sleepOnPerson.$

$true \rightarrow sleep.$

A Qu-Prolog implementation of a teleo-reactive agent is given in Clark and Robinson (2015).

The HAMMER architecture is a framework for online action-selection and intention recognition originally developed for robotics (Demiris and Khadhouri, 2006). This is based on a generative, simulationist approach to understanding actions by mentally rehearsing them from a motor-based perspective. It uses Inverse-Forward model pairs with an additional "Prediction Verification" module, in parallel, with feedback to help select the next action. The current state at time t is input to the Inverse Model to generate a plan (sequence of actions); this plan is input to the Forward Model to generate a predicted state at time $t+1$, and the Prediction Verifier compares the state prediction and state information at time $t+1$ to generate an error signal which is fed back to the Inverse Model.

However, HAMMER had been used not just in robotics for understanding and generating behaviours, but also in multi-agent systems (Butler and Demiris, 2008). HAMMER can be used both as a "controller" to plan and control one agent, and as a "predictor" to make predictions about the actions of the other agents. These are additionally fed into the Inverse Model to condition action-selection. HAMMER has also been extended with *affective anticipation* (Sanderson and Pitt, 2011) to reflect "emotional" reasoning (like a greater fear of a bad outcome) based on cognitive theories (Castelfranchi, 1999).

In Autonomic Computing, MAPE-K has been proposed as a reference architecture for the feedback-control loop of an embedded software agent (Huebscher and McCann, 2008). Autonomic Computing was a research and development programme initiated by IBM in response to the spiralling costs of data centres (while hardware costs had plummeted, personnel costs had remained constant, but energy costs had soared). Therefore, the self-management of resources was proposed, but there was a contest for those resources depending on goals: the performance manager wants to minimise response times and turn as many processors on as necessary; while the power manager wants to minimise energy usage and so turn off as many processors as possible.

The human autonomic system of self-regulation, which can maintain a homeostatic equilibrium while hiding the complexity of that process from the human herself, provided the inspiration for the proposal of Autonomic Computing. An autonomic element was implemented following the MAPE-K reference architecture, where MAPE identifies the different activities in an autonomic control loop: monitor the environment to build a model; analyse the model to assess the situation and detect any anomalies; plan a sequence of actions to restore a desired state from an anomalous one; and execute the plan to provide corrective action. The 'K' refers to knowledge shared between several autonomic elements.

1.5.2 Multi-Agent Systems

A multi-agent system is simply a system whose elemental components are agents as specified in the previous sub-section. The key differentiator here is, perhaps between distributed object-oriented systems and multi-agent systems, and between dynamical systems and multi-agent systems.[5]

---

[5]And perhaps between real-time and multi-agent systems. I once gave a seminar to a real-time systems group, and they were a *real* real-time systems group: i.e. they were interested in scheduling and guarantees that computations would finish before specified times. Even our gentle idea of *time-aware agents* (Prouskas and Pitt, 2004), designed to discriminate between time-constrained agent–agent, agent–human, and agent-mediated human–human interactions in socio-technical systems, was absolute anathema to them, let alone the idea that agents could control their own state and decision-making ("agents can say no", indeed (Odell, 1999)). Fortunately, I distracted them with a slide of some kittens and made good my escape, though I do still wonder if they knew that their bubbling vat of tar contravened all sorts of health and safety regulations. Mine, mostly.

In a distributed object-oriented system, one of the key concerns is the *physical* distribution of data and methods, which are location transparent and still (relatively speaking) tightly coupled. In a multi-agent system, one of the key concerns — especially in relation to situatedness — is the *logical* distribution of responsibility and control, loose coupling (in the sense that if one agent cannot be delegated a task, then another will), and location is significant (who did what action that affected which agent matters).

In a dynamical system, the focus is on states and transitions between states. The system is analysed by specifying stocks, which represent quantities that vary over time, and flows, which measure the rate of transition of stock from state to state, depending on factors which influence the speed, volume and direction of the flow. The system can be analysed by defining differential equations to represent the rate of change of the different stocks in different states. In contrast, a multi-agent system allows for a finer-grained analysis, with asynchrony, heterogeneity, learning and other distinguishing features of the 'stock'.

In both distributed and dynamical systems, a multi-agent system focuses on the organisation of individual and collective intelligence in the context of differing functionality and diverse knowledge; cooperation, coordination and competition; and planning and decision-making wrt. individual and joint goals.

The *sine qua non* of such organisation, as indicated by one of the assumptions in open systems, is *communication*. Unsurprisingly, perhaps, the model of communication required between 'intelligent' agents was somewhat richer than stigmergy (indirect coordination by side-effecting the physical environment) or through associative memory (as implemented by, for example, tuple spaces). Agent Communication Languages were, for a while, a subject of some contention. The particular model of agent communication used in this book is described in the next section.

1.6 Agent Communication

1.6.1 The Contract-Net Protocol

While Hewitt's open systems (Hewitt, 1986) approach to distributed artificial intelligence concentrated on organisational mechanisms, an alternative approach at the same time was instead focusing on market mechanisms.

One of the first such mechanisms to appear was the so-called contract-net protocol (Smith, 1980), which was a task-sharing protocol that became commonly used in distributed systems. The basic intuition behind the protocol is an auction. An agent needs to delegate a task, so it sends out a call for proposals to perform the task; some other agents bid for the job; the original agent evaluates the bids and selects one; the selected agent performs the task and gets 'paid' (job done; quite literally).

It is a very effective protocol, and indeed negotiations and auctions and other market mechanisms were an important aspect of early work in multi-agent systems (Rosenschein and Zlotkin, 1998); as indeed was the usefulness of structured exchanges of messages in the form of protocols as a basis for both systems engineering (Pitt and Mamdani, 1999a) and a possible route to formal semantics (Pitt, 2003). The contract-net protocol itself has been formally specified in numerous ways in modelling language for multi-agent systems (e.g. agent unified modelling language (AUML)). This is illustrated in Fig. 1.4: compare and contrast two specifications to be found on the web; the specification on the left is from the FIPA website,[6] and the specification on the right from the Wikipedia website.[7]

However effective the protocol for specific applications, there are (at least) two problems for specification. The first is that, as Fig. 1.4 shows, there are many subtle variations and differences in terminology, not just in pictorial representation, but in terms of roles, actions, replies, unicast or broadcast communication, timeouts, and so on. From the point of view of interoperability, this means that an agent using the contract-net protocol in application A could not be guaranteed to be able to use the same protocol in application B.

Secondly, and more importantly, the protocol diagrams specify structure, but not meaning. In these diagrams, it was not clear which action establishes the legal fact that a contract exists between two

---

[6] http://www.fipa.org/specs/fipa00029/SC00029H.html; last accessed 27/8/2021.

[7] https://en.wikipedia.org/wiki/Contract_Net_Protocol; last accessed 27/8/2021.

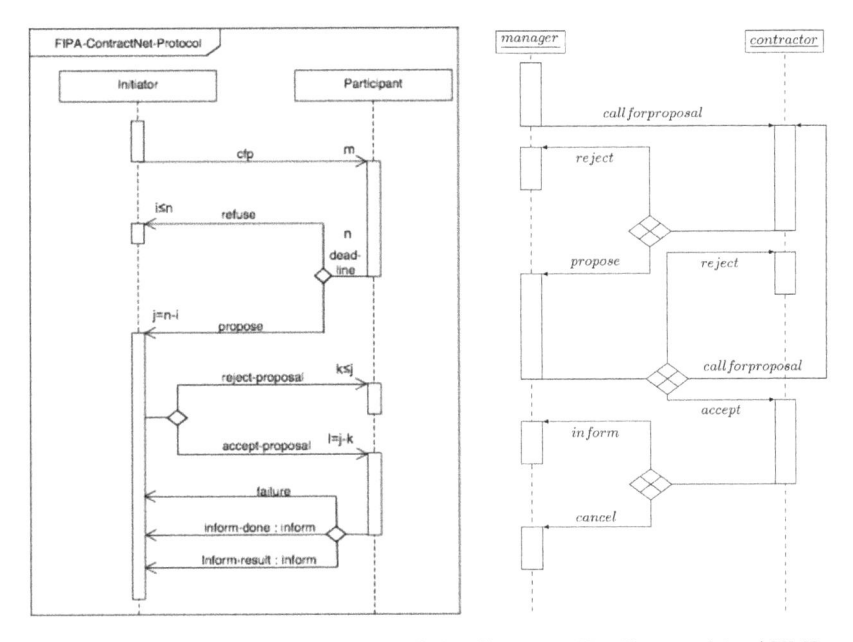

Fig. 1.4. Different Specifications of the Contract-Net Protocol in AUML

parties. In situated systems, this *does* matter: in the UK, for example, in different legal contexts, when a contract is formally recognised in law can depend on when a particular document was signed, when it was posted, when it was delivered, or when it was opened.[8] Knowing which action was of conventional significance is therefore critically important.

Faced with such problems, perhaps standardisation could help.

1.6.2 *Standardisation and FIPA ACL*

In 1996, the international standards body the Foundation for Intelligent Physical Agents (FIPA) held its inaugural meeting in London. Ostensibly intended to address the issue of interoperability in distributed systems with 'intelligent' agents (actually its implicit but

---

[8] One of my preferred dining establishments in London used to offer "garlic bread, with or without garlic". So garlic bread without garlic is? ... Which presumably means this is actually the contract-net protocol, but without the contract.

unstated purpose was to de-risk a potentially disruptive technology), one of its key technical specifications was for an Agent Communication Language (ACL).

At the time, there were two well-known ACLs, KQML (Finin et al., 1994) and ARCOL (Bretier and Sadek, 1996). Arguably (and the FIPA ACL Technical Committee did, relentlessly), KQML had a syntax but no semantics; and ARCOL had semantics but no real syntax. One might suppose that the compromise position and indeed best outcome would be to use KQML's syntax and ARCOL's semantics.

One might suppose that, and one would be wrong, because of a missing adjective: KQML's syntax and ARCOL's semantics were both *terrible*, the syntax was terrible for lightweight communication, the semantics was terrible for verification (i.e. compliance checking with a standard), and both were terrible for interoperability.[9] Most pertinently, without an explicit representation of which action has what conventional effect in which context, any use of multi-agent systems as a technology for situated systems in the emerging 'Digital Economy', with financial transactions and legal consequences, was going to be extremely problematic.

1.6.3 *Institutionalised Power*

A root cause of the problem with the FIPA ACL specification was that ARCOL's semantics was notionally based on Searle's Speech Act Theory (Searle, 1969). However, it over-emphasised a psychological element of Searle's work, where he tried to motivate performative actions with regards to beliefs, desires and intentions. This appeared to align with the BDI agent architecture (see above). As a result, the FIPA-ACL semantics were based on an internalised, 'mentalistic' approach (Pitt and Mamdani, 1999b), and missed the point entirely.

This is because this mentalistic approach overlooked Searle's primary, and more important, contention that speaking a language

---

[9]Still, some of us made a useful living out of criticism, e.g. Pitt and Mamdani (1999b). To the extent that when I first encountered the chairman of FIPA at the time, Leonardo Chiariglione, (internationally recognised for his work on many standards, including DAVIC and especially MPEG) in a lift in a hotel in Nice, and was introduced, he looked me up and down and said "Ah-ha! The Destabiliser".

is to engage in a rule-governed form of behaviour (like playing a game). Consequently, the FIPA ACL semantics omitted the *constitutive* aspect of conventional communication, in particular the idea of 'counts as'.

This 'counts as' is a consequence relation between the performance by agent A of some act of special significance (in particular, but not necessarily, a speech act) bringing about a state of affairs X which counts as, according to context, bringing about a state of affairs Y. For example, in the context of an auction house, the person occupying the role of auctioneer (and no one else) announcing "sold" counts as, in effect, establishing a contract between buyer and seller. Note that this explicitly ties a specific action with a fact of conventional (and legal) significance that was missing from the contract-net protocol; moreover, it need not involve speech — banging a hammer on a table can also 'count as' bringing about the same result.

Therefore, we know how to "get things done" with (physical) objects: given a hammer, a nail, and a bit of Newtonian physics, applying the hammer to the nail in the orthodox way brings about the expected result. We know how to "get things done" with (software) objects: if we send a message to the object, then depending on the semantics of the call, the object will change state (in computer memory). And how we "get things done" with words, i.e. speech acts), is also to bring about changes in state. It is just that these state changes are of a *conventional* kind not a physical kind.

Thus, Wittgenstein wrote at the start of the Tractatus that "The world is the totality of facts, not of things" (Wittgenstein, 1922). However, while he did divide the world into facts which could be true or false, he did not go on to distinguish further between two types of fact: *brute* facts which are true (or not) by physical reality, and *institutional* facts which are true (or not) by agreement or convention within the context of an institution (Searle, 1969). In this sense, speech acts are just another means of bringing about certain states of affairs in the particular context of an institution; and from this point of view, Speech Act Theory is better understood as a theory of *institutions* rather than of language.

However, by a curious temporal coincidence, in the same year as FIPA's inaugural meeting Jones and Sergot published their paper on formal characterisation of *institutionalised power* (Jones and Sergot, 1996). The term institutionalised power refers to this characteristic feature of institutions, whereby identified agents, acting in appointed roles, are empowered to create or modify facts of conventional significance in the context of institution (*institutional facts*), through the performance of a designated action, often a speech act. Jones and Sergot's formal characterisation was based on a logical consequence relation whereby an agent A sees to it that X (holds) counts as (if) institution I sees to it that Y (holds).

In this way: a person appointed to the role of auctioneer performing the speech act "sold" counts as a contract between a buyer and a seller according to the institution of the auction house; a person appointed to the role of priest performing the speech act "I pronounce you ..." counts as a marriage contract according to the institution of the church; and so on.

This formalisation of institutionalised power was a critical contribution to the logical specification of agent societies.

1.7 Specification of Agent Societies

1.7.1 *Norm-Governed MAS (NG-MAS)*

In the EU ALFEBIITE[10] project, an executable specification language was developed for a sub-class of agent societies (Artikis and Sergot, 2010). This language adopted the perspective of an external observer and viewed societies as instances of normative systems; that is, it described the permissions and obligations of the members of the societies, but took into account that the behaviour of agents in the society might deviate from the ideal (i.e. they might do what they were not permitted to, might not do what they were obliged to, and so on).

Moreover, the language explicitly referenced and represented the institutionalised powers of the member agents, which is a standard feature of any institutional or norm-governed interaction. Consequently, it also maintained the long established distinction, in the

---

[10]Pronounced $\alpha\beta$: the acronym stood for "A Logical Framework for Ethical Behaviour between Infohabitants in the Information Trading Economy of the Universal Information Ecosystem". No, me neither, and I was coordinating the project. Allegedly.

study of social and legal systems, between physical capability, institutionalised power and permission. Thus, physical capability referred to the ability of an agent to create or modify brute facts, institutionalised power referred to the ability of an agent to create or modify institutional facts, and permission qualifies both: an agent may (or may not) have the permission to exercise its physical capability, and may (or may not) have the permission to exercise its institutionalised power. Note that just as exercising physical capability without permission still changes the (physical) world, exercising institutionalised power without permission still changes the conventional world (institutional facts).

The specification of powers, permissions and obligations provided the 'building blocks' for specifying more complex normative relations such as rights and duties.

Finally, the specification language provided a declarative formalisation of these concepts by means of temporal action languages with clear routes to implementation: in particular (but not only) the EC (Kowalski and Sergot, 1986) (see below) but also C/C+. The specification could therefore be validated and executed at design-time and run-time, so that the system designers could animate and validate the specification, and the agents could inspect (and introspect on) their actions.

This sub-class of computational society, as a computational instantiation of the 'open agent society', was, over the next few years, the basis for exploring various ideas in virtual organisations and for piecemeal formulation of various different protocols (for auctions, voting, dispute resolution, argumentation, access control, etc.), until it coalesced in the concept of dynamic norm-governed multi-agent systems.

1.7.2 *Dynamic NG-MAS*

In some multi-agent systems, changes in environmental, composition or other conditions may entail modifiable specifications, i.e. specifications that are modifiable during the system execution (see also Sec. 2.5). To deal with run-time self-modification, this framework for agent societies was extended to support 'dynamic' specifications, that is, specifications that are developed at design-time but may be modified at run-time by the agents themselves (Artikis, 2012).

```
                  ┌─────────────────────┐
                  │  Level k−1 protocol:│
                  │   decision-making   │
                  │  over level k−2 rules│
                  └─────────────────────┘
                            ⋮
 transition       ┌─────────────────────┐    transition
 protocol:        │   Level 1 protocol: │    protocol:
 meta protocol    │   decision-making   │    object protocol
 initialisation   │   over level 0 rules│    rule modification
                  └─────────────────────┘
                  ┌─────────────────────┐
                  │  Level 0 protocol:  │
                  │   MAS specification │
                  └─────────────────────┘
```

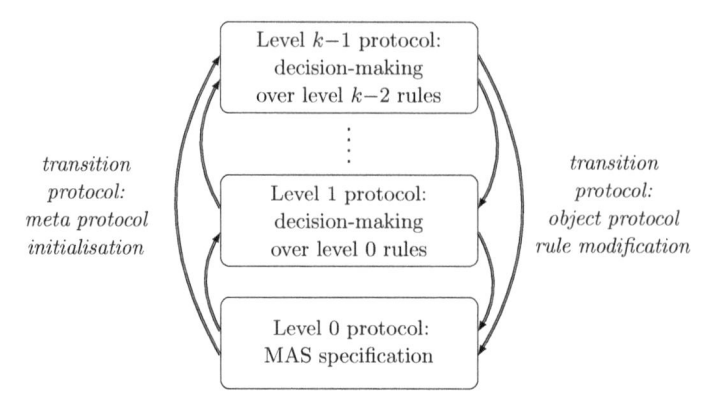

Fig. 1.5. A Framework for Dynamic Specifications.

A protocol for conducting business in a multi-agent system, such as an auction protocol for task delegation like the contract-net protocol, is classified as an 'object' protocol. This protocol may have a number of changeable parameters, as illustrated by the variations of the contract-net protocol shown earlier. At some point during the execution of the object protocol, the participants may initiate a 'meta' protocol in order to potentially modify the object protocol rules — for instance, it might change the value assigned to a parameter, or it might replace an existing rule-set with a new one. The meta-protocol may be any protocol for decision-making over rule modification, such as voting or argumentation.

This framework for dynamic specifications is displayed in Fig. 1.5. Note that the participants in a meta–protocol may initiate a meta–meta protocol to modify the rules of the meta protocol, and they may initiate a meta–meta–meta protocol to modify the rules of the meta–meta protocol, and so on. In general, in a k-level framework, level 0 corresponds to the main (object level) protocol, while a protocol of level n, $0 < n \leq k-1$ is created by the protocol participants of a level m, $0 \leq m < n$, in order to decide whether or not to modify the protocol rules of level $n-1$, and if so, how.

Although in principle this looks like infinite regress, in practice it is unlikely to arise. In any case, the regress can be halted at some level k by the simple expedient of declaring level k rules to be immutable (see Secs. 6.7.3 and 10.6.3). Another protocol could make an immutable rule mutable, modify it, and then declare it immutable again. Remember, these are conventional rules: we can pretend that they are as fixed and permanent as physical rules, if it is convenient; but also manipulate them as we see fit, if that is equally convenient. However, this does mean scrutiny and accountability are essential: rules do have to be followed, and be seen to be followed; and the justification for such behaviour (modifying 'immutable' rules) should be explainable to some appropriate authority (see Chapter 10).

Apart from object and meta protocols, the framework also includes 'transition' protocols (see Fig. 1.5). Transition protocols are procedures that express, among other things, the conditions under which an agent is permitted to initiate a meta protocol, the roles that each meta protocol participant will occupy, and the ways in which an object protocol is modified as a result of the meta protocol interactions. Furthermore, an agent's proposal for specification change can be evaluated by taking into consideration the effects of accepting such a proposal on systemic criteria, such as efficiency, effectiveness, fairness, congruence, or social welfare (utility). One approach to this is some form of *reflection* (Landauer and Bellman, 2003): components of the system have their own internal model of the system itself and can reason about the effects of proposed changes. Such reflection might be based on the representation of a dynamic specification as a *metric space* (Bryant, 1985).

A dynamic NG-MAS specification defines a set of rules, and for each rule, it identifies the *degrees of freedom* (DoF), that is, the changeable parameters and the range of values those parameters can take. Therefore, a set of rules R implicitly defines an n-dimensional *specification space* $\mathcal{L}$, where each instance of the specification space is characterised by a different assignment of values to each parameter in each rule. (The significance of the *size* of this space is considered in Sec. 2.5.)

A point in the specification space represents a complete dynamic specification — a *specification instance* — and is denoted by an n-tuple where each element of the tuple expresses a 'value' of a DoF. One way of evaluating a proposal for changing from one specification instance to another is to compute a 'distance' between different specification instances. Then the specification instance can specify rules about 'moving' in its own space: for example, certain configurations of parameter values may be considered unacceptable (invalid), or there may be constraints on how 'far' the specification can be

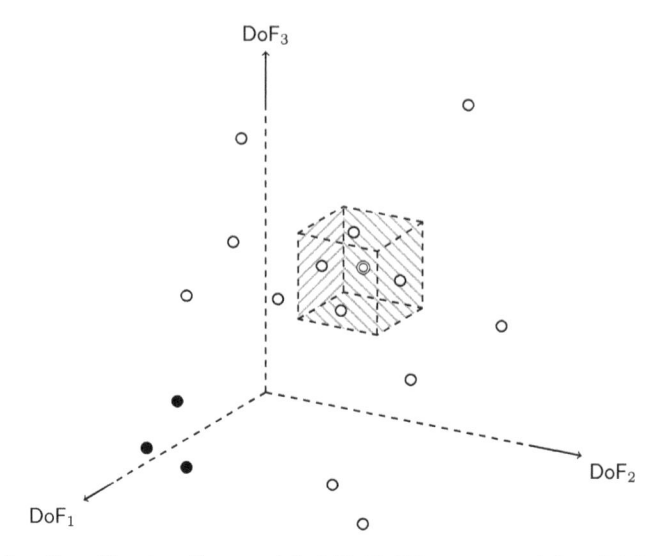

Fig. 1.6. Specification Space with 3-DoF, Distance, and Invalid Instances

changed, based on a distance metric d. Figure 1.6 depicts a specification with (an unlikely) three degrees of freedom, the bold circle is the current specification instance, filled circles are invalid, allowable changes are within the grey area. The enactment of proposals (for transitions to alternative specification instances) that do not meet the distance or difference criteria are constrained. However, rules about these criteria are also conventional and could be changed to make these instances accessible.

Note that one motivation for formalising such constraints in this way is to favour gradual changes of a system specification. This is akin to Popper's approach to dealing with social problems through gradual incremental change over time (to address reflective and standard software engineering questions such as: "are we building the right system?", and "are we building the system right?"), in preference to indiscriminate large-scale changes.

1.7.3 *Event Calculus*

Having established the basic concepts of, and a framework for, dynamic norm-governed systems, we need a formal language to represent and reason about action, agency, social constraints and change.

Table 1.1. Main Predicates of the EC

Predicate	Meaning
Act happensAt T	Action Act occurs at time T
initially $F = V$	The value of fluent F is V at time 0
$F = V$ holdsAt T	The value of fluent F is V at time T
Act initiates $F = V$ at T	The occurrence of action Act at time T initiates a period of time for which the value of fluent F is V
Act terminates $F = V$ at T	The occurrence of action Act at time T terminates a period of time for which the value of fluent F is V

There is a variety of action languages (Artikis, 2012); for clarity of exposition, for executable specification, and as a formal specification for implementation, throughout this book we use the Event Calculus (EC) (Kowalski and Sergot, 1986).

The EC is a logic formalism for representing and reasoning about actions or events and their effects. The EC is based on a many-sorted first-order predicate calculus. For the version used here, the underlying model of time is linear, so we use non-negative integer time-points (although this is not an EC restriction). We do not assume that time is discrete (the numbers need not correspond to a uniform duration), but we do impose a relative/partial ordering for events: for non-negative integers, $<$ is sufficient.

An *action description* in EC includes axioms that define: the action occurrences, with the use of happensAt predicates; the effects of actions, with the use of initiates and terminates predicates; and the values of the fluents, with the use of initially and holdsAt predicates. Table 1.1 summarises the main EC predicates. Variables, that start with an upper-case letter, are assumed to be universally quantified unless otherwise indicated. Predicates, function symbols and constants start with a lower-case letter.

A *fluent* is a property that is allowed to have different values at different points in time. Where F is a fluent, the term $F = V$ denotes that fluent F has value V. Boolean fluents are a special case in which the possible values are *true* and *false*. Informally, $F = V$ holds at a particular time-point if: either $F = V$ holds at the start, and has not *terminated* by some action in the meantime; or $F = V$ has been *initiated* by an action at some earlier time-point, and has not *terminated* by some other action in the meantime.

Therefore, events initiate and terminate a period of time during which a fluent holds a value continuously. Events occur at specific times (when they *happen*). A set of events, each with a given time, is called a *narrative*.

The utility of the EC comes from being able to reason with narratives. Therefore, the final part of an EC specification is the domain-independent 'engine' which computes what fluents hold, i.e. have the value *true* in the case of boolean fluents, or what value a fluent takes, for each multi-valued fluent. This can be used to compute a 'state' of the specification in terms of the fluents representing institutional facts. This state changes over time as events happen, and includes the roles, powers, permissions and obligations of agents.

Using the EC as a specification language, and reasoning with narratives, also allows the definition of a generic *monitoring* and *sanctioning* mechanism. This mechanism can be used for detecting behaviour that is not compliant with the rules. It will be illustrated in the definition of protocols for voting in Chapter 4 and dispute resolution in Chapter 5, but (using the literary device of ironic foreshadowing) the central importance of this mechanism will become clear in Chapter 6.

An EC action description for an NG-MAS is specified using axioms of the following form:

$$Action(Agent) \text{ initiates } F = V \text{ at } T \leftarrow Conditions$$

which are read as stating: the occurrence of action *Action* at time T initiates a period of time for which the value of fluent F is V, if the *Conditions* are satisfied. Typically, *Conditions* will include a reference to institutionalised power, so that the *Action* can only be (meaningfully, validly) performed by those agents empowered to do so, usually by virtue of occupying a designated role.

Generally, the conditions will include that the agent performing the action is empowered (has the institutionalised power) to do so. This is represented as:

$$\textbf{pow}(Agent, Action(\ldots)) = true \text{ holdsAt } T$$

Note that (institutionalised) power to perform an action often, but not always, implies permission to perform that action. Note that powers, as well as permissions and obligations, are also represented by fluents, so can be initiated (or terminated) for a period of time by such actions.

A *narrative* is a sequence of actions which happen at specific times:

$$Action_1 \text{ happensAt } T1$$
$$Action_2 \text{ happensAt } T2$$
$$\ldots$$

The EC does have its limitations: although it is very elegant, and the engine is 16 lines of Prolog code, long narratives can be challenging to process. So although the EC has 'clean' semantics, it has 'poor' performance; however, many of the languages used for event recognition had 'good' performance but not much in the way of semantics. A significant achievement has been the development of Run-Time Event Calculus (RTEC), which is a logic-based language with declarative semantics but capable of processing thousands of events per second (Artikis *et al.*, 2015); this language has been used in several applications such as city transportation and maritime monitoring (Pitsikalis *et al.*, 2019).

1.8 Simulation and Animation

The previous section dealt with the central part of the methodology, the formal characterisation of a theory. In this section, we consider the right-hand side of the methodology, the principled operationalisation via simulation and animation, using the software platform PreSage-2 as an exemplar.

PreSage-2 (Macbeth *et al.*, 2014) is one of many software platforms which are available for agent-based modelling or multi-agent based simulation. Alternative platforms which are also suitable for simulation and animation tasks include Netlogo (Wilensky and Rand, 2015), Repast (North *et al.*, 2006) and MASON (Luke *et al.*, 2005). The feature sets of these platforms are quite similar, although arguably Netlogo is more oriented towards less experienced programmers, with usage being largely graphical user-interface based; while

MASON and PreSage-2 sit at the other end of the scale, with powerful capabilities for more experienced programmers and all functionality being code-based. Repast lies somewhere in between these two points. A general survey of the basic features of agent-based modelling tools, which provides an indicative evaluation of which platforms are suitable for particular tasks, can be found in Nikolai and Madey (2009).

PreSage-2 itself is a second generation agent animation and multi-agent simulation platform, developed from the original PreSage platform (Neville and Pitt, 2009) and its variant PreSage-$\mathcal{MS}$ (Carr et al., 2009), which was specifically developed to work with the idea of metric spaces in dynamic norm-governed systems as outlined in the previous section. In this section, we briefly overview PreSage-2 only, but this illustrates the features needed when developing or selecting a simulation/animation platform for experimental purposes (see also Sec. 2.3.3).

PreSage-2 is designed as a prototyping platform to aid the systematic modelling of systems and generation of simulation results. Therefore, the platform has to: simulate computationally intensive agent algorithms with large populations of agents; simulate the networked and physical environment in which the agents interact, including unexpected external events; reason about social relationships between agents including their powers, permissions and obligations; support systematic experimentation; and support aggregation and animation of simulation results.

The platform is composed of packages which work together to control the execution of a simulation as illustrated in Fig. 1.7:

- **Core:** Controls and executes the main simulation loop and other key management functions;
- **State engine:** Stores and updates simulation state;
- **Rule engine:** Processes agent actions with respect to descriptions (e.g. as specified using the EC);
- **Environment and agent libraries:** Implementations of use cases which can be used in common environment and/or agent types;
- **Communication network simulator:** Emulates a dynamic, inter-agent communication network;

(a) PreSage-2 Architecture

(b) PreSage-2 Simulation Plan

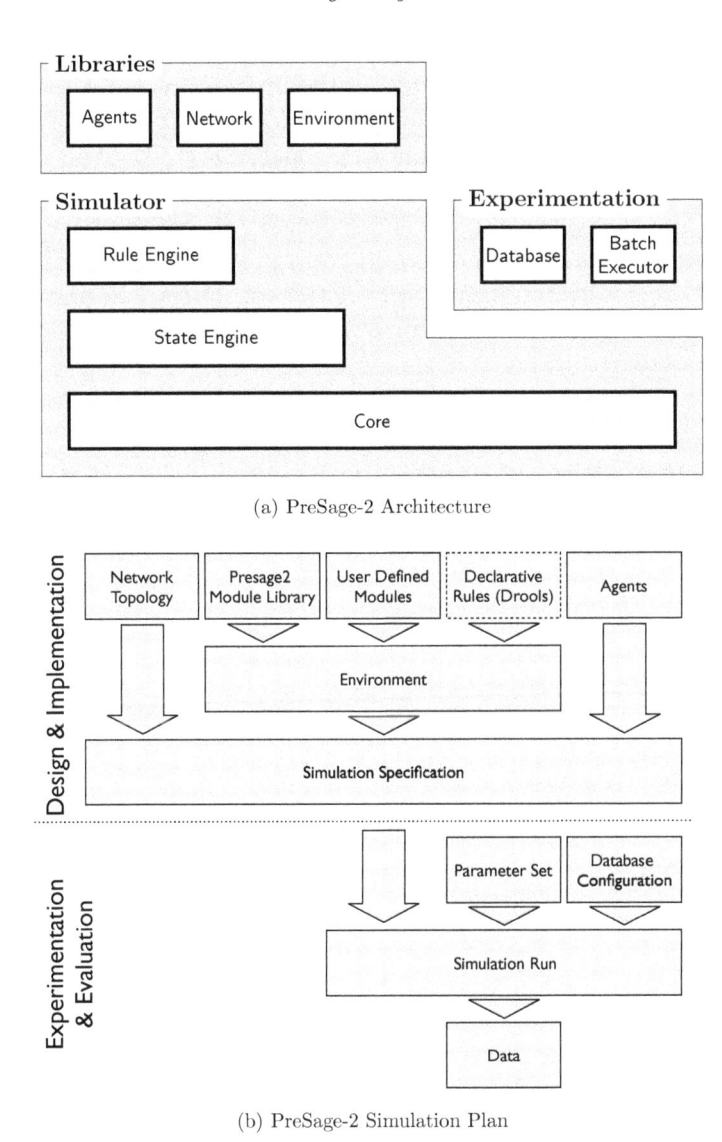

Fig. 1.7. PreSage-2 Agent Animator and Multi-Agent Simulator

- **Database:** Enables storage of simulation data and results for subsequent analysis; and
- **Batch executor:** Tools to automate batch processing (i.e. to enable multiple runs of systems with dynamics or randomness, measuring independent/dependent variables, etc.).

The PreSage-2 simulator's core controls the main simulation loop as well as the initialisation of a simulation from parameter sets. The simulation uses discrete time, with each loop being a single timestep in the simulation. At each timestep, each agent is given a chance to perform physical and communicative actions, and the simulation state is updated according to these actions as well as to any external events. Agent architecture and computational complexity is not limited (except by the limitations of the computer running the simulation). The platform waits for every agent's function to terminate before moving to the next time step.

A key concept of multi-agent simulation is that the agents share a common environment. The state engine package simulates this environment as a state space. This package allows the user to control two important functions: firstly, the observability of state for each agent, and secondly, the effect of an agent's action on the state. The former specifies what state an agent can read given the current environment state, while the latter determines a state change given the current state and the set of all actions performed in the last timestep. The user defines these functions from a set of modules. Each module can be seen as an independent set of rules regarding observability and/or state changes. This method allows for behavioural modules to be slotted into a system without conflict, building up complex system rules from the composition of modules. This modularity also supports re-use across different simulation environments and experiments.

An optional PreSage-2 configuration uses the Drools production rule engine, based on the Rete algorithm (Forgy, 1982), as the underlying state storage engine, encapsulating all features of the initial implementation plus additional benefits afforded by Drools. Drools allows structured and relational data to be stored in the state, providing for a much richer state representation. Moreover, Drools features a forward chaining rule engine, so that declarative rules (contained in the Rule Engine) can be used to modify the state stored in the State Engine. The declarative form of these rules is close to that of action languages such as the EC (and it is possible for the axioms of the Event 'engine' to be used in Drools directly (Bragaglia *et al.*, 2012)). It is practically possible to port a dynamic norm-governed specification in the EC into PreSage-2 via a translation into Drools, although so far this has only been demonstrated manually rather than through a compiler.

1.9 Summary

The narrative of this chapter started from the need to design and implement complex socio-technical and cyber-physical systems as part of the 'digital transformation' to the 'digital society'. Since both types of system involve autonomous components encapsulating some degree of computational intelligence, and *having* to interact with one another, we proposed to use the perspectives of both open systems and social systems to construct *societies of agents*. We then surveyed several aspects of that construction process: a methodology, technology, communication (and in particular institutionalised power and conventional facts), specification and simulation.

It remains the case though this "agent society" is a designed artefact, or, at risk of sounding slightly over-blown, a teleologically-created micro-universe. Whichever, the artefact was designed for a purpose but, as we have discussed, the designer has departed for (as the poet says) fresh woods and pastures new, leaving the agents facing an existential crisis, lost and alone in their own little micro-universes with the only meaning that which they can construct for themselves. Since we don't want our agents sending themselves *terminate* messages at the sheer absurdity of it all, and we can't make them read Camus (yet), we need some other solution to the issues of long-lived agent societies that can maintain and even modify their purpose, with respect to some sense of order and value. The solution we will consider is *self-organisation*.

Chapter 2

Self-Organising Systems

2.1 Introduction

In Chapter 1, we saw how embedded (cyber-physical) systems and situated (socio-technical) systems need to show some kind of responsiveness to prevailing operational and/or environmental conditions with respect to possibly competing goals and interests of the components.

Examples of embedded systems include data centres, sensor networks and cloud computing. In a data centre (as discussed in Sec. 1.5.1), a performance manager and a power manager traded off response time against power consumption. In sensor networks, a group of sensors have limited battery life before needing to recharge, and have to trade off accuracy and coverage against longevity: accuracy and coverage are maximised when all the sensors are on; longevity is maximised if the sensors are turned on one at a time. In cloud computing and "X as a service", the quality of that service can be traded off against total cost of ownership.

An example of a situated system was the community energy system (or SmartGrid) with renewable generation sources and Smart-Meters to represent households, businesses, etc. This allows energy generation, distribution and consumption to 'flip' from a supply-side model, where generators meet demand by increasing or decreasing production while maintaining voltage and frequency control, to demand-side response, involving the incentivised shift in energy consumption over time, usually to flatten peak demand or to account for stochastic generation from renewable resources. In 'islanded' grids, as envisaged by the community energy systems of Sec. 1.2.1, the general policy is to look upon the energy generated as a common-pool resource, and the "prosumers" have to decide the allocation and appropriation, as we have seen, between and by themselves.

The common feature of all these examples is that the system overall needs to show some form of modification or adjustment to meet new conditions. Moreover, that re-adjustment should improve some aspect of behaviour or performance, it should be the intended facet, and it should change in an expected way. In system design, this has been more explicitly defined as *self-** requirements, where the '*' is a wild card standing for a variety of properties, so self-managing, self-configuring, self-healing and so on. To achieve these self-* requirements, the general process that we propose to analyse, and operationalise, is *self-organisation*.

Self-organisation is a process that has been observed time and again in the natural sciences (i.e. physics, chemistry and biology) and the social sciences (e.g. sociology, anthropology and economics). Essentially, the process of self-organisation results in the appearance of some kind of global system order that emerges from local interactions between component parts of that system. The endpoint of global order may emerge from any initial situation of total disorder, it does not require intervention of control of any external authority, and may not be the intention of any of the interacting parts.

In biological science, self-organisation is observed in morphogenesis, social behaviour in insects, and flocking behaviour in fish and birds. More or less explicitly applying the methodology of biologically inspired computing (Andrews *et al.*, 2010) (*cf.* Sec. 1.4), this has led to algorithms for solving optimisation problems in networks based on pheromone-trail laying and stigmergy observed in insect behaviour (ant-colony optimisation (Dorigo, 1997; Dorigo and Stützle, 2004)), algorithms producing swarm behaviour (e.g. Schmickl and Crailsheim, 2008, and see Sec. 2.3.1), and computer applications for morphogenetic engineering (Doursat *et al.*, 2012).

This chapter begins in Sec. 2.2 (with what will become a running example set in the context of a SmartHouse) with an illustration of premeditated self-organisation, where the process itself is undertaken with intention, and is both the subject of deliberation, and subject to self-organisation. Section 2.3 differentiates systems in which self-organisation emerges spontaneously and those in which it arises deliberately (and deliberatively). This leads to a consideration in

Sec. 2.4 of both the 'self' and the 'organisation', providing the basis for an analytic framework of the 'dimensions' of self-organisation: the 'what', 'how', 'why' and 'evaluation' of self-organisation in Sec. 2.5. Section 2.6 offers a preliminary answer to the questions of 'what' and 'how'. The rest of the book is a deeper analysis of 'how', with corresponding explanation of 'why' and of 'evaluation'. The chapter concludes in Sec. 2.7 with some pointers towards strategic and social interaction.

2.2 Example: Same As It Ever Was

...And you may find yourself living in a beautiful house, a Smart-House as described in Sec. 1.2, and as illustrated in Fig. 2.1(a). And you may find your house is equipped with PV solar panels in the roof, and an array of gadgets and modern appliances in your tastefully furnished dwelling space (Fig. 2.1(b)).

And you may ask yourself, can you turn on all your gadgets and appliances, so that you can complete a list of tasks that you have mysteriously been asked to perform? In which case, you might first consult your SmartMeter, which is rather more accessible (although in this case slightly more intrusive, see Fig. 2.1(c)). This SmartMeter shows how much energy you are generating and have stored, and your current consumption, and projections show the former is greater than the latter. And so you may conclude that you can just turn on all your gadgets and appliances.

And you may ask yourself, what could possibly go wrong?

Quite a lot as it turns out, since if you were in the situation as described, then you might be playing *Social mPower* (Bourazeri et al., 2016), a Serious Game (Michaal and Chen, 2005) developed to investigate a further SmartGrid transition, not just from supply-side to demand-side, but now from demand-side response to *demand-side self-organisation*. It being a game, *cathedra mea, regulae meae*,[1] as it might be said, so next thing you know it is no longer a sunny day, there is no longer enough energy to power all those gadgets and appliances, and so you cannot win, it would seem.

---

[1] My game; my rules.

(a) dCES with Three SmartHouses and Local Generation

(b) Programmable Appliances Inside a SmartHouse

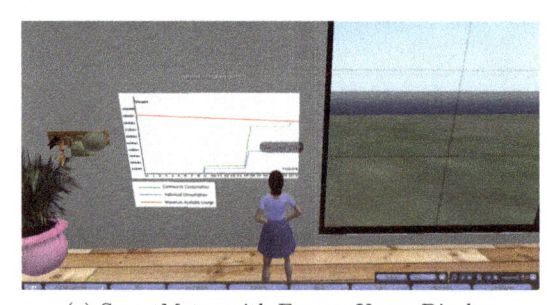

(c) SmartMeter with Energy Usage Display

Fig. 2.1. Self-Organisation of Resources in the Serious Game *Social mPower*

But hold on — this is a multi-player Serious Game: there are other occupants of houses much like yours, just over there. Perhaps they could turn out to be neighbourly, and 'lend' you some of their energy, for now, and you can repay the 'loan' later, when the weather is better, say.

And then over time, what would a visitor from another planet see, perhaps? That somehow, although each occupant did not have enough energy on her own to power all her appliances and gadgets immediately, all occupants did have enough energy collectively to power all their appliances and devices eventually. Yet, there was no one telling them what to do: instead some seemingly spontaneous collective order has emerged as a result of the various interactions between the haphazard collection of individuals.

This then is the essence of *self-organisation*. So, the question is, how do we implement self-organisation in a multi-agent system? Our answer begins with a study of *emergence* in *swarms* and *cellular automata*.

2.3 Emergence

In complex systems, *emergence* can be a global property of local interactions, or occurs when a collective entity is observed to possess or display properties which none of its parts have on their own. In the two examples described in this section, we firstly observe that swarming behaviour emerges as a consequence of interactions between separate entities, but none of the entities can produce the behaviour on its own; and secondly we observe that repeating patterns emerge as as a consequence of interactions between separate cells, but none of the cells can produce the pattern on its own.

2.3.1 *Swarms*

Boids (Reynolds, 1987) is an example of how leaderless, distributed flocking behaviour can be produced by each 'flockmate' following a set of simple rules relating its velocity and direction with respect to neighbouring flockmates. These rules are as follows:

- **Separation:** Move to avoid over-crowding local flockmates;
- **Cohesion:** Move towards average position of local flockmates;
- **Alignment:** Move towards average heading of local flockmates; and
- **Synchrony:** Move towards average velocity of local flockmates.

As an example, the pattern shown in Fig. 2.2 was produced with a Qu-Prolog implementation of the algorithms specified for these rules. This situated a flock of 20 'boids' in a grid 1000×1000 and changes a goal position every so often. The boids swarm to and around the goal until a new goal is set.

The flocking behaviour is creating order out of apparent chaos, producing global outcomes as a product of following local rules and

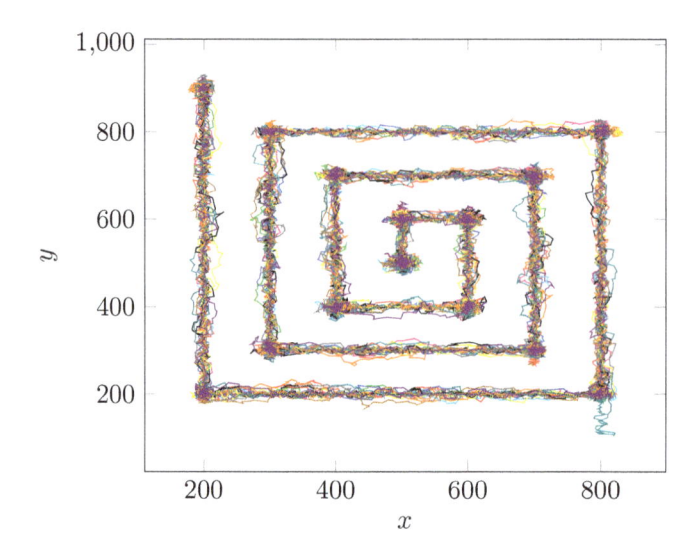

Fig. 2.2. Boids on the Wing

only local interactions. It shows that emergent behaviour can arise spontaneously without design or purpose, and in spite of whatever expectations the second law of thermodynamics might have supplied. Moreover, none of the boids has any goal or even any idea about flocking.

On the other hand, the spiral pattern is also an emergent feature, but this is one that has been designed by the programmer. However, it is only apparent and 'meaningful' to an external observer: again, none of the constituent parts had any knowledge or intention of creating this pattern. However, we are interested in self-organising systems where the parts *do* have an awareness of these global structures and an intention to construct them, and to determine by and for themselves rule-sets by which such global outcomes emerge from purely local interactions.

2.3.2 Cellular Automata

A cellular automaton consists of a set of cells arranged on a grid of specified size, shape and dimensions. Each cell is in one of a finite number of possible states, and each cell has a neighbourhood, defined by a distance relative to that cell. The state of the grid is called a *generation*. The automaton iteratively evolves through a series of discrete time steps according to a fixed set of rules, whereby the state of the ith generation is computed from the $(i-1)$th generation by visiting each cell in turn and updating its state by applying the rules to the state of the cells in its neighbourhood. Note that the actual update of the state of a cell occurs only after the state-update has been computed for every cell.

Cellular automata are perhaps best known or commonly encountered through John Conway's Game of Life (Gardner, 1970), either because of its foundational contributions to understanding of computation and philosophy, or because of simple aesthetically pleasing screen-savers used by 1980s Sun workstations, according to preference.

The Game of Life is a zero-player game (i.e. beyond the initial configuration, no further input is strictly necessary) which is 'played' on a finite 2D grid of size $M \times N$. The grid is a torus: so the left-hand edge is the right-hand 'neighbour' of the right edge (and vice versa); and the topmost edge is the lower neighbour of the lowest edge (and vice versa). Each cell has a status: dead or alive; but this status is not fixed and depends on what is going on around it (i.e. the status of its neighbours).

As stated above, the game is played in discrete time steps, each step defining a generation, with the successor generation computed from its predecessor by applying a fixed set of rules. The ruleset commonly used in the Game of Life includes the following:

- **Loneliness:** An alive cell with fewer than two live neighbours becomes dead;
- **Suffocation:** An alive cell with more than three live neighbours becomes dead;
- **Abiogenesis:** A dead cell with exactly three live neighbours becomes a live cell; and
- **Stet:** An alive cell with two or three live neighbours stays alive.

This set of rules has some interesting properties and gives rise to some remarkable behaviours. For example, because it is possible to build logic gates out of moving patterns, the game has a computational power equivalent to a universal Turing machine (Chapman, 2002). Theoretically, this implies that if something can be computed by an algorithm, then it can be computed by the Game of Life. Other properties include unpredictability (the nth generation should not be inferred from the 0th (i.e. initial) generation); the potential to reproduce itself; and simplicity.

A further remarkable property that followed from these rules is the range of possible outcomes. This includes: wipe-out (all cells are dead), stagnation (some cells are alive, but the cell pattern is unchanging from one generation to the next), stability (the cell pattern changes from one generation to the next, but after a fixed period returns to the original pattern), and quasi-stability (the cell pattern appears stable, but a 'disruptive' event occurs and the pattern goes through a period of seeming chaos, before settling down to another period of apparent stability, before another 'disruptive' event, and so on; quasi-stability is a feature derived from cybernetic systems (Ashby, 1952) and further discussed in Chapter 10).

However, perhaps the most remarkable (and sought after) behaviour is the ability of a pattern to reproduce and transpose itself. These patterns appear to be 'alive': one can see them moving across the screen. The simplest is called the glider: composed of just five alive cells in a 3 × 3 sub-grid, it repeats itself in four generations, during which time it moves one cell horizontally and one cell vertically (the direction depends on initial orientation). These gliders are the basis of the various complex behaviours, including the simulation of logic gates from which the game derives its computational equivalence to a universal Turing machine.

After the glider, numerous other types of patterns were discovered or programmed, including oscillators, spaceships (patterns like gliders, but larger, which move across the grid), and guns, which emit repeating patterns like gliders. This implies that not only are patterns reproducible, but they are also capable of infinite growth (second law of thermodynamics: eat your heart out).

Consequently, the Game of Life has been the source of much inventive programming and theoretical research into emergence and self-organisation, while cellular automata in general have found many applications in modelling of physical and biological systems. However, this is still not quite the self-organisation that we want.

2.3.3 Self-Organisation

In this book, we are concerned with *intentional* self-organisation produced by local interactions involving choice, coordination and decision-making. This might involve many processes, such as self-awareness, reflection or interoception, but the crucial feature is the contrast with 'pure' *emergence*. The basic idea underlying intentional self-organisation is that the system components organise themselves, by themselves and without outside interference, assistance or incentive (other than 'evolving' to be fit for, or congruent with, an environment in which they are embedded).

Emergence	Self-Organisation
the non-introspective application ...	the introspective application ...
of hard-wired local computations ...	of soft-wired local computations ...
with respect to physical rules and/or the environment ...	with respect to physical rules, environment and/or conventional rules ...
which result in unknown and/or unintended global outcomes.	to achieve intended and coordinated global outcomes.

For example, contrast the 'emergence' shown in Fig. 2.3. The figure shows, on the left, a flock of migratory birds in a particular formation, and on the right a football team in different tactical formations. Although there are some significant signalling and leadership functions in the former (the bird at the front is *not* the leader; there is one bird who is 'better' than the others at direction-finding which signals to the lead bird in which direction to fly), the birds appear to follow instinctive rules according to the state of the environment, and have

Fig. 2.3. Emergence vs. Self-Organisation

no more intention to create a 'V'-shaped formation than any other shape or structure, other than that the 'V' is aerodynamically well-suited to travelling long distances (the birds position themselves and phase their wingbeats close to the aerodynamic optimum, but they don't publish articles in *Nature* to prove it (Portugal *et al.*, 2014)).

On the right-hand side, the formation of the football team, whether orchestrated by a manager or the players themselves, is specifically adopted according to their personnel, the opposition, or the situation of a game. The team itself is composed of multi-functional components (some components are capable of occupying different positions); conventional rules are mutually agreed between competing composite entities (for example, there is a limit of eleven players, but there is no such numerical restriction on the birds); moreover, these rules are enforced by a third party (the referee); and the players plan the formation ahead of time (or adopt this, or a different formation, at 'run-time') with the intention of achieving a specific tactical or strategic outcome.

2.3.4 Planned Emergence

In boids and cellular automata, we see that:

- The 'agents' are homogenous;
- Their behaviour is hard-wired;
- Communication (if any) affects 'cognitive' state;
- There are no conventional rules;
- Emergence is unintentional; and
- Processing is lightweight (simple) (each agent is a point or particle which can be implemented as a cell in an array).

With self-organisation, we also expect there to be conventional (as opposed to physical) rules and exercise of institutionalised power; moreover, if these rules are changed (for example, the winning condition), different formations and behaviours (perhaps unintended) will emerge. Besides which, changes are made to the rules in response to environmental changes (for example, a change in the rules in response to technological advancement: for an extended discussion of VAR and the offside rule in soccer, see Singh *et al.* (2019)).

Therefore, for *intelligent* components (i.e. agents) of a self-organising multi-agent system, we want to see that:

- The agents are heterogenous;
- Behaviour is soft-wired (allows for learning);
- Communication affects 'socially-constructed reality' (e.g. through the exercise of institutionalised power (see Sec. 1.6.3));
- There are conventional (mutually agreed, mutable) rules (part of that socially constructed reality);
- Emergence is intentional and introspective (planned for); and
- Processing is 'heavy' ('heavier') (each agent requires a separate thread, machine, etc.).

In summary, we want the system components themselves to decide on and adjust the conventional rules by which local interactions produce an intended global outcome. We also want the following features:

- *Structuration* (Giddens, 1984): Structures are composed of agents, and agents have memory of structures;
- 'Proceduration': Rules are enacted by agents, and agents have memory of procedures;
- The conventional rules are themselves an emergent property of the system; and
- The organisation itself to be an agreed product of self-organisation (or self-determination).

In view of these requirements, we next take a closer (but still brief) look at the ideas of what the terms *self* and *organisation* are, or mean.

2.4 The Self and The Organisation

If we want to design and implement self-organising systems, then we should have a clear idea of what *self* and *organisation* mean. The fact that this has been a challenge for some of the finest minds for centuries is no obstacle to taking care of it in a couple of pages. So what follows is not (and could never be) an exhaustive review let alone a definitive statement: however, it does offer some pointers to the literature and offers hopefully, an intuition of both terms that makes it conceptually clear what sort of 'self' and what sort of 'organisation' we are trying to self-organise.

2.4.1 *The Self*

The concept of the *self* has been the subject of study in many different fields: philosophy, psychology, sociology, theology, political science, law and others.

In philosophy, starting with Descartes, Hume, Kant and others, there was the idea of *self-as-subject*, individual's knowledge of itself induced from its own sensory experience; synthesised with mind and imagination to give self-as-object. In Marx's writing, the concept of the self is situated within his theory of alienation, by which is meant a separation of an agent from meaningful agency, most commonly associated with productive labour from the means and benefits of production.

Alienation could be a barrier to the idea of *self-actualisation*. In psychology, self-actualisation is considered an innate need of every person and is concerned with the fulfilment of each person's potential. It is placed at the apex of Maslow's hierarchy of needs, spanning basic physiological needs at the base of the hierarchy, psychological needs in the middle, and finally, self-fulfilment needs at the top (Maslow, 1943). Although not without criticism, the theory has proved popular for considering how motivation, personality and behaviour can be correlated, thereby 'actualising' the self.

Also in psychology, the Mirror Test has been used in animal psychology to determine if an individual animal has the ability to recognise itself in a mirror, implying the mental capacity to construct a secondary representation of the 'self' (Gallup, 1970). This line of investigation has also been pursued in robotics, with the intention to build a robot capable of passing the Mirror Test, in particular enhancing self-knowledge about kinematics and self-calibration using self-observation (Hart and Scassellati, 2014).

From law, a couple of ideas of interest to understanding 'self' from a legal perspective are *habeas corpus* and *personhood*. *Habeas corpus* (literally, "you have the body") is a legal provision through which a case can be brought before a court in order to challenge the legality of a detention or imprisonment (i.e. *prove* "you (should) have the body"). The writ demands that the court should instruct whoever has detained someone to present that person before the court to examine whether or not the detention is lawful. However, *habeas corpus* seems only meaningful if there is a 'corpus' to be detained and released.

The concept of *personhood* defines the legal status of being a person. The notion of *legal personality* provides for rights, responsibilities and liabilities, and is not necessarily restricted to 'natural' persons (humans), but non-human entities too, like companies, corporations or government agencies. In this sense, a 'self' can be an 'organisation', too (see what follows).

From a computational standpoint, the concept of self has been examined in relation to *self-awareness* and *reflection*. Computational self-awareness (Pitt, 2014; Lewis *et al.*, 2016) is concerned with agents that can collect information about their state and progress, learning and maintaining internal models, which contain knowledge that enables them to reason about their behaviour. Reflection (Landauer and Bellman, 2003) is the capacity of a system to reconfigure itself in response to reflection upon and evaluation of its performance. This has been studied in such diverse contexts as self-improving systems for systems integration (Bellman *et al.*, 2014) and motivates the need for run-time models (Landauer and Bellman, 2016). The idea of reflection has also featured in recommendations for governance of socio-ecological systems (Dryzek and Pickering, 2017; Pitt *et al.*, 2020a).

Ultimately, the key feature of self for an agent that we require is slightly more than just reacting to local rules: an agent should have an internal model of the system (even partially), an awareness of its position and role within that system, and a capacity to reflect upon (reason about) its performance, both in the past, and projected into the future. The question then is how these individual 'selves' are capable of managing by themselves a system of themselves, i.e. forming an organisation, whatever that is.

2.4.2 The Organisation

The concept of the *organisation* has also been the subject of study in many different fields: management, politics, sociology, economics and law, among others.

Asked to define an organisation, many people will instinctively draw a hierarchical organisation chart, but such a structure does not define what an organisation is for, nor how it does it, nor any of the implicit processes occurring within it. For example, a drawing of the management hierarchy is not necessarily correlated with a drawing of the social network: the most connected node in the network may not be the 'boss' at the apex of the hierarchy. This implies that the most effective method to disseminate information throughout an organisation is not necessarily to tell the agent at the top.

In Richard Scott and Davis (2016), a sociological study, three different definitions of 'organisation' are offered, not out of obtuseness, but because different definitions from different perspectives provide a sharper focus on different salient aspects. The study starts by identifying the basic 'ingredients' of an organisation:

- **Its environment:** The specific physical, technological, cultural, and social context in which an organisation is embedded;
- **The formal organisation:** Structures, processes, etc.;
- **The informal organisation:** Including culture (patterns of values, norms, beliefs and expectations more or less shared by all members), social network (connections and communications between those members); and power/politics (the distribution of influence, control and 'social-reality' creation based on trading or sharing physical, informational, and conceptual resources and the exercise of institutionalised power);
- **The people/agents:** Basically the participants who make contributions in return for inducements; their knowledge, skills, needs, preferences, fitness for tasks; and aspects of leadership, roles, position in social networks;
- **Work/technology:** Every organisation does 'work' and possesses 'technology' for doing that work; and
- **Strategy/goals:** Define choices, basis of competition, specific tactics and intended outcomes.

Based on these ingredients, three definitions are provided from different perspectives, the Rational Systems perspective, the Natural Systems perspective and the Open Systems perspective.

The Rational Systems perspective defines an organisation as "collectivities oriented to the pursuit of relatively specific goals and exhibiting relatively highly formalized social structures". The focus here is on the normative structure of an organisation. The Natural Systems perspective defines an organisation as "collectivities whose participants are pursuing multiple interests, both disparate and common, but who recognise the value of perpetuating the organisation as an important resource". The focus here is on behavioural structure and social order, in particular, the trade-off between social consensus and social conflict. Social consensus concerns organisational stability and continuity and reflects the need for cooperative behaviour and the existence of shared norms and values. Social conflict results from the suppression of some interests by others, but recognises conflict as a basis for understanding instability and as a potential source of necessary change. The Open Systems perspective defines an organisation as "congeries [aggregations] of interdependent flows and activities linking shifting coalitions of participants embedded in wider material-resource and institutional environments". Of course, this perspective takes us back to the description and features of open systems introduced in Sec. 1.3.1.

As one of its goals and appreciating its contribution to self-preservation, every organisation seeks to narrow the gap between the potential and the actual value of its collective knowledge for 'correct' or 'optimal' decision-making capability. The gap is perhaps most widely known through the corporate lament "If only HP [Hewlett-Packard] knew what HP knows", recognising the difference between the organisation's actual performance with fragmented knowledge and the organisation's potential performance if that knowledge could be synthesised (Sieloff, 1999). This "knowledge gap" problem has deep historical roots in political science (Ober, 2008), social choice theory (List and Goodin, 2001), and organisational theory (Davenport and Prusak, 1998), and narrowing it is a crucial requirement for successful reflection.

At the root of this is a sense of recursion: for an organisation to self-organise optimally, it has to 'know' what its constituent selves know. This invokes the *viable system model* defined by Stafford Beer in his work on *management cybernetics* (Beer, 1959), which was concerned with how an organisation modifies itself to survive in a changing environment, maintains its identity (coherence), and fulfils its purpose. The rules for a viable system (Beer, 1981) include the recursive system theorem, which states that "In a recursive organizational structure, any viable system contains, and is contained in, a viable system". There are practical limits to this theorem.

2.5 The Dimensions of Self-Organisation

2.5.1 *An Analytic Framework for Self-Organisation*

In Bonabeau *et al.* (1999), it is proposed that self-organisation relies on four basic ingredients:

(1) strong dynamical nonlinearity, often though not necessarily involving positive and negative feedback;
(2) balance of exploitation and exploration;
(3) multiple interactions; and
(4) availability of energy (to overcome a natural tendency toward entropy, or disorder).

However, an alternative conclusion from this brief but wide-ranging discussion of 'self' and 'organisation' is, apart from there being no conclusive definition, that self-organisation implies that there is some 'ingredient' of an organisation the needs to be modified, and the process of self-modification has to come from within the system, i.e. as a product of self-awareness, reflection or interoception.

From this, we can propose instead a framework for analysis along four dimensions of self-organisation:

(1) The modifiers/modified — who or what is changed or modified?
(2) The mechanics — how is change or modification performed?
(3) The motivation — when and why is change or modification required?
(4) The evaluation — how is change or modification assessed?

In Sec. 2.5.2, we address the first of these questions, and after that in Sec. 2.6, use two examples to illustrate how change can be brought about. However, every chapter in the book can be seen as an attempt to address one or more of these questions, but particularly the third and fourth: knowing or understanding when and why change is required, and establishing criteria to evaluate the consequences or benefits of change.

2.5.2 *The General Setting for Self-Organisation*

The general setting for self-organising multi-agent systems is illustrated in Fig. 2.4. Essentially, a set of agents embedded in an

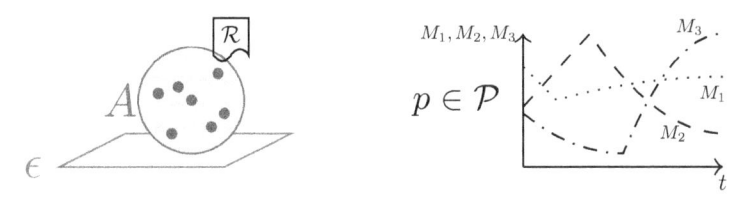

Fig. 2.4. Abstract Setting for Self-Organising Multi-Agent Systems

environment must select, modify and apply a set of rules in order to resolve some problems or achieve some objectives. For now (but see Chapter 6), we can define an institution $\mathcal{I}$ at a time t by:

$$\mathcal{I}_t = \langle \mathcal{A}, \epsilon, \mathcal{P}, \mathcal{R} \rangle_t$$

where:

- $\mathcal{A}$ is the collective set of agents;
- ϵ is their environment;
- $\mathcal{P}$ is a set of problems or goals for the collective;
- $\mathcal{R}$ is a set of rules, or policies.

Note that the environment ϵ_t consists of both brute facts (those facts true by virtue of physical reality) and institutional facts (those facts true by mutual agreement, i.e. it is a socially constructed reality). Therefore, the ruleset $\mathcal{R}_t$, which denotes the rules in force at time t, could be considered as a distinguished element of the (institutional) environment ϵ_t, although that is reserved for the archive of knowledge codification (Ober, 2008). For our purposes, this ruleset is the instance of the specification space defined in Sec. 1.7.2.

Given this general setting, the possible dimensions of change are:

- The physical environment ϵ:
  ○ in frequency, magnitude, and speed;
  ○ regularly or stochastically ('disasters'); and
  ○ naturally or by 'agent-made' intervention.
- Agents $\mathcal{A}$:
  ○ composition (current agents can leave, new agents can join);
  ○ capability (agents' performance can improve or deteriorate);
  ○ connectivity (the social network between agents); and
  ○ individual goals (e.g. maximising utility) and individual values (e.g. fairness).

- The problemset $\mathcal{P}$:
  - composition (problems can be solved, new problems can be created);
  - the relative weight or priority of metrics evaluating 'success'; and
  - the metrics themselves.
- The institutional rules $\mathcal{R}$ can be changed, by the agents A applying rules also specified in $\mathcal{R}$.

The problemset $\mathcal{P}_t = \{P_1, P_2, \ldots, P_n\}$ defines the overall 'mission' of the institution. Note that type of problem, as mentioned earlier, may be an ongoing collective action or coordination problem that needs a resolution encapsulated in the policy selection $\mathcal{R}_t$, and these can vary (e.g. coordination game, stag-hunt game, etc.: see Chapter 3); or it may be a more specific type of problem, which requires a one-off decision which needs to be made according to the structures and procedures specified in $\mathcal{R}_t$.

For example, in a community energy system, one problem (objective) P_1 may be to distribute resources, but achieving this objective might have multiple evaluation criteria and so require various different metrics — see Fig. 2.4. For example, one criteria might be to distribute resources *fairly*, as measured by a metric M_1 (e.g. the Gini index); a second criteria might be to distribute resources *sustainably*, as measured by a metric M_2 (e.g. using Daly Rules (Daly, 1994)). A third criteria, as measured by a metric M_3 (e.g. computational complexity), might be to distribute the resources *cost-effectively*, bearing in mind that in a system with endogenous resources the computation of the distribution must be 'paid for' from the resources being distributed (Pitt and Schaumeier, 2012).

A second example problem P_2 might be to make an investment decision, for example, how much the agents have to contribute individually so that the community can collectively invest in which renewable energy generator. Similarly, in a sensor network for environmental monitoring, there may be a standing policy to trade off accuracy, longevity and coverage; and occasional one-off decisions required to admit new sensors to the collective.

Therefore, turning to $\mathcal{R}$, a ruleset is required which enables the collective to be *multi-functional*, i.e. to solve concurrently multiple different types of problems. However, the relationship between $\mathcal{A}$,

ϵ and $\mathcal{P}$ and $\mathcal{R}$ is not clear. It is most likely the case that there is no optimal $\mathcal{R}$ for all combinations of $\mathcal{A}$, ϵ and $\mathcal{P}$, but even if there were, the number of possible specification instances (the size of specification space) is given by:

$$\begin{aligned} \mid \mathcal{R} \mid = & (V_{1,1} \times V_{1,2} \times \ldots \times V_{1,P_1}) \\ & \times (V_{2,1} \times V_{2,2} \times \ldots \times V_{2,P_2}) \\ & \times \ldots \times (V_{R,1} \times V_{R,2} \times \ldots \times V_{R,P_R}) \end{aligned}$$

where $V_{i,j}$ is the number of values that the jth parameter of rule i can take, P_i is the number of parameters of rule i, and R is the number of rules in the set. Considering the specification space as a search space, it would be far too 'large' for the agents to find the optimal configuration, no matter how 'long-lived' the system is.

2.6 The Mechanics of Change

Given a ruleset $\mathcal{R}$, if this were a 'static' specification: developed at design-time, there would be no support for run-time modification. However, due to environmental, social, or goal-oriented changes (ϵ, $\mathcal{A}$, $\mathcal{P}$, respectively) brought on by incongruence, inefficiency, malfunction or malpractice, it may be preferable, or even necessary, to alter the system specification during the system execution. Therefore, we want $\mathcal{R}$ to be a 'dynamic' specification: to be specified at design-time, but modifiable at run-time by system components.

This process is illustrated with two examples: firstly, by modifying a parameter, i.e. changing some $V_{i,j}$ for some rule $R_i \in \mathcal{R}$; and secondly, by modifying the ruleset, i.e. substituting some rule $R_i \in \mathcal{R}$ for some rule R'_i.

Note that there are many issues with the mechanics of change. For example, the process by which a particular $\mathcal{R}$ is selected has to take into account the different mechanisms by which this can be accomplished, for example, by majority preference (consulting everyone) or expert judgement (consulting just a few). This is significant, because some problems, like estimating the weight of an object, can be solved by averaging the opinions of heterogenous individuals (the *independent guess aggregation* (Ober, 2008) or *wisdom of crowds*

(Surowiecki, 2004)); but others, like selecting a chess move, require expertise.

Applying the wrong mechanism for a type of problem can cause issues: expertise can eliminate diversity and lead to 'groupthink'; while lack of domain knowledge can result in majoritarian tyranny. Decision-making by numbers alone is not a guarantee of correctness, and is one motivation for a *separation of powers* and the importance of review (i.e. executive reviewed by legislative; legislative reviewed by judiciary; judiciary reviewed by executive). This issue will recur throughout subsequent chapters.

2.6.1 Parameter Modification

This example is concerned with resource allocation in an ad hoc network (Carr and Pitt, 2009). An ad hoc network is a collection of connected, autonomous, heterogenous computing nodes, which need to work together to achieve their individual goals, i.e. to transmit messages. However, there are limited resources: battery power, processing time, memory buffers, available bandwidth, etc. Clearly, nodes need to reciprocate, but they are also competing for these resources.

Designating each node in the network as an agent, we can then define $\mathcal{M}$ as a multi-agent system (MAS) at time t:

$$\mathcal{M}_t = \langle U, \langle A, \rho, B, \mathbf{f}, \tau \rangle_t \rangle$$

where:

- U is the set of agents;
- $A_t \subseteq U$, the set of agents *present* at t;
- $\rho_t : U \to \{0, 1\}$, the presence function s.t. $\rho_t(a) = 1 \leftrightarrow a \in A_t$;
- $B_t : \mathbb{Z}$, the 'bank', the overall system resources available;
- $\tau_t : \mathbb{N}$, the threshold number of votes to be allocated resources; and
- $\mathbf{f}_t : A_t \to \mathbb{N}_0$.

The intuitive idea is that in any group of agents, if it is ad hoc, only a subset of them will be 'on', or in range (i.e. *present*) at any timepoint t. Abstractly, their collective resources (of all kinds) are denoted by B_t. Then resource allocation function $\mathbf{f}_t$ determines who gets allocated resources. The input/output relation of agents to resources is computed depending on the value of τ_t, a threshold value, and a pair of voting processes, as follows.

The system operation is divided into consecutive timeslices. During a timeslice t, each 'present' agent a will:

- **Phase 1:** Vote for a threshold value for τ (change a rule);
- **Phase 2:** Offer (O^a)/Request (R^a) resources $(R^a > O^a)$;
- **Phase 3:** Vote for a candidate(s) to receive resources; and
- **Phase 4:** Update satisfaction, reputation and value metrics.

The threshold value τ represents the threshold number of votes required to receive resources (at time t):

$$\mathbf{f}_t(a) = R_t^a, \mathbf{card}(\{b | b \in A_t \wedge \mathbf{v}_t^b(\ldots) = a\}) \geq \tau_t$$
$$= 0, \text{ otherwise}$$

Thus, the value of τ is context-dependent and crucial for 'collective well-being':

- If τ is too low, too many resources will be distributed, and this will result in the depletion of the resources; but
- If τ is too high, too few resources will be distributed, and this will result in depletion of the agents, as they will become 'dissatisfied' and leave the system.

Therefore, for Phase 1, the agents have to (learn to) change the system rule which states that *"the resource controller is obliged to grant access to the resource to a requester, if the number of votes for the requester is greater than or equal to τ"* by modifying by themselves the value of τ, according to circumstances.

In Phase 4, each agent updates various metrics for satisfaction, reputation and values. Agent satisfaction is computed by simple reinforcement of satisfaction in the new state as a product of satisfaction in the current state, and what happened to the agent:

$$\sigma_{t+1} = \sigma_t + (1 - \sigma_t) \cdot \varphi, \quad \text{if the agent is assigned resources}$$
$$\sigma_{t+1} = \sigma_t - \sigma_t \cdot \psi, \quad \text{otherwise}$$

where φ and ψ are agent-dependent coefficients (this equation will re-appear quite frequently in the following chapters).

We also want each agent to exhibit 'responsible' behaviour, by voting for a collectively beneficial value of τ and not necessarily one which maximises the apparent benefit to itself. This is because a naive but selfish (and potentially ruinous) strategy is to vote for

$\tau_t = 0$, in principle guaranteeing allocation of resources in the short term, but depleting the system in the long term.

An agent's opinion of the others, by which each agent establishes a 'reputation', depends on several factors, such as:

- How close the other's prediction was to the chosen τ;
- How close the other prediction was to its own voted τ; and
- The overall deviation from chosen τ and voted τ.

This in turn means that each agent needs a strategy for predicting a value of τ. One approach is to specify a set of randomly initialised prediction functions and assign a subset to each agent. Agents then use their predictor functions with historical information of what a good value of τ would have been in the previous timeslices, and verify this with what the best value would have been for the current timeslice. Functions returning a value close to this will be weighted more than less accurate predictors.

This approach results in an observable 'responsible' behaviour in comparison to, for example, an agent that always votes for $\tau = 0$, and so an increased reputation for the responsible agent. 'Responsible' agents with consistently accurate predictor functions could also emerge as *experts* and the task of deciding τ would be delegated to this sub-group rather than requiring the whole group to be involved.

Note that reinforcement learning, for example, Delayed Q-Learning, can be used to 'rehabilitate' an agent that presents selfish behaviour or inaccurate predictions, but improves over time.

As a preliminary exercise of a simple self-organising multi-agent system using a rudimentary form of reflection to maintain a form of self-control, this system demonstrates the basic principles of self-organisation through parameter-based modification. Of course, it gets a bit more complicated than this, as demonstrated by the next example of policy modification (and the following eight chapters).

2.6.2 Policy Modification

This example is based on a scenario due to Marek Sergot, who has made significant contributions to the computational logics of action and agency (e.g. Kowalski and Sergot (1986); Sergot (2001, 2007). In this scenario (Craven and Sergot, 2008), the primary concern is to characterise situations with a number of interacting components whose actions and interactions may result in some components being in different states, but some combination of those states is prohibited.

More specifically, the scenario involves two categories of agents (m_* and f_*) moving around a micro-world of inter-connected locations. For example, there may be two locations (l and r), and three agents: a Dangerous Intellectual f and two Surveillers m_1 and m_2.

Then, in Sergot's framework of labelled transition systems (Sergot, 2007), one can reason about normative and institutional aspects of a system, by specifying an action description that identifies which of its states are 'green' (permitted, allowed, valid, acceptable) and which are 'red' (not permitted, not allowed, invalid, unacceptable); and also which system *transitions* are green (permitted, etc.) and which are red (not permitted, etc.).

The scenario can be re-specified in the Event Calculus (only implicitly identifying the green/red states and transitions), but in such a way that which combinations of states, and narratives that produce those states, can be changed 'on the fly' by *policy modification*.

To begin with, we can identify the following fluents and action:

- A fluent $location(x) = l$ and $location(x) = r$, where x ranges over the agents (f, m_1 and m_2);
- A fluent $violation(x) = b$, where again x ranges over the agents (f, m_1 and m_2) and b is a boolean; and
- An action $move(x, l1, l2)$, where again x ranges over the agents, $l1$ and $l2$ range over locations (l and r), and a *move* action initiates or terminates *location* and *violation* fluents.

Thereafter, we can specify initiates axioms for the *move* action:

$move(A, L1, L2)$ initiates $location(A) = L2$ at T ←
    $location(A) = L1$ holdsAt T ∧
    $connected(L1, L2)$

$move(A, L1, L2)$ initiates $violation(A) =$ **true** at T ←
    $location(A) = L1$ holdsAt T ∧
    $connected(L1, L2)$ ∧
    not **per**$(A, move(A, L1, L2), T)$

Note this means that if an agent performs a *move* action which satisfies the conditions, it does change location. The question is whether or not the resulting state is permitted (allowed, valid, etc.). The *permission* to move is defined by the axiom:

$$\begin{aligned}
&\textbf{per}(m1, move(m1, L1, L2), T) \leftarrow \\
&\quad location(m1) = L1 \quad \textsf{holdsAt} \quad T \quad \wedge \\
&\quad location(m2) = Lm2 \quad \textsf{holdsAt} \quad T \quad \wedge \\
&\quad location(f) = Lf \quad \textsf{holdsAt} \quad T \quad \wedge \\
&\quad valid\_locations(L2, Lm2, Lf)
\end{aligned}$$

It is then possible to define different combinations of green or red states and transitions by defining different policies for *valid_locations*.

For example, Policy 1 could be "Don't leave the Dangerous Intellectual f alone with only one Surveiller (m_1 and m_2)". This means that either f has to be alone in one location, or all three agents have to be in the same location. The policy can be specified as:

$$\begin{aligned}
&valid\_locations(Lm1, Lm2, Lf) \leftarrow \\
&\quad Lm1 = Lf \quad \wedge \\
&\quad Lm2 = Lf \\
&valid\_locations(Lm1, Lm2, Lf) \leftarrow \\
&\quad \textsf{not } Lm1 = Lf \quad \wedge \\
&\quad \textsf{not } Lm2 = Lf
\end{aligned}$$

A state transition diagram for Policy 1 is shown in Fig. 2.5. This distinguishes between the allowed states (green) and disallowed states (red) and the allowed/disallowed (green/red) transitions between those states.

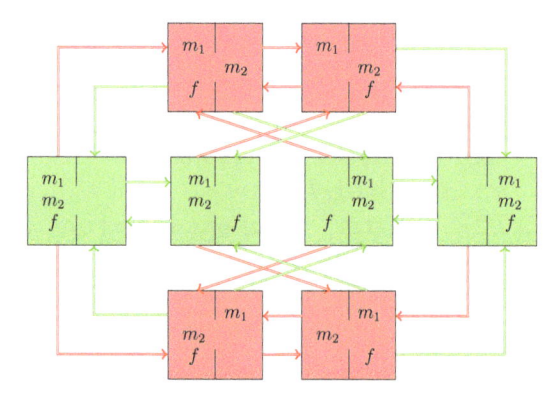

Fig. 2.5. Green/Red State Transition Diagram for Policy 1

Self-Organising Systems

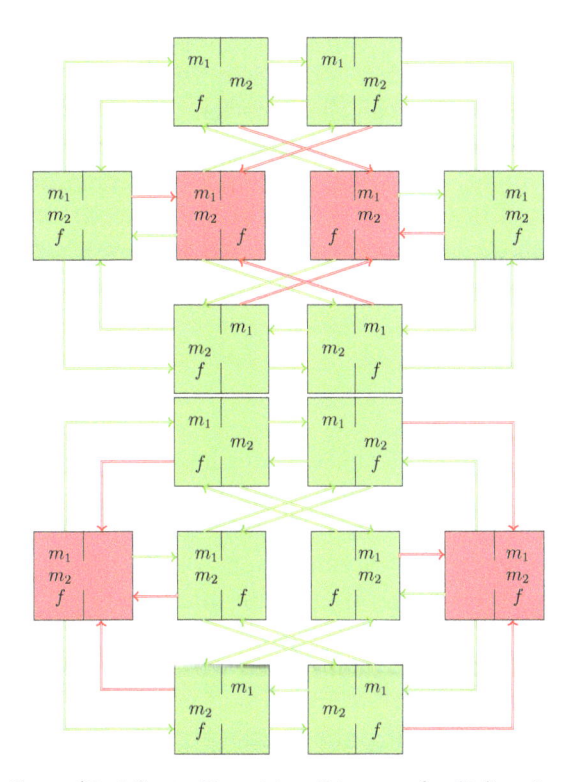

Fig. 2.6. Green/Red State Transition Diagram for Policy 2 and Policy 3

A second rule, Policy 2, could be "The Dangerous Intellectual must be accompanied by at least one Surveiller". This policy can be specified as:

$$valid\_locations(Lm1, Lm2, Lf) \leftarrow$$
$$Lm1 = Lf$$
$$valid\_locations(Lm1, Lm2, Lf) \leftarrow$$
$$\text{not } Lm1 = Lf \quad \wedge$$
$$Lm2 = Lf$$

Yet another rule, Policy 3, could be "The Dangerous Intellectual cannot be accompanied by both Surveillers". This policy can be specified as:

$$valid\_locations(Lm1, Lm2, Lf) \leftarrow$$
$$\text{not } (Lm1 = Lf \quad \wedge \quad Lm2 = Lf)$$

The state transition diagrams for these two policies are illustrated in Fig. 2.6.

In this way, the system can self-organise, if it has to, by substituting one policy for another. (This is quite straightforward to do in Prolog.) Of course, this begs the question of *why* the components of the system should want to change the policy, and whether the change was an improvement. An example related to Community Energy Systems is presented in Cardoso *et al.* (2019): indeed, this leads to the third and fourth questions of the analytic framework, the motivation for, and evaluation of, self-organisation.

2.7 Summary

The narrative developed in this chapter has picked up on the requirement for *agency* in cyber-physical and socio-technical systems, and extended it to include the requirement for *self-organisation*. However, we showed that self-organisation, or spontaneous order, is a phenomenon that has been observed in many physical, chemical, biological and social systems.

Here, we are particularly concerned with analysis of those discrete structures and processes that are to be found in complex social systems, on the understanding that these structures and processes do not actually exist outside of the 'minds' of the agents in that social system (except to the extent that they can be codified in some form (i.e. $\mathcal{R}$ in Fig. 2.4)).

We propose to use this analysis to establish the principles, necessary and sufficient conditions, and algorithmic foundations underpinning their formation, selection, modification, combination and continuation, or rather, perhaps, their self-formation, self-selection, self-modification, self-combination and self-continuation. Consequently, rather than emergence, we were concerned with processes that we called *planned emergence*. This in turn led to a discussion of the 'self' and identification of three key concepts:

(1) **Self-awareness:** The system has an internal representation of itself;
(2) **Reflection:** The system is able to evaluate its own performance; and
(3) **Interoception:** Senses paying attention to system well-being,

and a discussion of the 'organisation' identifying three key perspectives: that of rational systems, focusing on normative structure; of natural systems, focusing on behavioural structure; and open systems, focusing on interaction within the system and with the external world (environment).

Derived from this, the analytic framework of Sec. 2.5 gave four dimensions of possible change, and we briefly looked at two of them: the dimensions of change and the mechanics of change; and for the latter, rule modification and policy modification.

However, we next need to address the third question: the motivation for change. This, we contend, is actually a product of the *type* of interactions that take place in these social systems, and the problems that these interactions are intended to solve. These problems, as we have hinted, are problems of coordination, collective action and management of common-pool resources (CPRs) (like the 'bank' in Sec. 2.6.1), and the interactions are both *strategic* and *social*. We begin our study of strategic interaction with a review of *game theory*.

PART II
Strategic Interaction

Chapter 3

Game Theory

3.1 Introduction

The aim of this chapter is to examine strategic interaction through the lens of *Game Theory* (Nash, 1950; von Neumann, 1959; Binmore, 2005). Here, a game is defined as any situation in which two or more entities — entities such as people, animals, or software agents — are interacting; and each of these entities, or *players*, has to make a move, or choose an action, called a *strategy*. Like actions, strategies have consequences, and the outcome of all the players' individual selections (called a *profile*) yields a *payoff* for each player. To begin with, the theory assumes that each player is *rational* and prefers to maximise his/her payoff (as 'measured' by its *utility*), and selects a strategy accordingly.

Defining a game as "any situation" is very general, and so the scale of the game and the nature of the players (not just individuals, but countries or populations are possible entities, too) can be correspondingly large or small, concrete or abstract, important or parochial. So, a game of chess can still be analysed as a 'game' with two players, and Antonius Block was playing a rather high-stakes game against a forbidding opponent (see Fig. 3.1). A duel is a 'game', and if Galois had been as good at Game Theory as he was at Group Theory, he might have survived. Hitler and Stalin were playing a 'game', albeit a duel by proxy with an unfortunate million-strong cast of cannon-fodder. The strategic decision-making of countries, for example in the Cold War, can be analysed as playing a particularly dangerous 'game', called a game of deterrence. Thus, games can be 'one-shot', or iterated: sharing a living space, or working space, involves repeatedly playing a possibly endless series of 'games': with iterated games,

Fig. 3.1. A Scene from Ingmar Bergman's Film *The Seventh Seal* (The knight Antonius Block plays a 'game' of chess against Death: Antonius lives so long as he can keep the 'game' going)

the players' utilities may or may not change with each game in the series.

However, games don't always have to be adversarial or competitive: getting behind the wheel of a car and driving onto the road can be analysed as a 'game', but this is a game where it is in everyone's best interest to cooperate by driving on the same side of the road. Moreover, situations don't necessarily have to involve people, and indeed population dynamics of animal species can also be analysed as a 'game' (Maynard Smith, 1982). Computer security protocols, where the interacting entities are computer programs, can be analysed with Game Theory. Corporate decision-making can be analysed as a 'game' against the regulators: for example is the corporate payoff maximised by paying fines, or by recalling exploding cars, cheating on emissions testing, fixing the LIBOR rate, avoiding taxes, mis-selling pensions and mortgages, or poisoning water supplies?

The objectives of this chapter are therefore to:

- Formulate various different strategic interaction scenarios in game theoretic form: players, strategies/actions, and payoffs/utilities;
- Analyse such in terms of different *solution concepts*, such as the dominant strategy, Nash equilibrium and social welfare optimisation, in order to predict the outcome of particular games; and

- Interpret various implications, such as the significance of complexity results as the number of players and strategies increases, and inferences about rationality and the emergence of cooperation.

This chapter is organised as follows. Section 3.2 starts with a simple example of strategic interaction in a commonplace setting, a shared kitchen, to ground the subsequent discussion and development. Section 3.3 gives a brief overview of formal terminology and representation of games, before Sec. 3.4 presents the key analytic framework, using the idea of a solution concept, in particular the *Nash equilibrium*. These ideas are used to analyse the kitchen-sharing example, and this discussion is further extended in Sec. 3.5 with an analysis of the classic game The Prisoners' Dilemma, in both its one-shot and iterated forms, leading to some reflections on the nature of rationality and cooperation. Section 3.6 analyses other 2-player games, concluding with a discussion concerning the divergence of analytic results from observed results. Some further issues are briefly discussed in Sec. 3.7, specifically n-player games and evolutionary game theory, and the chapter concludes in Sec. 3.8, with signposts for the rest of the book.

3.2 Example: The Kitchen Stand-Off

Imagine you are living in a 2-person flat with a flatmate: you have your own bedroom but there are some communal spaces, such as the living room, the bathroom, and the kitchen. In the kitchen, you and your flatmate share three common appliances: one for perishable food storage (otherwise known as a fridge), one for heat transfer for edible food transformation (otherwise known as a stove), and one for utensil re-use preparation (otherwise known as a dishwasher). In addition, there are certain common tasks, like sweeping the floor, putting the rubbish out, and unstacking said dishwasher.

Sounds idyllic. What could possibly go wrong?

Over time, the fridge gets dirty, the washing-up stacks up, the stove gets encrusted, the floor gets crumby, and so on. If you both help to clean the kitchen, it will be cleaned quickly, and while you both spend time, you both get the benefit of a clean kitchen. If only one of you cleans the kitchen, it is slower, so the cleaner loses time, and the cleaner gets mucky while the other doesn't, but you both get the same benefit of a clean kitchen. If neither of you clean the kitchen, you save time but you still have the nastiness and inconvenience of a dirty kitchen, dirty appliances, dirty floors, and so on.

So: what should you do?

To start off, you could think of the situation as a **game**, but eschew too much creative thinking, and mis-apply Jacques Derrida (who did not say "il n'y a pas de hors-jeu", there is nothing outside of the game, but this is close to the idea that is needed). So, solutions like moving out, installing a new kitchen, or ringing your mum (which usually works, to be fair) are not allowed — basically if you shouldn't bring a knife to a gunfight, you shouldn't bring a flamethrower to a game of Catan either.

Instead, in a "game-like situation", you try to identify who the players are and what actions they might take (within the confines of the game); and then you try to predict what the outcome of various action-combinations might be. You might also consider if this situation is a one-off, never to be repeated, or it if will be repeated: kitchens do get messy on a fairly regular basis. With such predictions, you can decide what you should do (action to take or decision to make) in order to achieve a favourable outcome.

So if you were living with von Neumann, Morgenstern, Rasmussen or Nash (recognised as the founders of Game Theory), you would identify:

- P: The *players* of the game;
- A: The *actions* each player can take (their *strategies*);
- P: The *payoffs* each player would get for each combination of actions (their *utilities*); and
- I: The *information* set, all the possible actions that could have taken place in the game so far, given what that player has observed.

In Sec. 3.3, we define these notions more formally.

3.3 Game Theory: Terminology and Representation

3.3.1 *Utility and Preferences*

While the players and the actions can be plausibly extracted from the description of the game-like situation — for example, in the Kitchen

Stand-Off game, the players are *you* and *flatmate*, and their strategies are *clean* and *skive* — but the utilities might not be so clear.

Therefore, to be more precise about this idea of utility: it was originally a measure of pleasure or satisfaction used in the philosophical theory of utilitarianism (Burns and Hart, 1977), which promoted actions that maximised the happiness or well-being of those affected by such actions. While an interesting philosophical abstraction for exploring the nuances of motives vs. intentions, consequences vs. conformity, or total utility vs. average utility, in practice, utility is impossible to metricate (i.e. uniformly measure and quantify on a numerical scale). Moreover, there are 'real world' phenomena such as marginal utility: the utility of the first 90 mg of vitamin C of the day is good health, the utility of the second 90 mg is expensive urine.

Therefore, the way to interpret utility used here is from economics, that is, in terms of a utility function representing a consumer's *preference* ordering over a set of alternatives. There is one function for each player in the game, in the example u_{you} and $u_{flatmate}$, and the arguments to these functions will be the combination of actions that each player can take.

This means that some caution needs to be exercised: in comparison (is the difference between your first and second preferences the same as between your second and third? Does your first preference matter as much to you as your flatmate's first does to him/her?); in combination (is your first and flatmate's third preference the same as both your and your flatmate's second preferences?); and above all *utility is not the same as money*. Moreover, in economics, note that there is a difference between *ordinal* utility, which simply ranks a set of choices in order of preference, and *cardinal* utility, which also ranks choices in order of preference and expresses the magnitude of the preference for one choice over another.

Having said that, we will compare, add and numerically quantify anyway (with caution), primarily using a **preference relation** $\prec$ — provided we maintain consistency, and we accept that our players are behaving in order to maximise the value of "something", and if we don't actually define what that "thing" is, we label it *utility* instead (Binmore, 2005, p. 65).

Applying this to our example, we could surmise that your first preference is to skive off while your flatmate does the cleaning; but that an awareness of the germ theory of disease and an instinct for self-preservation means that your last preference is for both you and flatmate to skive off, leaving a filthy kitchen. That said, if you are going to have to clean, you would rather clean with flatmate than clean on your own. Thus the preference relation for *you* in this situation is as follows:

$$u_{you}(clean, clean) = 3$$
$$u_{you}(clean, skive) = 2$$
$$u_{you}(skive, clean) = 4$$
$$u_{you}(skive, skive) = 1$$

The ordering relation on $\prec$ is obvious: $u_{you}(skive, skive) \prec u_{you}(clean, skive)$, etc.

A **strategy** is a predetermined programme of play that tells a player what actions to take in response to every possible strategy other players might use. A **strategy profile** is an action for each player, e.g. $(skive, skive), (clean, skive)$, etc.

3.3.2 Games: Matrix Form and Extensive Form

In games, players take turns to make/play moves or choose/select actions. However, action-selection may be sequential or simultaneous, and this potential difference is reflected by different forms of representation: matrix form and extensive form.

In matrix form, a **payoff matrix** shows utility for each strategy profile. Assuming that *flatmate* has the same preference ordering as *you*, then the payoff matrix for the Kitchen Stand-Off game is shown in Fig. 3.2. Of course, there is more than one way to represent who gets which payoff: in the matrix on the left:

- *you* == the "row player": utility in the lower left of the cell;
- *flatmate* == the "column player": utility in the top right,

and in the matrix on the right:

- *you* == "row player": utility is first argument of the tuple;
- *flatmate* == "column player": utility is second argument.

From here on, we will use the representation on the right.

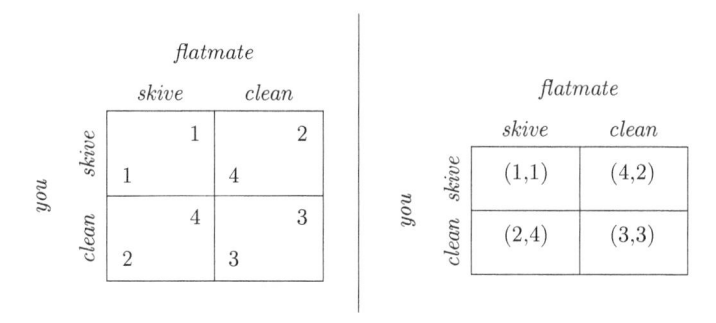

Fig. 3.2. Payoff Matrix for the Kitchen Stand-Off Game

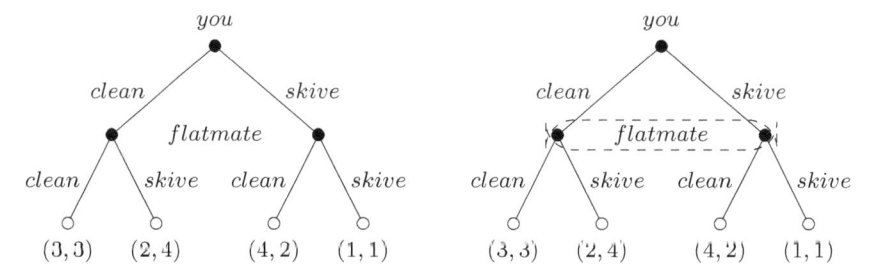

Fig. 3.3. Extensive Form for the Kitchen Stand-Off Game

The payoff matrix assumes that the two players choose their strategy simultaneously. In some games, the players choose sequentially. The **extensive form** representation is a tree whose nodes belong to players, arcs are labelled with an action-selection, and the leaves are the payoffs. This is illustrated in Fig. 3.3, where it is *you* to move first. Note that this gives two possibilities: either *flatmate* does, or does not know which action *you* have selected before she makes her choice. In the right-hand game, the dotted line shows the **information set** of *flatmate*. The key feature of an information set is that the player whose turn it is to select an action is unable to differentiate between those nodes, i.e. the player does not know which node has been reached and so is incognisant of the choices of other players that have led to this point.

Note that this allows games of perfect information (where every information set is a singleton set) and games of imperfect information. It also means that the extensive form on the right of Fig. 3.3 is equivalent to the matrix form of Fig. 3.2.

3.4 Solution Concepts

Definitions and representation are all very well, but we want to use them to get predictive leverage, i.e. to decide what action to take, or to predict what the outcome of a specific game will be. For this, we need a **solution concept**. A solution concept in Game Theory is a formal rule for predicting which strategies the players will adopt, and by extension what the outcome of a game would be (or identifying what it should (ideally) be). The predictions are called solutions and determine which strategies will be selected by which player. The solution concepts that will be examined in turn here are the dominant strategy, the Nash equilibrium strategy, the Pareto optimal strategy, and social welfare optimisation.

3.4.1 *Dominant Strategy*

A strategy s_i is **dominant** for a player i if, no matter what strategy player j chooses, i will do at least as well choosing s_i as it would choosing any other available strategy.

If there was always a dominant strategy, analysing game-like situations would be easy. But, there isn't always a dominant strategy, and sometimes, even if there is, it is not always the "best" strategy (as we will see).

3.4.2 *Nash Equilibrium Strategy*

The Nash equilibrium strategy is named after John Nash, who, among many contributions to mathematics, proved the properties of some foundational concepts in Game Theory. One of these is the eponymous equilibrium strategy, which is any profile of strategies — one action for each player — in which each player's strategy is the best response to the strategies selected by all of the other players.

In other words, two strategies s_i and s_j are in **Nash equilibrium** if:

- Assuming that player i chooses s_i, player j can do no better than choose s_j; and
- Assuming that player j chooses s_j, player i can do no better than choose s_i.

This means that neither player has any incentive to deviate unilaterally from a Nash equilibrium.

Informally, to verify if a strategy profile $\omega = (s_1, s_2, \ldots, s_n)$ is a Nash equilibrium, each player should ask itself "given that I know the strategies of the other players, and treating those strategies as set in stone, can I benefit by changing my strategy?" If all the players answer "no", then ω is a Nash equilibrium; if anyone answers "yes", then ω is not a Nash equilibrium.

A **pure strategy Nash equilibrium** is one where each player plays one specific strategy.

A **mixed strategy** is one where at least one player puts a probability distribution over alternative strategies. For example, *flatmate* might flip a coin to decide whether or not to *skive* or *clean*, so each strategy has $p = 0.5$. However, *you* might roll a dice, and choose *skive* if you throw a 6, so $p(skive) = 0.16$, $p(clean) = 0.84$.

A **mixed strategy Nash equilibrium** is one where every action played with positive probability must be a best response to other players' mixed strategies. A pure strategy is a restricted mixed strategy, with one strategy assigned a probability $p = 1$ and all other strategies assigned zero.

As with the dominant strategy, not every game has a pure strategy Nash equilibrium. Nash proved that every game with a finite number of players and a finite number of pure strategies has at least one Nash equilibrium. So, it is possible for a game to have more than one Nash equilibrium, raising the question of discriminating between alternative Nash equilibria. In addition, a game with infinitely many strategies might have no equilibria.

Nash also proved that for any game with a finite set of actions, at least one mixed strategy Nash equilibrium must exist. With a mixed strategy Nash equilibria, no player can improve their payoff by unilaterally changing their probability distribution. But then, which of flipping a coin or rolling a dice gives the mixed strategy Nash equilibrium for the Kitchen Stand-Off game? And also, is the mixed strategy Nash equilibrium even the 'best' equilibrium?

3.4.3 Pareto Optimal Strategy

The Nash equilibrium can be seen as a solution concept that focuses on the utilities to each of the individual players. Pareto optimality is a (sort of) solution concept that is primarily concerned with the utility that accrues to all of the players. We say "sort of" because although Pareto optimality is a formal rule, rather than predicting what the outcome will be (according to the mathematical inevitability of equilibria), it identifies what the outcome might ideally be if we were looking for a *socially optimal* outcome.

An outcome is said to be **Pareto optimal** (or Pareto efficient) if there is no other outcome that makes one player better off without making another player worse off. Or in other words, a Pareto optimal outcome cannot be improved because any change would 'hurt' at least one player.

If an outcome is Pareto optimal, then at least one player will be reluctant to move away from it (because this player will be worse off). On the other hand, if a strategy profile ω is not Pareto optimal, then there is another profile ω' that makes everyone as happy, if not happier, than ω.

3.4.4 Social Welfare Maximisation

In any game-like situation, there may be multiple equilibria, and there may be multiple Nash equilibria: one of these is the expected outcome. However, a curious feature of a Nash equilibrium is that while it may be an 'attractor', as it were, in general, it does not correlate with a socially optimal outcome. Therefore, there may be an outcome which is not an equilibrium but maximises the total amount of utility that all the players receive. It might be useful to know just how 'bad' this expected outcome is compared to the optimal outcome. To analyse this, there are various metrics that can be used based on the concept of **social welfare**.

The social welfare SW of a strategy profile ω is defined as the sum of the utilities that each agent gets from ω:

$$SW(\omega) = \sum_{i=1}^{n} u_i(\omega)$$

Then we can define two sets. First, for a game with n players, let S be the set of all possible strategy profiles $s_1 \times s_2 \times \cdots \times s_n$. Second, let E be the subset of S where each strategy profile is in equilibrium (i.e. the set of Nash equilibria).

The *Price of Anarchy* (Koutsoupias and Papadimitriou, 2009) can be defined as the ratio of the social welfare of the optimum strategy profile to the social welfare of the *worst* Nash equilibrium:

$$\text{Price of Anarchy} = \frac{\max_{\omega \in S} SW(\omega)}{\min_{\omega \in E} SW(\omega)}$$

If instead of welfare, which we want to maximise, we choose to measure efficiency (bearing in mind that 'efficiency' in micro-economics has a specific meaning relating to relative improvement/harm than the ratio of useful work to actual work), we can think in terms of costs that we want to minimise, and invert the ratio.

The Price of Anarchy therefore measures how much selfish behaviour degrades a system if the players choose a strategy to maximise benefit for themselves, rather than following a strategy that is chosen for them by a central authority (dictator, oracle) that would maximise the benefit for everyone.

Alternatively, in a cooperative game, the *Price of Stability* (Anshelevich *et al.*, 2004) can be defined as the ratio of the social welfare of the optimum strategy profile to the social welfare of the *best* Nash equilibrium:

$$\text{Price of Stability} = \frac{\max_{\omega \in S} SW(\omega)}{\max_{\omega \in E} SW(\omega)}$$

The Price of Stability measures the social welfare of the best Nash equilibrium and expresses how much worse it is than the optimal social welfare. It can be useful in a cooperative game with an objective authority that can have some influence on the players' behaviour.

3.4.5 The Kitchen Stand-Off, Revisited

We can now apply our solution concepts to the payoff matrix of the Kitchen Stand-Off game, as illustrated in Fig. 3.2. This reveals:

- There is no dominant strategy;
- There are two (pure strategy) Nash equilibria:
  ○ (*skive*, *clean*) and (*clean*, *skive*);
  ○ If *flatmate* chooses *skive*, *you* can do no better than *clean*;
  ○ If *flatmate* chooses *clean*, *you* can do no better than *skive*;

- All outcomes except (*skive*, *skive*) are Pareto optimal; and
- All outcomes except (*skive*, *skive*) maximise social welfare.

So where does this analysis leave us?

Suppose then that *flatmate* does decide to flip a coin. Then the probability p of picking either strategy is $\frac{1}{2}$.

In these circumstances, we can determine the **expected utility**, where the expected utility of an outcome is the payoff associated with that outcome multiplied by some relevant probability. In this case, if *you* choose *skive*, the expected utility is (overloading the function symbol u_{you}):

$$u_{you} = \left(\frac{1}{2} \cdot 1\right) + \left(\frac{1}{2} \cdot 4\right) = 2.5$$

whereas if *you* choose *clean*, the expected utility is:

$$u_{you} = \left(\frac{1}{2} \cdot 2\right) + \left(\frac{1}{2} \cdot 3\right) = 2.5$$

i.e. the expected utility is the same, no matter what action *you* choose.

This means that if *flatmate* chooses his/her strategy with this probability distribution, *it does not make any difference what strategy you choose* — your **expected utility** is the same!

Except: this game is symmetric, so if instead of rolling a die, *you* flip a coin too, then it makes no difference what strategy *flatmate* chooses.

What happens if the payoff matrix is changed? Suppose the utilities change to those in Fig. 3.4. The preference ordering is the same as before, but the new utilities can be interpreted as the relative strength of the preferences changing, or the 'value' of the time saved changing, and so on.

	flatmate p *skive*	$(1-p)$ *clean*
you skive	(0,0)	(8,2)
clean	(2,8)	(4,4)

Fig. 3.4. Payoff Matrix (With Probabilities) for the Kitchen Stand-Off Game

Examining Fig. 3.4, it is again possible to calculate a probability p for *flatmate*'s probability distribution that renders your expected utility to be the same, i.e.:

$$((0 \cdot p) + (8 \cdot (1-p))) = ((2 \cdot p) + (4 \cdot (1-p))) = \frac{2}{3}$$

If *flatmate* chooses *skive* with probability $\frac{2}{3}$, your expected utility is the same no matter what *you* choose. Of course, it still works for *you*, too: *you* can calculate a probability that makes *flatmate*'s strategy irrelevant to her expected utility, too.

There is something inexorably remorseless about this. In terms of maximising rational choice, *you* have a strategy that renders *flatmate*'s strategy irrelevant; but reciprocally, *flatmate* has a strategy that renders *your* own strategy irrelevant. Except: it is not much of a "strategy" — it didn't involve any cognition or insight, it is just a probability. So, is that it? — we must set our life upon a cast and stand the hazard of the die, and for all that, the cast of someone else's die?

3.4.6 The Hawk–Dove Game, aka Chicken

To answer the question from the previous sub-section: It would appear so. The form of the Kitchen Stand-Off game is a 'classic' (well-studied) game in Game Theory, called the Hawk–Dove game, or the Game of Chicken. This type of game has been studied in animal behaviour (Maynard Smith, 1982), and also appeared in the James Dean film, *Rebel Without a Cause*. In animal conflict, the Hawk–Dove game posits a contest over a resource. If both animals (players) back down, they avoid injury and share the reward. If only one backs down, it gets nothing and the other gets all the reward. If they both fight, they each pay a cost for fighting subtracted from their share of the reward.

In the James Dean film, and playgrounds all over the world, the Game of Chicken involves two people engaged in some dangerous activity: in the film, it was driving a car at top speed towards a cliff edge. If they both stop, nothing happens. If one stops, he is the chicken and the other the victor. If neither stop, it is the worst outcome for both of them.

	player$_j$	
	Hawk	Dove
Hawk (player$_i$)	$(\frac{V-C}{2}, \frac{V-C}{2})$	$(V, 0)$
Dove (player$_i$)	$(0, V)$	$(\frac{V}{2}, \frac{V}{2})$

Fig. 3.5. Payoff Matrix for the Hawk–Dove Game (of Chicken)

	player$_j$	
	q	$1-q$
p (player$_i$)	(X_1, X_2)	(W_1, L_2)
$1-p$ (player$_i$)	(L_1, W_2)	(T_1, T_2)

Fig. 3.6. General Form of Payoff Matrix for Anti-Coordination Game

The 'standard' form of the payoff matrix for the Hawk–Dove game is as shown in Fig. 3.5. It is assumed that the value of resource V is less than cost C of a fight, i.e. $C > V > 0$ (which partly explains why arguments in academia are so bitter: the difference between the cost of fighting and the value of the reward is so negligibly small that there is as much point in fighting as in yielding). Clearly, both players benefit if they both yield; but each player's optimal choice depends on the other: if the opponent yields, they should not; but if the opponent does not yield, they should.

In fact, the general form of any 2-player **game of anti-coordination** is shown in Fig. 3.6.

There are two probabilities p and q such that:

$$q = \frac{W_1 - T_1}{(W_1 + L_1) - (T_1 + X_1)}$$

$$p = \frac{W_2 - T_2}{(W_2 + L_2) - (T_2 + X_2)}$$

giving a mixed strategy Nash equilibrium (p, q).

Are all games, with different relational orderings on W, L, T and X, like this? We will look at some different games, starting with another 'classic' game, the Prisoners' Dilemma.[1]

3.5 The Prisoners' Dilemma

Imagine the following scenario. Zézinho and Skumbag are partners in crime. Unlike the Messiah, they also have been very naughty boys and have been arrested and jailed. They are being held in solitary confinement with no way of communication. Each one cares more for himself and his own freedom than the welfare of the other (or anyone else's for that matter).

The prosecution lawyer, being a generous soul, offers them a choice: Confess to the crime (*defect D* from partner), or stay silent (*cooperate C* with partner). She then tells each of them individually:

- The same offer has been made separately to both of you;
- If you both confess, you will be jailed for 2 years;
- If you confess and the other stays silent, you will be freed and the other will be jailed for 5 years; and
- No conferring.

But they both know, if neither confesses, there is only enough evidence to jail them for 1 year.

So, what do they do? Clearly, it is a game-like situation, so it can be formulated as a game and analysed using our solution concepts.

3.5.1 *Analysing the Prisoners' Dilemma*

The payoff matrix for the Prisoners' Dilemma is shown in Fig. 3.7. Analysis using our solution concepts gives:

- (C, C) maximises social welfare; *and*
- All outcomes except (D, D) are Pareto optimal; *but*
- D is the dominant strategy; *and*
- (D, D) is the only Nash equilibrium.

---

[1] Although part of the dilemma is where the apostrophe goes. Each prisoner does have a dilemma; or it could be argued they share a single dilemma. Or, if it were a title, it need not have an apostrophe at all, as in *The Grammar Pedants Club*.

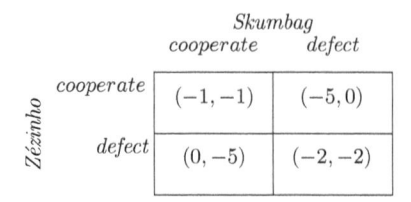

	Skumbag cooperate	Skumbag defect
Zézinho cooperate	(−1, −1)	(−5, 0)
Zézinho defect	(0, −5)	(−2, −2)

Fig. 3.7. Payoff Matrix for The Prisoners' Dilemma

	Player$_j$ cooperate	Player$_j$ defect
Player$_i$ cooperate	(R, R)	(S, T)
Player$_i$ defect	(T, S)	(P, P)

Fig. 3.8. General Form of Payoff Matrix for The Prisoners' Dilemma

There is seemingly only a slight change from the Hawk–Dove game to the Prisoners' Dilemma, but the solution concepts give radically different answers. Figure 3.8 shows the general form of the Prisoners' Dilemma.

For a strict Prisoners' Dilemma, $T > R > P > S$, so that:

- $R > P$ implies that mutual cooperation is better than mutual defection; and
- $T > R$ and $P > S$ imply that defection is the dominant strategy.

Thus, the payoffs can be characterised by:

- T is the "temptation";
- R is the reward;
- P is the punishment; and
- S is the "sucker's payoff".

The 'paradoxical' feature of the Prisoners' Dilemma is that all options are Pareto optimal except for the unique equilibrium, which is for both players to defect. This striking contrast between social optimality and the (predictable) Nash equilibrium, given that so many 'real world' game-like situations can be abstracted into a Prisoners' Dilemma,[2] has made the problem a primary object of study in numerous disciplines. In particular, the distinct separation between all the socially efficient outcomes and the equilibrium one, apparently demonstrates the dynamic tension between cooperation and competition. However, the illusion of this tension, with regard to the *emergence* (or *planned emergence*) of cooperation is demonstrated when we start 'tweaking' the scenario, for example by playing repeated (iterated) games, rather than playing the game just once.

3.5.2 The Iterated Prisoners' Dilemma

The solution concept for the Nash equilibrium predicts, mathematically, that the strategy profile $\omega = (defect, defect)$ will be the outcome for rational, utility-maximising, players. That said, intuitively, other solution concepts suggest alternative other outcomes are preferable, especially (*cooperate*, *cooperate*), which does not "waste utility", for example.

What does this tell us about human behaviour? That to err is human, to forgive is divine ... but *to defect is rational* — if "we" (humans) are rational and rational means "utility maximisation"?

It turns out that it is possible to fulfil this prediction about human behaviour in the laboratory, and on television shows. But not *always...*

So, why not?

Part of the explanation might lie in the artifice behind the scenario, for example in the assumption that the game is played once, and only once, and that the players will never encounter one another in any game-like situation in the future. Moreover, the game is set up so that defect is the dominant strategy, both players know that defect is the dominant strategy, and know that the other knows too, so of course defect is 'rational' (Binmore, 2005).

---

[2] A word to the wise: whatever utility one assigns to it, in the 'real world', no one ever wants the sucker's payoff.

The outcomes are different with an *iterated* Prisoners' Dilemma (and *iterated* Kitchen Stand-Off). In this situation, there are the same players, actions, and payoff matrix, but now the game is played multiple times, sequentially, and all the players can see the previous actions of others.

If the game is played exactly n times, and both players know this, then the optimal strategy is always to defect. This can be predicted by *backwards induction*. On the very last, nth, round, the best outcome for your opponent will be to defect. Therefore, you should defect as well. However, now your opponent knows on the $n-1$th round that you are going to defect on the nth. So she will defect on the $n-1$th round. But now you know this, too, so on the $n-1$th round, you...

Working back to the first round, this means the optimal strategy is to defect. But it turns out that the "always defect" strategy prediction *fails* to be confirmed always by empirical observations. For example, if the game is to be played n times, but the players *do not* know this, or the players are told that the game will be played indefinitely, then in any round m ($m < n$), if one player defects, then the other player can retaliate by defecting in the next $m+1$th round. This effect is called the **shadow of the future**, and it encourages cooperation or enables players to avoid prisoners' dilemma situations by deploying a strategy of conditional retaliation.

In a well-known experiment, Robert Axelrod asked researchers to submit computer programs to a Prisoners' Dilemma Tournament, in which each program would play the iterated Prisoners' Dilemma against every other. The programs implemented various strategies, from the complicated to relatively straightforward, like random, always-defect, always cooperate, and tit-for-tat (implemented by the rule: round 1 — choose cooperate; round n — copy opponent's strategy from round $n-1$).

Although 'defeated' in one-to-one play by the always-defect strategy, the tournament winner, defined as the best on average against all other strategies, was tit-for-tat.

Again, it's not much of a strategy, though, is it? And what does this tell us about human behaviour, cognition and rationality? Beyond the conclusions that Axelrod drew, which included: don't be envious, reciprocate, don't be the one to "start something", and don't try to be too clever. For sure: it is not worth trying to be too clever in a no-win situation, like the Prisoners' Dilemma as it is formulated; on the other hand, that does not mean we can't be clever in trying to create win–win situations instead.

3.5.3 *A Slight Digression on Rationality*

Folklore is defined as the beliefs and stories of a community, passed on by word of mouth. In the 1950s, in the game theory community, it was well known that in an infinitely repeated version of the Prisoners' Dilemma, provided players are sufficiently patient, there is a Nash equilibrium such that both players *cooperate* on the equilibrium path. Only that no one had *proved* it, and so therefore no one had published it. Therefore, the knowledge existed in the community, but not in the literature; hence, it was known as the *folk theorem*.

Various explanations have been proposed to explain the empirical behaviour, for example **superrationality**. A superrational player still seeks to maximise her own utility, but will also consider the possibility that other players are superrational. Faced with the same problem, one superrational individual will always come up with the same — better — solution as any other superrational individual; and therefore, against an 'ordinarily rational' player, a superrational player will defect, but against another superrational player, a superrational player will cooperate. However, quite apart from the old maxim — never underestimate someone's capacity for doing something stupid, just to prove they can do something stupid — the concept of superrationality seems to be looking in the wrong place for a solution.

In the iterated Prisoners' Dilemma, the optimal strategy depends upon the strategies of likely opponents, and how they will react to defections and cooperations. This requires modelling other players, either actual opponents or idealised players (e.g. "what would Jesus do?"). This implies certain requirements of self-modelling and indeed self-awareness (perhaps as discussed in Sec. 2.4.1). It also demands some sensitivity to context.

Alternatively, it could be that the paradox of rationality implied by the Prisoners' Dilemma is completely specious, and that rational players don't cooperate in the Prisoners' Dilemma simply because from the way the game is set up, the assumptions it makes, and the constraints it imposes, the conditions necessary for rational cooperation are completely removed (Binmore, 2005). It is important to bear this in mind when we look first at other 2-player games, then at n-player games, and finally at meta-games.

3.6 Other 2-Player Games

In this section, we will briefly examine a number of other 2-player games, including the Coordination game, Battle of the Sexes, Stag Hunt, Ultimatum game, and Focal Point games. For each one we will give a motivating game-like situation, present the payoff matrix, and analyse the matrix using our solution concepts. The two general observations of which to be aware are how seemingly relatively small changes in the preference ordering of the payoffs lead to substantive differences in the analysis, and how counter-intuitive (or even paradoxical) is the difference between the mathematical prediction and the socially optimal outcome.

3.6.1 (Pure) Coordination Game

In a (pure) coordination game, both players have to choose the same option, and if they do, they both get the same reward, otherwise, they both get nothing. There are many examples of this: for example wearing fancy dress to a party, driving on the same side of the road, and so on.

A typical payoff matrix is illustrated in Fig. 3.9 for the game-like situation where two players have to pick the same colour of t-shirt to wear, *red* or *blue*. Analysis with the solution concepts determines:

- There is no dominant strategy;
- (*red, red*) and (*blue, blue*) are both Nash equilibria, Pareto optimal, and maximise social welfare.

	$Player_j$ red	$Player_j$ blue
$Player_i$ red	(3, 3)	(0, 0)
$Player_i$ blue	(0, 0)	(3, 3)

Fig. 3.9. Payoff Matrix for a (Pure) Coordination Game

However, coordination games do have a mixed strategy Nash equilibrium; although, generally people are not observed driving in the middle of the road, or alternating between driving on the left or right...

3.6.2 Battle of the Sexes

The Battle of the Sexes is a lopsided coordination game. Player *She* wants to watch football and go to the pub for a few pints; player *He* knows the Royal Shakespeare Company is in town and would like nothing more than to pick over the finer points of *Troilus and Cressida*. A typical payoff matrix for such a game-like situation is illustrated in Fig. 3.10.

Analysis with the solution concepts offers two pure strategy Nash equilibria, and the usual mixed strategy Nash equilibrium. But all are unfair in some way: the two pure strategy equilibria are "unfair" to either one player or the other; but the mixed strategy equilibrium is "inefficient" because of *coordination failure*, i.e. the expected utility is less than the maximum utility of both players combined.

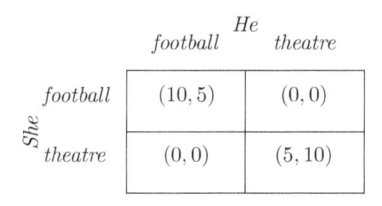

	He football	*He* theatre
She football	(10, 5)	(0, 0)
She theatre	(0, 0)	(5, 10)

Fig. 3.10. Payoff Matrix for Battle of the Sexes Game

3.6.3 Stag Hunt Game

The Stag Hunt game is associated with 18th century philosophers Rousseau and Hume. In particular, Rousseau wrote about a game-like situation involving a hunt to explore the conflict between the potential benefits of social cooperation versus the 'security blanket' of individual self-dependence (Skyrms, 2004).

In the stag hunt, each player must choose to hunt either stag or a hare, without knowing the choice of the other. The players need to cooperate to catch a stag, but if they do, they get the greatest

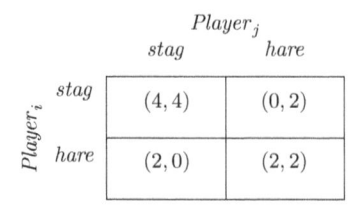

	Player$_j$	
	stag	hare
Player$_i$ stag	(4, 4)	(0, 2)
Player$_i$ hare	(2, 0)	(2, 2)

Fig. 3.11. Payoff Matrix for Stag Hunt Game

reward; although they can be sure of catching a hare on their own, the value (payoff) of a hare is less than that of a stag.

A typical payoff matrix for a Stag Hunt game is illustrated in Fig. 3.11.

Analysing this game, it can be seen that like the Prisoners' Dilemma, there is no dominant strategy, but unlike the Prisoners' Dilemma, there are *two* pure-strategy Nash equilibria: when both players cooperate and when both players defect. In both types of game, both players choosing to cooperate is Pareto optimal, and in the Stag Hunt game it is a Nash equilibrium; whereas in the Prisoners' Dilemma the single pure Nash equilibrium is when both players choose to defect.

The two pure strategy Nash equilibria are distinguished in the Stag Hunt game by:

- (*stag,stag*) is **payoff** dominant, i.e. all the players' payoffs are at least as good as, and at least one is better than, their payoffs from any other Nash equilibrium; and
- (*hare,hare*) is **risk** dominant, where the uncertainty over the others' actions means that one particular action yields a higher expected utility than any other action.

Generally speaking, it has been observed that people choose the less-risky option when they are guaranteed some pay-off, and end up in an equilibrium that has a sub-optimal (individual and social) payoff. Furthermore, the smaller the difference between risky and safe options, the more likely is the failure to coordinate on the socially preferable outcome.

From which it might be tempting to conclude that people prefer to be guaranteed some payoff. So what happens when the parameters are changed, as in the Ultimatum game?

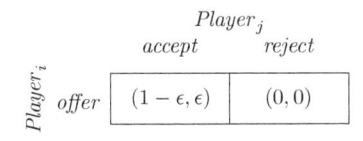

	Player$_j$	
	accept	reject
Player$_i$ offer	$(1-\epsilon, \epsilon)$	$(0,0)$

Fig. 3.12. Payoff Matrix for the Ultimatum Game

3.6.4 *Ultimatum Game*

In the Ultimatum game, two players are given a sum of money by a third party. They have to decide between themselves how to divide the money: first, player i makes proposal of the division. Second, player j can either *accept* or *reject* the proposal. The players' payoffs are specified as follows:

- If player j accepts, the money is split according to i's proposal;
- If player j rejects, both players receive nothing.

Note, the game is not iterated, so reciprocation is not an issue.

A payoff matrix for an Ultimatum game is illustrated in Fig. 3.12.

Analysing this game, if $\epsilon = 0$, player j is at best indifferent. Therefore, "rationally", player j should accept any proposal where $\epsilon > 0$. In which case, equally "rationally", player i should offer the smallest unit of money such that $\epsilon > 0$. However, in one set of experiments, it was reported that nearly half of those playing first offered an even split, about half of offers falling below $\frac{1}{3}$ were rejected, and over half of offers below $\frac{1}{4}$ were rejected.

This would suggest that there are some other parameters being factored into the decision-making rationale beyond purely mathematical reasoning, for example fairness norms (Binmore, 2005). Some of this reasoning is illustrated by Focal Point games.

3.6.5 *Focal Point Games*

In a focal point game, two (or more) players are presented with a set of choices. They are told that they get the reward V if they all make the same choice, no matter what the actual choice is (the payoff matrix for a two-player focal point game would have (V, V) in the north–west to south–east diagonal, and $(0, 0)$ everywhere else).

For example, make a choice from the following lists:

- 14, 15, 16, 17, 18, 100;
- 174, 296, 483, 666, 739, 837;
- Choose a meeting place in London: the Statue of Eros at Piccadilly Circus, the *Dog and Duck* pub in Peckham, Croydon Bus Garage, Hampstead cemetery by the grave of Karl Marx.

Such games were studied by Schelling (1960), without much in the way of formal mathematics. Instead, he observed that people 'solved' such games by identifying *focal points*, i.e. a choice that for social, cultural or psychological reasons was more salient or more pertinent than the others, even though the utility is the same for all the choices (V for all getting the same one, 0 otherwise).

A demotic conclusion: we'd all prefer the mathematical realm of pure abstraction, but sometimes you've got to wrestle the 'pig of human behaviour', and enjoy it as much as he does.

3.7 Beyond 2-Player Games

We conclude the technical development of this chapter by briefly considering games which involve more than two players. First, we describe some n-player games and an important complexity result; second, we describe a paradoxical example of how adding capacity to a network can actually cause congestion; and finally, we briefly mention *evolutionary game theory*.

3.7.1 *n-Player Games*

The games analysed so far have involved two players choosing between two actions. Such problems can be generalised to n-players choosing between m actions; however, the solutions concepts remain the same: the search for an equilibrium or socially optimal outcome. Examples considered here include the El Farol Bar problem, Cake Cutting, and the Pirate Game. Another n-player game, the Unscrupulous Diners Dilemma, is studied in Sec. 8.5.4.

The El Farol Bar problem is this (Arthur, 1994). There is a small, but popular, bar. It is popular because it is fun, but if it gets too crowded, it is not fun at all. The owner of the bar won't answer his phone, so no one can find out the state of the bar before they set off. Therefore, the client's regular clientele, on any given night, have to decide at the same time and without conferring, whether to go to the bar or not, subject to the outcomes that:

- If more than 60% go to the bar, it is too crowded, and they all have a worse time than if they had not gone at all; and
- If less than 60% go to the bar, it is uncrowded, and they all have a better time than if they stayed at home.

The key feature of the dilemma is that if everyone uses the same pure strategy, the players (the clientele) will all reason the same way, and the bar will either be packed or empty; either way, everyone will be having less fun than they could have. However, by iterating the game, the clientele can *learn* a mixed strategy which is a function of the number of players, the threshold for crowdedness, and the relative utilities of going to a crowded bar, going to an uncrowded bar, or not going at all.

The Cake Cutting game is the n-player variation of the 2-player game solved with the childhood strategy "I cut; you choose". There is an n-player solution, but it is slightly more complicated (Brams and Taylor, 1996). (Unsurprisingly, bigger and stronger siblings without parents who create the conditions for the emergence of cooperation tend to develop the rather simpler "I cut; I choose" strategy.)

The Pirate game is an n-player variant of the Ultimatum game. A ship of pirates has a hierarchy in the crew, from Ship's Captain at the top, down to Roger (the cabin boy) at the bottom. They have a certain amount of treasure to share among themselves. The most senior pirate proposes a distribution, and the crew vote. If a majority vote in favour, with the proposer having the casting vote in case of a tie, then the proposal is accepted, and the game ends. Otherwise, the proposer is made to "walk the plank", or otherwise thrown overboard, and the game repeats with the next most senior pirate. What distribution does the captain need to propose in order to survive and maximise his share of the treasure? For a hint: work backwards; for a discussion of the solution see Stewart (1999); and for a discussion of *voting*, see the next chapter.

n-player games can also produce paradoxical results. For example, Braess paradox is the observation that adding capacity to a network can increase congestion or diminish the overall traffic flow through it

(Braess et al., 2005). The paradox of enrichment is derived from predator–prey modelling in population ecology, where it was observed that increasing the amount of food available to the prey could destabilise the predator population (Rosenzweig, 1971), although other researchers have claimed that the paradox is not observed in nature (Roy and Chattopadhyay, 2007) and offered an alternative interpretation of the equations.

3.7.2 Coalitions and the Shapley Value

In n-player cooperative games, there is an option for a subset of the players to form a *coalition*, and share the payoff generated by cooperation. One way to determine how to share the payoff among the members of the coalition is to use the **Shapley value** (Shapley, 1953; Michalak et al., 2015).

The Shapley value is defined formally as follows. Given a set of N players, let $C \subseteq N$ be a coalition of those players. The payoff generated by that coalition is denoted by $u(C)$. The *marginal contribution* $mc(C,i)$ of player i to coalition C, as a measure of the relative importance or centrality of i to the achievement of C, is given by:

$$mc(C,i) = u(C \cup \{i\}) - u(C)$$

Then, assuming that all the players collaborate, the Shapley value defines one way to distribute the total payoff to those players. The Shapley value SV of player i with payoff function u is given by:

$$SV_i(u) = \sum_{C \subseteq N \setminus \{i\}} \frac{|C|!(|N|-|C|-1)!}{|N|!} mc(C,i)$$

The Shapley value is a 'fair' distribution, in that it satisfies certain properties including symmetry (if two players 'add' the same value to the same coalitions, then they get the same share), null-player (if a player's marginal contribution to all coalitions is zero, then its Shapley value is zero), linearity and efficiency. We will analyse 'fairness' in some detail in Chapter 7.

3.7.3 Evolutionary Game Theory

Having moved from 2-player games to n-player games, we can make one more move, and consider n-player games whose *population is dynamic*, and changes over time. This is the core of **Evolutionary Game Theory**.

Imagine an infinite population of individuals, in which each individual adopts a strategy for playing a game, and meets another individual at random. What would happen to such a population?

In such a situation, an evolutionary game theory analysis would:

- Define an initial population P_0 with some variation among competing individuals;
- Competing individuals in P_i meet in pairwise contests, and receive payoff/fitness according to the rules of the game;
- Based on its fitness, each individual undergoes death or reproduction: this function implements the **replicator dynamics**; and
- A new population P_{i+1} replaces the previous population, and the cycle repeats.

Rather than a Nash equilibrium, evolutionary game theory aims to identify an **evolutionarily stable strategy**. A strategy is evolutionarily stable if a mutant strategy cannot successfully enter the population and disturb the existing dynamic (which itself depends on the population mix).

3.8 Summary

In this chapter, we have studied Game Theory, using a variety of 2-player and *n*-player games, and used a variety of solution concepts for predicting and evaluating the outcomes of playing such games.

Game Theory has been described as the science of decision-making; but, as we have seen, it is a branch of economics and therefore something of an inexact science. It can be an incredibly powerful analytic and indeed accurate predictive tool; it can also turn around and bite you on the —, when what you see in the wild is not what you expected to see according to the equations or what happened in the laboratory.

Very loosely, when working with Game Theory, we are playing a game against the 'real world'. We can either be satisfied with the mathematics that tells us that the outcome will be the one predicted by the Nash equilibrium, or dissatisfied, in that we would prefer to achieve some alternative, socially optimal outcome. As our opponent, the 'real world' can either conform to the mathematics, or some other phenomenon will interfere, some assumption will not hold, and the outcome will be different. Whether or not this is actually the outcome we want, and indeed the utilities of these various outcomes, are yet other matters to consider.

Much effort has been expended by many influential scholars on the discrepancy between the predicted and the actual outcomes. Even more has been expended on warning against the over-reliance of models, mathematical modelling, and coarse assumptions regarding human behaviour (for example the disastrous policy-making of the UK government in its response to the COVID-19 crisis was informed by mathematical modelling and behavioural science rather than evidence-based public health interventions (Boseley, 2020)).

For example, Ken Binmore has written:

> Game theorists think it is just plain wrong to claim that the Prisoners' Dilemma embodies the essence of human co-operation. On the contrary, it represents a situation in which the dice are as loaded against the emergence of co-operation as they could possibly be. ... No paradox of rationality exists. Rational players don't co-operate in the Prisoners' Dilemma, because the conditions necessary for rational co-operation don't exist in the game. (Binmore, 2005, p. 63)

Similarly, Elinor Ostrom has written:

> What makes these models so dangerous — when they are used metaphorically as the foundations for policy — is that the constraints that are assumed to be fixed for the purpose of analysis are taken on faith as being fixed in empirical settings. ... [I'd] rather address the question of how to enhance the capabilities of those involved to change the [constraints] to lead to outcomes other than remorseless tragedies. (Ostrom, 1990, pp. 6–7)

What Ostrom observed is that a game-like situation can often be seen as a contest over a resource. She called this an operational-choice game. In an effort to break out of the remorseless attractor of the Nash equilibrium, people have invented — and call this super-rationality if you like — meta-level *political games*, which Ostrom called social choice and constitutional choice games (see Ostrom

(1990), Chapter 6, and also Binmore (2010)). The intention of these meta-games is to side-effect or contextualise a seemingly one-shot operational-choice game to divert it from its inevitable trajectory, or to create the conditions necessary for rational cooperation to occur.

The rest of this book can, from this perspective at least, be seen as the study of different intervention mechanisms by which autonomous agents can self-organise themselves using political meta-games, in order to change the constraints and avoid remorseless tragedies of object-level operational-choice resource-contest games.

Chapter 4

Social Choice Theory

4.1 Introduction

The aim of this chapter is to examine strategic interaction through the lens of *Social Choice Theory*. Social Choice Theory (List, 2013) is essentially the study of an input–output relationship: the inputs are a set of individual decisions, and the output is a collective (group) decision; so, a social choice relation aggregates the set of individual inputs — votes, expressed preferences, judgements — into a single output — the group's vote, preference or judgement. The requirement to do this arises in numerous areas of everyday life: committees, juries, deliberative assemblies, panels, friendship groups, family groups and so on. Not surprisingly, it is a common requirement in open multi-agent systems as well (Pitt *et al.*, 2006) and has been well-studied in the field of *computational social choice* (Chevaleyre *et al.*, 2007), besides being a critical feature of self-organisation.

There are (at least) two ways of looking at this. The first is to completely specify an input/output relation (or property of that relation), and then to design a process which correctly computes it. The second is to design a process, and then see what sort of input/output relation it computes. Either way, the object of study for a social choice theorist is the process or procedure for computing an input–output relation. This is not simply a matter of specifying the steps in the process, but also of *evaluating* the process itself. Such an evaluation may consider many criteria: correctness, of course, but also complexity and comprehensibility — and resistance to manipulation (how easily the process is rigged or fixed) and domination (if one voter determines all possible outcomes). It turns out that, among a sea of delightfully paradoxical outcomes, there is one highly influential result which is absolutely critical to understand and interpret properly.

The objectives of this chapter are therefore to:

- Understand strategic interaction from the perspective of social choice, and appreciate different voting methods for aggregating a set of individual preferences into a collective social preference;
- Evaluate these voting methods according to various criteria, and understand the significance of key results and theorems for (computational) social choice theory; and
- Specify and implement a protocol for preference selection (voting) in self-organising multi-agent systems, focusing on some normative and institutional aspects of voting.

The chapter is organised as follows. Section 4.2 begins with a simple, informal example, to ground the subsequent development. This development covers an overview of basic Social Choice Theory in Sec. 4.3, a description of various common voting methods in Sec. 4.4, and a survey of the various paradoxes uncovered by social choice theorists in Sec. 4.5. This will provide the foundations for the specification of (and an implementation route for) a voting protocol that could be used in a self-organising multi-agent system, as presented in Sec. 4.6. The chapter summarises and concludes in Sec. 4.7 with some practical advice about electoral system paradoxes, voting carts and value horses.

4.2 Example: The Big Breakfast Menu Variations

To motivate this section, we return to The Flat, where the flatmates have resolved the Great Kitchen Cleaning Stand-Off, and have decided to reward themselves with a celebratory breakfast. However, one flatmate would prefer the classic 'greasy spoon' heart-attack-on-a-plate big fry-up: fried eggs, bacon, etc. One would prefer the millennial 'avo-toast': mashed avocado on sourdough toast with free-range poached eggs and some sustainably sourced smoked salmon. A third would prefer a continental breakfast, before it is banned as unpatriotic in post-Brexit Britain. A fourth would prefer a Big Kahuna hamburger, the cornerstone of any nutritious breakfast. Yet another would prefer ... well, presumably the picture is got.

All the various preferences are exclusive. So the flatmates have to solve the n-person Big Breakfast Menu Variations Dilemma: they have to decide, by themselves (there being no Delphic Oracle or Demonic Over-Landlord to help them), which *one* of the many attractive alternative breakfast menus they are *all* going to prepare and eat. One option would be, of course, to formulate this dilemma as an n-player game. The flatmates would try to work out the equilibrium for each of the various utilities that each flatmate(/player) has for their own, and each other's, preferences. But aware of the possible difficulties this might entail, perhaps there is an alternative.

There is: each flatmate expresses his/her preference as a vote; they tally the votes for each preference; the preference with the highest number of votes wins; and this is the preference that the flatmates will chose to follow.

What could possibly go wrong?

It turns out: quite a lot — especially if the flatmates want the decision to be made 'sensibly', 'fairly', 'efficiently', etc.

This chapter will explain various different processes for resolving this commonplace type of strategic interaction, with respect to criteria such as 'sense', 'fairness', 'efficiency', and so on; and also desiderata (desirable properties) of such processes, such as resistance to manipulation, or dictatorial tendency. It will also explore some of the apparent paradoxes the various processes can produce (in fact, that *all* the various processes can produce) — the peculiar joy of Social Choice Theory — before presenting some fundamental results, notably Arrow's Impossibility Theorem (Arrow, 1951).

But even though Pizarro conquered the Incas because no one told him it was impossible, just because we know something is impossible does not mean we cannot do it or should not try to do it. So, the final part of this chapter will specify a voting protocol for a self-organising multi-agent system. But we begin with the description of a formal vocabulary of notation and terminology of Social Choice Theory.

4.3 The Vocabulary of Social Choice Theory

This section will define a number of *voting rules* and discuss some 'nice' properties of such rules. A key theorem shows that one of these rules, plurality, satisfies these properties. Job done?... Unfortunately not: with one small tweak, a bit of Latin, intrigue and political manipulation illustrate how it is possible to stray so far from these criteria, and desiderata.

4.3.1 Basics

We begin with some notations and terminology. At root, there is:

- A finite set of **voters** V;
- A finite set of **candidates** C; and
- A **voting procedure** (winner determination method).

A voting method is a function which selects as its outputs a subset of C (the **social decision**) from the inputs of V. The inputs from V are called **ballots** and can either denote a single candidate $c \in C$, or a linear rank order of candidates in C, $\langle c_1, c_2, \ldots, c_n \rangle$, where $\forall c_i, c_j \in C$, $c_i = c_j \Rightarrow i = j$, and $n \leq \mathbf{card}(C)$. Note that a rank order of candidates, as with a rank order of game outcomes, may be taken as an *ordinal* preference, or as a *cardinal* preference, where the magnitude of preference is also expressed. Here, we will assume an ordinal preference, but see Goel *et al.* (2018) for an analysis of social choice rules with ballots expressing cardinal preferences.

A **profile** is a sequence of ballots $\langle v_1, v_2, \ldots, v_n \rangle$, where v_i is the ballot of the ith voter in V, and $n \leq \mathbf{card}(V)$. This defines the domain of *profiles*, the set of all possible ballot sequences of length n.

In general, a voting procedure vp is a procedure:

$$vp : profiles \times methods \to 2^C$$

Note that a voting procedure may produce multiple winners, not just one; but perhaps more importantly, that different voting methods may produce different outputs from the same input. Hence, a voting procedure is parameterised by a method as well as a profile. The method computes an aggregation rule, which defines a mathematical relation, as discussed next.

4.3.2 Aggregation Rules

Now consider a situation with a set V of n voters $V = \{1, 2, \ldots, n\}$ and a set C of two candidates $C = \{c_1, c_2\}$. Let:

- $v_i = 1$ denote the ballot of voter $i \in V$ is for candidate c_1;
- $v_i = -1$ denote the ballot of voter $i \in V$ is for candidate c_2;
- $v_i = 0$ denote the ballot of voter $i \in V$ is an abstention.

If the output of the voting method is 1, then candidate c_1 is declared the winner; if its output is -1, then candidate c_2 is declared the winner; otherwise the result is inconclusive.

A **profile** p is a sequence of ballots (i.e. $p \in \{1 \mid 0 \mid -1\}^n$). If a social choice relation is a mathematical object which assigns a decision (i.e. an element of $\{1 \mid 0 \mid -1\}$) to a profile p, then an **aggregation rule** f is the object which identifies (i.e. computes) a particular social choice relation.

There are *many* possible aggregation rules (more on this in what follows), but a couple of (fairly) intuitive aggregation rules are *plurality* (greatest number of votes wins) and *dictatorship* (one voter's vote alone determines the winner). The aggregation rule for plurality is defined by:

$$f(\langle v_1, v_2, \ldots, v_n \rangle) = \begin{cases} 1, & \text{if } \left(\sum_{i=1}^{n} v_i\right) > 0 \\ 0, & \text{if } \left(\sum_{i=1}^{n} v_i\right) = 0 \\ -1, & \text{if } \left(\sum_{i=1}^{n} v_i\right) < 0 \end{cases}$$

and for dictatorship (of voter i) is defined by:

$$f(\langle v_1, v_2, \ldots, v_n \rangle) = v_i$$

Note that there are n dictatorship aggregation rules, one for each $i \in V$.

At this point, it might also be worth a slight clarification: we use the term *plurality* to denote a "relative majority", meaning that the number of votes received by the winning candidate is greater than the number for any one other option; and the term *majority* denotes an "absolute majority", meaning that the number of votes received by the winning candidate is greater than that for all other options combined. In the aggregation rule above, since we have allowed for abstentions, it is possible for c_1 to get more votes than c_2 (i.e. $\sum_{i=1}^{n} v_i > 0$), but also for $\mathbf{card}(\{i : v_i = 1\}) < \mathbf{card}(V)/2$.

In fact, this observation allows us to define a third aggregation rule, *majority*. A majority for 1 and -1 is defined as $\mathcal{M}$ and $\mathcal{M}'$ as follows:

$$\mathcal{M} = \frac{\mathbf{card}(\{i \mid v_i = 1\})}{\mathbf{card}(V)}$$

$$\mathcal{M}' = \frac{\mathbf{card}(\{i \mid v_i = -1\})}{\mathbf{card}(V)}$$

Majority:

$$f(\langle v_1, v_2, \ldots, v_n \rangle) = \begin{cases} 1, & \text{if } \left(\sum_{i=1}^{n} v_i\right) > 0 \wedge \mathcal{M} > \frac{1}{2} \\ -1, & \text{if } \left(\sum_{i=1}^{n} v_i\right) < 0 \wedge \mathcal{M}' > \frac{1}{2} \\ 0, & \text{otherwise} \end{cases}$$

We can refine the majority aggregation rule by specifying not just a majority of those eligible to vote, but a majority of those who actually voted (i.e. some proportion of those voted 1 or -1, discounting those that voted 0). Another example may require the vote to be *quorate*: a certain proportion of non-abstention ballots have to be cast. In a third example, suppose that to change a constitution, we require a *supermajority* — not just more than half, but more than some other fraction, say two-thirds. If the proposal fails to pass that threshold, then the alternative wins by default, and there is no chance of an inconclusive result. This is called an *asymmetric* supermajority.

Asymmetric supermajority:

$$f(\langle v_1, v_2, \ldots, v_n \rangle) = \begin{cases} 1, & \text{if } \left(\sum_{i=1}^{n} v_i\right) > 0 \wedge \mathcal{M} > \frac{2}{3} \\ -1, & \text{otherwise} \end{cases}$$

4.3.3 Some 'Nice' Properties

We can carry on like this — defining new aggregation rules — by adjusting the conditions. For example, the *supermajority* aggregation rule can be any fraction that we choose.

So, how many possible aggregation rules are there? Well, there are n individuals, where $n = \mathbf{card}(V)$; and there are m possible ballots, where $m = \mathbf{card}(C)+1$, (+1 since we are allowing abstentions). Then there are $k = m^n$ possible profiles, i.e. all the possible combinations of $\{-1, 0, 1\}$ for each of the n voters. Given that there are j possible social choices for each profile, where in this case $j = 3$, since the result may be c_1 (1), c_2 (−1), or inconclusive (0), there are j^k possible aggregation rules.

Therefore, the number of possible aggregation rules grows exponentially with both the number of voters and the number of choices. A lot of them are going to seem a bit 'random', i.e. no discernible pattern between the profiles and the social choice; and some are going to seem a bit arbitrary, like the aggregation rules that assign 0, 1 or −1 to all possible profiles.

So, how is it possible to select a 'meaningful' aggregation rule from this mass of possible aggregation rules; and even if we decide it is 'meaningful', how do we know if it is a 'good' one? The three rules given so far (majority, plurality and dictatorship) are all meaningful (in this intuitive sense), but the former two would, perhaps, be preferable to the latter for those less inclined to favour authoritarianism.

To facilitate such a selection, May (1952) identified some preferable constraints on the relationship between profiles and social choices:

- **Universality:** The domain of admissible inputs consists of all possible profiles, i.e. the aggregation rule is not a *partial* function, so that $f(v_1, v_2, \ldots, v_n) \in C$ for every ballot v_i, for every voter $i \in V$;
- **Anonymity:** Any profile that is a permutation of another produces the same result, i.e. $\forall p \in \textit{profiles} . p' = \mathbf{perm}(p) \Rightarrow f(p') = f(p)$;
- **Neutrality:** If each ballot in a profile is inverted, then the result is inverted, i.e. $f(-v_1, -v_2, \ldots, -v_n) = -f(v_1, v_2, \ldots, v_n)$; and
- **Positive responsiveness:** If some voters change their vote in favour of one alternative, the result does not change in favour of the other.

The universal domain constraint ensures that the aggregation rule treats all profiles equally; the anonymity constraint ensures that it treats all voters equally; and the neutrality constraint ensures that it treats all candidates equally. The positive responsiveness constraint is a sort of monotonicity for aggregation rules: if the profile is changed in favour of one candidate, then the social decision does not change in favour of any of the others.

Based on this, May proved the following theorem (May, 1952): An aggregation rule satisfies universal domain, anonymity, neutrality, and positive responsiveness if and only if it is a majority rule.

As well as providing four plausible criteria for advocating majority rule as the selection for the aggregation rule, the theorem also provides a framework for substantiating why other aggregation rules are not as 'good'. For example, a dictatorship rule violates anonymity, while asymmetrical supermajority rules violate neutrality.

Is that all there is to it? May's theorem appears fairly definitive. But throughout this discussion, it might have been noted that there has been a complicating factor: how to handle the possibility of abstention, as a third option for the ballot; and so "inconclusive" (0) being returned as the social choice, i.e. the set of social choices is greater than two.

So, what does happen when the set of candidates is increased? Bearing in mind that, all along, we have been specifying a mathematical relationship (the aggregation rule), and that a voting method computes — *or is supposed to compute* — the aggregation rule, welcome to a world of paradox, and of political manipulation.

4.3.4 The Condorcet Winner and Condorcet Loser

Consider a situation with *three* candidates $C = \{a, b, c\}$. Then a voter's preference (rank order) can be one of six possible linear orderings over C:

Preference	P_1	P_2	P_3	P_4	P_5	P_6
	a	a	b	b	c	c
	b	c	a	c	a	b
	c	b	c	a	b	a
# voters	n_1	n_2	n_3	n_4	n_5	n_6

We can now define a majority relation $\succ_m$ which ranks the candidates according to how they fare in one-to-one comparisons. Then $A \succ_m B$ means that more voters rank candidate A over candidate

B, and is defined by the following three conditions:

$$a \succ_m b \text{ iff } n_1 + n_2 + n_5 > n_3 + n_4 + n_6$$
$$a \succ_m c \text{ iff } n_1 + n_2 + n_3 > n_4 + n_5 + n_6$$
$$b \succ_m c \text{ iff } n_1 + n_3 + n_4 > n_2 + n_5 + n_6$$

The **Condorcet Winner**[1] is defined as the candidate that is *maximal* in the majority relation $\succ_m$, i.e. it wins more one-to-one comparisons than any other candidate. Correspondingly, the **Condorcet Loser** is defined as the candidate that is minimal in the majority relation $\succ_m$, i.e. it loses more one-to-one comparisons than any other candidate. The Condorcet Winner reflects not just the first preference of every voter, but also the relative preferences of each voter.

The idea of the Condorcet Winner is particularly salient when there are more than two candidates. The plurality aggregation rule is simple, intuitive and plausible; and indeed most likely to produce a winner. However, when there are more than two candidates, it loses information, especially the relative preference of voters for (or against) candidates. In fact, plurality can even result in the Condorcet Loser being declared the winner.

For example, consider the election with four candidates $C = \{a, b, c, d\}$, and the following proportion of voters which have the associated preference relations on these four candidates:

Preference	P_1	P_2	P_3	P_4
	a	b	c	d
	b	c	d	b
	c	d	b	c
	d	a	a	a
# voters	40%	25%	20%	15%

---

[1] The Condorcet Winner is named after Nicholas de Condorcet, who was an eighteenth Century liberal thinker and activist in the era of the French Revolution. Alongside Marx, Condorcet was a key figure of the political Enlightenment, and is closely associated with the origins of Social Choice Theory. For more information, see Baker (1975).

In a straight plurality vote, candidate a is the social choice, with 40% of the vote. But note that $b \succ_m a$, $c \succ_m a$, and indeed $d \succ_m a$. So clearly a is the Condorcet Loser.

Is this possibility really what we want? A progressive voter in the UK could point to the "first-past-the-post" electoral system and how it consistently elects a government on a minority of the vote that pursues social and economic policies which arguably do not reflect the relative preference of the majority. However, once we start to interfere in the process, it points the way to all manner of disagreeable conclusions.

4.3.5 Example: Skulduggery in the Roman Senate

The example in this section is loosely based on the description in Riker (1986). The various machinations and implications are worked through in more detail in that work: indeed, the whole book is an entertaining romp through some more egregious examples of political chicanery throughout history: until one reads Daley (2016), and realises that these are not historical curiosities, and with technology and data it is possible to engage in extremely precise gerrymandering. But this example in set in classical Rome in the time of Pliny the Younger.

A Roman Consul, who had been seriously ill, has now died, and his slaves stand accused of his killing. There are three plausible explanations for his death, and so three possible outcomes for the slaves:

- The consul committed suicide ⤳ acquittal.
- The slaves assisted his suicide ⤳ banishment.
- The slaves murdered the consul ⤳ death.

The Senate has to decide. The senators might reason as follows: given that acquittal and death are considered opposites, then if a senator thinks...:

- ...that the slaves are guilty, then their punishment should be death; but if not, then banishment is 'preferable' to acquittal;
- ...that the slaves are innocent then the outcome of the trial should be acquittal: but if not, then banishment is 'preferable' to death;
- ...that there is sufficient doubt, then the compromise is banishment; but if not, then acquittal is 'preferable' to death.

Three factions emerge in the Senate, with the following numbers and preference orderings:

- Faction D: 37%: Death $\succ$ Banishment $\succ$ Acquittal.
- Faction B: 35%: Banishment $\succ$ Acquittal $\succ$ Death.
- Faction A: 28%: Acquittal $\succ$ Banishment $\succ$ Death.

In which case, how does a Senator get the result that he prefers? Well, we have already discussed the difference between an aggregation rule, a voting method, and a voting procedure. Therefore, the unscrupulous political-operative Senator would try to fix the voting procedure.

If he is in Faction D: he should insist on a ternary vote, with plurality as the aggregation rule. Then D wins, with 37%, beating the other two.

If he is in Faction B: he should insist on the Condorcet Winner, by taking a pairwise comparison of votes, the maximal number of comparisons being the winner. The result is:

- A vs. B: B wins 72 to 28.
- A vs. D: A wins 63 to 37.
- B vs. D: B wins 63 to 37.

So option B wins overall.

If he is in Faction A: he should realise that there are, in effect, two votes: one for innocence or guilt, and if guilty, another for punishment (death or banishment). Therefore, he should arrange for two votes, but:

- Insist on holding the punishment vote *first*, and
- Have his faction *vote against their own preference*!

Then: death beats banishment in the first vote (65–35), but acquittal beats death in the second vote (63–37). Option A wins.

And there we have it: three candidates, three factions; and each faction can ensure that their faction's preference is also the social choice, according to some more-or-less plausible voting procedure (plausible in the sense that the procedure is justifiable, and the tactical voting is deniable).

Herein is the dilemma: the plurality aggregation rule had some 'nice' properties, but in multiple-candidate elections, some apparent drawbacks, like electing the Condorcet Loser. To avoid such situations, one alternative is to use another method; but that appeared to open another can of worms, through direct manipulation. But maybe there is another, even better method, that does possess all the desirable properties, doesn't have the disadvantages, and cannot be manipulated. In Sec. 4.4, we will look at several other voting methods in the quest for the 'perfect' one.

4.4 Voting Procedures

This section looks at various different voting procedures which compute some aggregation rule. To illustrate the methods, we will apply them to the same running example. The voting methods to be presented are plurality (to establish a common baseline), runoff, Borda Count, instant runoff, approval voting, and Copeland Scoring. For each procedure, there is an informal description and application to the running example, to see what social choice it returns. For some procedures a (partial) Prolog specification is given. A final method is given to determine multiple winners.

4.4.1 *Running Example*

For this running example, let $V = \{1, 2, \ldots, 7\}$ and $C = \{a, b, c, d, e\}$. For a particular election, the profile p of ballots $\langle v_i \mid i \in V \rangle$ is:

$$p = \langle [a, d, c, b, e], [a, e, d, b], [a, c, e], [b, c, e, d, a], [b, d, c, e],$$
$$[c, e, d, b], [d, c, e, b] \rangle$$

Recall that these ballots indicate a linear preference, and assume that if a preference is not available, then the next in line is the individual choice instead. So for v_1, the first choice is a, but if a is not available, then voter 1's vote goes to d, and so on.

4.4.2 *Procedures*

Plurality. Each voter selects one candidate, and the candidate with the most first-placed votes is the winner (as we know). A partial Prolog specification (implementation) is given in Fig. 4.1.

```
winner_determination( plurality, Profile, SocialChoice ) :-
      count_votes( Profile, [], [First|Rest] ),
      most_votes( Rest, First, SocialChoice ).

count_votes( [], VoteCount, VoteCount ).
count_votes( [[A|_]|T], SoFar, VoteCount ) :-
      increment_votesfor( A, SoFar, [], Further ),
      count_votes( T, Further, VoteCount ).

most_votes( [], SocialChoice, SocialChoice ).
most_votes( [(A,V1)|T], (_,V2), SocialChoice ) :-
      V1 > V2, !,
      most_votes( T, (A,V1), SocialChoice ).
most_votes( [_|T], BestSoFar, SocialChoice ) :-
      most_votes( T, BestSoFar, SocialChoice ).
```

Fig. 4.1. Partial Specification/Implementation of Plurality

Applied to the running example, plurality gives:

- Vote-count: $[(d,1),(c,1),(b,2),(a,3)]$ – sum of first choice votes;
- Result: a wins.

Runoff (Plurality$^+$). There are two rounds of voting. In the first round: each voter selects one candidate, and the two candidates with most first-placed votes are identified. If either already has a majority, this candidate is declared the winner, otherwise the method proceeds to a second round. In the second round: each voter selects one candidate (either of the top 2); the candidate with most votes now is the winner. Figure 4.2 gives a partial Prolog specification.

Applied to the running example, runoff gives:

- Vote-count, first round: $[(b,2),(a,3)]$ — same as plurality, but c and d are eliminated;
- Vote-count, second round: $[(b,4),(a,3)]$ — the votes of v_6 and v_7, whose first preferences were eliminated in the first round, are transferred to b;
- Result: b wins.

Borda Count. This method is named after Jean-Charles de Borda, a contemporary of Condorcet, and a proponent of his eponymous method as an alternative to majority voting. In this method, each voter rank orders all the candidates. With n candidates being ranked k scores $(n-k)+1$ Borda points. A candidate's Borda Score is the sum

```
winner_determination( runoff, Profile, Winner ) :-
        count_votes( VotesCast, [], VoteCount ),
        round_one_runoff( VoteCount, TopTwo ),
        round_two_runoff( TopTwo, Profile, Winner ).

round_two_runoff( (A,B), Profile, Winner ) :-
        already_majority( A, B, Profile, Winner ), !.
round_two_runoff( ((A,Va),(B,Vb)), Profile, Winner ) :-
        condorcet_winner( Profile, (A,0), (B,0), Winner ).

condorcet_winner( [], (A,Va), (B,Vb), Winner ) :-
        Va > Vb -> Winner=A ; Winner=B.
condorcet_winner( [Ballot|Rest], (A,Va), (B,Vb), Winner ) :-
        compare( A, B, Ballot ) ->
                (Va1 is Va + 1, Vb1 is Vb) ; (Va1 is Va, Vb1 is Vb + 1), !,
                condorcet_winner( Rest, (A,Va1), (B,Vb1), Winner ).
condorcet_winner( [_|Rest], (A,Va), (B,Vb), Winner ) :-
        condorcet_winner( Rest, (A,Va), (B,Vb), Winner ).
```

Fig. 4.2. Partial Specification/Implementation of Runoff

of all the Borda points for each ballot in the profile. The candidate with the highest Borda Score is the winner. Figure 4.3 gives a partial Prolog specification.

Assuming that the Borda points are shared between candidates that are not explicitly ranked, applying the Borda Count method to the running example gives:

- $bs(a) = 5 + 5 + 5 + 1 + 1 + 1 + 1 = 19$;
- $bs(b) = 2 + 2 + 1.5 + 5 + 5 + 2 + 2 = 19.5$;
- $bs(c) = 3 + 1 + 4 + 4 + 3 + 5 + 4 = 24$;
- $bs(d) = 4 + 3 + 1.5 + 2 + 4 + 3 + 5 = 22.5$;
- $bs(e) = 1 + 4 + 3 + 3 + 2 + 4 + 3 = 20$;
- Result: c wins.

Instant Runoff. In this method, each voter rank orders all candidates, and the candidate (or candidates) with the *least* number of first-place votes is eliminated. This is repeated until only one candidate remains.

Note that a tie-break may be necessary, as multiple candidates might receive the least number of first place votes. In the specification of Fig. 4.4, the Condorcet Loser is eliminated. However, there are alternatives: the *Hare Rule* eliminates *all* candidates with the least first-place votes. Instead of iteratively eliminating the candidate with

```
winner_determination( borda, Candidates, Profile, SocialChoice ) :-
     length( candidates, N ),
     borda_score_each_candidate( Candidates, N, Profile, [], BordaScores ),
     highest_borda_score( BordaScores, SocialChoice ).

borda_score_each_candidate( [], _, _, BordaScores, BordaScores ).
borda_score_each_candidate( [A|Rest], N, Profile, SoFar, BordaScores ) :-
     borda_points_each_ballot( Profile, A, N, 0, BordaA ),
     borda_score_each_candidate( Rest, N, Profile, [BordaA|SoFar], BordaScores ).

borda_points_each_ballot( [], A, _, Score, (A,Score) ).
borda_points_each_ballot( [Ballot|Rest], A, N, Sofar, BordaA ) :-
     borda_points( A, Ballot, N, BordaPoints ),
     Further is SoFar + BordaPoints,
     borda_points_each_ballot( Rest, A, N, Further, BordaA )

borda_points( A, Ballot, N, BordaPoints ) :- %ranked
     rank( A, Ballot, K ), !,
     BordaPoints is (N - K) + 1.
borda_points( A, Ballot, N, BordaPoints ) :- %not ranked
     length( Ballot, L ),
     Diff is N - L,
     sum1dotdotX( Diff, 0, Sum1X ),
     BordaPoints is Sum1X / Diff.
```

Fig. 4.3. Partial Specification/Implementation of Borda Count

```
winner_determination( instant_ro, Candidates, Profile, SocialChoice ) :-
     least_candidate_elimination( Candidates, Profile, SocialChoice ).

least_candidate_elimination( [SocialChoice], _, SocialChoice ) :- !.
least_candidate_elimination( Candidates, Profile, SocialChoice ) :-
     first_places( Candidates, VotesCast, FirstPlaces ),
     least_first_places( FirstPlaces, Profile, Least ),
     eliminate_candidate( Least, Candidates, NewCandidates ),
     eliminate_from_profile( Least, Profile, NewProfile ),
     least_candidate_elimination( NewCandidates, NewProfile, SocialChoice ).
```

Fig. 4.4. Partial Specification/Implementation of Instant-Runoff

the least first place votes, the *Coombs Rule* removes the candidate with the most last-placed votes.

Applying the instant-runoff method to the running example gives:

- $[(e, 0), (c, 1), (d, 1), (b, 2), (a, 3)]$;
- $[(c, 1), (d, 1), (b, 2), (a, 3)]$;
- $[(d, 2), (b, 2), (a, 3)]$;
- $[(d, 4), (a, 3)]$;
- Result: d wins.

Note that settling tiebreaks by eliminating the Condorcet Loser lets d off the hook, twice; moreover, d goes on to win. With the Hare Rule, d would have been eliminated along with c in the second iteration (yes, it was fixed — why?).

Approval. With this method, a ballot represents not a linear rank order of decreasing preference, but rather represents the set of candidates who are 'equally acceptable' to the voter. So, in the running example, voters 1 and 4 are seemingly indifferent to the social choice, whereas 3 seems to be altogether rather more choosy. So the method works by each voter selecting a subset of candidates, and the most-named candidate is the winner.

Applying the approval method to the running example gives:

- Vote-count: $[(e, 7), (c, 6), (d, 6), (b, 6), (a, 4)]$;
- Result: e wins.

Copeland Scoring. In this method, each voter submits a ballot with a linear rank order. A win–loss record, the Copeland Score, is calculated for each candidate $a \in V$ with respect to each candidate $b \in V'$ where $V' = (V - \{A\})$. This score is given by:

$$copeland(a) = \mathbf{card}(b \in V' \mid a \succ_m b) - \mathbf{card}(b \in V' \mid b \succ_m a)$$

4.4.3 The D'Hondt Method

The D'Hondt Method (named after its famous Belgian inventor, Victor D'Hondt) is designed to provide *multiple* winners, for example to return a number of representatives for a large constituency, according to principles of *proportional representation* (i.e. the number of winners is proportional to the share of the vote; bearing in mind the number of winners is discrete and the share of the vote is likely to be fractional).

Suppose that in an election for such a constituency, there are to be n winners. With this method, each party in the election submits a ranked list of n candidates. The voters cast their votes in favour of a *party*, not a candidate. Then the process is as follows:

- Divide votes-for-party by (number-of-winners-for-party + 1).
- Party with most votes gets 1 winner.
- Repeat until n winners.

For example, suppose the votes cast for five parties, Green, Red, Yellow, Blue and Purple, in an election are as shown in the following table. Suppose the intention is to elect four representatives. The process would be as follows:

Start	Green	Red	Yellow	Blue	Purple
n = No. of Winners + 1	1	1	1	1	1
Vote/n	100,000	80,000	45,000	30,000	10,000
Round 1: first Green candidate elected					
n = No. of Winners + 1	2	1	1	1	1
Vote/n	50,000	80,000	45,000	30,000	10,000
Round 2: first Red candidate elected					
n = No. of Winners + 1	2	2	1	1	1
Vote/n	50,000	40,000	45,000	30,000	10,000
Round 3: second Green candidate elected					
n = No. of Winners + 1	3	2	2	1	1
Vote/n	33,333	40,000	22,500	30,000	10,000
Round 4: first Yellow candidate elected					

At this point, $n = 4$ candidates have been elected as representatives for the constituency, as required, and the process stops. The winning candidates for successively greater values of n can be determined by extending the procedure in the same way.

4.5 Paradox Abounds

The previous section showed that five voting methods, all ostensibly plausible, could each return a different answer, given the same profile as input. But that is not the limit of the problems: in this section, we review some counter-intuitive, indeed paradoxical, results from Social Choice Theory, leading up to the key result, Arrow's Impossibility Theorem (Arrow, 1951).

4.5.1 *Condorcet's Paradoxes*

Clearly not content with the eponymous winner and loser, Condorcet also identified a couple of paradoxes which became known as Condorcet's Paradox and Condorcet's Other Paradox (Fishburn, 1974).

Condorcet's Paradox concerns preference ordering: he observed that a set of preference orderings which are transitive can be aggregated to give a majority preference ordering which is not (i.e. it is cyclic). Therefore, there is no Condorcet Winner.

It can be assumed that a 'rational' preference ordering must be transitive, so that if a is preferred to b and b is preferred to c, then a is preferred to c. Condorcet even argued that a voting method should ignore any voter with inconsistent preferences.

However: even if each voter's preference ordering is transitive, the majority ordering $\succ_m$ might not be. A very simple example shows this:

Preference	P_1	P_2	P_3
	a	b	c
	b	c	a
	c	a	b
# voters	1	1	1

This situation gives a majority cycle: $a \succ_m b \succ_m c \succ_m a$. There is no Condorcet Winner. The group's collective preference appears to be not 'rational', even though each group member's individual preference is.

The second paradox, called Condorcet's Other Paradox (Fishburn, 1974) is a bit more complicated. We have seen from the first paradox that there may not be a Condorcet Winner. However, we can make it a requirement of a voting rule that it should be **Condorcet Consistent**, meaning that if a candidate is the Condorcet Winner, then that candidate should always be elected.

However, it is possible to construct situations where the Condorcet Winner is different from the Borda Winner (and indeed Condorcet did just that; see also Regenwetter and Grofman (1998) for results from real elections). In such situations, the only way to elect the Condorcet Winner, using any scoring rule, is to award more points to second place votes than to first place votes, which just seems ever so slightly counter-intuitive.

Condorcet's example was generalised to the following theorem (Fishburn, 1974): that for all $m \geq 3$, there is some voting situation with a Condorcet Winner such that every weighted scoring rule (e.g. Borda) will have at least $m-2$ candidates with a greater score than the Condorcet Winner.

This means that no voting method that uses a scoring rule is Condorcet Consistent, unless it sometimes allocates more points to second place votes than to first place votes. This has led to the proposal of various methods which are guaranteed to be Condorcet Consistent. This includes Copeland Scoring, discussed earlier, but also Nanson's Method, Schwartz's Set Method and Dodgson's Method.

Nanson's Method works by iteratively removing candidates with a lower than average Borda score, until there is only one candidate remaining. Schwartz's Set Method can return multiple winners, as the winners are those in the smallest set of candidates who are not beaten in a two-candidate election by any of the candidates not in the set. Dodgson's Method is notable for its computational complexity (NP-complete) and for being devised by the same man who wrote *Alice in Wonderland*, which just goes to show the same stuff can inspire trippy literature as well as trippy voting methods.

In any case, like the following paradoxes, it is important not to misinterpret Condorcet's Paradoxes with regard to social preferences: just because something can go wrong, it does not mean it *will* go wrong, nor that one needs to dispense with the 'thing'.

4.5.2 Yet More Paradoxical Results

A good survey, with further examples and explanations, of these results can be found in Pacuit (2019). However, these results include a failure of monotonicity, the no-show paradox, Simpson's Paradox about multiple districts, and Anscombe's Paradox about multiple elections.

In fact, we have already seen how a failure of monotonicity can affect plurality with runoff, in the Roman Senate example of Sec. 4.3.5. One would expect that receiving increased support from the voters would be better for a candidate, but as the example shows, increased support (in the form of rising preference ranking) led to a different candidate being eliminated, and subsequent defeat by the other.

The no-show paradox is the mirror of this: that a candidate who wins when all voters participate, can be defeated when some of those voters that do not prefer her do not participate in the election.

Intuitively, one might have thought that decreasing preference for others implies an increased chance of winning, but not always. It turns out that a voting method which is Condorcet Consistent is exposed to potential failures of monotonicity like this (Moulin, 1988).

Simpson's Paradox is a product of some voting methods not being 'additive', in the sense that if an election is broken down with the voters divided into different constituencies (or districts), then a candidate who wins all the elections in each different constituency can still be the loser if all the constituencies are combined. Of course, this works the other way: a candidate who wins the single constituency election can find herself the loser depending on how the constituencies are drawn. The paradox admits all sorts of opportunities for unscrupulous behaviour (Daley, 2016).

Anscombe's Paradox is a paradox of multiple elections. For example, suppose a set of voters are asked to vote yes (1) or no (0) on three issues. The results are:

Preference	111	110	101	100	011	010	001	000
# **voters**	1	1	1	3	1	3	3	0

Counting up on a per-issue basis "no" wins 7–6 on all votes — but there is no support for 000. Equally, this can be manipulated the other way, too: for example by bundling an unpopular measure in with a set of popular ones, and claiming a mandate for every issue in the election (see for example, the 2020 "All-Russian Vote", which proposed 200 amendments to the 1993 constitution, including a change which would allow the incumbent president to run for two further presidential terms).

4.5.3 Arrow's Impossibility Theorem

If these paradoxical results, which have scope for all sorts of counter-intuitive results and underhanded manipulation, are not bad enough, then Arrow's Impossibility Theorem should finish the job.

The problem is this: we are given a set of individual preference orderings, and three or more distinct alternatives. Our objective is to define an electoral system that produces a complete and transitive social ranking of the three (or more) alternatives from the set of individual orderings. Arrow specified four 'reasonable' criteria for the 'fairness' of that system:

- **Universal Domain:** No preference ordering can be ignored;
- **Unanimity (Pareto Efficiency):** If all voters prefer candidate A to candidate B, then B should not be the winner;
- **Non-Dictatorial:** The social ranking should not be defined by the preference ordering of a single voter; and
- **Independence of Irrelevant Alternatives:** The social ranking of two candidates A and B depends only on their relative ranking.

Arrow proved that there is no social welfare function, or ranked voting electoral system of the kind that we have discussed, that can produce that output from the given inputs *and* satisfy all four reasonable criteria at the same time (Arrow, 1951).

4.5.4 *Gibbard–Satterthwaite Theorem*

The Gibbard–Satterthwaite Theorem generalises Arrow's Theorem, and uses it to show that if a voting rule has at least three possible outcomes and if it is non-manipulable, then it is dictatorial. In other words, one of the following properties must hold for any voting rule:

- The rule is susceptible to tactical voting; or
- The rule limits the possible outcomes to two alternatives only; or
- The rule is dictatorial.

Not quite what was wanted, perhaps.

This theorem is an impossibility result: it means that we cannot devise an electoral system with all the desirable fairness qualities. However, while it does say that something cannot be done, it also does not say that nothing can be done, and certainly not that we should give up on voting altogether.

So, it does not say, for example, that no decision will be reached in any given situation: we can always define a voting method which ensures that some candidate is selected as the winner (although it might be helpful to check that the method is not NP-complete). Moreover, in general the candidate so selected is 'better' than choosing a winner at random, and certainly better than dictatorship.

It also does not say that none of the social welfare functions discussed here are actually useful for the purposes to which they are put.

Just because something is not perfect, does not mean that anything which is less than perfect is not serviceable. If anything, it is also a warning against presumption or complacency, and carelessness in design and selection.

It might also serve as a warning that the pursuit of 'fairness' itself might have unintended consequences. For example, it has been suggested that by using the D'Hondt system for British European elections, on the grounds that a form of proportional representation was 'fairer' than the first-past-the-post method used for parliamentary elections, the initial platform was provided for the anti-European sentiment in the UK that was ruthlessly exploited by a number of commercial and extra-national interests.

4.5.5 *Comparison of Voting Methods*

In view of these paradoxes and theorems, it is reasonable to ask which voting method should be used; although this question can be embedded in a broader question about what sort of electoral system should be used. There are three main dimensions: plurality vs. proportionality; quantifiable or binary criteria; and systemic rules. Finally in this section, we will look at each in turn.

In the first dimension, the two poles of voting methods appear to be plurality and proportionality. The former is a system based on securing an absolute winner from a real majority or relative majority of the votes, while the latter is based on ensuring that the outcome is a refection of the votes cast. Each has its merits, of course. However, for national elections, the New Zealand Royal Commission on the Electoral System 1986 report was decisive in changing that countries' electoral system from first-past-the-post to mixed member proportional (a system in which voters get two votes: one to decide the representative for their single-seat constituency, and one for a political party). This might explain why in 2020 New Zealand had Jacinda Ardern as Prime Minister, and the UK had her political antipode.

In the second dimension, there are criteria that state that if certain conditions are true of the ballots, then a particular candidate must (or must not) win; an example is the Condorcet Winner criterion. There are also criteria that state that if one candidate wins in one set of circumstances, then the same candidate should win in a related set of circumstances. An example criterion here is the Independence of Irrelevant Alternatives; another is monotonicity. Thirdly, there are criteria relating to the process of counting ballots and determining a winner, which include the computational complexity and the methods for resolving ties (i.e. avoiding randomness).

In the third dimension, there are rules regarding the control and conduct of the election. This includes voter eligibility, candidate eligibility, election officials, how and when elections are scheduled and sequenced, and the conduct of political parties and officials, especially after the election, and especially the transfer of elected authority.

In Sec. 4.6, we will examine (some of) these issues in context of a voting protocol based on *Rules of Order* (Robert *et al.*, 2000).

4.6 A Voting Protocol

The previous sections have mapped out some of the theoretical terrain of Social Choice Theory, in particular identifying some of the pitfalls in the selection of a voting method, and the perils of strategic manipulation.

However, the output of a voting method, the social choice (or winner), is normative: in one sense, it specifies that, according to X aggregation rule with Y ballots, candidate Z *ought* to be declared the winner. In the implementation of a voting protocol for an open system, we have to ensure that Z *really is* declared to be the winner.

The use of terms such as 'winner' and 'declared' are indicative that these are, in fact, matters of convention: the candidate identified as the social choice by the voting method is 'the winner' by mutual agreement of all those that participate; and being 'declared' to be the winner is the result of an action performed by a designated agent with the institutionalised power to see to it that "this candidate is the winner" is a true statement (or rather, a mutually-agreed institutional fact).

We complete this chapter by giving an overview of a formal specification of a voting protocol. The protocol will be based on an informal specification given in *Robert's Rules of Order* (RONR, Robert *et al.* (2000)), the standard handbook of procedures for conducting business in deliberative assemblies and committees. The formal specification will use the Event Calculus (Kowalski and Sergot, 1986), as originally presented in Chapter 1. A thorough description of the protocol is given in Pitt *et al.* (2006).

4.6.1 Actions and Fluents

According to RONR, the sequence of actions for a committee to take a vote on a motion is as follows: the chair opens a session; a committee member requests and is granted the floor; the member proposes a motion; another member seconds the motion; there is a debate on the motion; the chair closes the debate and calls for a vote of those in favour, of those against, and those abstaining; the chair declares the motion carried, or not, according to the ballots cast and the standing rules of the committee.

Leaving aside the floor request (for now: see Chapter 5 and Artikis *et al.*, 2004) and the debate on the motion (*cf*. Artikis *et al.* (2007)), this description otherwise serves to identify the roles in the situation (e.g. chair, committee member), the actions performed by each role (see Table 4.1), the states of the protocol in which these actions are valid or 'meaningful' (see Fig. 4.5), and some key fluents which are changed by the performance of specific actions (see Table 4.2).

4.6.2 *Institutionalised Powers*

We are interested in specifying when an empowered agent performs a designated action in a specific context which creates or changes an

Table 4.1. Actions Performed in the Voting Protocol

Action	Indicating...
$open\_session(Ag, S)$	$close\_session(Ag, S)$
$propose(Ag, M)$	$second(Ag, M)$
$open\_ballot(Ag, M)$	$close\_ballot(Ag, M)$
$vote(Ag, M, aye)$	$vote(Ag, M, nay)$
$abstain(Ag, M)$	$revoke(Ag, M)$
$declare(Ag, M, carried)$	$declare(Ag, M, not\_carried)$

Table 4.2. Fluents Used in the Voting Protocol

Fluent	Range
$wdm(C)$	aggregation rule of committee
$status(M)$	$\{pending, proposed, seconded\ voting(T), voted, resolved\}$
$votes(M)$	$\mathbb{N}_0 \times \mathbb{N}_0$
$voted(Ag, M)$	$\{nil, aye, nay, abs\}$
$role\_of(Ag, R)$	boolean
$sanction(Ag)$	list of integers

institutional fact. In particular, it is actions of the chair (the agent occupying the role of the chair) which empower other agents (agents occupying the role of committee-member) to vote (they can 'vote' at other times as well; but at those times they are just making a noise that is institutionally meaningless).

Therefore, the chair is empowered to open the ballot on a motion after it has been proposed seconded:

$$\mathbf{pow}(C, open\_ballot(C, M)) = true \text{ holdsat } T \leftarrow$$
$$status(M) = seconded \text{ holdsat } T \wedge$$
$$role\_of(C, chair) = true \text{ holdsat } T$$

After the chair performs the *open_ballot* action, the committee members are empowered to vote, but note that the action also changes the protocol state and zeroes the number of votes for and against the

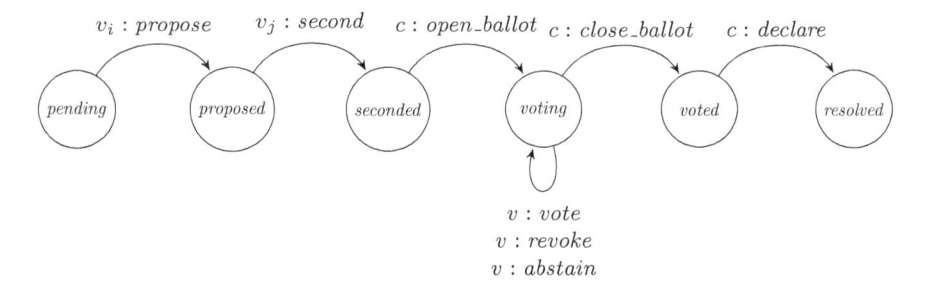

Fig. 4.5. State Sequence Diagram for the Voting Protocol

motion:

$$open\_ballot(C,M) \text{ initiates } votes(M) = (0,0) \text{ at } T \leftarrow$$
$$\mathbf{pow}(C, open\_ballot(C,M)) = true \text{ holdsat } T$$
$$open\_ballot(C,M) \text{ initiates } voted(V,M) = nil \text{ at } T \leftarrow$$
$$\mathbf{pow}(C, open\_ballot(C,M)) = true \text{ holdsat } T \wedge$$
$$role\_of(V, voter) = true \text{ holdsat } T$$
$$open\_ballot(C,M) \text{ initiates } status(M) = voting(T) \text{ at } T \leftarrow$$
$$\mathbf{pow}(C, open\_ballot(C,M)) = true \text{ holdsat } T$$

The committee members have the power to cast a vote:

$$\mathbf{pow}(V, vote(V,M,\_)) = true \text{ holdsat } T \leftarrow$$
$$status(M) = voting(\_) \text{ holdsat } T \wedge$$
$$role\_of(V, voter) = true \text{ holdsat } T \wedge$$
$$\text{not } role\_of(V, chair) = true \text{ holdsat } T \wedge$$
$$voted(V,M) = nil \text{ holdsat } T$$

The following axiom specifies the effect of an empowered agent casting a vote in favour (similar axioms are specified for other voting actions):

$$vote(V,M,aye) \text{ initiates } profile(M) = [1|Profile] \text{ at } T \leftarrow$$
$$\mathbf{pow}(V, vote(V,M)) = true \text{ holdsat } T \wedge$$
$$profile(M) = Profile \text{ holdsat } T$$
$$vote(V,M,aye) \text{ initiates } voted(V,M) = aye \text{ at } T \leftarrow$$
$$\mathbf{pow}(V, vote(V,M,\_)) = true \text{ holdsat } T$$

4.6.3 Permission and Obligation

Enfranchisement — being given the right to vote — is composed of two elements: having the right to vote, and having an entitlement associated with that right. Having the right to vote has three aspects:

- Having the power (being empowered) to vote;
- Denying anyone else the power to object to 'appropriate' exercise of this power; and
- Subjecting inappropriate removal of this power to sanction;

while the entitlements associated with the right also has three aspects:
- Being entitled to access the 'voting machinery';
- Being entitled to have the vote counted correctly; and
- Being entitled to a 'fair' outcome (i.e. the result is declared according to the way the votes were cast with respect to the standing rules (specifying the aggregation rule to be used) of the committee).

Some aspects of right and entitlement can be specified by specific axioms of power and obligation. For example, the *chair* has the power to close the ballot, but may not have *permission* to close the ballot at least until it is quorate, i.e. to give all the committee members sufficient time to vote, and for the number of members to be 'sufficiently' representative:

$$\begin{aligned}
&\mathbf{pow}(C, close\_ballot(C, M)) = true \text{ holdsat } T \leftarrow \\
&\quad status(M) = voting \text{ holdsat } T \wedge \\
&\quad role\_of(C, chair) = true \text{ holdsat } T \\
&\mathbf{per}(C, close\_ballot(C, M)) = true \text{ holdsat } T \leftarrow \\
&\quad role\_of(C, chair) = true \text{ holdsat } T \wedge \\
&\quad status(M) = voting(T) \text{ holdsat } T \wedge \\
&\quad quorate(M, T)
\end{aligned}$$

Similarly, an agent's entitlement to having its vote counted correctly is specified by the axiom above for an empowered agent casting a vote. The entitlement to have the result declared correctly is specified by an obligation on the chair:

$$\begin{aligned}
&\mathbf{obl}(C, declare(C, M, carried)) = true \text{ holdsat } T \leftarrow \\
&\quad role\_of(C, chair) = true \text{ holdsat } T \wedge \\
&\quad status(M) = voted \text{ holdsat } T \wedge \\
&\quad profile(M) = Profile \text{ holdsat } T \wedge \\
&\quad wdm(C) = Method \text{ holdsat } T \wedge \\
&\quad winner\_determination(Method, Profile, 1)
\end{aligned}$$

The last line invokes a winner determination method as specified in Sec. 4.4.

Note that agents that defy or violate the permissions and obligations associated with their roles, or who try to perform actions for which they are not empowered, can be sanctioned. However, one of the interesting features of RONR, reproduced in EC protocol specifications such as this, is "anything goes unless someone objects". This allows multi-agent systems to reflect the flexible interpretation of following conventional rules found in human societies (although *cf.* Graeber (2015)), which is further developed in Chapter 5, but also provides the basis for a system of graduated sanctions (Chapter 6), forgiveness as a mechanism to repair trust breakdowns (Chapter 8), and disobedience as a mechanism of change (Chapter 10).

4.6.4 *Implementation Route*

These axioms can be converted into executable Prolog code, and linked with an Event Calculus reasoner. Specific narratives of events can then be verified to ensure that agents did not violate their permissions and obligations. For full details, see Pitt *et al.* (2006).

4.7 Summary and Conclusions

This chapter has been concerned with Social Choice Theory, the study of strategic interaction in collective decision-making. We specified a simple decision rule, *plurality* (or relative majority) which seemed, in deciding between two alternatives, simple, intuitive, efficacious, and plausible (in the sense that it satisfied a number of desirable properties).

We then drove a truck through plurality by simply adding a third alternative and some human ingenuity in strategic manipulation. This led to an analysis of various voting methods and the various paradoxes that can befall any of these methods, ending up with Arrow's Impossibility Theorem, and the realisation that the quest for the 'perfect' voting system was somewhat quixotic, and chaotic.

"Dozens of possible voting methods have been devised, ranging from the imperfect to the abysmal", wrote the journalist George Monbiot (2017), which might seem a fairly reasonable way of surveying the landscape of voting methods and the slight sense of unease at some outcomes.

However, Arrow himself said: "Most systems are not going to work badly all of the time. All I proved is that all can work badly at times" (McKenna, 2008). Therefore, it is important to recognise that "there is no such thing as a fair voting system" is a misrepresentation of the Impossibility Theorem. Just as Gödel's Incompleteness Theorem demonstrates the inherent limitations of every formal axiomatic system for modelling basic arithmetic, so the Impossibility Theorem demonstrates the inherent limitations of every voting system for making group decisions. Nevertheless, we still do maths and logic; equally, we should still debate and vote.

Moreover, these surprising results (or paradoxes) do not mean that we have to abandon voting, or accept 'irrationality', or remove voters until there is a Condorcet Winner. It rather means that preferences, and in particular values, are not (and indeed should never be) an infallible, timeless and unquestionable *product* of votes. That is to say, it is not a matter of "we've had a vote, these are our social preferences, no more discussion", but rather living together requires an endless cycle of reflection, deliberation and voting, as well as meta-deliberation.

There are two implications of this. Firstly, while in theory no voting procedure can satisfy all the fairness criteria at the same time, this implies that the challenge is to design a voting procedure that minimises the likelihood of an unfair outcome. This entails understanding why some methods work better in some situations than others, but also applying an appropriate framework to evaluate, continually, the voting method being used.

Secondly, given the scope of strategic manipulation, there are other pertinent questions to ask. Social choice is not just a matter of how someone gets elected to a position of (institutionalised) power, but why they want it, how they got it, and what they do with it. Scrutiny and accountability are critical, and beware anyone elected to a position of authority who will not subject themselves to any level of scrutiny or refuses to be held responsible for their actions. In short, it is necessary to cause, and resolve, disputes.

Chapter 5

Alternative Dispute Resolution

5.1 Introduction

The aim of this chapter is to examine strategic interaction through the lens of *Alternative Dispute Resolution* (ADR). ADR is an umbrella term for a wide range of procedures, which are intended to enable two parties who are in disagreement over some issue to resolve their conflict without recourse to litigation, i.e. hiring lawyers and going to court.

We need these procedures, because in any strategic interaction in an open system, with multiple autonomous actors with competing or conflicting interests, there are going to be occasions when the outcome of the interaction is sub-ideal for one or other party. We have seen this with, for example defection, or the failure to coordinate in Game Theory, and manipulation of voting procedures in Social Choice Theory. Indeed, we stressed in the beginning that one of the features of open systems was the expectation of errors, whether inadvertent, necessary or malicious.

To regulate strategic interaction in open systems, we also proposed the use of conventional rules, but this type of rule, unlike a physical law (like gravity) can still be broken. So the scope for dispute, i.e. whether someone did or did not comply with a rule, how serious was the impact of any non-compliance, etc., is still wide.

Informally, in the days before Internet programming and Integrated Development Environments (IDE), it was reputed that computer code for desktop applications comprised one-third functionality, one-third interface, and one-third error handling. But any computer user will know that computers are prone to error: we have all experienced the blue screen of death, the revolving Catherine Wheel of Doom, and various other signifiers of malfunction. Moreover, resource conflict was expected in the design and manufacture of computer systems and networks, from priority queues in multi-tasking operating systems to network collision detection and overload protection.

Therefore, open multi-agent systems are error-prone, but the errors can occur with 'higher order' conventional rules, (which may also be changed at run-time, increasing the scope for inadvertent non-compliance) and normative constraints, like permission, obligation and prohibition. It would be preferable to avoid enforcement of rules by regimentation (as shown in (Jones and Sergot, 1993)), or a *reductio ad absurdum* in the interpretation of normative specifications (e.g. in the design of a computerised library, the requirement "no user is permitted to borrow more than four books" can be implemented by the simple expedient of not lending any). Similarly, it would be preferable to avoid 'algorithmic governance', where the space of possible actions is pre-ordained and an agent (human or software) can only select from the given options (König, 2020). It is also equally important to recognise the essential role of rule-breaking in exploration of a possible design space, self-improvement and breaking out of path-dependency, and the general contribution of disobedience to self-organisation and self-governance. Note that in some countries the right to protest is written into the constitution (and see Sec. 10.5).

Therefore, we need an appropriate form of error-handling in self-organising multi-agent systems, and this form, we argue, needs to take into account ideas from ADR. Consequently, the objectives of this chapter are to:

- Understand the 'expectation of error' feature of open systems, the range of causes and sources of possible errors, and the range of possible error-handling mechanisms;
- Specify protocols for 'on-line' and 'off-line' error detection in the framework of dynamic norm-governed multi-agent systems, in particular protocols for access control, regulatory compliance and dispute resolution; and
- Understand that 'errors' in open and self-organising systems are not necessarily events that can be prevented, nor is it even necessarily desirable to eliminate them completely.

The chapter is structured as follows. It begins in Sec. 5.2 with a scenario of domestic non-bliss in the SmartHouse kitchen. A brief overview of ADR is given in Sec. 5.3, while a test environment, called Coloured Trials, a grid-like micro-world developed to investigate intellectual property rights and disputes, is presented in Sec. 5.4. Using the framework of dynamic norm-governed systems, error management is discussed in three forms: error toleration through an access control protocol (Sec. 5.5), error retrospection through a protocol for regulatory compliance (Sec. 5.6), and error recovery through an ADR protocol (Sec. 5.7). The chapter summarises and concludes in Sec. 5.8, identifying the need for ADR in open systems, as well as its importance in the design of institutions for solving collective action problems, specifically common-pool resource (CPR) management.

5.2 Example: The Missing Sausage Quarrel

Mark and Jeremy occupy a shared flat. In this case, Mark owns the flat; or at least he will own the flat: he had the deposit to get the mortgage in order to buy the flat. Once he repays the mortgage, the flat is his. Jeremy is the lodger, and pays rent; by a curious coincidence, even at mate's rates, the amount of money that Jeremy pays per month to rent a room is about the same as the amount of money that Marks spends for the monthly repayments on the mortgage to own the flat. So in effect, Jeremy rents the flat, and Mark ends up owning it, but only because he had the capital to begin with. (For more on rentier economy, see Piketty (2014); for a discussion of fairness, those already outraged can see Chapter 7.)

That aside, although Mark and Jeremy live together, with the exception of the "big-shop" for items they both need, they foodshop, cook and eat separately. One day, Mark makes himself a big plate of sausages and mashed potatoes. He is enjoying this enviably nutritious feast, Jeremy (who is hungry) is looking on in envy, and at some point Mark puts his plate down to get ice-cream out of the fridge to pre-melt. While he is gone, Jeremy snaffles a sausage. Mark returns, and noticing the absence on the plate, exclaims "A sausage has gone! Oh my God, Jeremy, a sausage is missing!" The scene is set for a fair old dispute.[1]

---

[1] The actual scene is from UK TV Series *Peep Show*, Season 5, Episode 3.

It is arguable which has caused more disputes over the millennia: shared kitchens or the interpretation of sacred texts; certainly the latter, which have caused schisms, pogroms and inquisitional persecutions are much less serious than taking the last of the milk and not replacing it. Kitchens are also full of easily accessible sharp objects.

A disputatious arena with convenient proximity to makeshift weaponry: we are no longer asking "what could possibly go wrong?" — we know things can and will go wrong. Instead we are asking: what could we possibly do to make it right?

The answer, proposed by this chapter, lies not in reaching for the longest and sharpest knife in the block,[2] nor keeping your lawyer on speed dial. The answer is embellished with a consideration of *retributive justice* in Chapter 7, the idea of *forgiveness* in Chapter 8, and the importance of *disobedience* in Chapter 10, but it starts here with a study of ADR.

5.3 Alternative Dispute Resolution

ADR, especially online ADR, is another option to litigation, or court resolution, and usually takes the form of negotiation, mediation or arbitration (Pitt *et al.*, 2007).[3] The rise in importance of ADR methods over the past two decades is due to the numerous benefits offered to the parties involved in a dispute, coupled with the well-known shortcomings of litigation. Consequently, investigating and implementing ADR in the context of intelligent legal systems is an important focus of attention, and raises many key issues that citizens and businesses should consider when attempting to resolve a conflict.

---

[2]Besides which, my Robert Welch knives are to be used only for the purpose for which they were designed, and don't try otherwise. The same exclusion clause does not apply to the rolling pin (he says, bluntly).

[3]The "alternative" in "alternative dispute resolution" should not be interpreted in the same way as "alternative" in "alternative medicine", i.e. as an alternative to science, evidence and statistics. In fact the mechanisms described here should be considered the *primary* dispute resolution mechanisms and litigation as the *last* alternative. But then leaving lawyers in charge of dispute resolution makes as much sense as leaving software engineers in charge of interface design.

The problems of litigation have played a major part in the promotion of ADR to disputing parties, none more so than to firms, especially small to medium enterprises. Some reports indicate that very few lawsuits filed actually go to trial, and of this an even smaller proportion arrive at a verdict (WIPO Arbitration and Mediation Center, 2007). This is often due to a settlement being reached just prior to the end, or the case breaking down leading to a retrial. Equally, securing 'justice' for the individual citizen can be daunting when faced with the prospect of going to court, whereby the time, expense and hassle can easily outweigh the relatively small sums involved in the dispute. There are several initiatives to ensure that such minor cases can be resolved quickly, e.g. the Small Claims Court in the UK.

Even so, with many litigating cases reaching a settlement, they often come at a high price, in terms of money and time. In many cases, it can take years for a case to come to trial, time firms and individuals cannot afford to spend. During trial, companies and governments could be forced to wait for a prolonged period, impacting heavily on business. The significant capital expenditures make the litigation process expensive, with fees incurred for legal services, as well as the cost of court overheads. There is also the potential for appeals, which can add to both mounting delays and costs.

By contrast, ADR carries numerous benefits (Kowalchyk, 2006), including often being opportunistic and relatively quick. It also allows the parties involved to have more control over their dispute, and so settlement, as they choose the procedure and terms and conditions. In addition, any third party required — for example in a mediation and arbitration procedure — can be determined by those involved, and can come from within the system, so that juries are selected from a peer group with a genuinely shared experience, knowledge and understanding. Further distinctions between various types of dispute resolution appear in Fig. 5.1, which depicts a spectrum of procedures and their associated qualities.

Although not without its potential drawbacks (Carver and Vondra, 1994), ADR and related approaches have also been seen as important auxiliary services to mainstream legal and policing processes. This suggests *a priori* that ADR is an apposite approach to building an 'autonomic' system for dealing with disputes and norm-violations in *self-healing* self-organising multi-agent systems. However, as we have already mentioned, the need for disputes, and various dispute

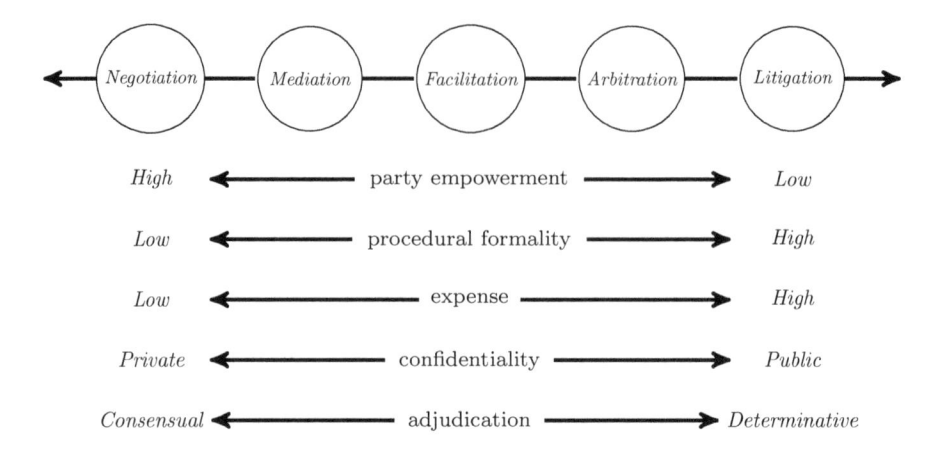

```
                Negotiation ── Mediation ── Facilitation ── Arbitration ── Litigation

       High    ←──────── party empowerment ────────→    Low
       Low     ←──────── procedural formality ────────→  High
       Low     ←──────────── expense ────────────→       High
       Private ←─────────── confidentiality ──────────→  Public
       Consensual ←─────── adjudication ──────────→      Determinative
```

Fig. 5.1. The Spectrum of ADR Mechanisms

resolution mechanisms, in the first place is a deeper issue and recurring theme. Indeed, while the processes identified here can be seen as dealing with errors, the role of argumentation and argumentation protocols (Artikis *et al.*, 2007) becomes intriguing when resolving inconsistent *beliefs*, e.g. through some form of dialectics, such as that proposed by Marx, for example (i.e. dialectical materialism).

5.4 Test Domain

This section describes the test domain for exploring ideas about ADR in self-organising multi-agent systems. It starts with an overview of the shift towards mass-participation content creation (i.e. blogging, video channels, photograph sharing) and *knowledge commons* (Hess and Ostrom, 2006), an electronic repository of knowledge created and maintained as a public good just like physical resources (Macbeth and Pitt, 2015). Based on the experimental system Colored Trails (Grosz *et al.*, 2004), we define the grid-like micro-world Colored Trails, for exploring intellectual property rights and disputes in multiple-authored works-of-mind and knowledge commons.

5.4.1 *Mass-Participation Content Creations*

Rather than passively viewing end-product content that has been produced by a studio for mass-consumption, we are living in an era of mass-participation content creation (MPCC), where 'prosumers' (acting as both content creators and consumers) collectively create 'works of mind' using collaborative tools for sharing, and building on, user-generated content. Examples include social networking sites, sites for image and video sharing, wikis, mashups and cloud services and web applications for computer-supported cooperative work. Increasingly, pervasive computing tools and technologies can be used to collect what is, in effect, also user-generated content, for example using A/V equipment such as cameras and microphones, wireless sensor networks, mobile phones, radio-frequency identification (RFID) tags in cards and implants, and so on.

This content can be used to develop hitherto unexpected applications, such as supplementing earthquake early warning systems through detecting the movement of mobile phone accelerometers *en masse* in a localised geographical space. This is an example of *implicit* user-generated content being aggregated in an application which can save losses in both economic and human terms.

However, with regard to user-generated content, a different approach to intellectual property and 'information economies' is required, for reasons relating to notions of copyright, ownership and credit, privacy concerns, and, as several BigTech companies have discovered, the substantial economic value to be derived from data-mining both implicitly- and explicitly-generated content while not actually paying for any of it (although distributed consensus technology does offer a promising approach for mapping micro-contribution to value creation). This is especially so when user-generated content is such a significant component of 'Big Data', the vast and interconnected datasets that make it possible, through search, data-mining and analytics, to spot business, social and cultural trends, as well as seismic tremors and the spread of disease.

Although it may be sensed by commercial organisations, this content is generated by users, and the potential benefits are such that it is necessary to democratise Big Data: as Buckingham Shum *et al.* (2012) observe: "the power of Big Data, models and the insights they yield should not remain the preserve of restricted government, scientific or corporate élites, but be opened up for societal engagement, critique and benefit. To democratise such assets as a public good requires a sustainable ecosystem enabling different kinds of stakeholders in society to engage, including but not limited to, citizens and advocacy groups, school and university students, policy analysts, scientists, software developers, journalists and politicians."

Furthermore, concepts of "fair use" need to be revisited, and the collection, storage and processing of user data should be subject to a core set of (internationally standard) 'fair' information practices (e.g. GDPR). Thus, for example, data should be collected fairly, lawfully and knowingly; data should only be used for the purposes specified during collection; and data should be disposed of, after its purpose is served. However, like all conventional rules (as we have seen, and will see again), they only 'work' if all parties agreeing to them also abide by them, and these fair information practices should be accompanied by design contractualism (Reynolds and Picard, 2004; Pitt and Nowak, 2014b) by which designers make specific moral or ethical judgements, encode them in system, and make such encoding visible and verifiable.

5.4.2 Colored Trails

Colored Trails is a computational testbed developed at Harvard, which was originally devised to investigate planning and decision-making strategies in task-oriented group activities (Grosz *et al.*, 2004), especially in situations where the group comprises both humans and agents (see also Sec. 8.7).

Colored Trails is a tileworld-like environment consisting of tiles of different colours. The objective is for players to compute and follow a path from a start location to a goal location. Informally, each player has a set of tokens: to move from one tile to another, a player has to surrender a token of the same colour as the tile to which it is moving.

In fact, the formal rules of Colored Trails are intentionally simple, and can be summarised as follows:

> Each player is given a starting position, a goal position on the board, and a set of chips in colors taken from the same palette as the squares. Players may advance toward their goals by moving to an adjacent board square. Such a move is allowed only if the player has a chip of the same color as the square, and the player must turn in the chip to carry

out the move. Players may negotiate with their peers to exchange chips. (Colored Trails website[4])

This simplicity allows experiments to investigate the behaviour and properties of interest, i.e. mechanisms and strategies for group behaviour under different operating conditions with different success criteria (i.e. if the players are trying to maximise individual self-interest or collective reward), without having to represent substantial and potentially complex application-specific details. Similarly, such abstraction is useful for investigating collective coordinated decision-making and action in the context of provision and appropriation to a knowledge commons.

5.4.3 *Coloured Trials*

To investigate the management of a knowledge commons, composed of user-generated content, from the perspective of dynamic multi-agent systems, an experimental testbed, called Coloured Trials, was implemented. The Coloured Trials testbed is itself a re-working and extension of the Harvard test environment presented in the previous section.

The analogy of Coloured Trials with user-generated content and MPCC is that a tile represents some form of content, a player represents a prosumer of such content, and a colour, associated with each player and each tile, represents a 'generated_by' relation between a tile and a player. The colour of a tile represents owned intellectual property and the presence of the tile indicates that the prosumer has made provision of the content to the knowledge commons. The surrender of a token represents compliance with intellectual property laws and appropriation of the content from the knowledge commons. Each player's goal is to create a composite 'work of minds' (e.g. a music playlist, illustrated collection, service mashup, etc.) represented by a path. A player in a Coloured Trials game is considered to be a member of an institution managing the CPR, i.e. the collective user-generated content represented by the tileworld.

---

[4]http://viki.eecs.harvard.edu/confluence/display/coloredtrailshome/.

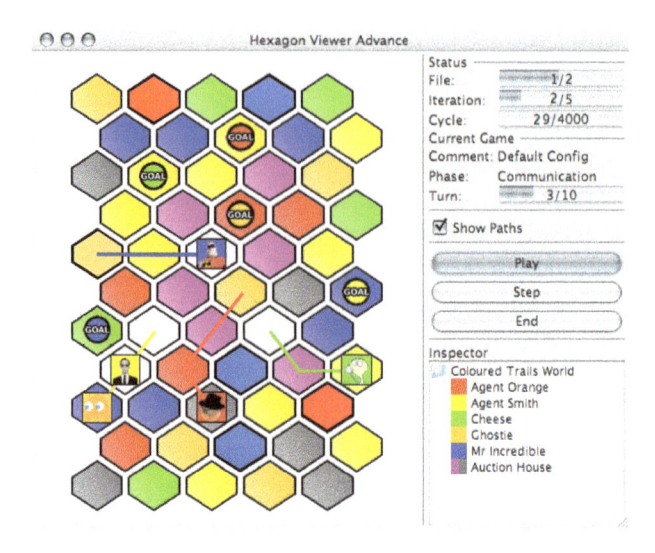

Fig. 5.2. Coloured Trials: Game Panel

At each move, the player has a choice whether to surrender a token (or not), and different versions of the game allowed for communication (or not), observation of behaviour (immediate or post-hoc), different scoring functions (maximise individual score vs. maximise collective score), different token models (fixed pool vs. dynamically available), and so on.

A basic platform for playing Coloured Trials was implemented using the multi-agent system simulator and animator PreSage (Neville and Pitt, 2009), the forerunner to the PreSage-2 system described in Sec. 1.8 (Macbeth *et al.*, 2014). Figure 5.2 shows a snapshot of a Coloured Trials game in progress. There are five agents, one random (for control) and four programmed with different strategies for path planning and decision-making. (A sixth (autonomous) agent represented an auction house which (in this version) auctioned new tokens as they became available randomly at run-time.)

The idea is that Coloured Trials is played in rounds. Each round consists of a 'game', where each player performs a sequence of actions, either to surrender a token, move to a new location, or communicate with another player. Actions are then checked to ensure that they comply with the regulations, and disputes arising from any non-compliant actions are resolved by the players. Then the next round begins and the cycle is repeated.

5.4.4 *Experimental Parameters in Coloured Trials*

The objective of Coloured Trials is the same as for Colored Trails: to provide an experimental testbed rich enough to explore the behaviour of interest in an abstract setting that is analogous to the domain of concern, in our case the provision and appropriation of MPCC in a knowledge commons.

Since the formalisation is based on the computational framework of dynamic norm-governed systems, which specifically identifies the degrees of freedom (DoF) in a dynamic specification, Coloured Trials can be parameterised to give experimental control over a number of different independent variables that influence the performance of different approaches to provision and appropriation of knowledge. The rule-based specification also allows for experiments in which certain features are, or are not, enabled, thus reducing or increasing complexity or isolating factors which do not affect the correlation between experimental parameters and observed outcomes.

For example, it allows for specification of different population profiles (with different propensities to comply, or not comply, with rules of the game), different reward structures, different systems of monitoring compliance with the regulations, different costs associated with monitoring and conflict resolution procedures, and sanctioning systems, including the number and severity of sanction levels, different organisational and management structures, and so on. There are other environmental variables which can also be controlled, including the provision of incorrect information (falsely coloured tiles), introducing a currency for tokens, changing the colour of tokens (to model open source software using copyleft, for example), and so on. The idea is to facilitate examination of how the trade-offs effect utility to the agents, the number of members belonging to the institution, compliance pervasion among the membership, the endurance and 'integrity' of the knowledge commons, and some notion of 'fairness'.

Each experimental instance of Coloured Trials needs to include a numeric scoring function, which can serve as a quantifiable metric of evaluation of the performance of the player strategies.

5.5 Error Toleration: Access Control

In this section, we specify a simple *role-based* protocol for error toleration in Coloured Trials through access control to shared resources.

The basic idea is that an agent requests access to a shared resource, which is granted access for a limited time by another agent, which is empowered to grant or revoke access in its role as the *resource controller*. However, while the requesting agent is supposed to yield the resource at the end of its allotted time-slot, if no other agent has requested it, it is more 'efficient' to let the agent carry on using the resource rather than making the agent yield the resource, re-apply, and re-compute granting. This is the same principle of "anything goes unless someone objects" underlying RONR (Robert *et al.*, 2000, and see Sec. 4.6), and allows us to distinguish between deliberate malpractice and a tolerable technical rule infraction. An Event Calculus (EC) specification will be given, but for a detailed specification, implementation and discussion of an EC-based resource-sharing protocol, see Artikis *et al.* (2004).

5.5.1 *Basics of Access Control*

In Collaborative Multimedia Computing (CMC) and Computer-Supported Co-operative Work (CSCW), the term *floor control* denotes a service guaranteeing that at any given moment only a designated set of users (subjects) may simultaneously work with or on the same objects (shared resources), thus creating a temporary exclusivity for access on such resources (Dommel and Garcia-Luna-Aceves, 1997). For purposes of simplicity in exposition, we will assume that exclusive access for a limited duration is being granted to a shared resource (represented by a non-owned coloured tile).

Granting exclusive access to a shared resource raises a number of questions and a number of opportunities to cause a dispute. We assume that one of the agents is assigned to the role of the chair — and note that this, reflexively, is exclusive access to a shared 'resource' — and that this assignment has been done legitimately. The agent occupying this role has the institutionalised power to prevent disputes over taking control of the resource, monopolising the resource, and so on. Ideally, the protocol would also satisfy a number of other properties, such as safety (every request to access the resource is eventually granted), and 'fairness' ('equal' access). See Chapter 7 for a discussion of 'fairness'.

Therefore, the Coloured Trials Access Control Protocol assumes the pool of agents can request exclusive access to a non-owned resource, and that one of their number has been appointed to the role of chair. Therefore, the actions that a ordinary agent can take, in the role of a *user*, include requesting access to a resource, releasing granted access to a resource, and withdrawing a request for access to a resource. The actions that the agent occupying the role of the chair may perform are to grant access to a resource, and to revoke access to a resource.

There are two points to note. Firstly, valid actions are intended to change the value of a fluent; and actions are valid if certain conditions are satisfied, generally determining whether or not the agent has the institutionalised power to perform that action. Secondly, a key element of error toleration is knowing what an agent is permitted to do, or obliged to do. We look at each of these points in turn.

5.5.2 *Fluents, Actions and Institutionalised Power*

The fluents in the Access Control Protocol are shown in Table 5.1.

A (user) agent seeks access to a resource by sending a request message to another agent. For the user agent to be empowered, both agents must occupy the appropriate roles, and the user agent A cannot already have been granted access to the resource. For the request to be valid, the agent must be empowered, and cannot already have made a request to access this resource. If these conditions hold, then agent A is added to the list of agents who have requested access to the resource:

$$request\_resource(A, C, R) \text{ initiates } requested(R) = [(A, T) \mid L] \text{ at } T \leftarrow$$
$$\mathbf{pow}(A, request\_resource(A, C, R)) = true \text{ holdsat } T \land$$
$$requested(R) = L \text{ holdsat } T \land$$
$$\text{not } member((A, \_), L)$$

Table 5.1. Fluents in the Access Control Protocol

Fluent	Domain	Description
$role(R, A)$	boolean	Agent A occupies role R
$status(R)$	$\{free, granted(A, T)\}$	Resource R is either free (no agent has access), or access to R was granted to A until time T
$requested(R)$	list	List of agent/time 2-tuples that have requested access to R

$$\begin{aligned}
&\mathbf{pow}(A, \mathit{request\_resource}(A,C,R) = \mathit{true}\ \mathsf{holdsat}\ T\ \leftarrow\\
&\quad \mathit{role}(A, \mathit{user}) = \mathit{true}\ \mathsf{holdsat}\ T\ \wedge\\
&\quad \mathit{role}(C, \mathit{chair}) = \mathit{true}\ \mathsf{holdsat}\ T\ \wedge\\
&\quad \mathbf{not}\ \mathit{granted}(R) = (A, T')\ \mathsf{holdsat}\ T
\end{aligned}$$

Note the difference between the conditions on being empowered and the conditions on computing the state change (change in the value of a fluent). Being granted access to the resource removes the power to make requests; making a request does not. However, making a second or subsequent request could be interpreted as an attempt at denial of service, and so subject to sanction (see later).

To release a resource, the agent needs to be empowered; to be empowered, a prior request needs to have been granted. A valid release-resource action sets the status of the resource R to free:

$$\begin{aligned}
&\mathit{release\_resource}(A, R)\ \mathsf{initiates}\ \mathit{status}(R) = \mathit{free}\ \mathsf{at}\ T\ \leftarrow\\
&\quad \mathbf{pow}(A, \mathit{release\_resource}(A, R)) = \mathit{true}\ \mathsf{holdsat}\ T\\
&\mathbf{pow}(A, \mathit{release\_resource}(A, R)) = \mathit{true}\ \mathsf{holdsat}\ T\ \leftarrow\\
&\quad \mathit{granted}(R) = (A, T')\ \mathsf{holdsat}\ T
\end{aligned}$$

The effect of withdrawing a request, and the power to do so, can be similarly specified.

These are the powers and effects of empowered actions on fluents for an agent in the role of user. For an agent in the role of chair, there are also two actions, to assign the resource and to revoke the resource:

$$\begin{aligned}
&\mathit{assign\_resource}(C, A, R)\ \mathsf{initiates}\ \mathit{status}(R) = \mathit{granted}(A, T')\ \mathsf{at}\ T\ \leftarrow\\
&\quad \mathbf{pow}(A, \mathit{assign\_resource}(C, A, R)) = \mathit{true}\ \mathsf{holdsat}\ T\ \wedge\\
&\quad T'\ \mathsf{is}\ T+5\\
&\mathbf{pow}(C, \mathit{assign\_resource}(C, A, R)) = \mathit{true}\ \mathsf{holdsat}\ T\ \leftarrow\\
&\quad \mathit{role}(C, \mathit{chair}) = \mathit{true}\ \mathsf{holdsat}\ T\ \wedge\\
&\quad \mathit{status}(R) = \mathit{free}\ \mathsf{at}\ T\ \wedge\\
&\quad \mathit{requested}(R) = L\ \mathsf{holdsat}\ T\ \wedge\\
&\quad \mathit{preferred\_user}(L, T, A)
\end{aligned}$$

$$\begin{aligned}
&\textit{revoke\_resource}(C,R) \text{ initiates } \textit{status}(R) = \textit{free} \text{ at } T \leftarrow \\
&\quad \mathbf{pow}(C, \textit{revoke\_resource}(C,R)) = \textit{true} \text{ holdsat } T \\
&\mathbf{pow}(C, \textit{revoke\_resource}(C,R)) = \textit{true} \text{ holdsat } T \leftarrow \\
&\quad \textit{role}(C, \textit{chair}) = \textit{true} \text{ holdsat } T \wedge \\
&\quad \text{not } \textit{granted}(R) = \textit{free} \text{ holdsat } T
\end{aligned}$$

This specification states that the *chair*-agent is empowered to assign the resource to an agent A, if the resource is free, access has been requested by A, and A is the 'preferred' user in the set of users that have requested the resource (whatever 'preferred' means in this context: the policy for determining 'preferred' could be a queue, a priority queue, or random, etc.; or it could be metricated according to the number of requests, duration of grants, number of sanctions, and so on).

Thus, the *chair*-agent is always empowered to revoke the resource. However, as we shall see in the next section, it is not always *permitted* to revoke the resource.

5.5.3 Permission and Obligation

The definition of which actions are permitted is application- (or protocol-) specific, and moreover, there is no fixed relationship between empowerment and permission. In some cases, power implies permission; in other cases, an agent can be empowered but not permitted (note it does not make sense to be permitted but not empowered).

Of the four actions specified in the previous section, if a *user*-agent is empowered to request or release a resource, then it is permitted to perform that action (i.e. power implies permission). However, after the time until which the agent has been granted the resource, it is obliged to release it:

$$\begin{aligned}
&\mathbf{obl}(A, \textit{release\_resource}(R)) = \textit{true} \text{ holdsat } T \leftarrow \\
&\quad \textit{granted}(R) = (A, T') \text{ holdsat } T \wedge \\
&\quad T > T'
\end{aligned}$$

If a *chair*-agent is empowered to assign a resource to the 'best' user that has requested it, then it is permitted to — and it is also obliged to. The *chair*-agent is empowered to revoke the resource. However, it is only permitted to revoke the resource after the time until which the *user*-agent has been granted access, and indeed is obliged to revoke the resource if that condition holds and another agent has requested it.

$$\mathbf{per}(C, assign\_resource(C, A, R)) = true \text{ holdsat } T \leftarrow$$
$$\quad \mathbf{pow}(C, assign\_resource(C, A, R)) = true \text{ holdsat } T$$
$$\mathbf{obl}(C, assign\_resource(C, A, R) = true \text{ holdsat } T \leftarrow$$
$$\quad role(C, chair) = true \text{ holdsat } T \land$$
$$\quad status(R) = free \text{ at } T \land$$
$$\quad requested(R) = L \text{ holdsat } T \land$$
$$\quad preferred\_user(L, T, A)$$
$$\mathbf{per}(C, revoke\_resource(R)) = true \text{ holdsat } T \leftarrow$$
$$\quad role(C, chair) = true \text{ holdsat } T \land$$
$$\quad granted(R) = (A, T') \text{ holdsat } T \land$$
$$\quad T > T'$$
$$\mathbf{obl}(C, revoke\_resource(R)) = true \text{ holdsat } T \leftarrow$$
$$\quad role(C, chair) = true \text{ holdsat } T \land$$
$$\quad granted(R) = (A, T') \text{ holdsat } T \land$$
$$\quad T > T' \land$$
$$\quad requested(R) = L \text{ holdsat } T \land$$
$$\quad \text{not } L = [\,]$$

5.5.4 Sanction

There are three key points to note. Firstly, the axioms are stating, at each time point, for each agent, what their powers, permissions and obligations are: what they can do, and what they should do. If the agents only did actions that were permitted, and always did actions that were obliged, then this would constitute a strong form of error prevention. Arguably, it would also be an over-strong form of error prevention.

This is because secondly, there is "wiggle room" in this specification. For example, if an agent is granted access to a resource, then after a certain time it is obliged to release it; but if no one else has requested it, then it might be considered reasonable to retain access until such time as another agent requests it. A violation of this obligation can be resolved with selective enforcement (although see Axelred, 1986) on non-enforcement of punishment norms). Similarly, the *chair*-agent is always empowered to revoke the resource, but not always permitted to do so. This means, for example, in an emergency it could revoke access, and it would then be in violation of its permission. Such a violation, and the reasons for it, could be examined afterwards. Clearly, we still need a dispute resolution mechanism.

Finally, processing one event at a time and restricting agents to only doing what they can or compelling them to do what they must is somewhat restricting the computational power of the EC. This is because one possible enforcement strategy is to devise additional controls (physical or institutional) that will force agents to comply with their obligations or prevent them from performing forbidden actions. This general strategy of designing mechanisms to force compliance and eliminate non-permitted behaviour is what Jones and Sergot (1993) referred to as *regimentation*. Regimentation mechanisms have often been employed in order to eliminate 'undesirable' behaviour in computational systems (see, for instance, the mechanisms listed in Artikis *et al.* (2004)).

However, Jones and Sergot (1993) argue that regimentation is rarely desirable in open systems. It produces a rigidity which goes against the maxim "anything goes unless someone objects", eliminates opportunities for discovering 'better' procedures, and suppresses dissent (see Sec. 10.5). Moreover, even in the case of a full regimentation of permissions and obligations, violations may still occur (consider, for instance, a faulty regimentation device). For all these reasons, we should not rely exclusively on regimentation mechanisms which supposedly prevent errors, but also mechanisms which allow us to tolerate errors. Moreover, we can use the EC to process narratives (sequences of events) to detect errors and apply sanctions (e.g. indicating an actual offence or a technical rule infraction), and use ADR to resolve the sanctions.

5.6 Error Retrospection: Regulatory Compliance

In this section, we specify an *ex post* (after the event) method for error handling through regulatory compliance, i.e. we let the agents play the game, creating a series of events called a *narrative*, and use the EC to check afterwards that the narrative complies with the rules and regulations of the scenario.

Effectively, regulatory compliance is pushing access control from a per event process to a per narrative process. The thinking here is in part inspired by "thinking fast and slow" (Kahneman, 2011). We are anticipating that there may be some situations where the agents need to be reactive, get the job done, and worry about the consequences and compliance with the rules afterwards; equally, there may be other situations where the agents need to be deliberative, proceed with more caution, and check compliance with regulations as the work progresses.

Recall that the idea in Coloured Trials is to create a trail from a start location to an end location. This necessitates computing a path, as a sequence of differently coloured tiles. The path itself can be seen as a series of 'moves', and each tile as some intellectual property (e.g. patent, copyright, etc.) required to create a composite 'work of mind'. To create a 'valid' ('legal', etc.) path, for each tile on the path, an agent must be the owner of the tile-colour, have and surrender a token of the tile-colour, or request and be granted access to the tile (as in the previous section).

There are now three further actions beyond requesting and granting access to a shared resource: move to a new location, surrender a token, and communicate with another agent to exchange a token. The following sub-sections specify the rules for each of these actions.

5.6.1 *Token Surrender*

Using the EC as the specification language, a *surrender* token action initiates new values for two fluents. First it reduces the number of tokens of the associated colour that a player *owns*, and secondly it increases the number of tokens that it has surrendered by one. The new fluent values are initiated if the agent is empowered to perform the action, and it is empowered to perform this action if it owns more than one token of the associated colour.

$$
\begin{aligned}
&surrender(P, Col) \quad \text{initiates} \quad owns(P, Col) = N \quad \text{at} \quad T \quad \leftarrow \\
&\quad \mathbf{pow}(P, surrender(P, Col)) = true \quad \text{holdsat} \quad T \quad \wedge \\
&\quad owns(P, Col) = N1 \quad \text{holdsat} \quad T \quad \wedge \\
&\quad N = N1 - 1 \\
&surrender(P, Col) \quad \text{initiates} \quad surrendered(P, Col) = N1 \quad \text{at} \quad T \quad \leftarrow \\
&\quad \mathbf{pow}(P, surrender(P, Col)) = true \quad \text{holdsat} \quad T \quad \wedge \\
&\quad surrendered(P, Col) = N \quad \text{holdsat} \quad T \quad \wedge \\
&\quad N1 = N + 1 \\
&\mathbf{pow}(P, surrender(P, Col)) = true \quad \text{holdsat} \quad T \quad \leftarrow \\
&\quad owns(P, Col) = N \quad \text{holdsat} \quad T \quad \wedge \\
&\quad N > 0
\end{aligned}
$$

Note that we do not care if a player performs a *surrender* action without having a token of the appropriate colour. This is just considered 'noise'. However, we do care if the agent moves location without being empowered and permitted.

5.6.2 Location Movement

A *move* location action, and the effect that it produces, depends on power and permission, as specified by:

$$
\begin{aligned}
&move(P, From, To) \quad \text{initiates} \quad location(P) = To \quad \text{at} \quad T \quad \leftarrow \\
&\quad \mathbf{pow}(P, move(P, From, To)) = true \quad \text{holdsat} \quad T \quad \wedge \\
&\quad location(P) = From \quad \text{at} \quad T \\
&move(P, From, To) \quad \text{initiates} \quad surrendered(P, Col) = N \quad \text{at} \quad T \quad \leftarrow \\
&\quad \mathbf{pow}(P, move(P, From, To)) = true \quad \text{holdsat} \quad T \quad \wedge \\
&\quad \mathbf{per}(P, move(P, From, To)) = true \quad \text{holdsat} \quad T \quad \wedge \\
&\quad colour(To) = Col \quad \text{holdsat} \quad T \quad \wedge \\
&\quad surrendered(P, Col) = N1 \quad \text{holdsat} \quad T \quad \wedge \\
&\quad N = N1 - 1
\end{aligned}
$$

$move(P, From, To)$ initiates $infr(P) = [(move, Col) \mid L]$ at T ←
$\quad$ **pow**$(P, move(P, From, To)) = true$ holdsat T ∧
$\quad$ not **per**$(P, move(P, From, To)) = true$ holdsat T ∧
$\quad colour(To) = Col$ holdsat T ∧
$\quad infr(P) = L$ holdsat T
pow$(P, move(P, From, To)) = true$ holdsat T ←
$\quad adjacent(From, To)$
per$(P, move(P, From, To)) = true$ holdsat T ←
$\quad colour(To) = Col$ holdsat T ∧
$\quad surrendered(P, Col) = N$ holdsat T ∧
$\quad N > 0$

These axioms state that if an agent is not empowered to move, then it is not going anywhere (although it is re-stressed, it is better to think, in this context, of movement creating a composite 'work of mind' rather than a change in physical space). If the agent is empowered to move, then it changes location, regardless of permission. If the agent is empowered and permitted to move, then it decreases the number of surrendered tokens of the corresponding colour. If the agent is empowered but not permitted to move, because it has not surrendered tokens of the corresponding colour, then (as Galileo said) it still moves anyway, but creates an infringement.

5.6.3 Communication: Token Exchange

The rules of the original Harvard testbed allow for communication between players in order to exchange tokens. Therefore, in Coloured Trials, we use the EC to define a small-state communication protocol for a simple negotiation, in order for agents to exchange tokens among themselves. This simple protocol allows a player *P1* to *offer* to trade a token of one colour to another player *P2* in exchange for a token of another colour. The receiving agent may either *accept* or *reject* the exchange.

The first player *P1* can only make a valid offer if it possesses at least one token of the offered colour (i.e. following the definition of Artikis *et al.* (2009), an action is valid at time T if and only if the agent that performed that action had the institutional power to perform it at time T). Similarly, the second player $P2$ is only empowered to accept the offer if it possesses a token of the offered colour.

$offer(P1, P2, O)$ initiates $trade(P1, P2, O) = made$ at T $\leftarrow$
  $\textbf{pow}(P1, offer(P1, P2, O)) = true$ holdsat T
$\textbf{pow}(P1, offer(P1, P2, (C1, C2))) = true$ holdsat T $\leftarrow$
  $owns(P1, C1) = N$ holdsat T $\wedge$
  $N > 0$
$accept(P2, P1, O)$ initiates $trade(P1, P2, O) = agreed$ at T $\leftarrow$
  $\textbf{pow}(P2, accept(P2, P1, O)) = true$ holdsat T
$\textbf{pow}(P2, accept(P2, P1, (C1, C2))) = true$ holdsat T $\leftarrow$
  $trade(P1, P2, (C1, C2)) = made$ holdsat T $\wedge$
  $owns(P2, C2) = N$ holdsat T $\wedge$
  $N > 0$
$reject(P2, P1, O)$ initiates $trade(P1, P2, O) = denied$ at T $\leftarrow$
  $\textbf{pow}(P2, reject(P2, P1, O)) = true$ holdsat T $\wedge$
$\textbf{pow}(P2, reject(P2, P1, O)) = true$ holdsat T $\leftarrow$
  $trade(P1, P2, O) = made$ holdsat T

There are four other axioms which increment and decrement the $owns$ fluents of $P1$ and $P2$ for the corresponding colours $C1$ and $C2$, which are similar to those above, and are omitted here.

In Coloured Trials, although a player does not have the power to make a valid $trade$, it is still an infringement if a player offers a trade when it has no tokens of the corresponding colour, or if it accepts an offer likewise:

$offer(P1, P2, O)$ initiates $infr(P1) = [(offer = 0, P2) \mid L]$ at T $\leftarrow$
  not $\textbf{pow}(P1, offer(P1, P2, O)) = true$ holdsat T $\wedge$
  $infr(P1) = L$ holdsat T
$accept(P2, P1, O)$ initiates $infr(P2) = [(accept = 0, P1) \mid L]$ at T $\leftarrow$
  not $\textbf{pow}(P2, accept(P2, P1, O)) = true$ holdsat T $\wedge$
  $infr(P2) = L$ holdsat T

5.6.4 *Outcome*

The outcome of passing a narrative through the EC will be to compute which player committed which infringements. This formalisation requires that to comply with the regulations, to perform a *move*, a player must have performed a *surrender* earlier in the narrative. Note that a player can perform a *surrender* without also performing a *move* (it is valid, if presumably wasteful); and can perform a *surrender* without a token and escape an infringement. Note also that the surrender does not have to immediately precede the move, it can occur any time earlier in the narrative. It is just performing a move without a prior surrender that is considered an infringement.

The next requirement is to address the infringements and resolve the issues without resorting to 'litigation', in other words (or protocols), by using some form of *ADR*.

5.7 Error Recovery: Alternative Dispute Resolution

In this section, we define a protocol whose intention is firstly, to avoid conflict, especially in the form of costly litigation, and secondly, to resolve disputes 'in house' (i.e. within the institution), to the satisfaction of both parties. This is important in MPCC to find a balance between 'fair use' without restrictive legislation (e.g. recent US proposals called SOPA and PIPA) and compensating voluntary contributions using incentive-based payment schemes (Regner *et al.*, 2010).

5.7.1 *Informal Specification*

The field of ADR covers a wide range of methods for conflict resolution such as negotiation, facilitation, mediation, arbitration and neutral expert determination. For the purpose of making a generalised specification, we group these methods into three general types: arbitration, mediation and negotiation.

Each method is distinguished by its characteristic protocol, the roles played by the players, and (possibly) the powers conceded to neutral third parties (who are invited to facilitate the process). However, we assume that the disputants have agreed, as a pre-condition of membership of the institution, that it is compulsory to use ADR in case of a dispute or conflict, and that refusing ADR can result in the ultimate sanction, i.e. exclusion from the institution. However, agreeing to use ADR does not bind the litigants to the specific method to be used. Consequently, ADR involves a pre-negotiation stage where the parties should agree on an ADR method. A method selection protocol involves a turn-taking process where one party proposes a method and the other party can either accept this method, reject it, or propose an alternative method.

In general, a negotiation protocol involves parties setting their demands as an upper limit for negotiation and then making concessions (proposals and counter-proposals) toward agreeing on a resolution agreement. A single issue or multiple issues under dispute can be included provided a notion of global utility is defined. Parties can then concede on some issues and gain on others as long as their global utility does not decrease.

Mediation makes use of the negotiation protocol with the extra benefit of having a neutral third party whose main role is to facilitate the negotiation. The mediation tasks are: (i) chairing the mediation session, (ii) identifying the main issues under dispute, (iii) aligning the issues with the demands and (iv) encouraging the adoption of proposals for resolution. The role and powers of the mediator should be defined before negotiation takes place. Some of these roles are mediation–facilitation, where the powers of the mediator are limited to enforce a floor-control protocol; mediation–recommendation, where the mediator has the power to make proposals; and mediation–arbitration, where the mediator is empowered by the parties to formulate a final and binding resolution.

Arbitration is an extension of the mediation–arbitration method where one or more arbitrators (panel) provide impartial resolution to a dispute based on expert legal opinion. As in litigation, the resolution (award) reached by the arbitration panel is final, legally binding and not open for negotiation. However, in contrast with negotiation, the parties have the power to choose the panel. The steps of the arbitration protocol are: (i) composition of an arbitration panel, (ii) definition of statements of claim and defence and (iii) issuance of an award through a process of opinion formation in the panel.

This rest of this section describes the formal-logical specification, in the EC, of an ADR protocol using arbitration, mediation and negotiation. There are three phases: initiation, method selection and execution. We will look at each phase in turn.

5.7.2 Phase I: Initiation

Again, we are following one of the principles underpinning Robert's Rules of Order (Robert et al., 2000), that "anything goes unless someone objects". Therefore, the process of regulatory compliance only detects an infringement of the rules. It is then up to the aggrieved party to *object* to the infringement. This initiates the ADR protocol.

We assume the status of any infringement is initially null. The initiation phase then sets up the frame for subsequent phases. Firstly, the roles of the two agents, $L1$ and $L2$, as the litigants who are involved in the dispute over infringement C, which will be relevant throughout the entire ADR protocol; and secondly, initialises the starting values for Phase II, which is the selection of the ADR method. The fluent $adr\_meth(C)$ is a 2-tuple, the chosen method (initially *null*) and a 'pool' of available methods.

$object(L1, L2, C)$ initiates $role\_of(L1) = litigator$ at T ←
$\quad$ **pow**$(L1, object(L1, L2, C)) = true$ holdsat T
$object(L1, L2, C)$ initiates $role\_of(L2) = litigator$ at T ←
$\quad$ **pow**$(L1, object(L1, L2, C)) = true$ holdsat T
$object(L1, L2, C)$ initiates $status\_of(C) = open$ at T ←
$\quad$ **pow**$(L1, object(L1, L2, C)) = true$ holdsat T
$object(L1, L2, C)$ initiates $adr\_meth(C) = (null, L)$ at T ←
$\quad$ **pow**$(L1, object(L1, L2, C)) = true$ holdsat T ∧
$\quad$ $all\_available\_methods = L$ holdsat T

An agent has the power to make an objection if it is the aggrieved party in an infringement:

$\quad$ **pow**$(L1, object(L1, L2, (move, Col))) = true$ holdsat T ←
$\qquad$ $infr(L2) = Infr\_List$ holdsat T ∧
$\qquad$ $includes(Infr\_List, (move, Col))$ ∧
$\qquad$ $colour(L1) = Col$ holdsat T ∧
$\qquad$ $status\_of((move, Col)) = null$ holdsat T

Similar axioms are defined for the other infringements identified above, e.g.:

$$\begin{aligned}
&\mathbf{pow}(L1, \mathit{object}(L1, L2, (\mathit{offer0}, L1))) = \mathit{true} \quad \text{holdsat} \quad T \quad \leftarrow \\
&\quad \mathit{infr}(L2) = \mathit{Infr\_List} \quad \text{holdsat} \quad T \quad \wedge \\
&\quad \mathit{includes}(\mathit{Infr\_List}, (\mathit{offer0}, L1)) \quad \wedge \\
&\quad \mathit{status\_of}((\mathit{offer0}, L1)) = \mathit{null} \quad \text{holdsat} \quad T
\end{aligned}$$

5.7.3 Phase II: ADR Method Selection

After the writ has been served, we allow either agent to make a proposal. The proposal may be rejected, in which case either agent is free to make a new proposal, or it is agreed, in which case it becomes the selected method for resolving case C.

Therefore, we have to track two values. Firstly, the status of the negotiation over the method. This may be either open for proposals, *open*, where we are waiting for either party in the suit to make a proposal; or *proposed*(L), meaning that agent L has proposed a method (tracked by the second value); or *agreed*, meaning that the two parties have reached mutual agreement on the ADR method.

Secondly, we track which ADR method is to be used to resolve the dispute. There are four possibilities, *null* (no method), *negotiation*, *arbitration*, and *mediation*. The value of this fluent is a 2-tuple, with the type of the first argument being a method, and the type of the second argument being a list of methods. The idea is that the first component represents a method that has either been proposed or agreed upon, the second argument a pool of methods that have not yet been proposed and rejected by either party.

Thus, an action to propose a method changes these values as follows:

$$\begin{aligned}
&\mathit{propose}(L, C, M) \quad \text{initiates} \quad \mathit{status\_of}(C) = \mathit{proposed}(L) \quad \text{at} \quad T \quad \leftarrow \\
&\quad \mathbf{pow}(L, \mathit{propose}(L, C, M)) = \mathit{true} \quad \text{holdsat} \quad T \\
&\mathit{propose}(L, C, M) \quad \text{initiates} \quad \mathit{adr\_meth}(C) = (M, R') \quad \text{at} \quad T \quad \leftarrow \\
&\quad \mathbf{pow}(L, \mathit{propose}(L, C, M)) = \mathit{true} \quad \text{holdsat} \quad T \quad \wedge \\
&\quad \mathit{adr\_meth}(C) = (\mathit{null}, R) \quad \text{holdsat} \quad T \quad \wedge \\
&\quad R' \quad \text{is} \quad R - M
\end{aligned}$$

Furthermore, either party has the power to make a proposal if they occupy the role of litigator (i.e. no other agent is empowered to act in this way) and the protocol is in the appropriate state, i.e. open for proposals:

$$\begin{aligned}
&\textbf{pow}(L, propose(L,C,M)) = true \quad \text{holdsat} \quad T \quad \leftarrow \\
&\quad role\_of(L, litigator) = true \quad \text{holdsat} \quad T \quad \wedge \\
&\quad status\_of(C) = open \quad \text{holdsat} \quad T
\end{aligned}$$

The action of rejecting a proposal resets the state of the negotiation back to the initial state, with the exception that the proposed method has been removed from the list of possible dispute resolution methods:

$$\begin{aligned}
&reject(L,C,M) \quad \text{initiates} \quad status\_of(C) = open \quad \text{at} \quad T \quad \leftarrow \\
&\quad \textbf{pow}(L, reject(L,C,M)) = true \quad \text{holdsat} \quad T \\
&reject(L,C,M) \quad \text{initiates} \quad adr\_meth(C) = (null, R) \quad \text{at} \quad T \quad \leftarrow \\
&\quad \textbf{pow}(L, reject(L,C,M)) = true \quad \text{holdsat} \quad T \quad \wedge \\
&\quad adr\_meth(C) = (\_, R) \quad \text{holdsat} \quad T
\end{aligned}$$

Note that this *reject* action is different from the action used in the communication protocol for the exchange of tokens used earlier.

As before, only two agents are empowered to reject a proposal, by virtue of the role, and the status, and only one at a time (i.e. an agent cannot reject its own proposal):

$$\begin{aligned}
&\textbf{pow}(L1, reject(L1,C,M)) = true \quad \text{holdsat} \quad T \quad \leftarrow \\
&\quad role\_of(L1) = litigator \quad \text{holdsat} \quad T \quad \wedge \\
&\quad role\_of(L2) = litigator \quad \text{holdsat} \quad T \quad \wedge \\
&\quad \text{not} \quad L1 = L2 \quad \wedge \\
&\quad status\_of(C) = proposed(L2) \quad \text{holdsat} \quad T \quad \wedge \\
&\quad adr\_meth(C) = (M, \_) \quad \text{holdsat} \quad T
\end{aligned}$$

There is also a restriction on this empowerment. Sometimes, power implies permission: if an agent is empowered to perform an action, then it is permitted to perform that action. In other instances, such as this one, although an agent is empowered to reject a proposal of an arbitration method, it is not permitted to do so. We do this for two reasons. Firstly, because the agent that made the offer has a 'right', or is entitled to, some form of appeal, and we consider the 'base case' for appeals to be arbitration. Secondly, the rejection will advance the state of the protocol, but the agent that rejected arbitration can be sanctioned for doing so (i.e. it violated its permissions), and as indicated above, the sanction for refusing ADR could be exclusion.

$$
\begin{aligned}
&\mathbf{per}(L1, reject(L1, C, M)) = true \quad \text{holdsat} \quad T \quad \leftarrow \\
&\quad \mathbf{pow}(L1, reject(L1, C, M)) = true \quad \text{holdsat} \quad T \quad \wedge \\
&\quad \text{not} \quad M = arb
\end{aligned}
$$

The action of agreeing to an arbitration method is structurally similar to rejecting. It sets the status of the negotiation to *agreed* at a specific time T, and fixes the method for dispute resolution as the one proposed. As with reject, only the two agents are empowered to agree to a proposal, and only then the one who was not the proposer.

$$
\begin{aligned}
&agree(L, C, M) \quad \text{initiates} \quad status\_of(C) = agreed(T) \quad \text{at} \quad T \quad \leftarrow \\
&\quad \mathbf{pow}(L, agree(L, C, M)) = true \quad \text{holdsat} \quad T \\
&agree(L, C, M) \quad \text{initiates} \quad adr\_meth(C) = (M, []) \quad \text{at} \quad T \quad \leftarrow \\
&\quad \mathbf{pow}(L, agree(L, C, M)) = true \quad \text{holdsat} \quad T \quad \wedge \\
&\quad adr\_meth(C) = (M, \_) \quad \text{holdsat} \quad T \\
&\quad \mathbf{pow}(L1, agree(L1, C, M)) = true \quad \text{holdsat} \quad T \quad \leftarrow \\
&\quad role\_of(L1) = litigator \quad \text{holdsat} \quad T \quad \wedge \\
&\quad role\_of(L2) = litigator \quad \text{holdsat} \quad T \quad \wedge \\
&\quad status\_of(C) = proposed(L2) \quad \text{holdsat} \quad T \quad \wedge \\
&\quad adr\_meth(C) = (M, \_) \quad \text{holdsat} \quad T
\end{aligned}
$$

In all these cases, power implies permission: an agent that is empowered to perform an action also has, by implication, permission to perform that action. However, there is also an obligation: when there is only one dispute resolution method left, the non-proposer is obliged to agree to this method (the other two having been proposed and rejected by either party).

$$\begin{aligned}
&\mathbf{obl}(L1, agree(L1, C, M)) = true \quad holdsat \quad T \quad \leftarrow \\
&\quad role\_of(L1) = litigator \quad holdsat \quad T \quad \wedge \\
&\quad role\_of(L2) = litigator \quad holdsat \quad T \quad \wedge \\
&\quad status\_of(C) = proposed(L2) \quad holdsat \quad T \quad \wedge \\
&\quad adr\_meth(C) = (M, []) \quad holdsat \quad T
\end{aligned}$$

In such cases, rejecting the final method causes an infringement:

$$\begin{aligned}
&reject(P, C, M) \quad initiates \quad infr(P) = [(adr, C) \mid L] \quad at \quad T \quad \leftarrow \\
&\quad \mathbf{obl}(P, agree(P, C, M)) = true \quad holdsat \quad T \quad \wedge \\
&\quad infr(P) = L \quad holdsat \quad T
\end{aligned}$$

5.7.4 Phase III: Execution

When the ADR method has been agreed, the final step is to execute the agreed procedure. Negotiation between two parties can proceed on the basis of the contract-net protocol specified in Artikis et al. (2002), while mediation can be specified using the argumentation protocol defined in Artikis et al. (2007).

The execution of the arbitration protocol requires three steps:

- Composition of the arbitration panel;
- Statements of claim and defence; and
- Determination of the decision and issuance of any penalty.

We look first at the composition of the arbitration panel. This in turn has four steps: nomination, veto, alternate strike, and finally appointment of a chair.

The first step is nomination. Each party in the case nominates a list of arbitrators in order of preference. The minimum length of the list is six (as each party will nominate six members of the institution making up an arbitration panel, or jury, of 12. However, these numbers of 6 and 12 can be varied by agreement), and the maximum length of the list is 12. Nominating a list of fewer or greater than these limits is not a valid nomination, and does not initiate the corresponding fluent value.

The next step is for each party to exert its right of veto on some arbitrators. There are a certain number of vetoes available to each party as previously defined by 'standing orders'; for the sake of argument we will assume three vetoes. A veto means that the nominated arbitrator can be replaced, but not by any arbitrator that has been vetoed by the party. To do this, we need to track four values: the number of vetoes left to each party, and the list of arbitrators vetoed by each party.

The third step is to strike out, in alternate turns, members from each list of nominees until the total number of members in each list is six. The way we will manage this is to specify that any agent can perform a valid strike, provided the other party has more nominees in its list, and the list has more than six members.

The final step is that the arbitrators appoint a chair. This can be accomplished by a role assignment protocol enacted between the 12 arbitrators (see, e.g. Dastani *et al.*, 2003; Pitt *et al.*, 2011c and subsequent chapters, recalling also that role is an essential element of institutionalised power). Then the statements of claim and defence, and deciding between the litigators, follow the same format as the argumentation.

5.8 Summary

This chapter has been concerned with errors in self-organising multi-agent systems: the range of sources and causes of errors, and a trio of techniques for error management. We defined a testbed, called Coloured Trials, for examining errors in the creation of intellectual property as a composite 'work of mind', and used this to examine error toleration, retrospection and recovery through protocols for access control, regulatory compliance and ADR.

Since the first ever 'bug' was found in a computer program, it was a goal of software engineering to eliminate errors, and a critical phase of software development is testing, as it should be. However, when it came to human–computer interaction, it was discovered that it was more disadvantageous to prevent system users from making what the system designers considered to be errors or the 'wrong' way to use their system. Consequently, interface design guidelines, such as Nielsen's 10 usability heuristics (Nielsen, 1994), balanced a tension between "user control and freedom" (to explore and make mistakes) against "error prevention" and helping users to "recognise, diagnose and recover from errors".

Furthermore, usability evaluations in human–computer interaction distinctly tried to distinguish between different types of error. For example, following Norman's Stages of Action (Norman, 1988), there is a distinction between having the right intention, but choosing the wrong actions to achieve it, called a slip, and formulating the wrong intention, based on a fundamental misunderstanding of the underlying computer model, called a *mistake*. Moreover, a critical contribution to interface design was the maxim "don't mode me in" (Tesler, 1981), based on the idea that computer interfaces should be *modeless*, whereby all actions should be enabled at all times, rather than modal, whereby a user should have selected a specific mode in order to perform a specific action.

Although we are still building distributed computer systems, agency and self-organisation require an approach to systems design much closer to modeless interface design than to engineering error-free systems (exceptions can be made for real-time and safety-critical systems). While we are not completely modeless, for example we might prohibit certain specification instances, or specify that certain actions can only be performed by agents in certain roles, the tolerance of error and "unless someone objects" do approximate this 'humanistic' style of operation much more effectively than, for example, regimentation. Moreover, when we move from cyber-physical to socio-technical systems, we are back in a domain of much richer human–computer interaction anyway, and we want the 'technical' to work like the 'socio', not compel the 'socio' to comply with the 'technical' (for more on this topic see Chapter 8 on *artificial social construction*).

Therefore, it is not just the case that we don't necessarily want to design and code errors out of our systems, but we also recognise that errors have potential positive advantages for self-organisation. This ranges from the toleration of technical rule infraction for the sake of efficiency or expediency, through exploration of a search space for serendipitous discovery and learning of new methods or processes to avoid path dependency, and on to the importance of dissent as a driver of change and in the prevention of various forms of potential tyranny (Chapter 10).

On the other hand, we are not advocating some totally anarchic free-for-all either. We do need to detect errors, and we do need to enforce sanctions. Up until now, we have talked about "institutionalised power", but it is time perhaps to put the institution in the institutionalised power. This is the subject of the next chapter, in which the analysis of games and political meta-games, of voting, and disputes will become clear: this will be the chapter in which things fall into place.

Chapter 6

Ostrom Institution Theory

6.1 Introduction

The aim of this chapter is to examine strategic interaction through the lens of a theory of *self-governing institutions* developed by Elinor Ostrom. Elinor Ostrom was an American political scientist whose research focused on addressing a particular type of strategic interaction called *collective action*, specifically *sustainable common-pool resource management*.

A collective action situation can be simply defined as one in which a group of people need to make common cause in order to achieve a shared objective. A collective action problem is a collective action situation in which it would be more beneficial for the group as a whole if they cooperated, but due to conflicting individual interests, they fail to do so.

Of course, Chapter 3 gave many examples of this: the n-player version of the Stag Hunt game demonstrates the difficulty of coordination *at scale* in the absence of *credible pre-commitments*, i.e. some trustworthy signposting that someone will pursue a particular course of action.

Indeed, voting (Chapter 4) at scale demonstrates elements of a collective action problem. In a national election, the probability of any one vote making a difference to the outcome is as close to zero as makes no odds, so there is no incentive for any individual to vote. However, if no one else is going to vote, just one vote is enough for a preference to win, so it is worth voting; but if everybody else thinks like this, the vote is meaningless again, there is no point bothering, etc. (Remind me: what time does the El Farol Bar open?...)

Most pertinently, the issue of anthropogenic climate change is a collective action problem at community, regional, national and international scales. Individually, recycling, re-usable containers, reducing car use, etc. are all actions that individuals can take to reduce their carbon footprint, but have no discernible impact on solving the problem. Thus, there is no tangible incentive to inconveniencing oneself (Robbins, 2019; Pitt, 2020a), especially if profligate consumption is the dominant political and advertising message. Similarly, and perhaps consequently, nationally, even if a country wanted to reduce its carbon emissions, if its neighbouring states will not do so as well, there is no incentive for political parties seeking election to impose upon or penalise their own citizens.

In this chapter, we are interested in a particular type of collective action called *common-pool resource management*. This is similar to an n-player Hawk–Dove game, in that there is a contest for, and potential conflict over, access to a shared resource (e.g. a grazing pasture, river-water for irrigation, fisheries, forestries, kitchens, and so on). In these game-like situations, the players have to contribute to the maintenance of the resource, called *provisioning*, in order to be able to withdraw from the resource, called *appropriation*. The problem is that excessive appropriation and insufficient provision (called *free riding*) maximises individual utility in the short term, but is unsustainable in the long term and results in *depletion* (i.e. destruction) of the resource. Everyone's utility from that point on is zero.

We will study a solution to this object-level operational-choice game based on meta-level political games, which specify a supplemental set of rules that impose additional constraints on the players' behaviour. We will call the object that defines and enforces these political games and associated rules an *institution*. These are the subjects of scrutiny and specification by Elinor Ostrom, and for this reason the chapter is entitled *Ostrom Institution Theory* — there are other subjects labelled 'institution theory' and 'institutional theory', and these really don't concern us here. Instead, we will focus on how autonomous and self-interested agents can self-organise *electronic institutions* for themselves, to manage (self-govern) their own affairs.

This chapter is organised as follows. It begins with a by now traditional example set in the kitchen of a house-share in Sec. 6.2.

Section 6.3 reviews collective action and common-pool resources (CPRs), and specifies an abstraction of these problems as a *linear public good* (*LPG*) game. Section 6.4 reviews Ostrom's theory of self-governing institutions (Ostrom, 1990) while Sec. 6.5 specifies elements of this theory in computational logic to define self-organising electronic institutions. Section 6.6 extends this analysis with an experiment on institutional boundaries and institution-environment congruence. Some further issues are discussed in Sec. 6.7, specifically minimal recognition of rights to self-organise, system of systems and polycentricity, and the paradox of self-amendment. The chapter concludes in Sec. 6.8 in a non-standard fashion.

6.2 Example: The Common-Pool Refrigerator

Imagine being back in the kitchen of a shared house: it is in fact the location (slash battleground) of many variations of collective action problems, and in particular CPR problems.

A typical example is the collective kitty for all the common household items: comestibles like tea, coffee, sugar and milk; cleaning products like soap, washing up liquid, pan scourers, and so on. Flatmates are supposed to provision money to the kitty, which is used to purchase these shared *common-pool* resources; and they then appropriate those resources. Everybody benefits if all cooperate (all provision and appropriate 'fairly', whatever 'fairly' means in this context (see Chapter 7)) Of course, there is always someone who does not contribute (this is free riding), someone chugs straight from the milk container, someone drinks the last of the milk and does not replace it, and so on.

Moreover, all of the kitchen appliances can be seen as CPRs. The cooker can be seen as a CPR: the flatmates provision to its cleanliness, they appropriate time for its use. Of course, there is a potential conflict of competing interests when more than one flatmate wants to use the cooker at peak meal-preparation times, i.e. conventional times for breakfast, lunch and dinner. The refrigerator can be seen as a CPR: the flatmates are indirectly provisioning its maintenance by contributing to the payment of the electricity bills and keeping it clean; they are appropriating space for storage of perishable food items (allocating one shelf per person might seem a plausible solution, but it is not the ideal way to distribute items at the best temperature. Just saying).

In fact, we have already seen one example: the kitchen-cleaning stand-off game (see Sec. 3.2). Of course, this is actually an iterated game rather than a one-off game, and there are always a number of chores to do: sweep the floors, do the washing up, unstack the dishwasher, put the bins out. One solution is the approach taken by Jayne, Simon Tam and Shepherd Book in *Firefly* (the best television series of this, or any other millennium), where they play poker (or some other card game) with their assigned chores as different-value betting chips. (Shepherd Book wins a round and says "That's a nice pile of things I don't have to do".)

Gambling is one solution to distributing the burdens of provision to and the benefits of appropriation from a CPR. However, as viewers of another television series, *The Big Bang Theory*, will perhaps be thinking, there is a more orderly solution — a contract known as the *roommate agreement* (or, to translate from the American, the *flatmate agreement*). Such a flatmate agreement is a set of conventional (i.e. made-up and mutually-agreed) rules by which the signatories voluntarily agree to constrain their behaviour. It is these contracts, or sets of rules, that we are going to call *Ostrom institutions*, that are the formal object of investigation and specification in this chapter.

However, both gambling and contractual solutions still encounter problems of non-repudiation, enforcement and free riding. For example, a group of first-year university students, who had moved into shared self-catered accommodation, were encouraged by college administration to self-organise their own arrangements for maintaining order in, and good condition of, their unit, one of many in a 'village' of such units. The flatmate agreement shown in Fig. 6.1(a) was negotiated, agreed and signed at Christmas by them all. The image on the right shows the state of the flatmate agreement by Easter, three months later...

It is to avoid this sort of degeneration that Ostrom institutions don't just have rules, but have special features that ensure that both the CPR, and indeed the institution itself, are sustainable.

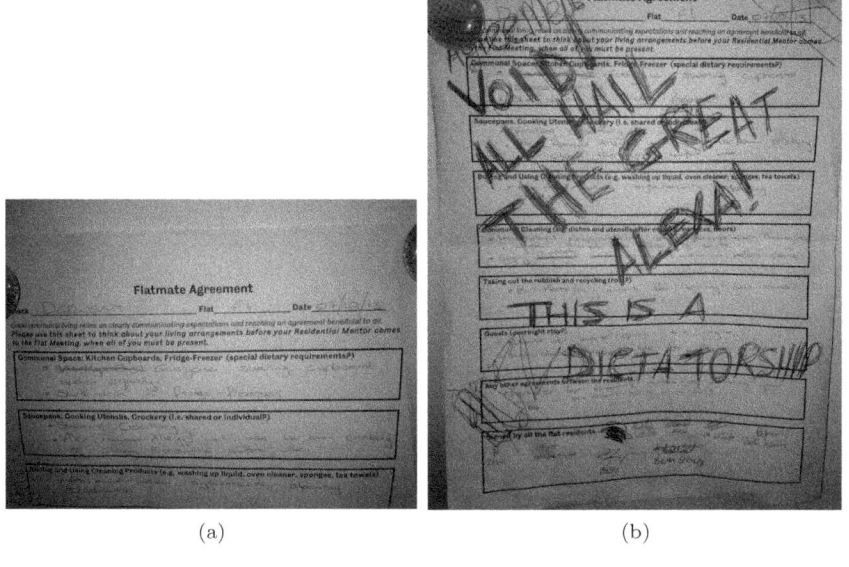

Fig. 6.1 A Flatmate Agreement, at Christmas (a) and by Easter (b)

6.3 Collective Action

This section reviews collective action more generally, considers CPR management more specifically, and then presents a form of game which serves as a useful abstraction capturing all the features of the various situations. Given our ultimate interest in multi-agent systems, from hereon we will refer to the players in this game as *agents*.

6.3.1 *Three Types of Collective Action*

It is possible to identify three types of collective action problems (*cf.* Ober, 2008), involving shared-resources and multiple independent actors, such as joint enterprises, coordination and public goods.

Firstly, in a *joint enterprise* problem, a group of individuals are all contributing their efforts to achieving a specific goal, but although costs are incurred by each individual, the rewards are accrued to all members of the group. This encourages free riding — but if everyone (or enough of the community) free rides, the group activity fails. A typical example is a collection for a leaving present or a birthday present: the cost of contributing to the collection is individual; the benefit of the thanks for the gift is shared.

Secondly, a *coordination* problem typically involves the organisation of separate and autonomous individuals as members of a larger group to work together to achieve some goal, in the possible absence of common knowledge and reliable communication, and the presence of conflicting personal interests. For example, for the rice farmers of Bali (Lansing and Kremer, 1993), pest dynamics dictates that crop-planting should take place at the same time, but water scarcity dictates that crop-planting should take place at different times. Solving this coordination problem informs the farming collective when to plant crops in order to maximise their overall rice yield, given that each farmer also wants to maximise his/her individual yield.

Thirdly, as discussed, in a *common-pool resource* (management) problem, each individual acts in order to maximise their short-term own interest, but if everyone does, then it depletes the resource which is contrary to their long-term interest. This problem is compounded by the impact of pro-social behaviour not being acknowledged and of anti-social behaviour that brings about depletion being *discounted*, i.e. the benefit of actions that contribute positively to resource sustainability are not directly perceived, while the cost of depletion is not experienced except by those actors that join the system later (think: anthropogenic climate change).

These types of problems are actually commonplace in computer networks, distributed computing and socio-technical systems. For example, in various types of networks, such as ad hoc networks, sensor networks, and vehicular networks, several computational resources have to be pooled: battery power, CPU time, memory buffers, transmission bandwidth, and so on. In cloud computing, there is a trade-off between quality of service and total cost of ownership. Similarly, in socio-technical systems, there is an issue of provision and appropriation to a common-pool in SmartGrids, which creates a common-pool of energy storage to even out the stochastic generation of electricity from renewable sources; and in participatory sensing applications, where the 'work' of collecting the data is done by the leaf nodes of the network, but the most significant benefits accrue to the aggregators of the data at the centre of the network.

Table 6.1. Typology of Common-Pool Resources (*cf.* Hess and Ostrom, 2006)

		Subtractability	
		Low	*High*
Exclusivity	*Difficult*	**Public goods** Air, Streetlighting Knowledge	**Common-pool** Libraries, Fisheries Irrigation systems
	Easy	**Toll or club goods** Journal subscriptions Day-care centres	**Private goods** Personal computers Cars, Doughnuts

6.3.2 *Common-Pool Resource Management*

The key issues to address in a CPR type of collective action are access to, benefits from and side-effects on a shared resource.

In terms of access, given the various types of collective action problems and the differing features that they can exhibit, and the wide range of CPR management problems, an attempt has been made to classify different types of problems in a typology (Hess and Ostrom, 2006). Table 6.1 shows a typology that classifies according to subtractability (rivalry) vs. exclusivity. Exclusivity determines how easy it is to exclude individuals from the benefits of the resource, either through physical or legal means; while subtractability determines the extent to which the benefits consumed by one individual subtract from the benefits available to others. Side-effects include the creation of *externalities*, as discussed in Chapter 8.

Considering the benefits, there is the following issue. There is sufficient resource to *satisfice* (satisfy minimally) some agents; although there is *not* enough resource to *satiate* (satisfy maximally) all agents. However, the micro-level (individual) goal of each agent is to maximise its *utility*, i.e. a rational self-interested agent will try to satisfy (itself) maximally. Herein lies the conflict: there is enough to satisfice if the agents can cooperate; there is not enough if they fail to do so.

Moreover, considering the side-effects, each agent trying to satisfy itself maximally may conflict with the macro-level (collective) goal, which is sustainability, of both the resource and the agents.

Thus, the agents need to be satisficed, at least to some degree (over time); furthermore, attempting to satisfy all the agents maximally may deplete the resource.

The difference between subtractability and exclusion is usually used to distinguish between CPRs and public goods. We are interested here in CPRs, even if the self-organised management of those resources will be studied in terms of a game that is called the *LPG* game (Gächter, 2007), because this game also demonstrates the conflict between micro- and macro-level utility maximisation.

6.3.3 Linear Public Good Games

The LPG game is a cooperation game for studying collective action that has enabled the study of issues such as voluntary contributions and opportunities for free riding.

In a typical LPG game, n agents form a group to achieve some collective goal. All group members (i.e. the agents) individually possess a quantity of some resource. Each group member $i \in \{1, \ldots, n\}$ decides independently to contribute resources $r_i \in [0, 1]$ to the public good. The contributions from the whole group are summed up and the utility (payoff) u_i for each agent i is given by:

$$u_i = \frac{\alpha}{n} \sum_{j=1}^{n} r_j + \beta(1 - r_i), \quad \text{where } \alpha > \beta \text{ and } \frac{\alpha}{n} < \beta$$

The first term represents the payoff from the public good (the 'public payoff'), whereby the sum of the individual contributions are distributed equally among the n group members. The second term represents the payoff from the resources withheld from the public good (the 'private payoff') irrespective of how much was contributed individually and collectively.

The coefficients α and β represent the relative weight of the public/private payoffs, respectively. If the above conditions on α and β hold, a rational but selfish agent has an incentive to contribute 0 to the public good, i.e. to free ride, so that:

- The dominant strategy is defect: the individual allocation is greatest when a member contributes 0 and every other group member contributes 1;

- The collective payoff is least when every group member contributes 0, but increases as contributions increase; and
- The collective payoff is greatest when all group members contribute fully (i.e. contributes 1).

However, the LPG game makes a number of assumptions, in particular that there is full disclosure, that no monitoring costs are incurred, that there is no cheating on appropriation, and that there are no diminishing returns. The assumptions have to be relaxed in open systems managing a CPR with an economy of scarcity, so to study resource allocation in this context, we utilise a variant game, LPG' (Pitt et al., 2012a).

The LPG' is still an iterated n-player game for a set of agents A, where $\mathbf{card}(A) = n$. This game is played in consecutive rounds, $t_0, t_1, \ldots, t_\infty$ (we omit identifying a round by a subscript t if it is clear from the context). In each round t, each agent i performs the following actions (see also Fig. 6.2):

(1) Determines the resources it has available, $g_i \in [0, 1]$.
(2) Determines its need for resources, $q_i \in [0, 1]$ (see first note in what follows).
(3) Makes a provision of resources, $p_i \in [0, 1]$ (see second note in what follows).
(4) Makes a demand for resources, $d_i \in [0, 1]$.
(5) Receives an allocation of resources, $r_i \in [0, 1]$.
(6) Makes an appropriation of resources, $r'_i \in [0, 1]$.

Note firstly that the LPG' game can impose an *economy of scarcity*, by insisting that each agent's need for resources is greater than those

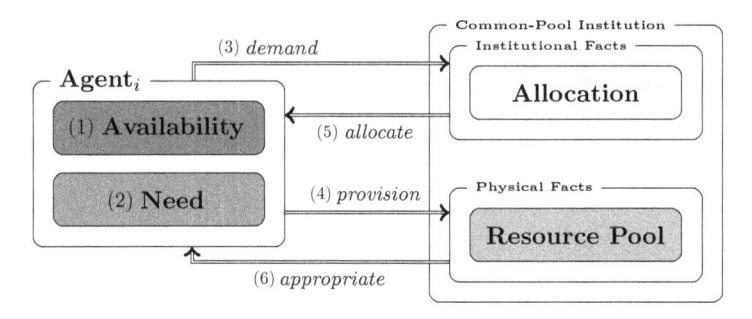

Fig. 6.2. Sequence of Actions in the LPG' Game

it is able to generate for itself, i.e.:

$$\forall i \in A. q_i > g_i \implies \sum_{i=1}^{n} q_i > \sum_{i=1}^{n} g_i$$

Thus, agents are necessarily dependent on others making a provision, but there is still an incentive to withhold one's own provision.

Note secondly that there is a *physical* constraint, that an agent cannot provision more resources than it actually has, therefore ($p_i \leqslant g_i$). The total resources accrued by an agent at the end of a round is given by R_i:

$$R_i = r'_i + (g_i - p_i)$$

i.e. R_i is the sum of the resources that are *appropriated* (rather than allocated) from the common-pool and the available resources that are withheld from the pool. The utility of agent i is then given by:

$$u_i = \begin{cases} \alpha_i(q_i) + \beta_i(R_i - q_i) & \text{if } R_i \geqslant q_i \\ \alpha_i(R_i) - \gamma_i(q_i - R_i) & \text{otherwise} \end{cases} \quad \text{where } \alpha_i > \gamma_i > \beta_i$$

Now, α_i, β_i and γ_i are *private* coefficients in $\mathbb{R}$ measuring, respectively, the relative utilities of getting resources that are needed, getting resources that are not needed, and not getting resources that are needed. The relation $\alpha_i > \beta_i$ reflects the diminishing returns of excess resources, while $\gamma_i > \beta_i$ reflects the line from the film *True Romance*: "it is better to have a gun and not need it, than to need a gun and not have it".

In addition, note that the acts of provisioning and appropriating resources are physical actions, which create or change 'brute' facts; whereas the acts of demanding and allocation are conventional actions, which create or change 'institutional' facts.

Finally, it will be assumed that appropriated resources do not accrue from one round to the next, so agents cannot stockpile resources.

6.4 Self-Governing (Ostrom) Institutions

There are two further points to note about the LPG' game. Firstly, dealing with an economy of scarcity, there are at least two approaches to resolving the conflict over access to a shared resource (as in the Hawk–Dove game). At one extreme, just have a fight, but as we have seen, fighting is costly. At the other extreme, just make up some rules for *resource allocation*, and resolve the potential conflict according to these rules.

Secondly, there are possibly other constraints that the agents may want to apply. For example:

- An agent should not demand more than it needs, $d_i \leqslant q_i$;
- An agent should provision all that it generates, $p_i = g_i$; and
- An agent should not appropriate more than it is allocated, $r'_i \leqslant r_i$.

In order to get all the agents to comply with these constraints, they should specify and agree to some rules (monitoring and enforcement are separate matters, as will be seen).

This specification and agreement of *conventional* (rather than *physical*) rules is the cornerstone of "Ostrom Institution Theory", as presented in this section. First it starts with a discussion of collective action, analytic and empirical perspectives, before giving an overview of Ostrom's theory of self-governing institutions and then briefly summarising her framework and methodology for Institutional Analysis and Development (IAD).

6.4.1 *Collective Action: Analytically and Empirically*

In one of the most influential studies of collective action, it was asserted by Mancur Olson, according to what came to be known as the *zero contribution thesis*, that "unless the number of individuals in a group is quite small, or unless there is coercion or some other special device to make individuals act in their common interest, rational, self-interested individuals will not act to achieve their common or group interests" (Olson, 1965, p. 2).

Olson therefore claimed that the argument that any 'large' group will ever organise itself to optimise a common good is completely specious. This theoretical analysis was supported by the subsequent work of Garret Hardin (Hardin, 1968) on the *tragedy of the commons*, essentially an n-player prisoners' dilemma which purports to show that a large group of actors will act to maximise their interests in the short term, even if that means depleting a CPR in the long term, which is in no one's interest.

These works were taken by some as 'proof' of humanity's innate selfishness, and the impossibility of solving collective action problems through cooperation. Especially at scale, the only solution was the coercive incentive of the centralised stick rather than any carrot. This also provided some of the motivation for *mechanism design*: the problem of finding an optimal system-wide solution to a decentralised optimisation problem with self-interested agents having private information about their preferences for different outcomes.

However, some 25 years later, Elinor Ostrom observed (and there may be some excess paraphrasing of a Nobel-prize winning body of research): "that's not what we always observe in the real world".

While the analytic results in terms of solution concepts like the Nash equilibrium pointed to inevitable depletion of a CPR through under-provision (free riding) or over-appropriation, the empirical analysis showed something quite different. Based on extensive fieldwork, Ostrom showed that throughout history and geography, from irrigation systems in Andalusia and California to fisheries and forestries in Japan and Switzerland, different communities had managed to sustain a CPR, without recourse to coercion, and for many generations.

Speaking demotically, it turns out that people (or communities of people) are very good at "making stuff up". Beyond legends and religions, people are also very good at making up and writing down conventional rules to (voluntarily) regulate, constrain or otherwise organise their own behaviour. It is the root of all game-playing, but it is also the essence of sustainable CPR management: communities had successfully managed and maintained a common-pool resource through the 'evolution' of *self-governing institutions*.

6.4.2 *Self-Governing Institutions*

Elinor Ostrom's research explains how people can solve a collective-action problem involving sustainable CPR management, by the formation of self-governing institutions (Ostrom, 1990). Ostrom showed that in spite of the zero-contribution thesis and the tragedy of the commons, there was an alternative to centralisation or privatisation of CPRs. She observed that in many cases, quite to the contrary of theoretical results, communities were able to manage their own affairs by 'evolving' *institutions* to self-govern their communal resource.

Ostrom defined an institution as a "set of working rules that are used to determine who is eligible to make decisions in some arena, what actions are allowed or constrained,... [and] contain prescriptions that forbid, permit or require some action or outcome" (Ostrom, 1990, p. 51). She also maintained that the rule-sets were conventionally agreed (ideally by those affected by them), mutable (i.e. the rules are changeable, and most importantly, those affected by the rules participate in the processes by which those rules are changed), and mutually understood (so the rules could be taken as common knowledge by all concerned). The rules also needed to be monitored for compliance and enforced in the case of non-compliance, and could not simply be repudiated. Membership of the institution implied accepting the rules and accepting punishment for transgressing the rules.

In addition, the rules were 'nested'. Ostrom (1990, p. 52) distinguished three levels of rules. These were, at the lowest level, *operational-choice* rules, which were concerned with the processes of resource appropriation, provision, monitoring and enforcement. At the middle level, *collective-choice* rules were concerned with selecting the operational rules, as well as processes of policymaking, role assignment and dispute resolution. At the highest level, *constitutional-choice* rules indirectly affected the operational rules by determining who is eligible to, and what specific rules are to be used to, define the set of collective-choice rules.

The nesting of rules was important for the process of *institutional change* for two reasons. Firstly, the changes which constrained action at a lower level (in what Ostrom at the time referred to as a *decision arena*) occurred in the context of an apparently 'fixed' set of rules at a higher level decision arena, i.e. there were conventional rules which were as ostensibly unbreakable as physical rules (*cf.* Binmore, 2010). However, these rules could yet be changed in another decision arena at an even higher level (whose rules appeared to be fixed), and so on. Secondly, lower level rules were easier, quicker and less 'costly' to change than higher level rules.

These two properties of nested rules increased the stability of strategies and expectations of those individuals having to interact with others in the context of the institutional setting. It can also be seen that this nesting of rules corresponds to the embedding of object-level 'resource' games within meta-level 'political' games, as discussed in Chapter 3.

Importantly, Ostrom also observed that there were occasions when the institutions were *enduring*, and the resource was sustained, and others where it was not. She was then able to identify eight common (sic) features of the enduring institutions, one or more of which were absent from those that were not. From there, she took one further, critical, step which was to say that if community were ever confronted with a collective action problem of this kind, then it should not rely on 'luck' to 'evolve' an institution with the necessary features, instead *supply* or *design* an institution for the problem such that it possesses those features *ab initio*.

Accordingly, eight design principles, each principle corresponding to one of the features, were specified as guidelines for designing institutions to ensure that self-management of CPRs would endure. These principles are summarised in Table 6.2 (Ostrom, 1990, p. 90).

It was partially in recognition of this foundational contribution to economic and political science that Ostrom shared the award of the 2009 Nobel Memorial Prize in Economic Sciences. In her later

Table 6.2. Ostrom's Design Principles for Enduring Self-Governing Institutions

1 Clearly defined boundaries: those who have rights or entitlement to appropriate resources from the CPR are clearly defined, as are its boundaries.

2 Congruence between appropriation and provision rules and the state of the prevailing local environment.

3 Collective-choice arrangements: in particular, self-determination, whereby those affected by the rules participate in the selection, modification and enforcement of those rules.

4 Monitoring, of both state conditions and appropriator behaviour, is by appointed agencies, who are either accountable to the resource appropriators or are appropriators themselves.

5 A flexible scale of graduated sanctions for resource appropriators who violate communal rules; i.e. violation should be proportional to the severity, frequency or necessity of the offence.

6 Universal access to 'fair', rapid, low-cost, light-weight conflict-resolution mechanisms.

7 Minimal recognition of the right to self-organise (see Sec. 6.7.1).

8 Systems of systems: layered or encapsulated CPR, with local CPR at the base level (see Sec. 6.7.2).

years, she was very concerned with climate change; in particular, the perspective that the issue of climate change could be analysed as a collective action problem (Ostrom, 2010), in which the 'players' were nation-states and various trans-national organisations, and binding protocols (like the Kyoto Protocol and the Paris Agreement) constituted the institution. The planet, as the CPR at stake, was, and is still being, depleted (opening up the potential criticism that the principles do not scale, and that Olson was right after all: at scale, coercion is required).

However, these features and design principles have been shown to be robust through a meta-analysis (Cox *et al.*, 2010), and have been reproduced in sustainable servers for the online computer game Minecraft (Frey and Sumner, 2018). Minecraft enables players to host their own servers, and it has been possible for people to create graphical constructions of remarkable complexity and beauty. To do so requires cooperation though, at scale. The 'vanilla' server allows players licence to do anything, but servers can be self-customised and self-configured using rules defined by *mods* and *plug-ins*. The study of Frey and Sumner (2018) showed how the servers which endured were those whose self-configuration implemented rules which conformed to Ostrom's principles. Thus, even the most anti-social group on the planet (teenage boys), faced with a collective action problem, did not go all *Lord of the Flies* but instead evolved Ostrom institutions to protect, promote and sustain their common interest.

We want to design and develop Ostrom institutions for computer networks and distributed systems, which requires an analytic framework. Ostrom herself proposed such a framework, called Institutional Analysis and Development (IAD) (Ostrom, 2005).

6.4.3 *Institutional Analysis and Development*

The IAD framework can be used to analyse the relevant factors in an institution which manages a commons, allowing the evaluation of institutions with respect to Ostrom's eight principles, and facilitating comparison with respect to other institutions which have been analysed in the same way. The framework can also be used for the design (or development) of institutions. The basic components of analysis and design are illustrated in Fig. 6.3.

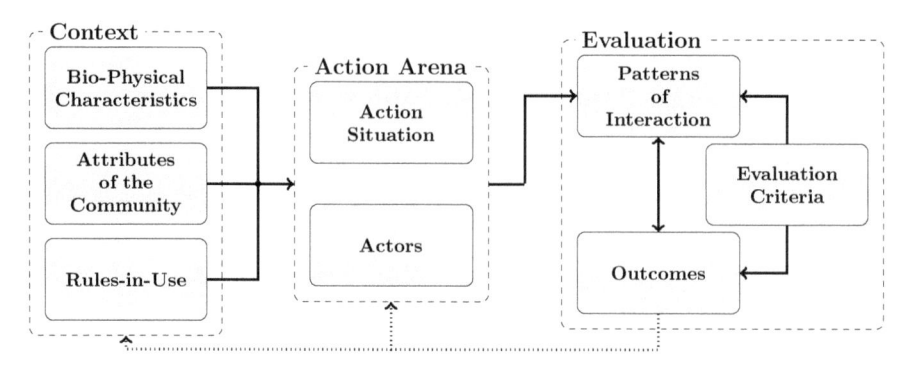

Fig. 6.3. Ostrom's IAD Framework

The IAD is split into eight areas of analysis. The left side of the framework looks at context: what the resource and the community using it is like, and which institutional arrangements have been created for resource and institution management. The middle section deals with where interactions occur and who these interactions are between, i.e. the 'action arena'. The right-hand side observes the interaction patterns, and evaluates the outcomes. A feedback loop conveys this evaluation back to the community, and reinforces characteristics, attributes or the rules.

More specifically, the biophysical characteristics are concerned with establishing the physical attributes of the resource, in terms of *flow* and *facility*. This distinction separates the resource units (*flow*) from where they are stored and generated (*facility*). The attributes of the community concerns identifying interest groups, especially providers and appropriators, but also policymakers. Policymakers constitute a more diverse and abstract group of community decision-makers: providers and appropriators can be policymakers, and vice versa, but equally, membership of those groups is not a requirement. The rules-in-use dictate what users must, must not or may do in an organisation. IAD breaks these rules down into three nested levels, as has been discussed: operational choice, collective choice and constitutional choice.

The action arena describes the various decision arenas and the actors involved. This could include, for example, identifying any decision-making committees, their remits and the actors involved (or what roles are involved). The patterns of interaction identify the information flow and learning conditions, which feed into the evaluative criteria, whereby outcomes are analysed and fed back to the community.

The creation of an institution in order to manage a CPR in a practical scenario is certainly non-trivial. However, IAD has been successfully applied, for example, in applications as diverse as free software (Schweik, 2007), land management (Nigussie *et al.*, 2018) and knowledge commons (Macbeth and Pitt, 2015). Nevertheless, there is a fundamental problem of *supply* (Ostrom, 1990, p. 42): someone must provide the initial organisational structure and institutional rules. Furthermore, rulesets which satisfy Ostrom's eight principles are often very specific to the resource characteristics, so there may not be a pre-existing 'library' of rules available when looking to 'supply' an institution with which to manage a new resource. Finally, the paradox of self-amendment and the entropic tendency to oligarchy demonstrates the difficulty of implementing effective collective governance structures.

Section 6.5 considers the problem of 'supply' by defining a set of protocols, specified in computational logic in the framework of dynamic norm-governed systems, which could be re-used in *self-organising electronic institutions* for different computer-based applications. The paradox of self-amendment is considered in Sec. 6.7.3, while the entropic tendency to oligarchy is a recurring theme in Chapters 9 and 10.

6.5 Self-Organising Electronic Institutions

Besides IAD, there are many approaches to analysing and representing institutions. With specification in NG-MAS as a target, the approach proposed here captures some minimal structural, functional and procedural elements of an institution, but especially its roles and institutionalised powers.

6.5.1 *Structural and Functional Specification*

In terms of structural representation, the general case is depicted diagrammatically in Fig. 6.4(a). This shows an action situation (Ostrom, 2005), originally called a decision arena in Ostrom (1990), to be

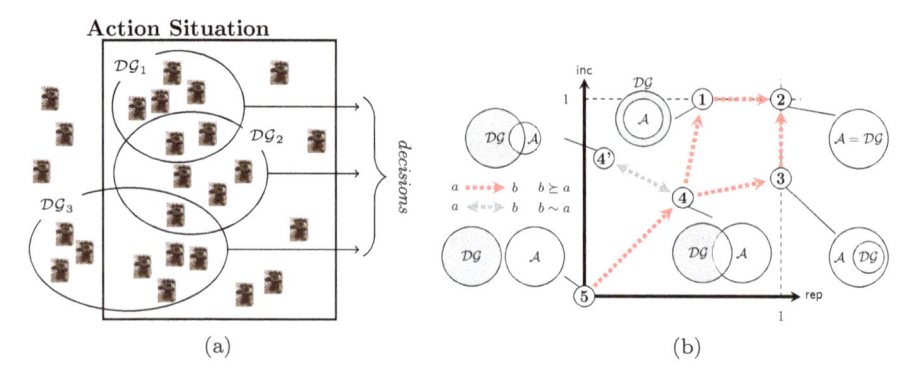

Fig. 6.4. (a) Action Situation Decision Groups and (b) Participation Space

regulated by a set of conventional rules, with clearly defined boundaries (determining who is and is not an appropriator belonging to the situation). Within any action situation there are 'decision groups' (DG: here for example there are three). These groups make decisions of conventional significance to the institution; i.e. there is a procedure for making a decision, which is declared by a distinguished member occupying an identified role and performing a designated action in the appropriate context, i.e. by the exercise of *institutionalised power* (Jones and Sergot, 1996).

The relationship between the membership of the institution and its constituent action situations (Fig. 6.4(a)) and its decision groups is shown in the 'participation space' in Fig. 6.4(b). This two-dimensional space 'plots' representation against inclusivity (rep×inc), showing the possible relationships between $\mathcal{A}$ (institution membership) and $\mathcal{DG}$ (group membership). DG_1 and DG_2 are points on the line between (2) and (3), whereas DG_3 is in the space 'near' (4). Note that $b \succeq a$ denotes that point b is preferred to point a, while $a \sim b$ denotes indifference between a or b. This means that the most participative case (2) is when the decision group membership ($\mathcal{DG}$) is identical with the institutional membership ($\mathcal{A}$), although forms of representative democracy or deliberative assembly are 'below' this. The most extreme case (5) is when all decisions are taken outside the DG.

In terms of functional representation, an institution's rules can be divided into three levels, from lower to higher (Ostrom, 1990): *operational-choice rules* (OC) are concerned with the provision and

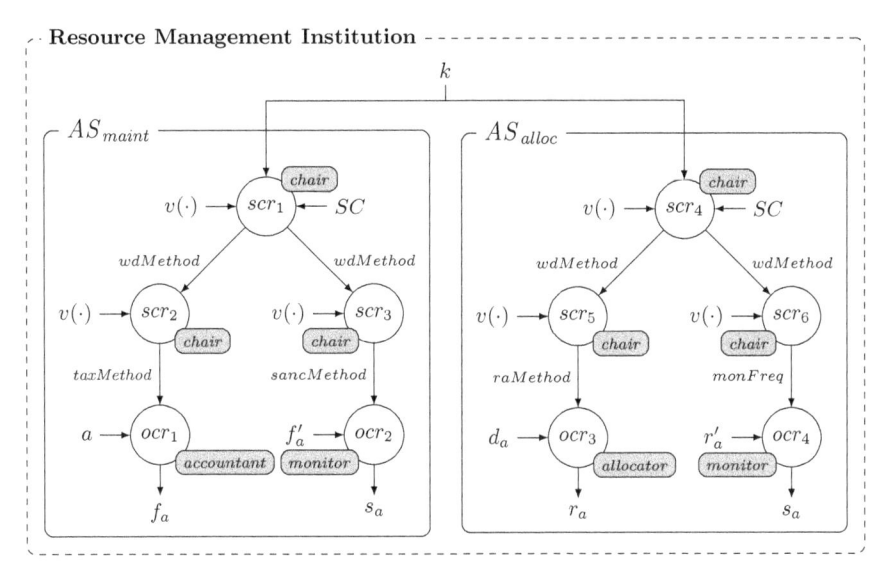

Fig. 6.5. Rules Relationships: Nodes Represent Rules, Edges Their Inputs/Outputs, and Shaded Rectangles the Role Empowered to Execute the Function

appropriation of resources, as well as with membership, monitoring and enforcement; *collective-choice rules* (SC) drive policymaking and selection of operational-choice rules; and *constitutional-choice rules* (CC) deal with formulation of the collective-choice rules.

For example, Fig. 6.5 illustrates a resource management institution with two action situations, one for *infrastructure maintenance* (AS_{maint}) and one for *resource allocation* (AS_{alloc}).

In the infrastructure maintenance action situation AS_{maint}, there are two operational-choice rules: ocr_1 which applies the *taxMethod* (which could be licence fee, progressive, etc.) and is administered by the agent in the *accountant* role; and ocr_2 which applies the sanctioning method (lenient (low cost for first offence), stepped (equal cost for each offence), deterrent (high cost for first offence), etc.) administered by the agent in the *accountant* role. The selected methods are decided by scr_2 and scr_3, respectively, by a vote according to the winner determination method specified, in each case, by scr_1.

In AS_{alloc}, there are two operational-choice rules: ocr_3 *allocates* the resource to the users, according to their demands and some allocation method (*raMethod*); ocr_4 applies *monitoring* to identify any users that appropriate more resources than they have been allocated.

For the social collective-choice rules, scr_5 selects the resource allocation method ($raMethod$); scr_6 selects the monitoring frequency; and scr_4 selects the *winner determination* method to be used in the voting procedures of ocr_1 and ocr_2.

For the procedural representation, we have used the EC and institutionalised power, as discussed in the following.

6.5.2 Procedural Specification

By applying the methodology of sociologically inspired computing (or, if it is preferred, in a curious serendipity like taking random slices of Emmental cheese and rotating them such that all the holes align so that a pencil can pass through them), the statement of Ostrom's first six design principles aligned with the axiomatic specification of protocols undertaken in a series of separate studies are as follows:

(1) P1 (boundaries) ⇝ role assignment (membership) and access control protocols as in Sec. 5.5 and Artikis *et al.* (2004);
(2) P2 (congruence) ⇝ meta-protocols for changing protocol parameters and policies (as in Sec. 1.7.2), or changing the protocols themselves (note that evaluating and ensuring congruence is an issue of reflection and justice, both procedural and interactional — see Secs. 7.6 and 9.6, respectively);
(3) P3 (collective choice) ⇝ voting protocol as in Sec. 4.6 and Pitt *et al.* (2006);
(4) P4 (monitoring) ⇝ event recognition being, in effect, the essence of the EC; and so the machinery for regulatory compliance Sec. 5.6 and Pitt *et al.* (2007);
(5) P5 (graduated sanctions) ⇝ sanction mechanism, as a standard feature of various protocols as described in Secs. 4.6 and 5.3, while a socio-cognitive approach based on shame and embarrassment was considered in Pitt (2004);
(6) P6 (appeals) ⇝ argumentation and alternative dispute resolution, as in Sec. 5.3, and Artikis *et al.* (2007) and Pitt *et al.* (2007).

Note that Principle 8 (system of systems) is concerned with structure and Principle 7 (minimal recognition of rights to self-organise) is concerned with a constraint on that structure. These two principles are discussed in Sec. 6.7.

This alignment meant that the features of self-governing institutions that successfully sustained a CPR could not only be reformulated as Ostrom's institutional design principles for supply of an institution, but now the design principles themselves could be reformulated as axiomatic specifications in computational logic for supply of an electronic institution to be used for sustainability by a norm-governed MAS.

Since these specifications were syntactic sugar for a Prolog program, the specifications were their own implementation, and so this meant that the protocols could be directly executed. In other words, such a specification provided an algorithmic basis for sustainable CPR management through self-governance. Note that this formalisation also meant that institutionalised power was a principal component of analysis, which did not feature at all in Ostrom's work, even in her ADICO *grammar of institutions*, which identified norms as a component of institutions alongside rules and shared strategies (Crawford and Ostrom, 1995).

6.5.3 Self-Governing Institutions and Sustainable MAS

From this alignment, and slightly extending the definition of Sec. 2.5.2, a self-organising electronic institution can be defined at time t by:

$$\mathcal{I}_t = \langle \mathcal{A}, \mathcal{C}, \mathcal{N}, \mathcal{R}, \mathcal{P} \rangle_t$$

where (omitting the subscript t if it is clear from context):

- $\mathcal{A}$ is the set of all agents;
- $\mathcal{C}$ is the set of (collective) action situations;
- $\mathcal{N}$ is a binary *nesting* relation on $\mathcal{C}$;
- $\mathcal{R}$ is the norm-governed specification of a set of protocols; and
- $\mathcal{P}$ is the set of all problems being addressed by each $C \in \mathcal{C}$.

Following the dynamic norm-governed system framework of Artikis (2012) (refer back Sec. 1.7), a number of degrees of freedom (DoF) for each of the protocols in $\mathcal{R}$ can be identified. Thus, recall that $\mathcal{R}$ defines a specification space, where each specification instance is defined by a different set of values assigned to the DoF. In the context of the LPG' game, one degree of freedom is the operational-choice rule by which the resources are allocated (e.g. at random, by ration, or in turn); another degree of freedom is the winner-determination method used to elect an agent to occupy a role; another degree of freedom is the appointment to the role itself. Some of the degrees of freedom may be changed by rules contained within the action situation, and some may be changed by decisions made in the action situation with which it is nested, as determined by the nesting relation $\mathcal{N}$, and so on.

Each (collective) action situation $C_{i,t} \in \mathcal{C}_t$ is defined by:

$$C_{i,t} = \langle \mathcal{M}, L, \epsilon, P \rangle_t$$

where (again omitting the subscripts when clear from context):

- $\mathcal{M}$ is the set of members, such that $\mathcal{M} \subseteq \mathcal{A}$;
- L is a specification instance of $\mathcal{R}$;
- ϵ is the action situation's local environment, a pair $\langle Bf, If \rangle$; and
- P is a set of problems or goals for this collective.

Regarding the environment ϵ, Bf represents the set of 'brute' facts whose values are determined by the *physical* state, including the sum of CPRs P as a result of provision by the agents. If represents the set of 'institutional' facts, whose values are determined by the *conventional* state, i.e. are asserted by the exercise of institutionalised power.

This implies that a self-governing institution for the sustainable management of CPRs can be specified as a self-organising multi-agent system. In doing so, a key experimental result using multi-agent simulation and the LPG' game showed that *the more principles that were axiomatised in this way, the more likely it was that the institution could maintain 'high' levels of membership and sustain the resource*. Full details can be found in Pitt *et al.* (2012a). For aligning holes in Swiss cheese, it is possible to win Best Paper awards (Pitt *et al.*, 2011a).

6.6 Boundaries and Congruence

A further consideration of sustainability involves the appropriation and provision of endogenously-generated resources across *multiple* non-nested ($\mathcal{N} = \emptyset$) action situations, and *conflicting* 'optimisation' criteria. These criteria can affect collective/choice arrangements (Principle 3) regarding institutional membership (Principle 1), which trades off cost-of-ownership (keeping membership high keeps cost low) against quality-of-service (keeping membership low keeps service-quality high). Such considerations typically arise in cloud computing and *-as-a-service business models.

6.6.1 *Experimental Setting*

In this context, we equate 'action situation' with 'institution' (this is essentially a system of systems issue). Then, to investigate institutional development and agent preferences with respect to this trade-off, we define two operational-choice rules (ocr_i) for role assignment, (with, in parenthesis, the role responsible for its enactment and enforcement), and four collective-choice rules (scr_i) for assigning an agent to a role, and for choosing an access control method (*acMethod*) and exclusion method (*exMethod*). (Note that the actual values of *acMethod* and *exMethod* determine the specification instance L in the specification space defined by $\mathcal{R}$.) Let $V(\cdot)_{a \in \mathcal{M}}$ stand for a set of expressed preferences on an issue by each *member* agent in institution C (where $C \in \mathcal{C}, \mathcal{C} \in \mathcal{I}$), then these six rules are:

$$(gatekeeper) \quad ocr_1 : \mathcal{M}^c \times acMethod \to Bool$$
$$(monitor) \quad ocr_2 : \mathcal{M} \times V(\cdot)_{a \in \mathcal{M}} \times exMethod \to Bool$$
$$(head) \quad scr_1 : V(\cdot)_{a \in \mathcal{M}} \times wdMethod \to \mathcal{M}$$
$$(head) \quad scr_2 : V(\cdot)_{a \in \mathcal{M}} \times wdMethod \to acMethod$$
$$(head) \quad scr_3 : V(\cdot)_{a \in \mathcal{M}} \times wdMethod \to \mathcal{M}$$
$$(head) \quad scr_4 : V(\cdot)_{a \in \mathcal{M}} \times wdMethod \to exMethod$$

Thus, the collective-choice rule scr_1 and scr_2 use a winner determination method (*wdMethod*) to map a set of votes onto, respectively, an agent (who is appointed to the role of *gatekeeper*) and one of the two access control methods. Similarly, the social collective choice rule scr_3 and scr_4 use a winner determination method to map a set of votes onto, respectively, an agent (who is appointed to the role of *monitor*) and one of the two exclusion methods. These collective-choice arrangements are all applied by the agent occupying the role of *head*.

The operational choice rule ocr_1 is applied by the *gatekeeper* to map an application to join from an agent not in $\mathcal{M}$ (i.e. the set complement $\mathcal{M}^c$) to a boolean outcome depending on the access control method. A true result means the applicant can be assigned the role of *member*. Similarly, the *monitor* agent uses the exclusion method specified in rule ocr_2 to exclude (or not) a non-compliant agent in $\mathcal{M}$.

6.6.2 Specification Space

The rules in $\mathcal{R}$ effectively define four DoF: the selection of the *acMethod* and the selection of the *exMethod*, and the assignment to the *gatekeeper* role and the assignment to the *monitor* role. Since no agent can occupy both roles *monitor* and *gatekeeper* in an institution C with n members, it follows that there are $4n^2 - 4n$ possible specification instances. Rather than dynamically computing the entire space for each institution and trying to determine the 'optimal' configuration, we separate the 'specification instance' selection function into two dimensions.

For the first dimension, the decision of which agent to assign to the role of *monitor* or *gatekeeper*, we define a family of preference functions, some based on relevant properties of the agent (e.g. compliance probability, time already spent in the role, etc.) and some not (e.g. random, nominative proximity, etc.). Each agent is associated with a subset of these functions, and applies them when voting for either *monitor* or *gatekeeper*. The *head* is empowered to assign the role to the agent with the most votes according to a winner determination method.

For the second dimension, the selection of *acMethod* and *exMethod*, we define two criteria. The first criterion is a *target* membership: this value is a trade-off between total cost of ownership (which is too high if the *headcount* is less than the target) and the quality of service (which is too low if the *headcount* is more than the target). The second criterion is the average probability of compliance in the LPG game. For each agent, we define a probability distribution for voting for a change in the specification according to these criteria. As a result, the selected specification instance falls into one of the quadrants *1–4* as shown in Fig. 6.6.

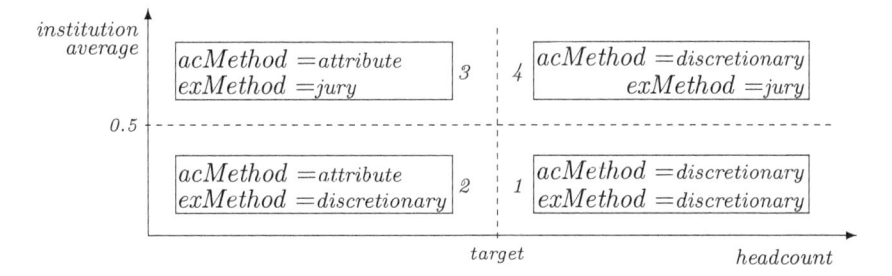

Fig. 6.6. Specification Space

6.6.3 Policy Specification

The EC specification of the operational choice rule ocr_1 is given by a role-assignment protocol for membership. An agent can apply for membership to an institution C if it does not occupy a role in any other institution, while the gatekeeper agent is empowered to admit the agent to this institution by an *assign* action, depending on the access control method:

$apply(A, C)$ **initiates** $applied(A, C) = true$ **at** $T \leftarrow$
$\quad$ **not** $role\_of(A, \_) = member$ **holdsAt** T
$assign(G, A, member, C)$ **initiates** $role\_of(A, C) = member$ **at** $T \leftarrow$
$\quad$ **pow**$(G, assign(G, A, member, C)) = true$ **holdsAt** T

The gatekeeper agent is empowered to assign according to the rules:

pow$(G, assign(G, A, member, C)) = true$ **holdsAt** $T \leftarrow$
$\quad applied(A, C) = true$ **holdsAt** $T \wedge$
$\quad acMethod(C) = attribute$ **holdsAt** $T \wedge$
$\quad role\_of(G, C) = gatekeeper$ **holdsAt** $T \wedge$
$\quad role\_conditions(member, A, C) = true$ **holdsAt** T

pow$(G, assign(G, A, member, C)) = true$ **holdsAt** $T \leftarrow$
$\quad applied(A, C) = true$ **holdsAt** $T \wedge$
$\quad acMethod(C) = discretionary$ **holdsAt** $T \wedge$
$\quad role\_of(G, C) = gatekeeper$ **holdsAt** T

For the game rule, this can be defined by a rule on the provide action, assuming this can be monitored and monitoring is for free (but see the following):

$provide(A, R, C)$ initiates $provision(A, C) = R$ at $T \leftarrow$
    $\mathbf{pow}(A, provide(A, R, C)) = true$ holdsAt T

$provide(A, R, C)$ initiates $sanctioned(A, T, C) = true$ at $T \leftarrow$
    $\mathbf{pow}(A, provide(A, R, C)) = true$ holdsAt T ∧
    $provision(A, C) = R$ holdsAt T ∧
    $institution\_average(C) = Ave$ holdsAt T ∧
    $R < Ave$

$\mathbf{pow}(A, provide(A, R, C)) = true$ holdsAt $T \leftarrow$
    $role\_of(A, C) = member$ holdsAt T

The *monitor* is empowered to exclude a *member* that does not comply with the rules of the game G. For each iteration of G, agents should contribute resources in the interval $[ave_I, 1]$ to comply, where ave_C is the average contribution of resources from the previous iteration (the value of the fluent $institution\_average(C)$).

If the *exMethod* is discretionary, then the *monitor* agent G can exclude the applicant A (or not) as it decides. If the *exMethod* is jury, then the *monitor* must call for a vote on the issue of excluding the sanctioned agent. In either case, the agent must be sanctioned for the *monitor* to be permitted to use its institutionalised power:

$exclude(G, A, member, C)$ initiates $role\_of(A, C) = none$ at $T \leftarrow$
    $\mathbf{pow}(G, exclude(G, A, member, C)) = true$ holdsAt T

$\mathbf{pow}(G, exclude(G, A, member, C)) = true$ holdsAt $T \leftarrow$
    $role\_of(G, C) = monitor$ holdsAt T ∧
    $exMethod(C) = discretionary$ holdsAt T

$\mathbf{pow}(G, exclude(G, A, member, C)) = true$ holdsAt $T \leftarrow$
    $role\_of(G, C) = monitor$ holdsAt T ∧
    $exMethod(C) = (jury, WDM)$ holdsAt T ∧
    $ballot(exclude(A), C) = V$ holdsAt T ∧
    $winner\_determination(WDM, V, true)$

$$\mathbf{per}(G, exclude(G, A, member, C)) = true \text{ holdsAt } T \leftarrow$$
$$role\_of(G, C) = monitor \text{ holdsAt } T \wedge$$
$$sanctioned(A, T', C) = true \text{ holdsAt } T \wedge T' < T$$

Note that the *monitor* is empowered to exclude any *member*, but it is only *permitted* to exercise that power when that member has been sanctioned (and, when, the exclusion method is *jury*, only when the vote is in favour of exclusion). This means that when the monitor excludes an agent, that agent really is excluded and it has no role in the institution. In a richer setting, an excluded agent could appeal against an invalid use of the power, the *monitor* could be removed from the role, and so on. Here, we see the entanglement with the system of retributive justice, which was beyond the scope of this experiment.

6.6.4 *Experimental Results*

An experimental testbed was written to simulate the iterated LPG game with multiple institutions and a randomly-generated population of agents, whereby a bundle of information is associated with each agent. This includes its name, up-time, down-time, initial institution and role assignment (may be none), and its strategy for the LPG game. This strategy is given by a probability of complying with the rules of the game. Therefore, the contribution $r_{i,t}$ that an agent i makes at time t is given by:

$$r_{i,t} = \begin{cases} Ave_{(t-1)} + rnd \cdot (1 - Ave_{(t-1)}) & \text{if } rnd \geqslant pc_{i,t} \\ rnd \cdot Ave_{(t-1)} & \text{otherwise} \end{cases}$$

where $pc_{i,t}$ is the probability of i's compliance at t and $Ave_{(t-1)}$ the average institution contribution from the last time-point. As a result, the contribution is in the interval $[Ave, 1]$ if a random number rnd generated in the interval $[0, 1]$ is greater than the probability of compliance, and is in the interval $[0, Ave]$ otherwise.

The agents update their probability of compliance in the next time-point according to a form of social influence. Letting $|C|$ denote the *headcount* for the number of agents in institution C and $|C|^+$ denote the number of agents in C which complied in the current round, then:

$$pc_i(t+1) = \begin{cases} pc_i(t) + \alpha \cdot (1 - pc_i(t)) & \text{if } (|C|^+ / |C|) \geqslant 0.5 \\ pc_i(t) - \beta \cdot pc_i(t) & \text{otherwise} \end{cases}$$

where α and β are globally defined coefficients in $[0, 1]$ determining the rate of positive and negative *reinforcement*, respectively. If a majority of agents comply in the current round, then the likelihood of each one complying in the next round is increased, and vice versa.

The results (reported in Pitt *et al.*, 2011b) demonstrated the positive effect of clearly defined boundaries and collective choice arrangements. It turns out that the optimal strategy is to behave like the majority, i.e. if everyone else is complying, then the cost of exclusion from not complying is greater than the benefits gained from not complying (especially when the exclusion method is jury and the 'moral majority' is likely to vote for exclusion). On the other hand, if everyone else is cheating, it is a mug's game not to cheat as well. In our experiments, it was observed that institutions would form whose rules oscillated around specification points 3 and 4 (i.e. the average compliance was greater than 0.5, and in fact tended to 1.0); the institutions themselves were stable and enduring; and that compliance pervasion emerged even from low level of initial compliance (even with an initial probability of compliance for all the population of 0.2, institutions eventually formed in which the compliance approached 1.0).

6.7 Dignity, Polycentricity and Self-Amendment

Collectively, Ostrom's eight principles could be broadly considered as two groups of four: one group dealing with internal self-regulation, and the other dealing with self-regulation with respect to external agencies. In the first group are Principles 3 (social choice and self-determination), 4 (monitoring), 5 (graduated sanctions), and 6 (conflict resolution), i.e. the basic mechanics of ADR as discussed in Chapter 5. In the second group are Principles 1 (resilience to external agencies of equivalent competence), 2 (resilience to environmental change), 7 (resilience to external authorities), and 8 (resilience to the 'institutional system'). In this section, we consider three open issues concerning the second group. These are Principle 7 (minimal recognition of the right to self-organise) and the *zone of dignity*; Principle 8 (system of systems) and *polycentricity*; and finally the *paradox of self-amendment*.

6.7.1 Principle 7 and the Zone of Dignity

Some forms of corporate governance have introduced the concept of *guardrail*. The idea of a guardrail is that in a hierarchy, the 'upper' (management) layer specifies that within specific boundaries, the 'lower' (implementation) layer can make any decision, or take any action, it wants, in order to complete a given task. Moreover, the guardrails are not necessarily fixed: if the 'lower' layer needs to go outside the guardrails, it seeks permission from the 'upper' layer.

The idea of a guardrail can be seen within Ostrom's Institutional Design Principle 7, which states that, in a system of systems, the minimal recognition of the right to self-organise should be observed. In fact, many of the failures to sustain a CPR, reported in Ostrom (1990), could be traced to a failure of this principle. The idea of a guardrail is also present in Ober's Demopolis (Ober, 2017), in a discussion of the continuum of distributive justice from full equality to complete liberty. Dignitarian considerations set limits on how far the libertarian and egalitarian tendencies can push equality and liberty. The avoidance of indignity for a democratic regime defines the zone of dignity (ZoD), which determines the acceptable range of policy options for distributive justice, i.e. not too coercive, not too heartless. This raises the question of why there is not a maximal recognition of the right to self-organise, as this implies that in a system of systems, unlimited rights to self-organise do not affect the sustainability of a local CPR. Maybe this is true, but it does not necessarily augur well for the political regimes 'at the edge', i.e. the leaf node of a hierarchy or regions on the periphery of a state, e.g. some 1970s UK academic departments, organised crime, warlordism, feudalism, etc.; see for example (Weber, 1965).

The ZoD therefore represents a kind of preference meta-consensus (or guardrails) on the acceptable range of (institutional) policy options. To specify a deliberative process for algorithmic reflexive governance based on the ZoD requires three components: a coordinate plane, metrics to locate an object in that coordinate plane, and meta-rules to control the trajectory of an object (i.e. a set of

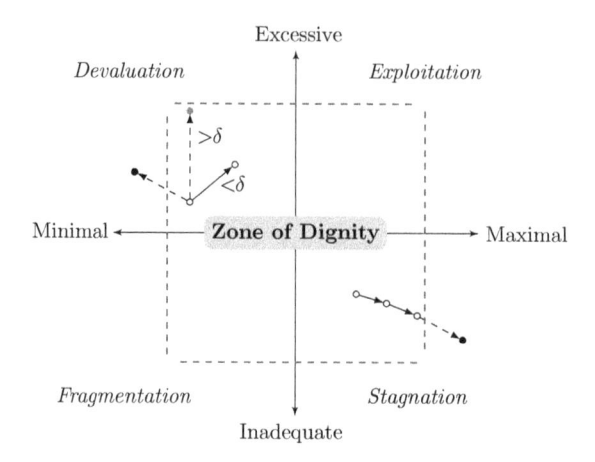

Fig. 6.7. Principle 7 and the Zone of Dignity

rules) as it moves within the plane. The proposed coordinate plane extends the ZoD from a linear one to a two-dimensional plane, by also including an axis of *resource extraction* or taxation, that the 'upper' institution imposes on the 'lower' (*cf.* Acemoglu, 2005).

As shown in Fig. 6.7, this characterises four quadrants of indignity that can bring about systemic collapse: exploitation, brought about by excessive tax and excessive control (tyranny); stagnation, brought about by inadequate tax and excessive control (no resources for top-down policies, no freedom-of-manoeuvre for bottom-up initiatives); devaluation, brought about by excessive tax and inadequate control (a system providing benefits without responsibilities is destined to fail); and fragmentation, brought about by inadequate tax and inadequate control (e.g. a weak state without a monopoly on violence produces factionalism (e.g. warlordism)). This plane defines the space in which to locate systemic configurations and evaluate their trajectories, and identifies the acceptable boundaries in this space.

The second component is to apply ideas from metric spaces, as used in the specification of dynamic norm-governed multi-agent systems (again, see Sec. 1.7, *cf.* Artikis, 2012). The idea is to use the framework of procedural justice to identify an institutional configuration as a point in the ZoD, and then either to implement meta-rules on the movement in that plane, or to evaluate the trajectory of the configuration in that plane. These meta-rules could, for example, prohibit movement from one configuration to another if it exceeds a certain distance (δ), or prohibit movement to a particular configuration altogether if it lies outside the boundaries of the ZoD (see upper left quadrant of Fig. 6.7: dashed transitions are impermissible, either because the resulting configuration lies outside the ZoD, or the distance exceeds δ). Alternatively, observing the speed and direction of a configuration's trajectory might trigger reflective deliberation which alters its course before the anticipated trajectory leaves the ZoD (see lower right quadrant of Fig. 6.7).

The third component is to use ideas of procedural justice for the evaluation of institutional configurations to locate them within this space. Procedural justice is generally concerned with fairly, accurately and efficiently evaluating procedures and the actors enacting those procedures. It has been used, for example, in dispute resolution to determine the trade-off between 'adequate' participation in the process and the 'accuracy' of the outcome, and in public health, to determine the costs and benefits of the authorities imposing decisions on the populace. The procedural justice framework for evaluating self-organising electronic institutions proposed in Pitt *et al.* (2013) tried to metricate three principles: the participation principle, i.e. the purposeful activities in which actors take part in relation to governance (not just voting); the transparency principle, i.e. the amenability of procedures to be subject of investigation and analysis to establish facts of interest; and the balancing principle, i.e. the proportionality of relative benefits and burdens. This framework, including both principles and metrics, is considered in more detail in Sec. 7.6.

6.7.2 *Principle 8 and Polycentricity*

A criticism often levelled at Ostrom's theory is that it does not apply at scale, similar perhaps to the way Newton's Laws of Motion are a satisfactory approximation for bodies moving much slower than the speed of light, but otherwise theories of relativity are required (and even then ...). It was true that Ostrom was primarily concerned with analysis of micro-change and modification of constraints by metagames, as opposed to macro-change of the kind promoted by Marx (Wall, 2014); in this sense perhaps Ostrom could be classified as 'evolutionary' rather than 'revolutionary', and closer in philosophical approach to Popper than to Marx.

However, Ostrom was concerned with macro-operation of the commons, and this was in effect the eighth design principle, concerning a *system of systems*. In a system of systems, the relationship between systems (i.e. the institutional architecture) can (in extremis) be either hierarchical (single centralised decision-maker) or polycentric (multiple autonomous centres of decision-making). In a hierarchical system, loosely speaking, information flows 'up' and policies flow 'down'. In an ideal world, perfect information drives appropriate policy formation, i.e. evidence-based policymaking. In a sub-ideal world, information is abstracted up the hierarchy, and policies are reinterpreted down the hierarchy.

For example, in the UK, a policy of restorative justice, a process that tries to resolve disputes to the mutual satisfaction of all concerned parties through negotiation, was introduced by a regional UK police force (Stockdale, 2015). The policy was interpreted differently by different groups: senior management understood the theoretical concepts, key values and nuanced differences between *instant restorative disposals* and *restorative conferencing*; middle management were focused on performance; and uniformed officers "on the beat" applied the policy as frontline practitioners. The latter group found themselves conflicted between pressures to resolve disputes without involvement of the criminal justice system, but also having to increase the number of 'detections' (the number of cases resolved with a ticket, charge, caution, etc.).

The tendency to drift from decentralised to centralised governance has been observed in human society, in organisations and in technology. For respective examples, as a consequence of the cognitive revolution (the evolution of imagination), it has been argued that as tribal size increased so the requirement for hierarchy and authority-bearing roles increased (Harari, 2014). Similarly, the repeated observation that any organisation, no matter how 'democratically' it was founded, eventually run by a small group in their own narrow interests rather than for the common good, led to the stipulation of the *iron law of oligarchy'* (Michels, 1962 [1911]). Regarding technology, most notably the Internet, it has been suggested that the lack of memory, structure and regulation in the technical layers of the Internet (in order to maximise throughput, minimise delays, and treat all data traffic equally) have, in conjunction with "network effects", enabled the centralisation of control and the economic dominance of just a small number of "tech giants" at the application layer (Special Report, 2018).

There can be good reasons for making this transition from decentralised to centralised control, such as standardisation and distribution of best practice; economies of scale which can reduce the time taken for, and cost of, consultative deliberation and decision-making; and dealing with crisis situations (for example, operating systems use random allocation of the CPU to tasks in overload conditions: random allocation can be no less unfair but much cheaper to compute than priority scheduling — which also consumes the very resources that are needed to cope with the overload).

However, as the size of a centralised system increases, absolute centralisation brings with it certain disadvantages: for example it can undermine principles of self-determination, rights to self-organise and willingness to take responsibility or show initiative. This removes 'edge' benefits such as localisation, rapid and appropriate response to local environmental conditions, and the diversity that promotes resilience. Certain processes that might have been effective at small scale (like word-of-mouth, and monitoring (compliance checking)) are no longer effective at larger scales. Unsurprisingly, perhaps, to counter the drift from centralised to decentralised control, there are counteracting mechanisms such as devolution, federalism and subsidiarity.

In addition, there can be other reasons for making a transition from centralised control to decentralised decision-making. The latter is arguably most effective when it occurs with certain boundaries. For example, the concept of academic freedom works best when the institution sets an overall mission statement and establishes boundaries for, but not prescriptions on, academic inquiry, thought and publication. Equally, corporate governance is often most effective when executive management sets guardrails which establish limits on decision-making: within those limits all behaviour is acceptable; moreover, action outside the guardrails is not necessarily prohibited, but needs instead to be justified, negotiated and approved.

Other examples of providing a top-down infrastructure with freedom of manoeuvre (with respect to its governance policy) within that infrastructure include the computer game Minecraft, which enables players to deploy their own servers within the parameters of the game rules and software architecture, but provides plugins for each host to configure their server to customise their game environment to their own taste (Frey and Sumner, 2018). Ostrom's institutional design Principle 7 (Ostrom, 1990) states that self-governing institutions should have minimal rights to self-organise, i.e. for sustainable common-pool resource management, one precondition is some minimal control over self-determination, i.e. the opportunity for groups and communities who are affected by a set of rules to participate in their selection, modification and enforcement.

However, excessive decentralisation can lead to fragmentation, disassociation and an inability to form relational bonds that transcend transactional bonds (as seen for example in the gift economies or the Trobriand islands (Malinowski, 1920), which can be crucial in times of crisis). Furthermore, from a complex systems perspective, decentralisation may make it impossible to coordinate in order to achieve macro-level outcomes, i.e. the coordination of micro-level behaviour through meso-level, mechanisms, which result in the creation of global structures or achievement of high-level goals by intention or design. This has been referred to as planned emergence (Pitt and Nowak, 2014a). Such meso-level mechanisms can take many forms from strict reporting structures to informal mechanisms such as joint social activities including sports clubs, choirs and dining facilities. The existence of strong cultural structures has been noted as one of the prerequisites of a successful organisation (Kay, 1993), while the decline of social capital associated with communities has been identified as contributing to the decline in quality of civic and democratic institutions (Putnam, 2000).

Therefore, the choice of centralised vs. decentralised governance is a false dichotomy. There is no single, perfect "one size fits all" model of governance that fits any and every situation. Given the myriad of known and unknown parameters and the spectrum of complexity and dynamics, there is no way of computing the most appropriate model either. Both centralised and decentralised governance models have their advantages and disadvantages, but it is possible, with a bit of introspection and (restricted) freedom for self-modification, to shift between the two, so that rules and the application of rules are both congruent with the environment.

In the long term, the critical requirement is not just the ability to shift between the two as circumstances require, but the ability to shift back and forth along the spectrum between the two, and not get stuck in either of the two extreme attractors. In addition, the ability to make, recognise and correct mistakes is required. Indeed, as was seen in Chapter 5, any policymaking body should have the opportunity to make mistakes. Not because mistakes are especially desirable, but because overzealous adherence to procedures which do not allow that mistakes can have occurred, restricts initiative, minimises judgement and cannot be corrected. On top of this, polycentricity is required, to acknowledge all the decision-making stakeholders in the situation and ensure that those who are affected by a set of rules participate in their selection, modification, application and enforcement.

6.7.3 The Paradox of Self-Amendment

The *paradox of self-amendment*, as studied and termed by Suber (1990), was the consequence of an inquiry into sets of rules that can specify their own amendment. The question addressed by Suber is essentially that if a rule-set has an amendment clause, can that clause be used to modify itself? For example, suppose a rule-set contains a clause that states "all rules can be changed, including this one"; which is then changed (by whatever legitimate process) to the clause which states "no rules can be changed". Is this, in whatever sense of the words, allowable, permissible, desirable?...

Suber called this the paradox of self-amendment. It is not restricted to theoretical legal systems either: for example, consider the two Prolog programs shown in Fig. 6.8. The two programs are logically equivalent, but the order of two rules has been swapped. As a result, their behaviour is entirely different. The program on the left answers **true** to the query `?- p.`, while the program on the right answers **false**.

This is a consequence of Prolog's semantics and its top-down, left-to-right procedure for query satisfaction. In the left-hand program,

```
p :- q, t.              p :- q, r, s.
p :- q, r, s.           p :- q, t.
q.                      q.
r :- retract( q ).      r :- retract( q ).
s :- fail.              s :- fail.
t.                      t.
?- p.                   ?- p.
true                    false
```

Fig. 6.8. Two Prolog Programs

the goal p breaks down into goals for q and r, both of which are in the database as facts, and the goal succeeds. In the right-hand program, the order of clauses for p is reversed. Now, Prolog tries to prove q, s and t. The goal q succeeds as before, r succeeds, but retracts q from the database, and s fails. However, backtracking over r does not undo the destructive update and so q is not restored to the database. Now, when the second clause to prove p is tried, the query q fails (even though it had previously succeeded), there are no more rules with p as the head, and so the goal p fails.

Based on Suber's work, we proposed what we called Suber's Thesis: "that any rule-based system which allows *unrestricted* self-modification of the rules will end in paradox (contradiction, indeterminacy, etc.)." We emphasised the "unrestricted" because it actually requires energy (time and effort) to monitor the proposals for consequences of self-modification. A group of agents specifically motivated to avoid paradox might be able to do so, but without a specific intention to avoid paradox, and careful execution, their modifications to the rules will be subject to a probabilistic or entropic tendency to the paradox of self-amendment.

Suber's thesis, if true, has several implications for designers of open, self-organising, rule-based systems, if their concern is that the system should operate within a 'corridor' of behaviour (Nafz et al., 2013), should avoid certain non-normative states (Artikis, 2012), or there is a risk of unintended consequences, for example undesirable pernicious outcomes like inconsistency, deadlock or exploitable loopholes, the paradox of self-amendment, or the iron law of oligarchy (Michels, 1962 [1911], and see Chapter 10).

The question is: does Suber's thesis also apply to self-organising, rule-based multi-agent systems? That is, does any self-organising rule-based system (with components of 'sufficient' intelligence) which allows unrestricted self-modification, end in paradox, contradiction, indeterminacy, etc.?

To investigate this question, we developed a multi-agent system to play Peter Suber's *Game of Nomic*. Nomic is an n-player turn-based game in which the rules of the game include mechanisms by which the players change the rules. Players start with zero points and take it in turns to propose a rule modification. The proposal is voted on, the result is enacted (either the change is made if it is agreed), and the player throws a die to determine an addition to his/her score.

The first player to 100 points wins. While the game deliberately incentivises 'interesting' rule changes, the primary motivation was to make a point about legal or parliamentary systems, that eventually the system would result in rules which amended themselves.

An important distinction was made between *mutable* and *immutable* rules. For example, Rule 202 was mutable and Rule 103 was immutable:

- 202. One turn consists of two parts in this order: (1) proposing one rule-change and having it voted on, and (2) throwing one die once and adding the number of points on its face to one's score.
- 103. A rule-change is any of: (1) the enactment, repeal, or amendment of a mutable rule; (2) the enactment, repeal, or amendment of an amendment of a mutable rule; or (3) the transmutation of an immutable rule into a mutable rule or vice versa.

However, a rule-change proposal could make an immutable rule mutable (and vice versa), whereupon it could subsequently be changed (or not).

The main ideas in the PreSage-2 simulator implemented to play the *Game of Nomic* (Holland *et al.*, 2013) were that each agent tried to model what the other players were like (or trying to do), that rules had 'flavours' which indicated its properties, and each simulated agent would propose a rule-change by 'inventing' a rule change, and then called a PreSage-2 sub-simulation to test its effect.

The system could not 'prove' Suber's thesis, indeed it is probably unprovable. However, some simulations did produce 'unexpected' results. For example, in one game, one agent 'invented' a rule-change which meant that it was always that agent's turn, and the other agents voted in favour of accepting it. But thereafter they blocked every proposal it made. This is the kind of unintended and unanticipated outcome of allowing dynamic specifications to be modified (by agents at runtime), of which the agents themselves need to be aware, for example by reflection.

6.8 Summary

Instead of the usual chapter summary, I am going to break the textbook fourth wall and finish this chapter with a trio of first-person Ostrom anecdotes. Warning: there may be some irony ahead.

Anecdote 0 (Computer Science: when it suits us, we start counting from zero). I gave Elinor Ostrom a lift in my car once.

Anecdote 1. I have used this remark in one of my own papers, Sara Santos and Pitt (2013), that if your only tool is an Ostrom-shaped hammer, then every problem is a collective action-shaped nail. I did get so wrapped up in the works of Ostrom that every presentation I made would be "Ostrom-this, Ostrom-that", every other slide. So much so that my friends in the scientific community invented this game that they called *Ostrom Bingo*, where on the first slide in my presentation that I mentioned Ostrom, someone would call out "Bingo". Oh how we laughed: the long afternoon presentations simply flew by.

One time I offered a reward to the person who could find all six references to Ostrom on the slides of one presentation. Some were in plain sight, others were in tiny fonts in pictures, one was the first letter of six bullet points which spelt out O-S-T-R-O-M. Fortunately, I did not have to give the reward, which in any case I did not have, because no one spotted when I talked about a system we had developed which we called Massive Online Real-Time Self-Organisation (MORTSO).

Oh how I laughed. I might have even chortled.

Anecdote 2. I did once have a sort of conspiracy theory about the award of the Nobel prize. Not about whether it was deserved, merited or a remarkable achievement, because it surely was. But the year was 2009, so the year after the great financial crash of 2008, which contrary to UK Conservative (right wing) narrative was due to deregulation of the financial industry and sub-prime mortgage selling, and *not* due to Labour (left wing) "profligacy" in government.

Nevertheless, it was rather hard to award the prize to one of the usual suspects whose financial instruments or economic theories had contributed to the crash, so it was awarded to someone who had been pointing out that there was a viable alternative to the economic orthodoxy which had turned out (almost literally given that it was hardly much different from gambling (Lewis, 2010)), to be something of a busted flush. Moreover, admitting as much would be a bit embarrassing and open the door to all sorts of disagreeable conclusions, such as perhaps a bit more equity in wealth distribution, or maybe a touch more state intervention, oversight and regulation, would not be such bad ideas after all. So it was a useful distraction to point out that Ostrom was the first woman to win this prize, rather than draw attention to what she actually won it for.

I was once giving a seminar expounding this theory in my usual reasonable, level-headed and see-both-sides style, when someone put up his hand, and said "I was on the prize awarding committee that year, and we never considered that."

Oh well. Not the first time a beautiful theory has been slain by an ugly fact, and surely not the last. Still, intentional or otherwise, this was the effect: the focus has been more often on form more than content. In any case, the committee got their own back a few years later by awarding the prize to William Nordhaus. Think Kissinger, Nobel Peace prizes, and the death of satire (*cf.* Pitt, 2019a).

Anecdote 3. The first time that I met Elinor Ostrom was at her Workshop at Indiana University. I was on my way to present the paper on the formalisation of the design principles in computational logic at the SASO 2011 conference in Ann Arbor, Michigan. Therefore, Indiana was close, at least by North American standards. So I emailed to ask if I could visit, and Ostrom, who was quite the kindest and most generous person with her time and her wisdom, said yes, that was fine.

Wow. Anyway, entering the Workshop is like walking into someone's living room, except instead of paintings on the walls, there are a multitude of awards; and instead of a mirror over the fireplace there is a Nobel prize (oh that's what they look like). With characteristic generosity, Ostrom maintained it was a prize for the Workshop and always acknowledged the contribution of others, in particular her husband, Vincent Ostrom.

From the reception area, various colleagues came to greet us,[1] and we were taken down into the kitchen for the ritual academic coffee. A few minutes later Elinor Ostrom joins us, there are introductions, a bit of chat about flights, and then she turns to me and asks directly "So: tell me why you are here".

---

[1] "Us" in this context being me and my PhD student Julia Schaumeier, one of the co-authors on the paper. To any PhD students reading this: has your supervisor ever taken you to meet a Nobel prize winner? No? Am I looking good right now? (And to the rest of my PhD students who didn't get to meet a Nobel prize winner... Sorry.)

No pressure there then. So I started to explain about the formalisation of her principles in computational logic and how the property about sustainability seemed to apply to electronic institutions as much as human ones. In the course of the explanation, I threw in the hilarious line that the first paper that I had published on her work was in 2008, and she was awarded the Nobel prize in 2009, so obviously these two events were correlated (I was yet to formulate the conspiracy theory above, which was probably just as well).

Cue all-round deep intake of breath from her various colleagues. Ice ages came and went for me as Ostrom continued to look at me and I could just *see* her thinking: "He's English, the English are supposed to have a sense of humour, so he's probably joking. I'll laugh". So she laughed.

Followed by a deep exhale of relief disguised by laughter from her various colleagues. Still, note to self: if you ever meet another Nobel prize winner, let them tell the jokes about it.

Sadly, I only met Ostrom once more, when I gave her a lift in my car, in case I hadn't mentioned that. Still, there was sufficient time to be in awe of someone whose abundant humanity, greatness of intellect and generosity of spirit confirmed that if there were ever a genuine tragedy of the commons, it is that Elinor Ostrom was taken from us while, in her words, there is still "much to be done".

PART III
Social Interaction

Chapter 7

Computational Justice

7.1 Introduction

The aim of this chapter is to study n-agent social interaction through the lens of *computational justice*. The concept of *justice* itself has been analysed by philosophers from Classical Greece (Plato, Aristotle), through the enlightenment (Hobbes, Kant, Bentham), and on to the modern day (Rawls, Binmore, Rescher). Therefore, defining a concept of 'justice' would be, perhaps, hard enough; even before attempting to give an algorithmic specification and programmed operationalisation of that concept as *computational* 'justice'. Yet, that is what we will attempt in this chapter.

The motivation for the study of computational justice is relatively straightforward. If we design (or supply) an Ostrom institution, as presented in Chapter 6, we can achieve *sustainable* common-pool resource management. This means that the resource allocation procedure can distribute the resources among the agents (by the agents) in such a way as to sustain the common pool, the agents and the institution itself.

But this raises at least two further issues. Firstly, ensuring that the allocation is 'just' or 'fair' — although that begs subsidiary questions such as determining what is meant by 'justice' and 'fairness' in this (or indeed any other) context, and according to whom? For example, in some countries, collective bargaining negotiations between management and unions over redundancies can be preceded by agreeing whose fairness metrics are to be used in making the decisions: the unions' metrics according to seniority or ability, or the management's metrics according to productivity.

Secondly, ensuring that the allocation procedure is efficient and effective, or more broadly 'fit for purpose'. For example, in deciding the fairness question, the members of an institution could develop an algorithm that everyone agrees is totally 'fair', but turns out to be NP-complete, so it may not terminate before the universe ends with either a crunch or a whimper (depending on the value of Ω). Thus, the perfect 'fairness' algorithm might be based on the finest theory of 'justice', but might not work in practice.

It is these two questions, *inter alia*, that computational justice is intended to address. Therefore, computational justice can be loosely defined as the specification and operationalisation of some conception of 'correctness' in the outcomes of algorithmic deliberation and decision-making. Since we have now included in the definition of 'justice' a notion of 'correctness', computational justice is perhaps better understood not by what it is, but by what it does: it is not so much a 'thing' as a *programme* of research that lies at the intersection of Computer Science and the Social Sciences, in particular economics, philosophy, psychology and jurisprudence. As a programme, it comprises several different *processes*, such as the formal representation of judicial systems, policy administration and social organisation; the implementation of computer models based on these concepts in self-organising multi-agent systems; and also exporting and evaluating these ideas back to the design and development of socio-technical systems composed of people and software agents.

Accordingly, the objectives of this chapter are to:

- Provide an overview of different theories of justice from an interdisciplinary perspective;
- Use computational logic to specify and operationalise different perspectives on justice, in particular *distributive* justice but also *retributive* justice and *procedural* justice; and
- Develop a general framework for applying concepts of computational justice to common-pool resource management in the context of Ostrom institutions.

The chapter is then structured as follows. A simple motivating example is given in Sec. 7.2. Section 7.3 gives a brief sample of different theories of justice; clearly, this cannot be an exhaustive survey, and is not. However, based on the ideas reviewed in this section, we formalise a theory of distributive justice as proposed by philosopher and logician Rescher (1966) in Sec. 7.4. The following two sections consider the formalisation of retributive justice (Sec. 7.5) and procedural justice (Sec. 7.6). The chapter concludes with the discussion of a general framework for computational justice in Sec. 7.7 and summarising remarks in Sec. 7.8, emphasising why we need justice in social interactions.

7.2 Example: The Biscuit Distribution Dilemma

Imagine there is a shared living space with three flatmates, call them a, b and e. They have negotiated a satisfactory flatmate agreement and the kitchen is kept clean all the time, they synchronise their use of resources, and they share a common pool of commonly used products for which everybody pays an equal share and consumes a reasonable amount. The landlord d is so happy that she gives them a packet of chocolate Hobnobs for all of them to share. It is a question of *distributive justice* to decide who gets how many biscuits.

Now, suppose that the landlord sells the house to the Demonic Landlord, call him c. Unfortunately c is less benign and rather lacking in judgement, and insists that the flatmates accommodate a new flatmate, call him g; despite the fact that g had twice applied for a room in the house, and twice failed the interview (must have violated a principle, e.g. (Sutton, 2008)); and despite the fact that g, to borrow Rescher's phrase, puts them all "quite into the shade in point of nastiness" (Rescher, 1966, p. 47). Suppose also that the Demonic Landlord rips up the flatmate agreement and unilaterally imposes g as the determiner of all decisions in the house.

What could possibly go wrong?

Suppose there is a pool of resources to distribute, various metrics for determining a possible allocation of those resources to the flatmates, and a *procedure*. The input parameters of this procedure are the resources, the set of flatmates, and the various metrics, and its output is a declared (actual) allocation. g now has control of this procedure.

Suppose that there are two alternative metrics, metric 1 and metric 2, which compute different resource allocations, as shown in Fig. 7.1. Further suppose, in contrast to a, that g prefers a majority share of a smaller resource pool than a minority share of a larger

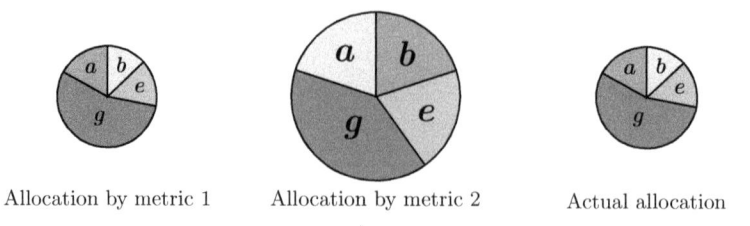

Fig. 7.1. Possible Allocation by Different Metrics; and Actual Allocation

pool, so g compels the others to accept resource allocation according to metric 1 in preference to metric 2. This results in a reduced total allocation of resources, even if this means g himself also gets fewer resources overall. As a collective decision, this is the tragedy of the anti-commons (Heller, 1998), where a group of appropriators under-utilise (and so waste) a resource; but is also a violation of Ostrom's Principle 2, that the resource allocation should be congruent with the environment, and goes against the principle of utility, expressed as "the greater good of the greater number".

Alternatively, suppose that there are several concurrent metrics by which the productivity of a flatmate could be measured, for example, metric 3 and metric 4, and these metrics compute different allocations of the total resources, as shown in Fig. 7.2. However, rather than averaging the proportional contributions of both metrics, g *unilaterally* insists that one specific metric (i.e. metric 3, that favours him) be used in determining the allocation, rather than taking into account additional metrics (such as metric 4, that might be favoured by the other flatmates). Therefore, the actual allocation only uses metric 3, although presumably the others would prefer the alternative metric, or at least a combination of the two, but do not have a say in the choice of the allocation method. This can be seen as a violation of Ostrom's Principle 3, that those affected by the provision and appropriation rules should participate in the selection of those rules, and can lead to an allocation method which a, b and e might consider 'unfair'.

Finally, imagine that a unfortunately leaves the flat, providing a windfall of resources to be distributed among the remaining flatmates. Rescher (1966, pp. 108–112) discusses the distribution of windfalls at some length and notices an indeterminism because of the plausibility of distributions based on either claims approaches

Productivity by metric 3   Productivity by metric 4   Actual allocation

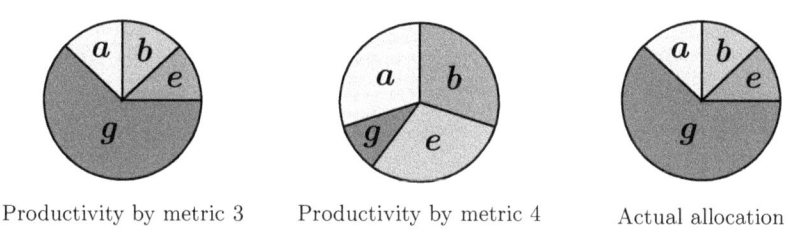

Fig. 7.2. Declared Allocation Using Only One of Several Metrics

or egalitarian-oriented approaches. However, suppose g allocates the entire windfall to himself ... because he can. Basically g stole a's legacy, and c allowed it.

7.3 Justice and Fairness: A Brief Overview

Intuitively, each of the examples in the previous section had an outcome that could be seen as 'incorrect' or 'unfair', from c's imposition of g as a flatmate and appointment as the sole determiner of rules, through to the allocation of resources according to metrics favourable only to g.

However, while it is possible to give reasons why c's actions violated constitutional- or collective-choice rules, or why the application of operational-choice rules produced 'unfair' outcomes, it is another matter to define rules which do produce 'fair' outcomes. This is a matter of *distributive justice*, the method of, and justification for, allocating resources among a group of individuals. But, as we shall see, there are other aspects of justice, including *retributive justice* and *procedural justice*, as well as *interactional justice* (studied in Chapter 9).

However, suppose for now we have a set of n agents having to share a divisible pool R of some resource, where each agent i makes a demand $d_i \leqslant R$ for some portion of the resource. There are many different ways of determining the set of allocations r_i based on the set of demands, see e.g. Brams and Taylor (1996). For example, a dictatorial solution might satisfy the demand of the dictator first, then allocate what is left equally to each remaining member. A competitive solution could be found based on auctions (Murillo *et al.*, 2011). A more collaborative solution could be based on giving an exactly equal share to each of the n agents. More elaborate algorithms can refine rationing by re-allocating an excess (i.e. if $r_i > d_i$) to an agent with a greater need.

In all cases, given a vector of demands, $\langle d_1, d_2, \ldots, d_n \rangle$, suppose some algorithm produces a pairwise vector of allocations, $\langle r_1, r_2, \ldots, r_n \rangle$. Whereupon, the principal questions are: what principles of justice informed whatever algorithm was used; and is the allocation that is produced *fair*?

In this section, we give a brief overview of theories of distributive justice from Aristotle to Rawls via Marx, consider various definitions of 'fairness', and finish with a summary of Rescher's theory of distributive justice.

7.3.1 *A Brief Review of Distributive Justice*

Distributive justice dates back, at least, to Ancient Greece, with Aristotle's maxim, also referred to as principle of distributive justice, stating that "equals should be treated equally, and unequals unequally, in proportion to the relevant similarities and differences" (Bartlett and Collins, 2011).

Since that time, the question of distributive justice has been addressed by many different philosophers of the Enlightenment, such as Hobbes, Mills, Kant and Rousseau. Consequently, there are many different theories. However, these can generally be classified into three main groups: firstly, *equality* and *need*; secondly, *utilitarianism and welfare economics*; and thirdly, *equity and desert*.

The first group, *equality and need*, is characterised by its concern for the welfare of those least advantaged in the society. This inspires the *need principle*, which seeks for an equal satisfaction of basic needs. Theories in this family include, *inter alia* egalitarianism, Marxism and Rawls' theory of justice (Rawls, 1971), among others. Egalitarianism can be broadly described as the doctrine that all people are equal and warrant equal resources, rights and opportunities. The distributive element of Marxism can be, again *very* broadly, summarised by the well-known phrase "from each according to his abilities; to each according to his needs".

Rawl's theory of justice stems in part from his analysis of the *veil of ignorance*, a thought experiment which asks people what sort of society they would prefer to live in (egalitarian, monarchical, authoritarian) if they *did not know* what social status (position or rank) they would occupy in such a society. From this Rawls derived two central principles: the principle of Greatest Equal Liberty, and the twin principles of Difference and Equal Opportunity. In articulating these principles (see Rawls, 1971), Rawls was formulating a theory of politics and socio-economics as much as philosophy.

The second group, *utilitarianism and welfare economics*, relies on the *efficiency principle*, which seeks to maximise the global surplus (also referred to as outcome, utility, satisfaction) of the society. Hence, it does not deal with individual outcomes, but in the aggregation of these. In this group there are, among others, the utilitarianism theory (Bentham, 1948 [1789]), Pareto-principle-based theories and envy-freeness, some of which have previously been encountered in the discussion of evaluating game outcomes (see Chapter 3).

The third group, *equity and desert*, advocates for a dependence of allocations on the actions of each individual, according to the *equity principle*. This principle states that an individual should receive an allocation that is proportional to her contributions (either positive or negative) to the society. Theories in this family include *equity theory*, which compares the ratio of costs and benefits to each individual concerned, and Nozick's entitlement theory of justice (Nozick, 1974). Entitlement theory states that given a just distribution d, then any distribution d' derived from d by legitimate means is also just. Legitimate means included voluntary transactions, rectification of a previous wrong, and appropriation, provided what is appropriated does not have an owner and would not disadvantage others. This group also includes a theory of retributive justice called *desert theory* (Walen, 2020), which essentiality states that the punishment should be proportional to the offence (although the theory is considerably more nuanced than that).

This classification is also reviewed by Moulin (2003), who defines four principles of distributive justice: *compensation*, *fitness*, *reward* and *exogenous rights*. The principle of *compensation* is related to the *equality and need* family; that of *fitness* to *utilitarianism*; and the *reward* principle to *equity and desert*. The fourth principle, *exogenous rights*, is not linked to any of the three groups mentioned above, and it takes into account aspects that are not related to the consumption or production of the resources being distributed. It can be subdivided into *equal exogenous rights* (e.g. right to vote, right to access health care, etc.), and *unequal exogenous rights* (e.g. related to private property, social level, etc.).

A more detailed description of these groups and the different theories in each of them can be found in Konow (2003). In his work, Konow also mentions that justice is context-dependent, and that one cannot use a justice theory in isolation, but should also take into account aspects such as culture, historical context, specificities of individuals or groups, etc.: this is what is referred to as local justice (Elster, 1992). This includes the question of whether or not the algorithm respected the principles of justice, community values and various other objective and subjective metrics. (See, in this context, Jasso's theory of distributive justice (Jasso, 1978), which proposes that justice evaluations are a two-step process: a cognitive formulaic step, and an 'emotive' step involving logarithms of the cognitive step; this theory has its critics (Soltan, 1981).)

Thus, while two justice systems may use the same underlying principles, they may end up producing completely different outcomes, depending on the context in which each of them is actually used. Konow also points out that the choice of a justice theory should not be limited to one belonging to one family or another, but that different theories may be combined, in what he calls *pluralistic justice*.

7.3.2 *Fairness*

Regarding fairness in Computer Science, much work has been done in the area of communication networks. However, the main goal of having fair allocations in this case is to improve the system's performance, usually through load balancing and flow control (Mazumdar *et al.*, 1991; Kelly *et al.*, 1998). Motivated by the network scenario, Lan *et al.* (2010) presents a set of axioms that define some families of fairness measures, including many of the previously described metrics in other works, capturing also principles and theories of fairness coming from social sciences (e.g. Gini, Jain, Atkinson indices, entropy, α-fair utility). However, the work presents *how to define* fairness measures, but not *how to achieve* such fair allocations. Furthermore, in the network domain, there is an absolute control of who can and cannot use the resources at any given time, thus the problem of non-compliant agents does not need to be addressed.

More generally, fairness in Computer Science has been linked to increasing system efficiency (Nagle, 1987; Mo and Walrand, 2000). This is specially the case for network or grid computing systems, where a fair distribution of work among different nodes or servers is sought not to keep the servers 'happy', but because it leads to an increased throughput or performance. Lately, however, there has been more interest in including the social aspects of fairness into computational systems. For instance, the field of Computational Social Choice (Chevaleyre *et al.*, 2007) builds the bridge between some aspects of Social Sciences and the area of Multi-Agent Systems, wherein a specific concern is to define metrics and design computational models that encourage (or compel) rational agents to determine an optimal or fair allocation of resources (i.e. mechanism design).

The issue of fairness has been studied both in Social Sciences (Philosophy, Economics and Political Science) and Computer Science (especially Networks and Multi-Agent Systems). While the underlying question in both areas is the same, *is the allocation or distribution of resources among the participants fair*, the rationale for seeking such a fair distribution varies between fields.

However, regarding a formal definition of fairness, there is no agreement on what precisely it is and how it can be measured. Fairness embraces a number of different aspects, including (for n agents), for example, the following properties of a method and its outcomes:

- **Proportional:** Each agent receives $1/n$th of the resource allocation;
- **Envy-free:** No agent i 'prefers' the allocation of any agent j;
- **Equitable:** Each agent derives the same utility from its allocation;
- **Efficient:** The greatest good of the greatest number; those who need resources most or can make maximum use of them, receive them;
- **Cost-effective:** Computing the distribution does not 'cost' a disproportionate amount of resources (especially critical in systems with endogenous resources where the computation of the allocation must be 'paid for' from resources to be allocated); and
- **Timely:** The computation terminates sufficiently quickly for the resources to maintain their utility.

There is also a tension between these different properties: a proportional distribution might not be efficient; a cost-effective and timely method might not produce an equitable or envy-free distribution, and so on. Moreover, in most of the literature these properties are used to analyse static problems (i.e. distribute the set of resources to the set of agents at a given instant), and therefore do not take into account temporal aspects (e.g. a sequence of allocation problems involving the same agents). This is of great importance when dealing with an economy of scarcity, since by its own definition (i.e. fewer available resources than those required) almost any distribution at one time would be considered unfair according to the above-mentioned properties, due to some agents not receiving any resources.

Some theories from Social Sciences conflate fairness with justice, in the sense that a fairer distribution of wealth or resources leads to a more just society (Konow, 2003). In this context, fairness mechanisms focus on keeping the participants as happy or satisfied as possible, thus avoiding situations where unsatisfied participants start misbehaving, with all the negative effects that could cause to the society (although see Sec. 10.5). However, most approaches remain monistic, with only one fairness criteria being used at any given time. Moreover, as pointed out by De Jong (Jong and Tuyls, 2011), some of the designed fairness models cannot be actually realised, either because of their computational complexity, or due to the fact that one cannot force autonomous agents to behave fairly. This latter observation is very relevant to open systems, where the agents' behaviour is not controlled by the system's designer, which creates opportunities for non-compliant agents that may not be willing to act according to the system rules. Even in De Jong's work, which tries to avoid such shortcomings, the resulting model is still monistic.

Therefore, conflating fairness with justice simply transfers the question of "what is fairness" to one of "what is justice", and does not explain why one would have two terms for the same 'thing'. However, the planet Venus has two denotations, depending on context, as the Morning Star or the Evening Star. So, while some treat the terms as synonymous, others draw a distinction between justice and fairness. For example, one distinction is to define justice as the adherence to rules of conduct, and fairness as individuals' moral evaluation of this conduct (Goldman and Cropanzano, 2014). The approach we will follow is to think of it as much the same 'thing', it just depends when or how you look at it. So we will more or less go with the idea that the issue of justice is concerned with deciding which principles and criteria are to be used to determine what is, and is not, due to one person (relative to others), akin to an adherence to the rules of conduct; while the issue of fairness is concerned with evaluating whether or not that person did indeed receive what was due, i.e. individuals' moral evaluation of this conduct (and to complete the self-referentiality, answering the question "in all fairness, was justice done"?). Then, instead of picking one particular criteria, resource allocation should be made according to several criteria: Rescher's Theory of Distributive Justice, as reviewed next, does just that. An evaluation of fairness from an external perspective through procedural justice is given in Sec. 7.6, while an internal evaluation using interactional justice will be studied in Chapter 9.

7.3.3 *Rescher's Theory of Distributive Justice*

The preceding reviews of both justice and fairness both effectively reached the same endpoint: the need for a pluralistic approach. Therefore, any theory of distributive justice needs to allow for multiple different criteria (i.e. principles) to be combined, and in self-organising multi-agent systems, allow the agents to select the criteria, and give them the option to define and change how each criteria is weighted, thus accounting for any context dependency in the agent society.

We propose to use Rescher's Theory of Distributive Justice.

Rescher's analysis of distributive justice concludes that the Principle of Utility, taken as a fairness metric expressed as "the greater good of the greater number", is but one of many prevailing considerations which need to be taken into account when determining a 'fair' allocation of resources. Rescher then argued that an adequate theory of distributive justice requires coordination of the concepts of justice, construed in terms of fairness and equity, and of utility, in the sense of general welfare.

Rescher observed that distributive justice had been held, by various sources, to consist of treating people wholly or primarily according to one of seven *canons* (established principles expressed

Table 7.1. Rescher's Canons of Distributive Justice

1	Treatment as equals.
2	Treatment according to their needs.
3	Treatment according to their actual productive contribution.
4	Treatment according to their efforts and sacrifices.
5	Treatment according to a valuation of their socially useful services.
6	Treatment according to supply and demand.
7	Treatment according to their ability, merit or achievements.

in English). These canons are summarised in Table 7.1, as the canons of equality, need, ability, effort, productivity, social utility and supply & demand.

Rescher argued that each canon, taken in isolation, was inadequate as the sole dispensary of distributive justice. Instead, his position was that distributive justice was found in treating people according to their *legitimate claims*, both positive and negative, with respect to which canons are relevant. This placed the emphasis for distributive justice onto the questions of: what the legitimate claims are, how they are accommodated in case of plurality, and how they are reconciled in case of conflict.

In the next section, we consider the algorithmic representation of legitimate claims in the context of a scenario with provision to and appropriation from an endogenous resource, and how to deal with plurality and reconciliation of those legitimate claims.

Essentially, Rescher's idea of legitimate claims gives us principles and criteria of distributive justice for specifying an algorithm for deciding an allocation of resources (Rescher, 1966, p. 81ff). Moreover, an algorithmic specification of Rescher's legitimate claims will be used to distribute the resources, the metric for computing the actual fairness of its outcome can be completely independent from the actual distribution method. For this purpose, there are many quantitative metrics for calculating 'fairness' objectively, including some metrics from the communication networks field, such as the Jain index (Jain et al., 1984) or the Max–Min metric (Cao and Zegura, 1999), as well as from Social Sciences, with the income inequality measures such as the Atkinson index (Atkinson, 1970), the Hoover index (also called the Robin Hood index) or the Gini index (Gini, 1912).

These income inequality metrics measure the statistical dispersion of a distribution, that is, how close or far apart the values of the distribution are. For a distribution where every individual has the same income, the dispersion is null. As the difference of incomes among individuals increases, so does the dispersion (inequality) measure. Among the mentioned measures, the Gini index is the most widely used, being commonly found in studies not only on economics (e.g. the Organisation for Economic Co-operation and Development (OECD) uses this index to measure income inequality), but also in other fields such as ecology (e.g. to measure biodiversity), education (e.g. to measure differences between universities) or health care (e.g. to compare quality of life), to name but a few. In this chapter, in order to measure fairness, we will use the Gini index; however, an alternative approach based on *interactional justice* is given in Chapter 9.

7.4 Distributive Justice

In this section, we will describe the formalisation and operationalisation of an Ostrom institution (Chapter 6) with a set of n agents playing an iterated Linear Public Good game (LPG') under an economy of scarcity (Sec. 6.3). First, we introduce a new agent metric, *satisfaction*, which will be used to determine an agent's 'pleasure' or 'displeasure' at the outcome of a round of resource allocation and the basis for their continued participation; and second, introduce a new agent behaviour, *compliance*, which determines whether or not an agent will conform to the institutional rules on provision and appropriation actions.

Then we will address Rescher's three questions in this context: firstly, the representation of legitimate claims in this context; secondly, how to accommodate multiple claims in the case of plurality, for which we give an algorithm detailing how claims are used to determine the resource allocation; and finally, how to reconcile claims in the case of conflict, for which, assuming *ab initio* an equal weight on each claim, we then show how the present allocation is used by the agents to re-assign the weights on the claims to give 'fairer' future allocations. We end with a summary of some experimental results. For full details, see Pitt *et al.* (2014).

7.4.1 Satisfaction and Compliance

Independent of its utility, each agent i in a collective action situation (institution) C makes a *subjective* assessment of its *satisfaction* $\sigma_{i,C}$, represented as a value in $[0, 1]$, based on its allocation in relation to its demands. Each agent increases its satisfaction in the next round if it is allocated at least the same as its demand in the current round, and decreases it otherwise:

$$\sigma_{i,C}(t+1) = \begin{cases} \sigma_{i,C}(t) + \varphi \cdot (1 - \sigma_{i,C}(t)) & \text{if } r_i \geqslant d_i \\ \sigma_{i,C}(t) - \psi \cdot \sigma_{i,C}(t) & \text{otherwise} \end{cases}$$

where φ_i and ψ_i are also private coefficients in $[0, 1]$ which determine the rate of reinforcement of, respectively, satisfaction and dissatisfaction. By choosing different values of φ and ψ, we can model different "personalities" of the agents (e.g. a high φ and a low ψ would model an excessively optimistic agent; both high φ and ψ would model a mood-swinging agent, and so on). We also define a threshold or cut-off value τ and an interval value m, such that if for m consecutive rounds, an agent i evaluates $\sigma_i(C, t) < \tau$ as true, then it will leave institution C. It will not re-join an institution it has previously left. Given this leaving condition, the value of ψ has a direct impact on the endurance or volatility of the system (i.e. high ψ values will make the agents be dissatisfied more quickly, and therefore they will probably leave the system earlier than with lower values of ψ).

Agents are implemented with a simple strategy regarding compliance with the LPG' game rules. Each agent has a fixed probability of cheating $pCheat$ each round and a cheating strategy $cheatOn$. The latter denotes which action they will cheat on, *provision*, *demand* or *appropriate*. A compliant agent i will provision what they generate ($p_i = g_i$), demand what they need ($d_i = q_i$), and appropriate what they are allocated ($r'_i = r_i$). The cheating behaviour for each of these actions is as follows:

- $p_i = g_i * rand(0, 1)$ — Reduces the usual provision (equal to the resources generated by the agent in this round) by a random factor between 0 and 1.
- $d_i = q_i + rand(0, 1) * (1 - q_i)$ — Randomly increases the quantity demanded above what the agent needs.
- $r'_i = r_i + rand(0, 1) * (1 - r_i)$ — Increases the quantity appropriated above what the agent has been allocated.

Note that the five coefficients (three for calculating utility and two for calculating satisfaction) and the satisfaction threshold values (τ, m), as well as the cheating strategy, need not be the same for every agent. The experiments in Sec. 7.4.5 do use homogeneous populations with all the agents having the same coefficient values, although there will be mixed populations of compliant and non-compliant (cheating) agents.

7.4.2 Representing Legitimate Claims

In the context of a self-governing institution for endogenous resource provision and appropriation according to the LPG' game, we note that there individual facts are made public, i.e. the demand, d_i, and the allocation, r_i. We assume that the provision p_i and appropriation r'_i are monitored, and 'normative' satisfaction σ_i (i.e. what the satisfaction should be for an 'ordinary' agent if it had a generic α and β, irrespective of its actual, internal satisfaction). The basic role of *prosumer* determines which agent is and is not a member of the institution, and there is one distinguished role, the *head*, who is responsible for the allocation.

Using this information, the legitimate claims, each of which determine the relative merit of the member's claims, can be defined by the following functions that compute a total order over the set of members. Note that T denotes the total number of rounds of the LPG' game played in an institution C, and $T_{\{i \in C\}}$ denotes the number of rounds that agent i has played (been present) in that institution. This is shown in Table 7.2.

7.4.3 Computing a Resource Allocation

This deals with the question of representing legitimate claims. To accommodate multiple claims, each canon f_* is treated as a *voter* in a Borda count protocol. Under Borda count voting, each vote ranks the list of candidates in order of preference. Borda points are assigned to each candidate in the list: for example, with n candidates, rank k scores $n-k+1$ Borda points. Borda points from each vote are summed to give a total Borda score for each candidate. The Borda count protocol satisfies a number of mathematical voting system criteria, and is often described as a consensus voting system because it tends

Table 7.2. Representation of Legitimate Claims in LPG'

Equals	↑ Average allocation ↑	$\frac{\sum_{t=0}^{T} r_i(t)}{T_{i \in C}}$
	↑ 'Normative' satisfaction	σ_i
	↑ Allocation frequency	$\frac{\sum_{t=0}^{T}(r_i(t)>0)}{T_{i \in C}}$
Needs	↑ Average demands	$\frac{\sum_{t=0}^{T} d_i(t)}{T_{i \in C}}$
Contribution	↓ Average provision	$\frac{\sum_{t=0}^{T} p_i(t)}{T_{i \in C}}$
Effort	↓ Number of rounds present	$|\mathbf{T}_{\{i \in C\}}|$
Social utility	↓ Time as $head$	$|\{t | role\_of(i,t) = head\}|$
Supply & demand	↓ Compliance	$|\{t | r'_i(t) = r_i(t)\}|$
Ability, merits...		n/a

to elect broadly acceptable candidates rather than those preferred just by a majority. This makes it well-suited as a voting protocol returning multiple winners.

In our case, each voting function f_* rank orders all the agents in a candidate list according to the relative grounds for their claims, and the Borda score for each agent is computed from the accumulation of Borda points associated with each vote. Normally, in a Borda count protocol, the candidate with the highest Borda score wins, but we may have multiple 'winners', so we form a Borda point queue in descending order of Borda score, and allocate resources to the front of the queue until there are no more to allocate.

To reconcile conflicts between multiple claims, a *weight* $w_* \in [0, 1]$ is attached to each function $f_* \in F$. The Borda score B of agent i under a set of functions F is given by:

$$B(i, F) = \sum_{*=1}^{|F|} w_* \cdot bpts(f_*(i))$$

where $f_*(i)$ computes the rank order assigned to agent i by each f_*, $bpts()$ computes the Borda points for that rank, and w_* is the weight attached to the corresponding function.

Figure 7.3 shows a flow diagram of how the legitimate claims are combined to compute *Borda_ptq*. The full procedure is specified in Algorithm 1. Note that the function **Borda_count** computes the Borda score B for each agent i and returns the monotonic list *Borda_ptq*.

$$A = \{a_1, a_2, a_3\}$$

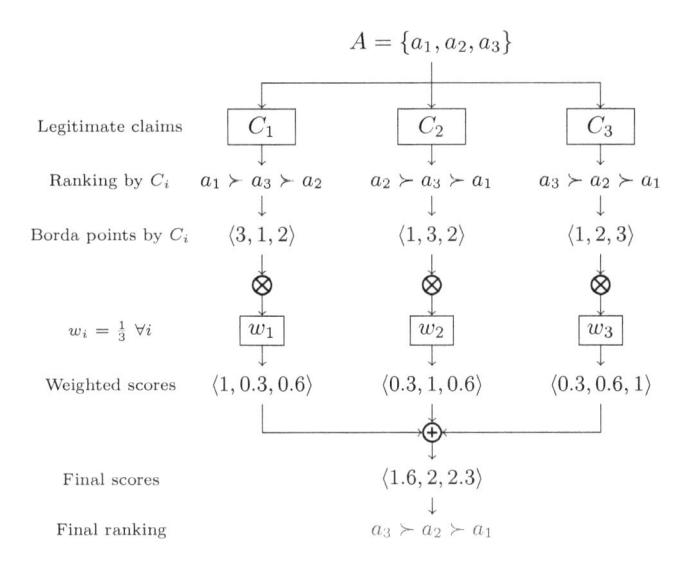

	C_1	C_2	C_3
Legitimate claims			
Ranking by C_i	$a_1 \succ a_3 \succ a_2$	$a_2 \succ a_3 \succ a_1$	$a_3 \succ a_2 \succ a_1$
Borda points by C_i	$\langle 3, 1, 2 \rangle$	$\langle 1, 3, 2 \rangle$	$\langle 1, 2, 3 \rangle$
$w_i = \frac{1}{3} \forall i$	w_1	w_2	w_3
Weighted scores	$\langle 1, 0.3, 0.6 \rangle$	$\langle 0.3, 1, 0.6 \rangle$	$\langle 0.3, 0.6, 1 \rangle$
Final scores		$\langle 1.6, 2, 2.3 \rangle$	
Final ranking		$a_3 \succ a_2 \succ a_1$	

Fig. 7.3. Schematic View of the Computation of Agent Ranking Using Legitimate Claims

7.4.4 Self-Organising the Weights

At the end of each round of the LPG' game, the agents self-organise the weights on the voting functions. There are three motivations to be considered in this self-organisation: maximising self-interest, avoiding path dependency, and restoring a homeostatic equilibrium. Therefore, we define three functions for computing new weights. The first function assumes that the agents vote for self-interest (i.e. for the functions that give them each the highest rank). The second function aims to resist entrenched self-interest and avoid path dependency based on the 'distance' between the voting function's output and the actual allocation. Finally, the third function applies an autonomic mechanism via a form of 'institutional homeostasis' on the legitimate claims.

Each voting function f_* outputs a rank order of the agents, which is effectively a vector represented by $\mathbf{f}_*$. We denote by $idx_C(i, \mathbf{f}_*)$ the index position of each agent i participating in the institution C in vector $\mathbf{f}_*$.

Assuming that each agent i votes for its preference for which function should have more weight in the next round according to its

ALGORITHM 1: Resource Allocation with Legitimate Claims

input : $A \leftarrow$ set of n agents
input : $F \leftarrow$ set of m voting functions f_* each with weight w_*
output: allocation $R : A \to \mathbb{R}$

1 **foreach** $\textit{agent } i \in A$ **do**
2 $\quad d_i \leftarrow i.\text{demand}$;
3 $\quad p_i \leftarrow i.\text{provision}$;
4 $\quad r_i \leftarrow 0$;
5 $P \leftarrow \sum_{i=1}^{n} p_i$;
6 $\textit{rank\_orders} \leftarrow [\,]$;
7 **foreach** $\textit{function } f_* \in F$ **do**
8 $\quad \textit{rank\_orders} \leftarrow \textit{rank\_orders} \cup f_*(A)$;
9 $\textit{Borda\_ptq} \leftarrow \mathsf{Borda\_count}(\textit{rank\_orders}, F)$
10 **repeat**
11 $\quad i \leftarrow \mathsf{head}(\textit{Borda\_ptq})$;
12 $\quad \textit{Borda\_ptq} \leftarrow \mathsf{tail}(\textit{Borda\_ptq})$;
13 $\quad$ **if** $P \geqslant d_i$ **then**
14 $\quad\quad r_i \leftarrow d_i$;
15 $\quad\quad P \leftarrow P - d_i$;
16 $\quad$ **else**
17 $\quad\quad r_i \leftarrow P$;
18 $\quad\quad P \leftarrow 0$;
19 **until** $P == 0$;

position in the rank order of this round, each agent i's vote is a rank order of the functions, which is effectively a vector represented by **i**. Note that:

$$idx_C(f_x, \mathbf{i}) < idx_C(f_y, \mathbf{i}) \to idx_C(i, \mathbf{f}_x) \leqslant idx_C(i, \mathbf{f}_y)$$

The Borda points for each function is given by the sum of the indices in **i** of the functions which gave that agent the same position, divided by the number of those functions. For example, suppose we had four functions which ranked agent i second, third, third and fourth. Then agent i's vote would give the first function 4 Borda points, the second and third functions 2.5 Borda points each (i.e. a half share of $3+2$), and the fourth function 1 Borda point. We denote by $Borda(f, \mathbf{i})$ the Borda points assigned to function f by the vote of i.

For each function $f_* \in F$, its total Borda points with respect to institution C is then given by:

$$Borda(f_*, C) = \Sigma_{i \in C} Borda(f_*, \mathbf{i})$$

and the updated weight w_* of each f_* is given by:

$$w_*(t) = w_*(t) + w_*(t) \cdot \frac{Borda\,(f_*, C) - AvgBorda}{TotalBorda} \quad (7.1)$$

A voting function which does better than average will get a higher weight in the next round, while those that do worse than average will get a lower weight. Note that the new weights are summed and normalised to 1.

To counter the self-interest that agents will continue to vote for (and increase the weight on) functions that work best for them, the weights on functions that are closer to the final rank order ($Borda\_ptq(C)$) are reduced, while for those functions that were less 'accurate', the weights are increased. This is computed by taking the Hamming distance (hd) between $\mathbf{f}_*$ and $Borda\_ptq(C)$ and updating the weights on the functions in the next round:

$$w_*(t) = w_*(t) + w_*(t) \cdot \frac{hd\,(\mathbf{f}_*, Borda\_ptq\,(C)) - AvgHD}{TotalHD}$$

Note again that all the new weights are summed and normalised to 1.

Finally, assuming that the 'equilibrium state' to be one gives equal weights to each legitimate claim, then we want to restore that state. If all the agents in the institution comply with the rules, i.e. $|C|$ is the same size as the set that comply according to canon f_6, then each function weight is moderated by the following equation:

$$w_*(t+1) = w_*(t) + \delta \cdot \left(\frac{1}{|F|} - w_*(t)\right) \quad (7.2)$$

Here, δ is a coefficient controlling the tendency of the autonomic mechanism towards either over- or under-compensation.

Determining the weight associated with each claim is an outcome of *self-organisation*: we propose that the agents themselves determine the weights using the collective-choice rules of a self-organising electronic institution.

7.4.5 Some Experimental Results

Two experimental testbeds have been written: one in Prolog and one using the multi-agent simulator and animator PreSage-2 (Macbeth et al., 2014).

The first testbed was a relatively small-scale one implemented in Prolog, with the intention to explore the animation of the EC specification, for rapid prototyping of the algorithms, and to validate the basic properties of the approach (Pitt et al., 2012b).

For example, one set of experiments compared the performance of each of the canons of legitimate claims individually (f_*), in subsets and all together (f_{all}), with f_{1a}, f_{1b} and f_{1c} being distinct claims. f_{all} has two variants, 'fix', which gives all distinct claims equal weight ($w_*(t) = 0.125$), and 'SO', which uses self-organised function weights. One such subset consisted of the two legitimate claims' average demands (canon of needs) and average provision (canon of productive contribution), intuitively corresponding to the Marxist dictum "from each according to his ability; to each according to his needs". It didn't work. In fact, only the full set of all eight claims with the agents self-organising the weights (rather than being fixed) consistently produced sustainable institutions that favoured the compliant agents.

Figure 7.4 shows how the weights on each canon develop in a game with the f_{all} (SO) allocation. The compliant majority's preferences cause higher weights on f_3 and f_6, both of which penalise cheating agents (recall that agents cheat on provision so a lower average provision, as measured by f_3, implies more cheating). Further experiments showed that self-organisation is robust to different cheating

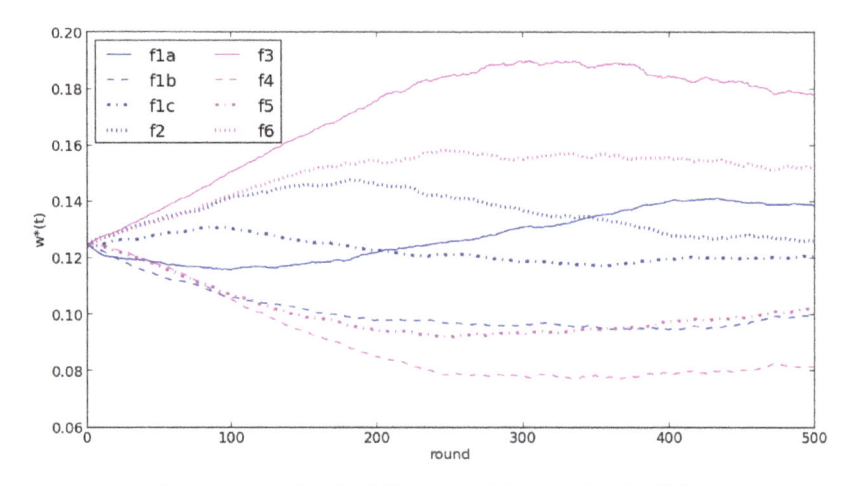

Fig. 7.4. Individual Function Weights for f_{all}(SO)

strategies, i.e. the weights were adjusted to favour whichever canons discriminated against non-compliant agents.

The second experimental platform was implemented using PreSage-2, as a basis for experiments at scale, i.e. with a larger number of agents, over a longer period of time, with multiple institutions; and with greater scope to explore the parameter space, given that the number of independent variables in the agent population alone included:

- The number of agents, and the proportion of non-compliant agents;
- The propensity of non-compliant agents to cheat on provision and/or appropriation;
- The initial satisfaction of agents, and their dissatisfaction threshold before they quit; and
- The coefficients α, β, γ (determining utility), φ and ψ (reinforcing satisfaction), and δ (controlling autonomic mechanism).

However, perhaps the critical variable was the resource allocation method: here there were four values: allocation by random; allocation by ration; allocation by legitimate claims with fixed weights; and allocation by legitimate claims with self-organised weights.

The dependent variables were: the utility of the compliant/non-compliant agents; the endurance of compliant/non-compliant agents and institutions; and the fairness of the resource allocation method.

The full results are detailed in Pitt *et al.* (2014), but in summary allocation by legitimate claims with self-organised weights was as follows:

- The only method that produced enduring institutions, and which benefitted compliant agents over non-compliant ones;
- The fairest method, using the Gini inequality index over accumulated allocations to measure fairness; and
- The method 'preferred' by the compliant agents (i.e. they joined and maintained institutions using this resource allocation method).

A striking outcome was that legitimate claims with self-organised weights led to a fair overall allocation over time, even after a series of relatively unfair allocations (see Fig. 7.5). This shows that, even with decision-making that in the short-term seems 'bad', self-organisation can ensure that in the long-term the outcome emerges as 'good'.

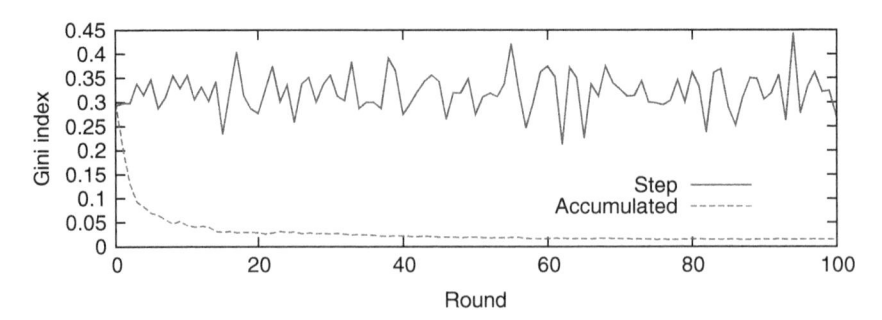

Fig. 7.5. Distributive Justice with Rescher's Legitimate Claims: How a Series of 'Unfair' Allocations Can Produce a 'Fair' Allocation Over Time

7.5 Retributive Justice

In Chapter 5, we considered dealing with expectation of error in open systems with protocols for monitoring regulatory compliance and alternative dispute resolutions. In Chapter 6, we saw how essential monitoring, graduated sanctions and dispute resolution were to the institutional design principles. In this section, we try to contextualise these protocols and design principles with respect to the idea of *retributive justice*.

There is a cultural tendency according to which, when an agent does something wrong, such as non-compliance with a normative system, then the wrongdoer should deserve punishment and, on the contrary, good behaviour should be rewarded.

The philosophers of punishments traditionally distinguish retributivism from utilitarianism. The retributivist perspective holds that punishment is a necessary consequence of committing an offence (the punishment of past wrongdoing). Retributivists assert that non-moral agency deserves to be punished in order to maintain a moral order: Kant asserted that no principle but retribution was a legitimate basis for punishment. This contrasts with the utilitarian notions of justice according to which punishment is justified by its potential benefits, in particular, the avoidance of future wrongdoing. From the most common utilitarian perspective, a punishment should bring some loss of utility to the wrongdoing agent; and the justification for the punishment is that this loss of utility acts as a deterrent to future wrongdoing, both to prevent recidivism (the same agent repeating the wrongdoing) and to encourage other agents to refrain from offending.

Whatever justification for punishment is established, practical questions then arise regarding the design of a punishment system. This includes the forms of punishment, e.g. whether the sanction should be a fine or the suspension of a licence, and the principles of punishment, e.g. a commonly-held principle is that a punishment should be proportionate to the severity of the wrongdoing. In this view, Ostrom (1990) maintained that a system of *graduated sanctions* was a necessary condition for enduring commons, but also that there should be a fast and effective dispute-resolution system. There are also different compensation strategies for *restorative* justice, i.e. making good for loss suffered as a consequence of wrongdoing and to favour forgiveness. As a concrete example of possible restorative alternatives, when there is a breach of contract, one may consider the position where the victim would have been in if the contract had been fulfilled or, alternatively, if the contract had never been signed.

7.5.1 *Experimental Setting*

Recall that one of the reasons for moving from the LPG game to the LPG' game was the idea that the former makes several 'unrealistic' assumptions:

- That in the general setting of an open system, there is no *full disclosure* of agents' internals to check compliance;
- There is no opportunity to cheat on appropriation, so that what is allocated is what is appropriated: however, in practice agents can 'cheat' on appropriation by taking more than they are allocated;
- It is assumed that monitoring costs are essentially 'free', but in a computational system with endogenous resources, the cost of monitoring (and of computing the resource allocation) has to be 'paid for' using the same pool of resources as those to be allocated.

Therefore, we consider an institution C in which it is impossible for any agent to 'audit' another for compliance, agents can break the conventional rules on provision and appropriation, and monitoring is not cost-free.

The resource allocation rule for C is $Ration^+$. This is a mapping from an (indexed) set of demands (for resources) by the agents in C

to an (indexed) set of allocations, given by:
$$Ration^+ : \{d_i\}_{i \in C} \to \{r_i\}_{i \in C}$$
Three further operational choice rules are designed to regulate the agents' participation in C. These are as follows:

(1) *Provision* rule — an agent must provide what it has available:
$$ocr_p : \forall i \in C, p_i = g_i$$

(2) *Appropriation* rule — an agent must not appropriate more than it has been allocated:
$$ocr_a : \forall i \in C, r'_i \leqslant r_i$$

(3) *Moderation* rule — an agent must not demand more than it needs:
$$ocr_m : \forall i \in C, d_i \leqslant q_i$$

Of the six values involved in these three rules, we can distinguish between:

- Two *internal* values, g_i and q_i, whose values, we assume, cannot be determined except by disclosure or an audit of agent i's local state.
- One *externalised* value, d_i, whose value is determined individually and disclosed (as an institutional fact) by each empowered agent i (in the role of *prosumer* in institution C).
- One *computed* value, r_i, which is an institutional fact whose value is determined by the resource allocation rule and initiated by one empowered agent, h, who occupies the role of the *head* of the institution.
- Two *physical* values, p_i and r'_i, which can be asserted as institutional facts, either objectively by monitoring the corresponding provision and appropriation actions (at a certain cost), or subjectively by disclosing the corresponding action (which we assume is verified 'for free').

Assuming that the physical values can be monitored but the internal values cannot be audited, it is possible to monitor an agent's provision but impossible to verify compliance with the rule. Therefore, we only have one monitoring function for the appropriation action:
$$monitor\_ocr_a : \forall i \in C, (i, r_i, r'_i) \to Boolean$$

The monitor rule takes an agent, its allocation and its appropriation, and returns *true* if the appropriation is larger than or equal to the allocation (i.e. the agent has been caught 'cheating'), and *false* otherwise. Related to the monitoring rule is the cost of applying the rule, which can be used to inform a decision about the frequency of monitoring, up to a certain maximum level. (Recall monitoring has to be 'paid for' from the same resources that are being appropriated.) These values, like those for the graduated sanctions, are determined by collective-choice rules.

7.5.2 Policy Specification

The policy specification for monitoring in this action situation is, as before, given by a set of domain-dependent EC axioms which define the institutionalised powers of the agents to initiate or terminate institutional facts. (In this specification, we use a different representation of *role*. There are multiple ways of representing role and the choice of representation depends on whether agents belong to multiple institutions, whether they can have multiple roles, etc. There is nothing contingent on this.)

In this action situation, there is scope for intentional or unintentional error, therefore the *report* action is performed if an agent detects a violation. This occurs when it is unable to collect its full appropriation, and is inevitable if some other agent violates the appropriation rule by taking more than it was allocated. An agent is empowered to report a violation if it is a *prosumer* in the institution, and secondly, if it appropriated less than it was allocated (because the common pool was exhausted):

$report(A, Rule, G, C)$ initiates $reported(A, Rule, G, C) = true$ at $T \leftarrow$
  $\mathbf{pow}(A, report(A, Rule, G, C)) = true$ holdsAt T

$\mathbf{pow}(A, report(A, Rule, G, C)) = true$ holdsAt $T \leftarrow$
  $current\_game(C) = G$ holdsAt $T \wedge$
  $allocated(A, G, C) = Ri$ holdsAt $T \wedge$
  $appropriated(A, G, C) = R'_i$ holdsAt $T \wedge$
  $R'_i < R_i \wedge$
  $reported(A, Rule, G, C) = false$ holdsAt $T \wedge$
  $role(A, prosumer, C) = true$ holdsAt T

The axiomatic specification can be directly expressed in Prolog to give an executable specification. At the end of one round of the LPG' game, it is used to compute the institutionalised powers of the agent occupying the role of *head*. For example, consider the following narrative (extract) comprising actions performed by agents g, h and p, occurring between $T = 1610$ and $T = 1678$ in the 21st round of the LPG' game played in the institution called cluster1 (note that the syntactic sugar of the specification the infix happensAt predicate has been replaced by the prefix happens):

```
happens(demand(p,0.4040986,21,cluster1),1610).
happens(demand(g,0.93242,21,cluster1),1622).
happens(allocate(h,p,0.4040986,21,cluster1),1631).
happens(allocate(h,g,0.409146,21,cluster1),1646).
happens(disclose(g,0.2780482,21,cluster1),1670).
happens(monitor(h,p,0.53519,21,cluster1),1675).
happens(report(g,ocr_a,21,cluster1),1677).
happens(gameover(h,21,cluster1),1678).
```

Then the Prolog findall query returns the following results:

```
?- findall( PAction, holdsAt( pow( h, PAction )=true,
1679 ), IP ). IP=[increment(h, ocr_a, 21, cluster1),
sanction(h, p, ocr_a, cluster1)].
```

This means that in cluster1, agent h occupies the role of *head* and is empowered both to increase the monitoring frequency of the ocr_a rule (as reported by agent g), and to sanction agent p which violated the ocr_a rule.

The fluents with which we were particularly concerned for the system of retributive justice were as follows:

Fluent	Dom	Description
$maxmf(C)$	$\mathbb{N}^0$	Maximum monitoring frequency of C
$mf(C)$	$\mathbb{N}^0$	Current monitoring frequency of C
$mfct(G,C)$	$\mathbb{N}^0$	Number of *monitor* actions performed during G
$decmf\_ctr(C)$	$\mathbb{N}^0$	Number of rounds since last reported violation

For any institution C, $maxmf(C)$ was fixed, but $mf(C)$ could be incremented or decremented by an empowered agent (e.g. h in the narrative above) performing the appropriate action to increment (or decrement) this value, for example:

$increment(A, Rule, G, C)$ initiates $mf(C) = F1$ at $T \leftarrow$
  $\mathbf{pow}(A, increment(A, Rule, G, C)) = true$ holdsAt T $\wedge$
  $mf(GC) = F$ holdsAt T $\wedge$
  $maxmf(C) = M$ holdsAt T $\wedge$
  $F < M$ $\wedge$
  $F1 = F + 1$ $\wedge$
  $role(A, prosum, C) = true$ holdsAt T

This meant that when a violation was reported, the head agent could increase the number of monitoring actions performed in any game round G, up to the maximum monitoring frequency $maxmf(C)$. If no violations were reported for a certain number of rounds, the same agent was empowered to decrement the number of monitoring actions.

7.5.3 Experimental Results

A variation of the testbed described in the previous section was implemented to investigate self-organisation of the system of retributive justice in the context of the LPG' game. There is one institution playing iterated rounds of the game. Each round follows the steps outlined previously. In each round, each agent generates (privately) its available and needed resources and declares (publicly) its provided and demanded resources. Each agent now had a new parameter $pCheat$: with probability $pCheat$ an agent will provide fewer resources than it has available (i.e. it violates rule ocr_p, although the violation cannot be detected). The resources are pooled, the monitoring costs are subtracted, and the allocation computed using a rationing rule (each agent is allocated an equal share; if its share exceeds its demand, the excess is re-allocated equally to those that have received less, and so on).

The findings of these experiments are reported in Pitt and Schaumeier (2012). The maximum monitoring frequency was required, otherwise if cheating was sufficiently frequent, then the agents would increase the current monitoring frequency uncontrollably, and exhaust all their pooled resources on monitoring, leaving nothing left to allocate. However, the optimal values of maximum monitoring frequency and sanctioning method critically depended on the profile of the agent population: excessive monitoring resulted in unnecessary costs and overall it would have been better to tolerate a 'low level' of non-compliance; however, stronger sanctions are not necessarily better for a generally compliant population — it seems that it is as easy to wreck a self-organising system by excessive monitoring and over-strict sanctioning as it is by non-compliant behaviour.

These results replicate findings on enforcement in open systems reported in Balke *et al.* (2013). Both these studies show that specific decisions need to be made about the retributive justice system, but that this system should be subject to the same collective choice processes (i.e. participation in election by those affected by them), and that it also needs to be congruent with the environment — and the environment includes the behaviour of the agents themselves.

7.6 Procedural Justice

The three previous sections have addressed the first question presented in this chapter, the principles and criteria for determining an allocation of rewards, or punishments, that is 'fair'. We turn now to the second question, ensuring that the allocation *procedure* itself is *fit-for-purpose*.

This is the domain of **procedural justice** that is concerned with ensuring that rules and procedures are not just satisfying the requirement for 'fairness', but also satisfy a range of other criteria such as 'transparency', efficiency and cost. For example, recall that *Robert's Rules of Order* (Robert *et al.*, 2000) being a comprehensive manual of procedures for conducting business in a deliberative assembly (i.e. a group of individuals making a decision about some policy or course of action, and mutually agreeing on some conventional rules and procedures which regulate how that decision is to be made) has achieved its longevity and status not just because consultation is effective, but also because the application is effective.

Concepts of procedural justice, i.e. what makes a procedure fair and effective, are of concern to many other fields of human endeavour as well as political deliberation, including dispute resolution in law, public health, organisational psychology, and philosophy. This has led to a number of different definitions, for example, procedural justice is ...:

- ... a theory of procedural fairness for civil dispute resolution (Solum, 2004) (and see Chapter 5);
- ... a requirement for a community to engage in a democratic process to determine which public health functions the authorities should maintain, with respect to a trade-off between costs and benefits (Kass, 2001) and a justification for their decisions (Uphsur, 2002);
- ... a four-component model derived from the interaction of procedural function and source (Blader and Tyler, 2003); and
- ... subject to a graded distinction between perfect, imperfect and pure procedural justice (Rawls, 1971).

Solum (2004) contends that a theory of procedural justice must address two problems, an 'easy' and a 'hard' one. The 'easy' problem is to produce accurate outcomes at acceptable cost, what has been referred to as the balancing model of procedural justice. The 'hard' problem is concerned with solving how, if perfect accuracy is unattainable, people feel compelled to comply with what they perceive as a mistaken judgement. The resolution to this issue is for two principles of procedural justice to work in harmony: the *participation* principle, which ensures that the procedural arrangements provide 'adequate' participation, and the *accuracy* principle, which ensures that the procedural arrangements provide 'maximum' likelihood of achieving the 'correct' outcome.

Kass (2001) argues that achieving population-oriented (macrolevel) goals in public health (as opposed to individual goals) requires a trade-off between the benefits and effectiveness of a proposed health policy to the population as a whole against the burdens (costs) and possible infringements of civil liberties imposed on the individuals separately. Fair procedures should be used to determine which burdens are acceptable to the community in return for the benefits.

Also in the field of public health, Uphsur (2002) cites the *transparency* principle, that public health authorities are obliged to communicate the grounds for their actions and decisions, and allow an appeals process (again, a capacity for review).

The four-component model of procedural justice (Blader and Tyler, 2003) contends that people use four types of judgement to evaluate group procedures. These judgements involve evaluating how the formal rules (for group procedures) treat group members and how decisions are made; and evaluating how the group authorities make decisions and treat group members. As such, this is a relational model of procedural justice based on subjective assessments of a procedural function (decision-making) and its source (the group authorities).

Rawls (1971) differentiates between *perfect* procedural justice, which holds if there is an independent criterion for determining a fair outcome of a procedure and a method which guarantees that the fair outcome will result from execution of the procedure. *Imperfect* procedural justice exists if there is such a criterion, but no method that is guaranteed to produce it; and *pure* procedural justice exists if there is no criterion but the procedural method itself.

Based on these definitions, a framework for evaluating institutional status (in terms of its 'fitness for purpose') according to three criteria of imperfect procedural justice, *participation*, *transparency* and *balancing* (i.e. we have defined criteria for evaluating outcomes, but no guarantee that our procedures will achieve 'just' outcome). These three principles can be informally defined as follows.

Firstly, the *participation principle* requires that arrangements for the allocation of resources, the selection of collective-choice methods and the resolution of disputes should be structured to provide each interested party (i.e. each appropriator) with the right to 'adequate' participation. Secondly, the *transparency principle* is the requirement for those making the decision to communicate the justification for their actions and allow for an appeal, by ensuring that any disinterested third party could validate the outcomes from a specification of the process and the given inputs. Thirdly, the *balancing principle* is the requirement to select methods for 'fair' resource allocation and sanction which balance out the relative benefits and burdens (for example, in systems with endogenous resources, the most scrupulously fair method may be prohibitively expensive to compute).

7.6.1 *Participation Principle*

To measure the degree of participation or engagement afforded to the agents by a set of institutional rules, we can identify four dimensions, three of 'space' and one of time, that address the following questions:

- *Empowerment*: What is the distribution of (institutionalised) power within the institution?
- *Inclusivity*: How many of the agents affected by the rule have a saying on how to choose it?
- *Representation*: Are the decisions made solely by agents affected by the rule, or is there any external influence?
- *Decision frequency*: How often a decision about the rule is made, in relationship to its application frequency?

In this section, we will define some possible metrics for each of the principles.

One metric for empowerment could be based on the distribution of institutionalised power among the agents. This would measure the degree and variance in the distribution of institutionalised power within a self-organising electronic institution.

During a given time window W, let $\mathcal{P}$ denote the totality of institutionalised powers available to all the roles, i.e. the set of actions that an agent might be empowered to perform during W, let $\mathcal{P}(i)$ denote the subset of $\mathcal{P}$ that agent i is both empowered and permitted to perform in the window, and let $N(p)$ be the number of agents with power and permission of exercising p (i.e. $N(p) = |\{i \mid p \in \mathcal{P}(i), i \in \mathcal{A}\}|)$.

Then, for a window with start point t_s and end point t_e (i.e. $W = [t_s, t_e]$), the relative (institutionalised) power of each agent in W (in some institution) can be represented in the following generic form:

$$\text{RelIP}_W = [\mathcal{P}; p_1, \ldots, p_n]_W$$

where (dropping the subscript W for the window as is obvious from context):

$$p_i = \sum_{p \in \mathcal{P}(i)} \frac{w_p}{N(p)}$$

where w_p is the relative weight (importance) of power p. For the moment, we assume $w_p = 1$ for all p.

For example, consider a self-organising electronic institution with the above EC specification, with $\mathcal{A} = \{a, b, c, d, e\}$, all of whom occupy the role of *prosumer*. Suppose in some window W that a is assigned to the role of *allocator*, so it is empowered to perform *announce* and *allocate* actions; that b is assigned to the role of *head*, so it is empowered to perform *cfv* and *declare* actions; and that there are insufficient resources to satisfy e's demand so its allocation is zero ($r_e = 0$), so while e is empowered to *appropriate*, it is not permitted to *appropriate*. Then:

	prosumer				*allocator*		*head*		
	provide	demand	appropriate	vote	announce	allocate	cfv	declare	p_i
a	✓	✓	✓	✓	✓	✓			2.85
b	✓	✓	✓	✓			✓	✓	2.85
c	✓	✓	✓	✓					0.85
d	✓	✓	✓	✓					0.85
e	✓	✓		✓					0.6
$1/N(p)$	0.2	0.2	0.25	0.2	1	1	1	1	

Therefore, for this window W:

$$\mathrm{RelIP}_W = [\mathcal{P}; 2.85, 2.85, 0.85, 0.85, 0.6]_W$$

The RelIP can be analysed in various ways. One property to test for is 'fairness', for which the Gini index (coefficient) can be used. The Gini index measures the statistical dispersion of values in a frequency distribution, such as the number of institutionalised powers of a group of agents.

For example, the index of institutional power IPX for a window W is given by (where $\mu = mean(\{p_i\})$):

$$\mathrm{IPX}_W = gini(\mathrm{RelIP}_W) = \frac{1}{2}\frac{1}{\mu}\frac{1}{|\mathcal{A}|^2} \sum_{i=1}^{|\mathcal{A}|}\sum_{j=1}^{|\mathcal{A}|} |\, p_i - p_j \,| \qquad (7.3)$$

while the cumulative IPX for a series of Windows $W_1, \ldots, W_n$ is given by:

$$\mathrm{IPX}_{[W_1, W_n]} = gini\left(\frac{\sum_{i=1}^{n} \mathrm{RelIP}_{W_i}}{n}\right) \qquad (7.4)$$

An IPX coefficient of zero would indicate 'perfect' fairness (every agent has the same 'amount' of power), while a coefficient of one would indicate 'complete' unfairness (one agent has all the powers).

This then is a metric for empowerment: we next consider metrics for inclusivity and representation. Note that the previous sections assumed that the constituency of all three decision groups (for resource allocation, reconciling competing legitimate claims by weighting them, and for role assignment) was $\mathcal{A}$, i.e. the set of all agents. However, as was shown in Fig. 6.4, decision groups can be more varied and structured, so metrics for inclusivity and representation need to take this into consideration.

For an inclusivity metric, let $\mathcal{DG}$ be a decision group in an institution, and let $\mathcal{A}$ be the non-empty set of institution members affected by the group's decisions. The degree of inclusivity of a decision group, $\text{inc}_{\mathcal{DG}}$, is the ratio of the number of appropriator agents in the relevant decision group to the number of appropriators:

$$\text{inc}_{\mathcal{DG}} = \frac{|\mathcal{A} \cap \mathcal{DG}|}{|\mathcal{A}|} \tag{7.5}$$

The maximum ratio of inclusivity, $inc_{\mathcal{DG}} = 1$, indicates that all the appropriator agents take part in the decision-making, thus satisfying Ostrom's third principle: "those affected by the operational-choice rules participate in selection and modification of those rules". The minimum ratio, $inc_{\mathcal{DG}} = 0$, would indicate that no appropriator agents are involved in the decision outcome of the rule.

Representation. Inclusivity is a relative measure of the involvement of the appropriators in the decision groups. Its counterpart is representation, which is a relative measure of the involvement of those *not* affected by the rules yet who still participate in their selection. The degree of representation, $\text{rep}_{\mathcal{DG}}$, is the ratio of the number of appropriator agents in the decision group to the size of that group (assuming the group is valid, i.e. non-empty), e.g.:

$$\text{rep}_{\mathcal{DG}} = \frac{|\mathcal{A} \cap \mathcal{DG}|}{|\mathcal{DG}|} \tag{7.6}$$

A degree of representation of $\text{rep}_{\mathcal{DG}} = 1$ denotes that there is no external influence in the decision-making. This would partially fulfil Ostrom's seventh principle: "Existence of and control over their own institutions is not challenged by external authorities".

For each rule, the inclusivity and representation metrics define a two-dimensional space, as was shown in Fig. 6.4(b), and a point in that space calculated by:

$$increp(\mathcal{DG}) = \mathsf{inc}_{\mathcal{DG}} \times \mathsf{rep}_{\mathcal{DG}} \tag{7.7}$$

If there are n decision groups in an institution, this defines an n-dimensional hypercube, and a point in this space — what we might call the 'Democratic Participation Index' (DPX) — during a window W, is computed by representing each decision-group's point in inclusivity/representation space in a vector, and the coefficient given by multiplying all the elements of the vector together:

$$\vec{\mathrm{DPX}}_W = \langle increp(\mathcal{DG}_1), increp(\mathcal{DG}_2), \ldots, increp(\mathcal{DG}_n) \rangle \tag{7.8}$$

$$\mathit{coeff}(\mathrm{DPX})_W = increp(\mathcal{DG}_1) \times increp(\mathcal{DG}_2) \times \ldots \times increp(\mathcal{DG}_n) \tag{7.9}$$

7.6.1.1 A Metric for Decision Frequency

To account for the fact that the result of applying a rule may be used in various other rules, we proceed as follows. Let r be the rule being analysed. Then, for each rule $r' \in succ(r)$, where $succ(r)$, is the set of children of r (i.e. the edges of the graph in Fig. 6.5), we compute how often a decision (i.e. use of rule r) about rule r' is made:

$$freq(r, r') = \frac{exec(r)}{exec(r')} \tag{7.10}$$

where $exec(r)$ indicates how many times rule r has been executed.

7.6.2 Transparency Principle and Balancing Principle

In order to define metrics to measure the transparency of an institution, we propose four further properties of institutions, addressing questions of:

- *Singularity*: To what extent is the principle of 'one agent, one vote' upheld, or do some agents have multiple votes?
- *Justifiability*: Is membership of decision-making bodies disclosed, are their procedures available, and are their workings revealed?

- *Accountability*: Do decision-makers benefit equally (rather than excessively) from the outcomes, and are they liable if they go wrong?
- *Temporality*: Are decisions appealable, and are they repealable?

There are already metrics for measuring singularity, for example, the Banzhaf power index for weighted voting systems. For justifiability, an EC specification could be useful, if the specification was made open and public, in order that a disinterested third party could replicate the deliberations and verify decisions of a particular group. The problem of accountability is particularly complicated (Thompson, 1980) and, in its totality, not necessarily directly addressable using the mechanisms outlined here; however, there is progress towards action languages for collective action and agency, see Sergot (2007). The idea of temporality considers that, on the assumption that procedures may not be perfect, decisions are not 'written in stone' but can be repealed if shown to be incorrect. Note again the application of a guiding principle of *Robert's Rules of Order* (Robert et al., 2000): "anything goes unless someone objects".

For the Balancing Principle, metrics should determine the proportionality of relative benefits and burdens. This includes:

- *Cost*: What is the cost (in whatever 'currency', which could be time) of operating a procedure?
- *Accuracy*: Does the procedure ensure the correct outcome (Rawls, 1971)? (See also, of course, Chapter 9.)
- *Consistency*: Does a procedure produce equal outcomes for different individuals under the same circumstances?

One approach to cost would be to analyse the computational complexity of each of the procedures and protocols used by the decision groups. For example, as has been seen in Chapter 4, there are many alternative winner determination methods for voting protocols. These vary in their robustness (i.e. resistance to strategic manipulation (Tideman, 2006)), but also in their complexity, from plurality to instant runoff.

The cost element of the Balancing Principle is particularly important for monitoring procedures in a system with endogenous resources where the cost of monitoring is not free. As seen in the previous section, it is possible to ruin a common-pool resource system by over-monitoring, thereby expending all the resources on monitoring and leaving little or nothing to distribute for 'real' tasks.

One of the problems exposed with some machine learning algorithms has been training on biased datasets, so that the bias is reproduced in classification (Asaro, 2019). This suggests that care should be taken in applying machine learning and data analytics in the administration and evaluation of justice, as opposed to the symbolic reasoning used here.

7.6.3 Procedural Justice: On Reflection

An experimental testbed has been written to test the use of procedural justice, and some results are reported in Pitt *et al.* (2013). Although it only implemented the IPX coefficient described above, so it was a very limited framework, we conclude that the 'fairer' role assignment conditions (such as allocating at random or in turn) could be distinguished from the 'unfair' role assignment conditions (such as always allocating the role to the same agent), both in comparative magnitude and in 'trajectory'.

In previous experiments with the LPG' game in an economy of scarcity and using legitimate claims as the resource allocation method (Pitt *et al.*, 2014), a measure of subjective 'satisfaction' was used by each agent to evaluate its benefit from belonging to an institution. If its subjective satisfaction fell below a personal threshold, the agent had no alternative but to 'vote with its feet'.

However, this is too coarse to distinguish between unfair treatment and extreme scarcity. It turns out, though, it is not the case that a horizontal trajectory at mid-value IPX is necessarily 'bad' — a platonic benign dictator would show the same empowerment metric profile, but would distribute resources fairly.

This leads to two conclusions. Firstly, that a range of indices is required, which can be used as pointers to possible issues. In addition, to observe Ostrom's seventh principle (minimal recognition of right to self-organise), the agents themselves have to be able to use the metrics for evaluating 'fitness for purpose', by mapping its index observations to its own assessment. To leverage this assessment, the agents need to communicate with each other. This proposal is investigated using the framework for interactional justice presented in Chapter 9.

Secondly, we conclude also that a framework for reflection — enabling an institution to reflect on and evaluate its own performance — could be partially built on the principles of procedural justice.

7.7 A General Framework

In Pitt *et al.* (2015), the collective choice rules were addressed by considering aspects of 'natural' justice, distributive justice and retributive justice; while it was proposed that the congruence of these rules to the environment was to be addressed by considering aspects of procedural justice and interactional justice.

These different aspects of justice can be summarised as follows:

- Natural justice: Concerned with rights to participate in and access information related to the decision-making processes that affect the lives and well-being of a group;
- Distributive justice: Concerned with processes for, and evaluating outcomes of, the distribution of rewards among the individuals belonging to (members of) a group;
- Retributive justice: Concerned with processes for, and evaluating outcomes of, the enforcement of sanctions for wrong-doing by the individuals belonging to (members of) a group;
- Procedural justice: Concerned with ensuring that those rules and procedures are 'fit-for-purpose'; and
- Interactional justice: Concerned with how 'well' those who are responsible for executing procedures or determining outcomes treat those who are subjected to them.

The relationship between these different elements of justice, and relation to Ostrom's institutional design principles, is illustrated in Fig. 7.6. Note we are using the more detailed description of Ostrom's original formulation (Ostrom, 1990) offered in Cox *et al.* (2010), which breaks down design principle 2 (congruence between appropriation and provision rules and local conditions) into two parts:

- 2A: Appropriation rules restricting time, place, technology, and/or quantity of resource units are related to local conditions; and

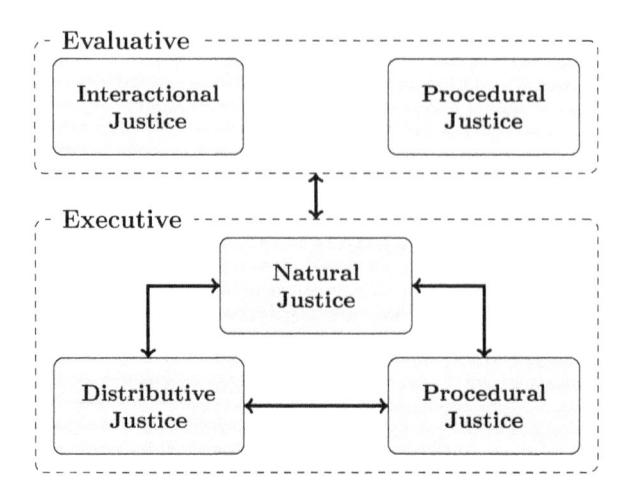

Fig. 7.6. Interdependence of the Qualifiers of Justice and Ostrom's Principles

- 2B: The benefits obtained by users from a common-pool resource, as determined by appropriation rules, are proportional to the amount of inputs required in the form of labour, material or money, as determined by provision rules.

Frameworks for the first four aspects of justice have been studied and formalised in the previous chapter (natural justice), and in this chapter (distributive, retributive and procedural justice). The missing piece of the 'justice jigsaw', interactional justice, is studied in Chapter 9. Prior to that, the next chapter develops another aspect of social interaction, specifically social construction, which is a prerequisite for interactional justice. The conventional rules of institutions, and values underpinning justice, are both social constructions, as are various other conceptual resources like trust, forgiveness and 'social capital'.

7.8 Summary

This chapter has studied computational justice, the algorithmic specification and operationalisation of principles and criteria of administering and evaluating justice and fairness. Different qualifiers of justice were analysed, for natural, distributive, retributive, procedural and interactional justice, and frameworks for each qualifier were developed. The framework for distributive justice has been generalised and extended in a series of works culminating in Burth Kurka *et al.* (2019), while retributive justice has been studied further in Riveret *et al.* (2013) and Zolotas and Pitt (2016).

In the context of Ostrom Institution Theory, a general framework for computational justice integrating these qualifiers was proposed. However, we showed in Pitt *et al.* (2011a) that the 'optimal' short-term distribution of resources was less important than the sustainability of the resource itself, and that sustainability was a product of self-organisation. As it happens, the capacity to change is an essential ingredient of (long-term) utility, i.e. "systems that ... allow for change may be suboptimal in the short run but prove wiser in the long run" (Hess and Ostrom, 2006, p. 68). We believe that this 'wisdom' consists of maximising not just sustainability but also justice. We argue that it is self-organising systems which allow for both justice and change that may prove to be wisest and most judicious in the long run.

This is a belief that appears to echo an opinion voiced by Binmore (2010):

> I think that we evolved the capacity to entertain fairness norms because they allowed our species a quick and efficient way to solve the coordination problems that inevitably arise when a group is faced with a new situation. For example, how should a novel source of food be shared without fighting or other wasteful conflict? If I am right, then fairness can be seen as evolution's solution to the equilibrium selection problem that arises in certain games with multiple equilibria.

What we are trying to do with computational justice is to develop an algorithmic approach that allows agents a quick and efficient way to solve their coordination problems. To do this, we have proposed the different qualifiers of justice, defined principles and algorithms for each qualifier, and emphasised a pluralistic approach — in the belief that is not a single, unique, universal dispensary of justice.

Moreover, a question has to be asked of any system dispensing justice: *how does the loser feel?* As we are unable to ask Donald, to address this question we first consider (artificial) social construction and the general idea of values, which will lead us on to a framework for knowledge management and interactional justice, and finally to governance.

Chapter 8

Artificial Social Construction

8.1 Introduction

The aim of this chapter is to examine n-agent social interaction through the lens of *social construction*. Social construction is a sociological theory analysing and explaining how shared assumptions about 'reality' are jointly constructed through (repeated) communication and coordination. We are interested in seeing how the joint construction of these shared assumptions can mitigate the complexity of, and risks associated with, strategic interaction involving decision-making under uncertainty, and mitigate the adverse consequences of making the wrong decision.

Although earlier sources are acknowledged, the 'foundation stone' of social construction was laid by Berger and Luckmann (1966) who argued that 'reality' was socially constructed (literally, the title of the book: *The Social Construction of Reality*). They argued that all knowledge is a product of, and reinforced by, repeated social interactions; where "all knowledge" included everything from the most basic perceptions of everyday reality, through to knowledge of seemingly obvious, but actually quite complex, social constructs like "money" (Searle, 1997), and onto knowledge of seemingly complex, and actually very complex, constructs that have already been studied, like *institutions* (Chapter 6) and *justice* (Chapter 7).

For Berger and Luckmann, a social interaction or social relation is defined as any relationship between two or more individuals. Therefore, according to the theory, when people interact, they do so on the implicit understanding that their individual perceptions and knowledge of "reality" are coincidental; and coincidental not in the sense of 'by accident', but in fact quite the opposite: the same thing at the same time, i.e. "common knowledge", arrived at by deliberation, and indeed, quite deliberately. In other words, an action, which in itself might seem pointless or worthless (e.g. exchanging a lump of inedible metal for an edible product, giving an object because of some arbitrary temporal recurrence) gets meaning and significance because of the prior social relations and common knowledge that have been constructed, which the action itself constructs.

Since this common knowledge is created and negotiated by and between people, mental constructs and social relations themselves come to be seen as, and accepted as, part of a mutually-agreed objective reality. Moreover, as people act upon this shared understanding of their common knowledge of reality, that reality is both maintained, reinforced and perpetuated through repeated interactions and through education.

This is why some people can sometimes talk about "the law" or institutions ("My organisation/university/religious-assembly wants me to ...") as if they physically exist (a perception not knowingly under-confused by granting corporations some of the same legal statuses as natural persons). However, this is also precisely why the philosophical underpinning (Searle, 1969) and the logical formalisation (Jones and Sergot, 1996) of institutionalised power are based on the idea of 'counts as', i.e. an empowered agent performing a designated act in a specific context *counts as* if the institution itself performed the act (which of course it cannot: it does not exist in the same way as a person does; but it does exist as a social construct).

This 'existence' distinction is quite crucial. What is of interest and importance to social construction is not whether some phenomenon is fictional or factual, or physical or mental, but rather how knowledge of the phenomenon is generated through social interaction, how that knowledge is interwoven into the social fabric (Ferscha *et al.*, 2011), and how that fabric becomes a determinant of social behaviour and social practice. In this chapter, the phenomena to be studied are *trust*, *forgiveness*, conceptual resources (often called *social capital*), and *values* more generally.

The motivation is that trust is an important factor in enabling social relations to begin. However, trust may help you make the right decision, but it won't stop you making the wrong decision. Therefore, we study forgiveness as a process which enables social relations to endure or improve (complementary to processes of dispute resolution (Chapter 5) and retributive justice (Chapter 7)).

Trust and forgiveness between two agents are used in the context of strategic decision-making, which is another social interaction in itself and has two outcomes. Firstly, it provides feedback, which is used to maintain and reinforce the shared understanding; and secondly, it creates *externalities*, which are of benefit to other agents in the system. These externalities are, of course, also social constructs, i.e. common knowledge constructed by social interaction. Consequently, we can begin to see how social relations and conceptual resources in 2-agent social interactions can serve to support the effective functioning of communities and social groups in resolving n-agent collective action problems. Resolving these makes a critical contribution to one more social construct: a shared set of congruent *values*.

After the obligatory kitchen-oriented example, the structure of this chapter follows the motivation: trust — forgiveness — social capital — values. The objectives of the chapter are:

- To study how decision-making under uncertainty can make use of various forms of socially constructed conceptual resources;
- To show how such conceptual resources can be transformed into computational artefacts that can be formally represented, and reasoned with, by agents/algorithms; and
- To explore the nature and function of institutions, the 'state' and qualitative human values in a socially constructed digital world (or, perhaps: a digitally constructed social world).

Note how the study of institutions in Chapter 6 and justice in Chapter 7 were in effect precursors to this study of social construction. These two strands plus this chapter will be woven together in the study of knowledge management (and interactional justice) in Chapter 9 and self-governance (i.e. the 'state') in Chapter 10, respectively.

8.2 Example: The Cheese-and-Wine Controversy

Meanwhile, back in the house, the housemates decide to hold a cheese and wine night — once they had spent some time and energy deciding first which night; and then even more time and energy deciding that it was a "cheese and wine" night rather than a "wine and cheese" night. Still the issue was *very* important.

After all that, the potential for surprise wins out over the quotidian mundanity of coordination, so they quickly reach an agreement that everyone separately buys a bottle of wine, a selection of cheese, and some complements, like bread, celery, pickles and so on, and brings that on the appointed night.

What could possibly go wrong?

Well, each housemate now has a dilemma. They now have to decide whether to go to some expense and bring a fine wine and some artisanal cheese; or be cheap and lazy and bring a bottle of Chardonnay and a lump of mouldy cheddar. If a housemate goes for the cheap option and everyone else goes for the expensive one, then he gets a good meal at low expense. If a housemate goes for the expensive option and everyone else goes for the cheap one, then she gets a poor meal at high expense.

Of course, this is a scenario that is acted out in shared houses and group birthday dinners, that everyone has experienced, and everyone has tales of injustice, free-riding and bringing a cheap packet of stale pitta bread while getting drunk on everyone else's wine.

In fact, the situation is so common and needs little abstraction and few assumptions to cast as a game: this is called the Unscrupulous Diner's Dilemma. This game will be studied extensively in Sec. 8.5.4, but (spoiler alert) the answer depends, and what it particularly depends on is social construction (so it wasn't much of a spoiler). In these situations, we observe the construction of social relations like trust; the construction of social processes like forgiveness; and the construction of conceptual resources like social capital. Underpinning all this, though, is the social construction of qualitative human values.

8.3 Trust

The concept of *trust* is similar to the concept of justice studied in the previous chapter, in so far as everyone knows intuitively what it is, but no one can provide a universal definition or formalisation. However, it was recognised that in open multi-agent systems, something approaching the concept of trust was needed (Marsh, 1994), and a substantial body of literature on trust and trust frameworks has been produced subsequently. It is not an intention to review that literature, instead we highlight three key works that have influenced the trust framework described in this section. These come from:

- **Cognitive science** (Castelfranchi and Falcone, 2002)**:** Trust as a willingness to expose oneself to risk, and the various criteria and contextual factors involved in that risk-assessment;
- **Analytic philosophy** (Jones, 2002)**:** Based on an observation of situations where one would ordinarily say "A trusts B", the common features are that A *believes* that there is a rule, and A *expects* B's behaviour to comply with the rule; and
- **Data science and human computer interaction** (Marsh *et al.*, 2020)**:** Rather than prescriptive definitions, look at functions instead, and identify criteria that allow for conceptual differentiation (selection of principles or evaluation according to those principles, as with the differentiation between justice and fairness as discussed Chapter 7).

However, in this context, it might help to think of trust as a socially constructed conceptual resource that helps people to coordinate expectations in situations of social and strategic interaction with different degrees and dimensions of uncertainty, and we are looking for algorithmic models which enable agents to do the same.

8.3.1 *Making Decisions Under Uncertainty*

A particular feature of open systems is co-dependence: one component has to rely on one or more other components in order to successfully complete its own tasks. For example, in an ad hoc network, one node has to rely on a network of other nodes to transmit its messages across that network (Cho *et al.*, 2010); in a distributed supply chain, one manufacturing component has to rely on the timely delivery and quality of the goods delivered in order to satisfy its own commitments to the chain (Easwaran and Pitt, 2002); in desktop grid computing, components have to delegate tasks to each other (Klejnowski *et al.*, 2013); and so on.

This requires a decision to be made about the reliability of the network, other suppliers, etc. This is, essentially, decision-making under uncertainty, because the decision-maker has no control over the autonomous behaviour of the components on which it chooses to rely. Furthermore, a decision *has* to be made: inaction implies inevitable failure to complete one's own task.

This is a *trust* decision, loosely defined as a willingness (or necessity) to expose oneself to risk, with the intention to reduce the doubt involved in the decision and so mitigate the risks involved. However, this assessment of risk concerning reliance on someone or something outside one's control is a potentially 'expensive' computation; furthermore, it is one that needs to be performed frequently and in some cases replicated — in which case it would be pointless to repeat the computation, but in any case there would be new information (i.e. the outcome of the previous interaction).

Therefore, in dealing with such a trust decision, a framework is required which takes into account Weisberg's (2014) two dimensions of uncertainty: doubt and ambiguity. Doubt measures the degree of belief in a proposition; ambiguity reflects an understanding of that proposition. Doubt is derived from those aspects that cannot be controlled, such as randomness, chaos or non-observability; ambiguity stems from having only a partial understanding of the situation. Doubt, according to Weisberg, can be quantified, typically by statistical measures; but ambiguity is essentially qualitative and requires logical reasoning.[1]

In retrospect, this combination of doubt and uncertainty (although not couched in those terms) is a feature of the trust framework developed by Neville and Pitt (2003), 10 years prior to the publication of Weisberg's book. Effectively, this framework tried to deal with the quantitative element of doubt about the outcome by means of *economic* reasoning, i.e. in terms of utilities, cost/benefit analysis, and on on; and the qualitative element of ambiguity in the process by means of *socio-cognitive* reasoning, i.e. in terms of confidence in beliefs, experiences, recommendations, the interpretation of signals (such as reputation) and so on. The resulting trust-decision

---

[1] Although Weisberg's key, and highly cogent, point, is that in the pursuit of the elimination of doubt by data analytics and machine learning, some researchers appear to have neglected the pragmatic need for disambiguation and choose to remain *wilfully ignorant* of this component of uncertainty.

framework brought together both socio-cognitive and socio-economic reasoning.

8.3.2 A Socio-Cognitive Trust Framework

Applying the methodology of Sec. 1.4, the socio-cognitive reasoning element of this framework was based on the formalisation of a trust theory from cognitive science. In this case, computational representation of an agent's trust belief is based on the formal model of Falcone and Castelfranchi (2001). The essential conceptualisation is as follows: the degree to which agent A trusts agent B about task τ in (state of the world) Ω is a subjective probability $\mathbf{DoT}_{A,B,\tau,\Omega}$. This is the basis of agent A's decision to rely upon B to "get τ done". The framework incorporates this stance, but computes 'trust' as this (subjective) probability of one agent's expectation regarding the performance of another, as a product of its direct experiences of that other party, and from the recommendations of its peers (i.e. reputation). In both cases, qualitative information is being used to reduce the ambiguity and risk.

The economic model used by a decision-making agent focuses on estimating the utility gained by the agent from a successful outcome of the trust decision, and estimating the utility lost in the event of an unsuccessful outcome. In situations where there may be a number of possible partners from whom to select (e.g. a trading partner in a supply chain, next hop in an ad hoc network, etc.), the agent should choose to trust the potential partner with the highest positive expected utility $\mathcal{E}$, i.e.:

$$\mathcal{E} = \mathbf{DoT}_{A,B,\tau,\Omega} \times \mathbf{U}(\text{succ})_{A,B,\tau,\Omega} + (1 - \mathbf{DoT}_{A,B,\tau,\Omega}) \cdot \mathbf{U}(\text{fail})_{A,B,\tau,\Omega}$$

An overview of the operation of the framework, as illustrated in Fig. 8.1, is as follows (for a detailed description, including formulas and algorithms, see Neville and Pitt (2003)).

Given an opportunity (or requirement) to trust a peer, an agent uses its economic model to calculate its outcome utilities (2,3). These outcome utilities are the economic influence on the decision to trust (5), and represent the payoffs of accepting the risk in relying on the peer. The other parameter in the decision to trust is the agent's trust belief (4) conditioned by its confidence in that belief (14), this being the agent's subjective evaluation of the probability of a successful

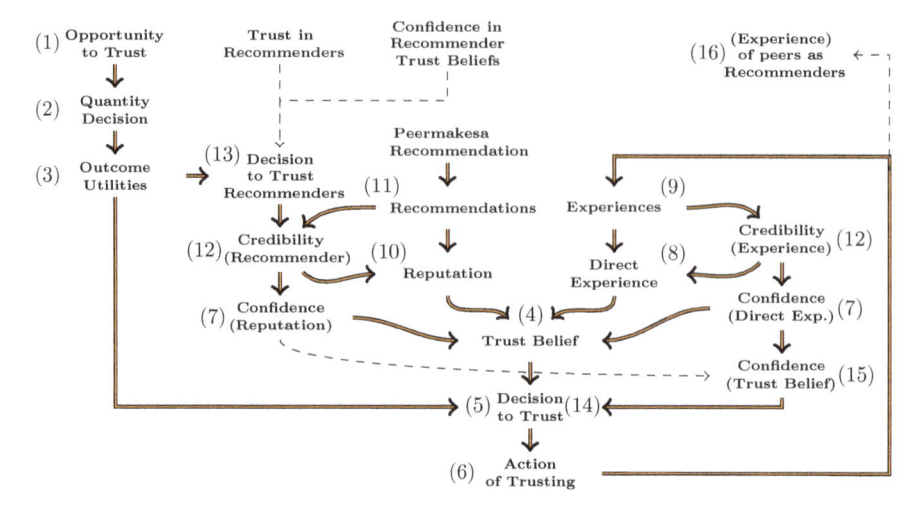

Fig. 8.1. Trust Framework Based on Socio-{Economic|Cognitive} Reasoning

outcome of trusting the peer. The agent's trust belief is computed from the combination of the agent's belief about its direct experiences (8) and the reputation of the potential trustee (10). The relative influence of these beliefs on the trust belief is determined by the agent's confidence in their respective accuracies (7). Direct experience represents a distillation of its set of prior first-hand interactions with the trustee into one belief (9). Likewise, the agent's opinion of the reputation of the potential trustee is informed by the recommendations of its peers (11). The credibility assigned to an experience or recommendation, and hence its weight of influence during the distillation process, is a function of the currency of the belief and it is also dependent upon the agent's decision to trust the source of the belief (12). This opportunity to trust a peer as a source of recommendations is handled in the same manner as defined here for the generic case (13). The agent will look to its experiences of the peer as a recommender and at what its peers recommend about them as recommenders. We will assume that the agent can trust itself not to lie about or distort its own experiences (although we do not rule out the possibility of self-deception).

In the cases where the resultant trust belief is enough to decide to trust the potential trustee, and given there are no better opportunities available, the agent will act upon its decision (6). The resultant experience of the trustee is added to the agent's set of prior experiences (15). Experiences are also formed about those agents that have made recommendations referring to the trustee and subsequently the agents that recommended them, and along the chain of recommendations (16).

8.3.3 *Trust in a Producer–Consumer Scenario*

The trust framework has been tested in a producer–consumer scenario with unreliable producers. For details of the simulation, experiments and results, see Neville and Pitt (2004), but the main result was that consumer decision-making with the fully-featured trust framework produced a close approximation to a 'safe' market (i.e. one with no malicious or unreliable producers). Another feature of the framework was its anytime computation based on 'sufficient confidence': this demonstrated that the agents' reasoning shifts over time and experience from 'risk' trust, an 'expensive' computation for decision-making in first encounters, to 'reliance' trust, which shortcuts such computations (by the confidence metric) for nth encounters, i.e. sufficient prior direct experience is such that there is an expectation of a beneficial outcome without needing to consider others' recommendations.

Of course, this is open to exploits, but this is a characteristic of 'stings' in human commercial transactions. However, the fact a trust decision, based on a trust relationship, *can* be exploited, raises another question — *what happens when the outcome of the trust decision is wrong, or is contrary to expectation?* One answer to this question is proposed in the next section.

8.4 Forgiveness

Possibly, the rhetoric of binary oppositions (like "thinking, fast and slow", "salt and pepper", "Tom and Jerry") led to the association of 'trust' with 'reputation'. But as we have seen, 'reputation' is a component of the trust decision. Therefore, in early computational trust frameworks, when there was a trust breakdown, the response was to damage the reputation of the transgressor, but this was not curative, nor constructive. Instead, we argued that the 'proper' binary opposition should be "trust and *forgiveness*". This section presents a computational framework for forgiveness.

8.4.1 *Trust Breakdowns*

Trust has been (informally) identified as a willingness to expose oneself to a risk; indeed, the computation of the 'degree of trust' (in the trust framework of the previous section) explicitly took into account the utility of successful and unsuccessful outcomes. In this case, as in many trust frameworks in the multi-agent systems literature (Pinyol and Sabater-Mir, 2013), 'trust' is a measure of probability, or an indicator of the doubt involved in a certain transaction or relationship. Therefore, many of these trust frameworks attempt to reduce the level of doubt — but it is impossible to eliminate it altogether, otherwise it would hardly be a trust decision. Therefore, if there is always some risk of an unsuccessful outcome, the key question becomes, as previously posited, what is a component in an open system to do, when it misplaces its trust, so that the outcome of its trust decision is wrong, or contrary to expectation? Critically, this does not imply that the use of trust itself is necessarily misguided, and that the entire trust framework should be abandoned, but instead some complementary mechanism for dealing with a particular trust breakdown is required.

A possible explanation for the trust breakdown is that there has been a violation of a norm, or from the truster's perspective, a violation of the *expectation* that the trustee's behaviour will comply with a norm, which is believed to be 'in force'. This follows from the Jones (2002) account of trust, mentioned before, where it is proposed that the act of trusting has two components, a *belief* component and an *expectation* component, and that one ordinarily says of a particular situation that "A trusts B" if A has the *belief* that there is a norm, or rule (to be complied with in this situation), and A has the *expectation* that B's behaviour will indeed comply with the norm.

Typically, then, in multi-agent systems research, and indeed in social systems for e-commerce, the reaction to a trust breakdown has been to damage or diminish the reputation of the violator. Notice, though, that reputation is a factor that is part of the trust-decision framework, and as such is a quantitative punishment mechanism which only serves to reduce doubt. It does not do anything to deal with the *ambiguity*, i.e. taking into account the truster's understanding of the situation, or why it is that the trustee has violated the norm, or how serious the offence was, or any of many other factors that pertain to the complexity of a trusting relationship.

Therefore, what is required instead is a *qualitative repair* mechanism, i.e. one that tries to take the ambiguity into account, and instead try to restore the system to a (kind of) homeostatic equilibrium. In fact, there is a well-established social mechanism for achieving precisely this effect — *forgiveness* (McCullough, 2001). Forgiveness is a pro-social motivational change in someone who has incurred a transgression. It implies giving up resentment and desire to punish someone. When people forgive, they become motivated to engage in relationship-constructive, rather than relationship-destructive, actions towards the offender. Forgiveness is influenced by psychological processes such as empathy for the transgressor, attributions and appraisals, and rumination about the transgression.

In social systems, forgiveness allows the truster (victim of the violation) to distinguish between intentional and unintentional violations (and a range of infractions in between), to consider the seriousness of the offence, and to take into account the dependence on whether this was a 'risk' trust vs. a 'reliance' trust decision (one might be more forgiving towards someone with whom one had an established beneficial relationship, than someone who violated in a 'first encounter' situation). Forgiveness is also known to stimulate voluntary acts of recompense from the violator.

8.4.2 *A Forgiveness Framework*

Consequently, in self-organising multi-agent systems, we require a forgiveness framework which reduces negative predisposition towards offender, and accentuates positive motivations for self-repair. In Vasalou *et al.* (2006), just such a forgiveness framework was proposed and developed. Based on a survey of the psychological literature on forgiveness, a conceptual model was proposed which begins with a negative evaluation that is subject to four positive motivations which might reverse an initial negative reaction into a positive one (see Fig. 8.2).

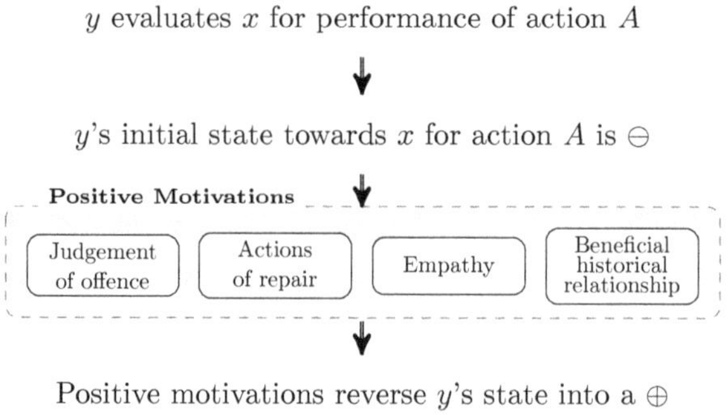

y evaluates x for performance of action A

↓

y's initial state towards x for action A is $\ominus$

Positive Motivations

| Judgement of offence | Actions of repair | Empathy | Beneficial historical relationship |

↓

Positive motivations reverse y's state into a $\oplus$

Fig. 8.2. Conceptual Model for Forgiveness

The four positive motivations for forgiveness — empathy, reparation, judgement of offence and prior beneficial historical relationship — were themselves broken down into eleven constituent signals as follows:

- **Judgement of offence:** Offence severity, offence frequency, intent;
- **Reparation:** Apology, actions of repair;
- **Beneficial historical relationship:** Benefits utility, benefits frequency; and
- **Empathy:** Visible acknowledgement, prior familiarity, similarity, propensity to embarrassment.

This conceptual model was formalised in a computational forgiveness framework as follows. With the exception of 'propensity to embarrassment', for each constituent signal, a formula was specified to identify the 'strength' of the signal (see Vasalou *et al.*, 2006, for full details). For example, the signal j for the frequency of a particular offence was computed by:

$$j = \frac{\left(\frac{n_{offence\_kind}}{n_{offences}} + \frac{n_{offences}}{n_{collaborations}}\right)}{2}$$

where $n_{offence\_kind}$ denotes the number of the offender's offences of the current kind, $n_{offences}$ is the offender's total number of offences across time, and $n_{collaborations}$ is the offender's total collaborations within the community. Note that two aspects of frequency are encapsulated in this formula: the frequency of the current offence is computed with the first division and the frequency of the offender's total past offences is computed with the second division. Among other possibilities, this formula intends to capture the instances where an agent has infrequently violated a particular norm, but at the same time frequently violates many others, i.e. it is trying to accommodate different aspects of ambiguity in the appreciation of the situation. The same holds for the other signals (note that 'propensity to embarrassment' resisted formulation in this way, although some attempts have been made to define a formal model of 'digital blush', e.g. Pitt (2004)).

Each constituent signal was then input into a fuzzy inference system (FIS), each of which consisted of rules of the following form:

```
IF severity IS low
AND frequency IS low
AND intent IS high
THEN judgement_of_offence IS 0.4
```

There were four such FIS, one each positive motivation of the conceptual model, which were combined in a fifth FIS to output a final forgiveness decision d, as in Fig. 8.3. Note that the weight of each input to FIS1 is equally divided between the four positive motivations (hence 25%); furthermore, the weight on each signal input to

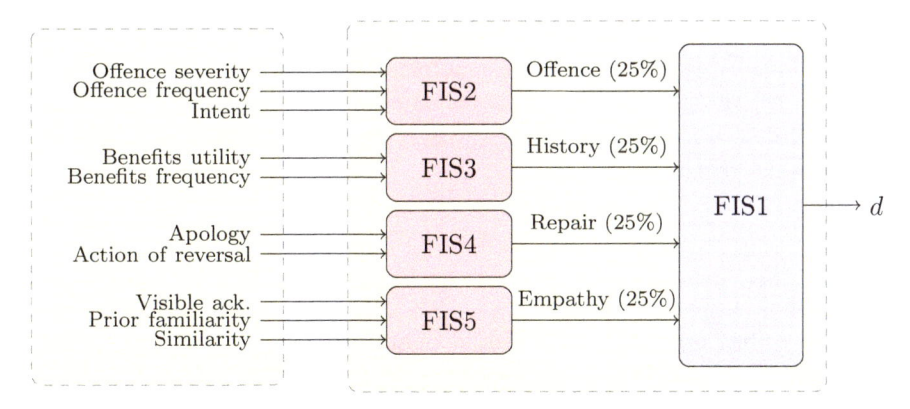

Fig. 8.3. Fuzzy Inference System for Computing Forgiveness Decisions

FIS2–FIS4 was equal. This was a design decision based on assumption that the importance of the ten signals and the four motivations were equally strong. That need not be the case; moreover, a learning agent could quite reasonably modify the weights at runtime according to experience. (There is nothing in the framework that dictates these weights should be equal or immutable.)

8.4.3 *Forgiveness in Computer-Mediated Communication*

The computational framework for forgiveness has been used as a decision-support system for unintentional violations in computer-mediated communication (CMC) (Vasalou *et al.*, 2008). This showed that it is possible to enhance CMC interface design with mechanisms to encourage pro-social behaviour (in this case, avatars which exhibited shame or embarrassment at non-compliance), suggesting that it is not simply anonymity that encourages anti-social online behaviour, but the absence of cues that activate self-awareness in a social setting. The framework has also been used in a socio-technical system to improve pro-social behaviour and reduce workplace civility in, for example, open plan offices (Sara Santos and Pitt, 2013).

One of the other features of forgiveness is that it can even *increase* the strength of a social relationship (in the same way that a broken bone re-knits more strongly).[2] This is because not only can the truster rely on the trustee, but it can also rely on being able to resolve an issue if the trust relationship is misplaced. As a result, qualitative social value can be created, even in an open system, which transcends purely quantitative transactional information. These social values are, in fact, parameters to trust decisions, forgiveness decisions, and so on, and can be formalised as social capital, as discussed in the next section.

---

[2]It has been pointed out that previously broken bones also ache in stressful situations, such as cold weather — a reminder of the break. This may be stretching the analogy, but forgiving and somehow not quite forgetting, so that caution could be exercised in important situations, could be a beneficial feature of a future forgiveness framework.

8.5 Electronic Social Capital

The term 'social capital' is not ideal, as 'capital' implies something that can be owned, traded and spent, and 'social capital' does not really work like that. Therefore, the term 'social potential' was preferred in Bellman *et al.* (2017), and in other work the term 'conceptual resource' is used (Uslaner, 2002; Christoforou, 2012). However, for historical reasons, we will use the term social capital in this section. We start by looking at dishwashers doing favours for each other.

8.5.1 *Favours*

Consider a decentralised community energy system (CES), such as that described in Chapters 1 and 2 (Pitt *et al.*, 2014a), where there are a number of interconnected 'SmartHouses', each with their own renewable energy generation mechanism, but no local storage mechanism, and a number of domestic appliances which need to be operated. When generation and consumption are in balance, all is fine; unfortunately, some times, if generation exceeds consumption, then it needs to be burnt off, which is wasteful and potentially harmful, and at other times, if generation is less than consumption, then the house will experience a blackout. Collective action is required to avoid these undesirable situations.

Therefore, SmartHouses aggregate together to form a CES. However, these CES require a method of lowering the consumption peaks in flattening the demand, reducing the difference between peaks and troughs in electricity usage by creating a levelled usage pattern that lessens the deviation from the average usage. One way of doing this is to create an 'internal market' in the CES, where the SmartHouses trade energy. An alternative way is a self-organising flexible demand system where SmartHouses can offer, demand and exchange an amount of electricity for a period of time in an exchange arena.

Such an exchange arena is presented in Petruzzi *et al.* (2013, 2014). In these works, the SmartHouses in a CES require resources at specific time-slots, but are allocated, by some predefined method, some other set of time-slots. However, in the exchange arena, they can exchange these time-slots. The key factor in the exchange is that a successful exchange counts as a *favour*, and that if an exchange makes it better for both SmartHouses, that counts as *two* favours.

Favours could then be used to gain a preferred allocation, Experiments showed that a CES consisting of 96 'selfish' SmartHouses, which only agreed to exchange time-slots if it made their own allocation better (but not otherwise, even if no worse) were outperformed in the long term by a CES consisting of 96 'pro-social' SmartHouses, using the favour-based exchange arena.

The favour-based exchange arena demonstrates that in the absence of a centralised controller, command structure or other form of orchestration, an open system can nevertheless use both mutually agreed *conventional* rules, and equally intangible mutually agreed social relations (such as 'owing a favour'), as incentives to participate, contribute or select an action which serves the collective, rather than individual, utility.

Furthermore, successful trust and forgiveness decisions in a two-party interaction can, as we have seen, also create a positive externality of benefit to third parties. For example, in a producer–consumer market of products or services with m producers and n consumers, it is mutually believed by all $m+n$ participants that there are some norms, and each has the same expectation, that others' behaviour will comply with those norms. As a consequence of a successful interaction between one producer–consumer pair, and of a failed interaction which is subsequently repaired, the belief in and expectations of the norms are reinforced, and so are more useful to other producer-consumer pairs in subsequent transactions.

8.5.2 *Social Capital*

These favours are a form of *social capital*. Social capital has been described as "the features of social organisation, such as networks, norms and trust, that facilitate coordination and cooperation for mutual benefit" (Putnam, 1993), and more recently as the "attribute of individuals that enhances their ability to solve collective action problems" (Ostrom and Ahn, 2003). In this latter work, it was observed that social capital has multiple forms, of which they identified three:

- *Trustworthiness*, as distinct from trust, and related to reputation, being a shared understanding of someone's willingness to honour agreements and commitments;

- *Social networks*, including strong and weak ties, identifying both channels through which people communicate or other social relations; and
- *Institutions*, identified as sets of conventional rules by which people voluntarily and mutually agree to regulate their behaviour.

They also suggested that *trust* itself was the 'glue' that enabled these various forms of social capital to be leveraged for solving collective action problems (see Chapter 6), for example, the sustainability of a common-pool resource. Social capital generates 'reliance' trust, as mentioned earlier, and, where reliance trust can be seen as a complexity-reducing decision-making short-cut which also helps resolve collective action problems.

More generally, social capital can be considered as an 'umbrella term' for a range of socially constructed conceptual resources that help people coordinate expectations and self-organise. As with trust and forgiveness, we seek to define an algorithmic formulation of *electronic social capital*.

8.5.3 *A Social Capital Framework*

Based on the Ostrom–Ahn social capital model (Fig. 8.4), we want to define an effective algorithmic framework which acts as a conventional incentivisation mechanism for cooperation that creates positive externalities that reinforce the same sorts of incentives. Therefore, in Petruzzi *et al.* (2014), a formal framework was proposed to represent and reason about (an electronic version of) social capital. The framework comprises an observation model in which actions enhance or diminish the different forms of social capital, and a decision-making model which uses the information from the forms of social capital to decide to cooperate or not with another agent.

Figure 8.5 shows a schematic view of the framework. Agents sense from the environment different events that they translate into Social Capital Information. This information is the input of the Social Capital Framework and includes information about when an agent cooperates or not; what messages are sent or received and all the institutional actions such as joining, leaving, sanctioning, etc. The three forms of social capital (Trustworthiness, Networks and Institutions) will store the information received and aggregate it.

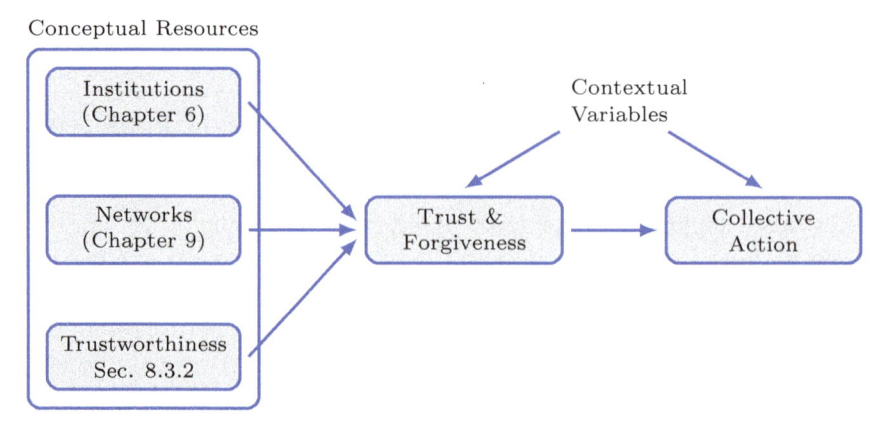

Fig. 8.4. Extension of Ostrom and Ahn's Social Capital Model

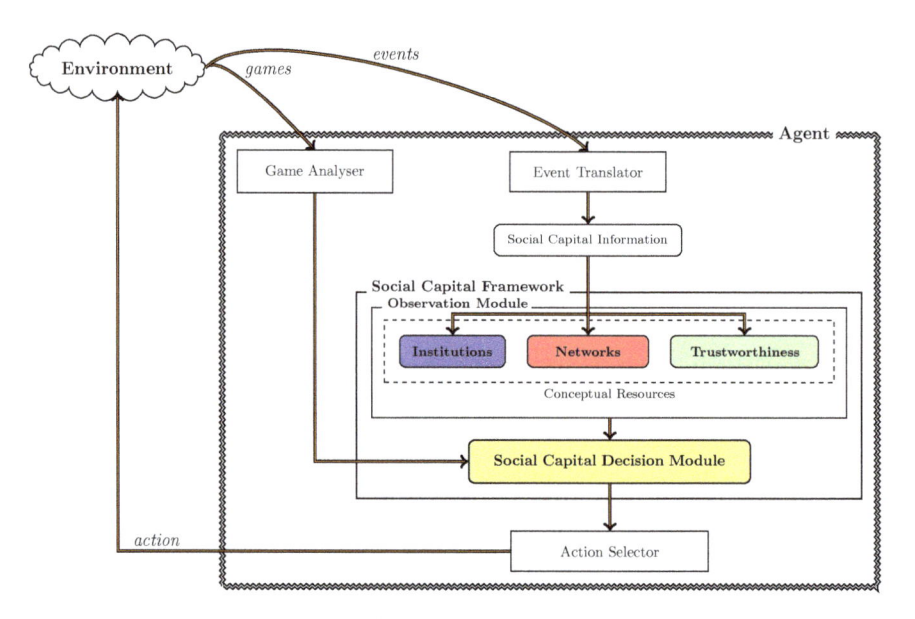

Fig. 8.5. Social Capital Framework

When the agent needs information about another agent or an institution, it will query the Social Capital Decision Module which will combine all the information from the forms of social capital into a value from zero to one, where zero is *no cooperation* and one is *full cooperation*.

To evaluate the Social Capital Framework, we defined a theoretical scenario called the Cooperation Game. The Cooperation Game is a strategic game where a population of agents is repeatedly randomly paired to play a game against each other. At every round, each player has a randomly designated opponent and a two-player strategic game to play. Once paired, players must choose either to *Cooperate*, *Defect* or *Refuse to play* (in this scenario, we allow 'sitting out' as an option). Then, the payoff matrixes are applied and they receive or lose points depending on what they have played. If one of the players refuses to play, the game is cancelled and agents do not receive or lose any points. A global count of points is kept for all the players and it is used to evaluate their performance over time.

An experimental testbed has been implemented to evaluate the social capital framework in this scenario, which was used to compare the performance of different types of agents' behaviours in different environments (represented by the games). The experimental results show that the use of social capital incentivises cooperation and enhances collective action: the use of any combination of the three forms of social capital results in higher cooperation among agents, outperforming the dominant strategy that would be suggested by a game theoretic analysis.

However, it was also concluded that while social capital is fine as a concept, as a term it is potentially misleading, as it suggests something that can be owned, traded or (even worse) 'spent'. Therefore, to define social capital in terms of concrete attributes runs the risks of commodifying the concept, with the concomitant loss of the actual 'value' or leverage that social capital has or can achieve (*cf.* Pitt and Nowak, 2014b). In other words, it is more important not to focus so much on what social capital is, but on what social capital does; and what it does is to coordinate expectations (Peyton Young, 2008) and provide a basis for community governance (Bowles and Gintis, 2002). Therefore, any framework for electronic social capital which can be used to support successful collective action in self-organising open systems will need not just to define, in computational form, the attributes that agents need to represent and reason with, but also the processes by which those same agents can coordinate their expectations and govern their *communities*.

Accordingly, in Petruzzi *et al.* (2015), there was further investigation into using alternative economic arrangements for addressing demand-side self-organisation in decentralised community energy systems, generally focusing on relational rather than transactional information, and specifically on a formal representation of electronic social capital rather than market-based approaches, such as auctions.

8.5.4 The Unscrupulous Diners' Dilemma

The framework for electronic social capital in multi-agent systems has been further refined based on this understanding of what social capital does rather than on what social capital is. As stated earlier, one function it 'does' is to coordinate expectations, so reducing the complexity of decision-making in collective action situations. To examine this proposition, a simulator was developed for an open, self-organising multi-agent system playing the unscrupulous diners' dilemma (Glance and Huberman, 1994), an n-player game as discussed in Sec. 3.7.

The Unscrupulous Diners' Dilemma involves a group of people in a restaurant. Each diner can order an expensive meal or inexpensive meal, knowing that the bill will be split equally. An expensive meal that has to be paid in full is less enjoyable than an inexpensive one. So the dilemma is this. Either: order an expensive meal, and either the others subsidise it by ordering inexpensive meals; or they order expensive meals too and minimise everyone's enjoyment. Or: order an inexpensive meal, and either enjoy that meal if other diners also order inexpensive meals, or, subsidise the other diners' expensive meals (which is no fun at all). Analysis proves that ordering the expensive meal is the unique Nash equilibrium and the dominant strategy, so like the Prisoners' Dilemma, everyone is worse off in the unique equilibrium than with other socially preferable solutions.

This simulator was also developed using PreSage-2, the large-scale multi-agent system introduced in Sec. 1.8 (Macbeth *et al.*, 2014). This allows the definition of different types of agents participating in the game; these experiments had three types: random players which arbitrarily chose their action; dominant strategy agents which selected the Nash equilibrium action; and social capital players, which use some form (or forms) of social capital as an input to their decision-making process. The three forms were trustworthiness, social networks and institutions, and social players could use some combination of all three. Experiments were run with different populations of types of agents, averaging 50 simulation runs per population distribution to average out the effects of randomness and nonlinearity in the system. The aim of the experiments was to investigate, *inter alia*, the performance of agents using social capital in a heterogenous population, the effects of scale, and a comparative evaluation of different combinations of social capital.

Full details of the experimental results can be found in Petruzzi *et al.* (2015), but the general observations that follow from these simulations were that the use of social capital in n-party collective action situations is:

- Optimal in the long term, as agents using the social capital framework outperform agents using the dominant strategy or other simplistic strategies;
- Computable, as all the framework updating mechanisms are 'offline' and the algorithms for computing the social capital metrics are mostly linear (note there is no known polynomial-time algorithm for finding the Nash equilibrium in general n-player, k-strategy games (Papadimitriou and Roughgarden, 2005)); and
- Scalable, because the complexity of individual social decision-making is independent of the size of the collective population.

The significance of this work is that it shows, as with trust, forgiveness (both as above), and with models of Ostrom's institutional design principles for self-organising common-pool resource management (Pitt *et al.*, 2012a), how formal representations of social concepts and processes could be used to regulate interactions between autonomous agents in a relational economy based on reciprocity (rather than a purely transactional one based on prices), which is also computable and scalable. This has positive implications for self-organisation in large-scale collective action situations, precisely those encountered in the decentralised community energy systems (which were introduced earlier).

8.6 Values

8.6.1 *Depreciating Values*

Throughout, this book has implicitly recognised the centrality of transactions in the conduct of human affairs, and by extension the corresponding centrality of transactions between agents in open multi-agent systems.

In contrast, this chapter has explicitly recognised the importance of socially constructed, qualitative *values* associated with those transactions, conceptual resources such as trust, favours, forgiveness, norms, institutions, justice and social capital. Although 'money' is also a social construct, all these values are non-monetary, insofar as they cannot be printed or traded, and are non-fiat, intransitive and non-fungible. For example, if a owes b £5 and b owes c £5, then a can pay c £5 and the debts are cleared. However, if a does b a favour and b does c a favour, it does not mean that c needs to do a a favour; and even if c does, it is not clear what sort and size of favour is of comparable value and acceptable to a.

However, when we move to multi-agent systems, and to sociotechnical systems, we also have to recognise that when technology is introduced to social relations, or applied to a social construct, it can be an amplifier of benefits, but the potential drawbacks can be correspondingly amplified, too. So technology can facilitate transactions, but it can also quantify (commodify, metricate, enumerate) the qualitative essence of those transactions. Here, we discuss four pernicious effects of technology on values.

Firstly, recent years have witnessed the increasing metrication of public and professional life, taking the management consultancy maxim "everything can be measured; and anything that can be measured can be managed" a bit too far and altogether too seriously. The disservice done to medicine, education and governance is well-documented in detail in Muller (2019). Moreover, the damage, distortion and disruption of the social fabric is clear as individual professionals, tradespeople and businesses are compelled to focus on (and the less scrupulous, to manipulate) maximising ratings or meeting arbitrary targets as much as they are on delivering their occupational service.

As much as it is inane to imagine that every social interaction, with all its parameters and contextual factors for both parties, could possibly be mapped onto a 1–5 rating scale, a more disturbing outcome is given by Goodhart's Law from economics: that once a metric becomes a target, it ceases to carry any meaning. So the misuse of metrics is doubly harmful: not only does it change the behaviour of the individuals so measured, but the metric itself loses meaning.

Secondly, there has also been an increase in the commodification of social relationships and concepts. An unintended consequence of social media is the way that social relations are denuded of their original content and replaced instead with a purely numeric, and so monetisable, value. For example, for an older generation, 'friends' were people they could count on; for the Facebook generation, 'friends' are people they could count up. And the more 'friends' one has, the more a targeted advertiser would be willing to pay for product endorsement, or even for the entire site. And thus was the aspiration for a career as a 'social media influencer' born (and never was a 'career' more inevitably guaranteed, because of the network effect, to result in very few getting nearly everything and very many scrapping for, well, scraps). The idea of 'loyalty', too, was critically inverted, from a mutual relationship to one-way lock-in and dependence (Pitt, 2020b).

Thirdly, there is the dissolution of values. This means that values generated by interactions and pro-social behaviours in one context do not translate, or are not transferable, to values in another; moreover, values that are generated in the analogue world do not translate, or are not transferable, to values in a digital sphere. This is especially so with regards to expertise: while there can be benefits to anonymity on the Internet, it is relatively difficult for expertise to establish itself, but relatively easy for false expertise to proclaim itself. Genuine expertise admits doubt, while false expertise sells doubt (Oreskes and Conway, 2010): the latter flourishes on the Internet (for example, the anti-vaccination movement (Hussain *et al.*, 2019).

Fourthly, 150 years ago Marx was protesting against the private ownership of the means of production: in 2020, he would be protesting against the private ownership of the means of social coordination. It has been argued that an unintended consequence of decentralisation of the Internet at the network layer, but the so-called network effect at the application layer (popular nodes become more popular and no other can compete), has resulted in the creation of mega-platforms for a particular domain of service (e.g. Google for search, Amazon for eCommerce, Facebook for social media, etc.) to the exclusion of all competition.

This monopoly has many disruptive social effects, including the reduction of individuals to revenue streams, and the elimination of empathy for, and 'othering' of, those individuals. This has developed into a kind of neo-colonialism (Lofgren, 2012): because of weak national governments in the face of supra-national organisations, these organisations can extract wealth without restriction or compassion. When governments conspire, the ruling elite are effectively colonialists: "in the place and ruling it, but not of it". Indeed, it has been observed that, with the UK leaving the EU, the English people are finding out what it is like to be ruled by the English.

8.6.2 Reinventing Values

The corollary of these processes, such as the metrication, commodification and monetisation of values, is to undermine trust, trust being the 'glue' that links forms of social capital (or conceptual resources) to successful collective action, in the Ostrom–Ahn framework. The dissolution of trust diminishes, to the point of obsolescence, all these socially constructed conceptual resources; the obsolescence of social capital diminishes the prospect of successful collective action. Without prospects and strategies for collective action, we cannot properly address local or global issues, like climate change, fuel poverty, plastic over-use, air quality, food inequality, and so on.

Therefore, we need to use ICT to fundamentally re-think — re-invent — re-discover — and represent conceptual resources in a trustworthy form, as a precursor to restoring (and going beyond) trust and empowering collective action. To do that, we need to address three interrelated questions: what are human values; how do values relate to processes; and how do values relate to exchange mechanisms. It is then that we can begin to design and implement computer systems that represent and reason with values in a qualitative way.

The study of what are human values is the subject of *axiology* and has intersected with numerous domains of inquiry, nor surprisingly (and not limited to) psychology, sociology, philosophy, anthropology and economics: see for example Schwartz (1992), Graeber (2011), Kropotkin (1902), Malinowski (1920). It is not proposed to review this work here, although for a preliminary investigation into *computational axiology*, see Pitt *et al.* (2018a) (where axiology is the philosophical study of value of valuation).

On the relation between values and processes, it needs to be understood that some processes are designed to achieve certain values, but very often these are only implicit in the execution of the process. For example, a fundamental question of jurisprudence is: which system is better: System A, which convicts all of the guilty but some of the innocent; or System B, which only convicts some of the guilty, but none of the innocent. In the UK, at least, the system purportedly tries to ensure the latter, and over the years a set of procedures, protocols, requirements and indeed rituals for trying court cases has emerged to avoid a miscarriage of justice for the innocent, even if this means occasional miscarriage of justice the other way, if the (actually) guilty are acquitted.

These rituals are time-consuming and ostensibly otiose and are very costly. Consequently, there are proposals for "fast track justice" and the use of data science and machine learning, even though caution is needed (Asaro, 2019). Moreover, it is these 'slow' mechanisms that help ensure the desired property: 'fast track justice' prioritises 'value' in purely base financial terms and assumes a cheaper system is more 'preferable' to one that derives its value from qualitative principles of jurisprudence.

On the relation between values and systems of exchange, it is important to note that within communities, the added-value of information, reciprocity or other pro-social behaviour is indeterminate, and/or the qualitative nature of traded services is subjective and cannot simply be measured by kilowatts, tons, etc. In the Digital Transformation, these values are not being realised as benefits for the participants, and there is an asymmetry between those at the edge, and those in the middle. For example, in Participatory Sensing applications, the users generating the data are not the primary beneficiaries, the data aggregators are; in Sharing Economy applications, most of the work is done at the edge, but most of the benefits accrue to the platform owners; and so on.

This requires understanding what is being exchanged, who is benefitting from the exchange (and by how much), and understanding again the implicit benefits of the exchange, all of which are lost if everything is diminished to an asymmetric financial transaction in a monetary economies. There are, in fact, different kinds of economies — for example, gift economies (Malinowski, 1920) and economies of esteem (Brennan and Pettit, 2005) — and the exchanges have added-value, in the sense that units of exchange are a force multiplier and create externalities. By a force multiplier, a unit of currency can be spent more than once, thus creating a chain of exchanges, each of which creates externalities. This is why it is called a currency and it is said to be "in circulation": but this currency can be drained from a local economy if a transnational corporation takes 20% of every transaction. Like the air under a wing creates lift, transaction-chains and the externalities so generated serve to enhance social cohesion and lay the foundations for successful collective action.

An increasingly dominant approach to developing open systems requiring distributed consensus is based on blockchain technology, which is essentially a protocol for building a reliable, verifiable distributed ledger. The ledger records transactions between any two parties, although more generally it in effect records anonymous multi-party transactions where each party's share is recorded. The integrity of the ledger is usually maintained by a peer-to-peer network of miners, who validate and timestamp those transactions. This avoids the need for a trusted third party, and ensures that any one block in the chain cannot be altered without altering subsequent blocks. The transaction is based on the exchange of tokens. Although the idea of a tradeable, traceable digital token was originally intended for an electronic currency (i.e. a cryptocurrency, for example Bitcoin), the token could represent an asset of any kind, e.g. a share, an identity, a contract — indeed a value of any kind.

In one sense, blockchain is arguably just a realisation of earlier protocols developed to solve similar problems, e.g. Paxos to maintain consistency in distributed databases (Lamport, 1998), or logical inference with inconsistent distributed knowledge bases (Kowalski, 1988), or interoperability in multi-agent systems (recall Sec. 1.6.2). It is only recently that the computing power to implement the processor-intensive validation procedures in a 'reasonable' time has become available (and has coincided with a number of pressing economic and financial drivers). However, the potential to represent a value of any kind is fundamentally transformative: it is arguably equivalent to the stored-program concept (where sequences of 0 and 1 could be interpreted by the computer to mean anything the programmer wants it to mean, i.e. data, or an instruction). The corresponding intuition could be called the *stored value concept*: the token can be interpreted to mean (can be imbued with meaning) anything a community wants it to mean.

Therefore, distributed consensus technology presents an interesting technological candidate for implementing electronic forms of conceptual resource. While at the time of writing this is an open question, the key warning here is not that technological offerings like cryptocurrencies and smart contracts are a replacement for trust, but actually they are a *displacement* of trust. The trusting relationship is no longer underwritten by a third-party institution, but a programmer. You are warned.

8.7 Artificial Social Constructionism

We finish this chapter with one more observation: for all that has been written about the singularity, and when computational intelligence overtakes human intelligence, it will be an interesting day indeed when intelligent agents, whether software or robotic, start to practice (rather than have programmed) social construction between and for themselves.

It will be an equally interesting day, for all that has been written about socio-technical systems, human–computer interaction and human–agent–robotic teamwork, when intelligent agents, whether software or robotic, can interact with people, and can participate in social situations, through a common understanding of a socially constructed reality.

In order for computers to respond to humans in the same way as humans respond to humans, the computers have to understand social construction and have shared values. This question is increasingly pertinent as progress is made towards lethal autonomous weapons (Bhuta *et al.*, 2014), social robotics (Gillet and Leite, 2020), automated policing and judicial systems (Asaro, 2019), drones, driverless vehicles and mobility-as-a-service (Pitt, 2019c), and voice-activated virtual assistants (Robbins, 2019). Questions of morality and ethics are then paramount (Winfield *et al.*, 2019).

A contribution to answering this latter question is being made through the development of a theory of *artificial social construction*, call it *artificial social constructionism* (Milanovic and Pitt, 2018). Particularly targeted at dealing with systemic failures, where failure of the automation bias seems to engender deep human mistrust of an automated system, this theory is examining three interlinked issues:

- **Norms:** Establishing norms is the first step to allow agents to learn the behaviour required to keep operating within a system;

- **Education:** Evolution of norms over time is used to teach new agents how to behave through observation and imitation (i.e. social learning for collective action (Lewis and Ekárt, 2017)) without having to encode specific rules; and
- **Values:** Holding values as a goal as opposed to a quantitative metric enables the system to adjust to a changing composition of agents and environments.

Values are where the norms and educations come into focus: failures to achieve, satisfy or maintain values can be identified as breaches of system norms and corrected through them (e.g. through forgiveness), and future avoidance or mitigating behaviour established (through education). For further details of the theory, see Milanovic and Pitt (2018). A series of online games has been designed to test each component of the theory, which is ongoing work. Some preliminary results suggest that humans playing a focal point game with an Artificial Intelligence 'opponent' can be led into doubting their own performance and erroneously blaming themselves when a mismatch over the choice occurs. This could lead to 'overtrust' when self-doubt induces people to delegate to a machine a decision that requires cognition, attention or critical thinking.

8.8 Summary

This chapter has studied social construction, the sociological theory proposing how shared assumptions about reality are jointly constructed through communication and coordination. We explored how social construction could be used to enrich social interaction in self-organising multi-agent systems through the specification of algorithmic frameworks for trust, forgiveness and social capital.

This showed how social construction can be used to create conceptual resources which help to reduce the risk and complexity of decision-making and collective action under uncertainty. However, we finished the chapter with a discussion of two open research questions: technology for the general representation of, and reasoning with, socially constructed values as part of computational axiology, and a broader investigation into a theory of artificial social construction.

In the discussion of values, if there was one point to stress, it would be about the monetisation of socially constructed values, with the consequence that everything is for sale. There are two concerns with this, as analysed in Sandel (2013): inequality and corruption. Widening inequality would not matter so much if it were only luxuries that were inaccessible, but once all goods and services of value are for sale, and necessities are only accessible to those with affluence, then social inequality becomes a cause of social instability. For the issue of corruption we have already seen an example: the ability to buy 'friends' demeans and corrodes the value, meaning and significance of friendship.

On a more positive note, if, frankly, it were deemed imaginative to make up rules which people can use to voluntarily regulate their behaviour, then it is a work of genius to associate positive qualities with people who comply with those rules. But beyond that, it is an act of true enlightenment to derive benefits from some forms of non-compliance with those rules, in particular by coming to a shared understanding of how values (perhaps implicitly referenced) are, or are not being served by those rules. This is the basis of *interactional justice*, as studied in Chapter 9.

Chapter 9

Knowledge Aggregation

9.1 Introduction

The aim of this chapter is to examine n-agent social interaction through the lens of *knowledge aggregation*. Knowledge aggregation is the process of combining data, information or knowledge from multiple diverse, heterogenous sources into a single unified base. The effectiveness, or perhaps the ineffectiveness, of the process is reflected in the corporate lament "if only HP [Hewlett-Packard] knew what HP knows", which recognises the gap between an organisation's actual performance with fragmented knowledge and the organisation's potential performance if that knowledge could be properly aggregated and synthesised (Sieloff, 1999).

In the context of self-organising multi-agent systems, the problems of knowledge aggregation include both incompleteness *and* inconsistency. In a diverse and heterogenous group of agents, each agent may individually have only partial knowledge, i.e. each agent's knowledge-base may be an incomplete model of the system, of the environment, or of each other; and yet the agents collectively may also have conflicting knowledge, i.e. the union of all the agents' knowledge-bases may produce an inconsistent model of the system, environment and each other.

This has been an issue in Computer Science almost from the moment two computers were first networked together, and interactions between them were asynchronous, in parallel and peer-to-peer. As we have seen and discussed, the problem has arisen already in some form or other, in the discussions of consistency in open systems and distributed databases, interoperability in multi-agent systems, and distributed consensus technology, and knowledge commons. Indeed, the problems of knowledge management are vast and varied: see for example the survey in Fakhar Manesh *et al.* (2020).

In this chapter, we will be primarily concerned with three questions of *knowledge aggregation*. Firstly, how is it that, in a distributed system without a source of 'true' knowledge, a group of agents, each with their own local, partial, subjective assessments (of a situation, or a question), can pool their expertise to establish, a common, aggregated, objective assessment of that situation. Secondly, how agents can use such aggregated assessments to decide on, and act upon, an appropriate course of action. And thirdly, how does the *social network*, i.e. the underlying connectivity between the agents, affect the products of the other two dimensions.

In addressing this issue, this chapter is set in the context of an Ostrom institution (as in Chapter 6), and brings together ideas from social choice theory (Chapter 4) and computational justice (Chapter 7) as the basis for a computational model of *interactional justice*. Interactional justice in sociology (Schermerhorn *et al.*, 2011) and organisational theory (Greenberg, 1993) deals with the interpersonal treatment of the members of an institution according to the outcomes produced by its rules, structures and decision-makers. Building on this work, we will develop an algorithmic characterisation of interactional justice which emphasises two aspects of interaction: firstly, interaction between each member and the institution (personal treatment), and secondly, interaction between the members themselves as they compare their treatment relative to others (interpersonal treatment).

The process of interactional justice uses opinion formation over a social network with respect to a shared set of congruent values (see Chapter 8), to transform a set of individual, subjective self-assessments into a collective, objective, aggregated assessment. That assessment has a *purpose*: for example, a negative collective assessment could provide an interoceptive stimulus (i.e. a reaction to a stimulus generated from within) for institutional self-organisation (*cf.* Pitt and Nowak, 2014a), perhaps either by reformation of the rules, or by re-assignment of the appointments to roles.

Therefore, the objectives of this chapter are as follows:

- To extend the discussion of social choice theory to include judgement aggregation and opinion formation (warning: there will be some more paradox);
- To provide a specification (and, since it will be in Prolog, a (partial) implementation) of algorithms for generating different types of social networks with different properties; and
- To define an algorithmic characterisation of interactional justice for self-organising multi-agent systems.

The structure of the chapter is aligned with these objectives. Section 9.2 starts the chapter with the by-now obligatory intuitive example from the shared kitchen. Section 9.3 extends the study of social choice theory from preference aggregation to judgement aggregation, while Sec. 9.4 surveys some work in the field of opinion formation, i.e. the transmission of information and exertion of social influence that causes people to exercise their judgement in one way rather than another. Section 9.5 is concerned with the algorithms for the generation of different types of social networks, and their different properties which can affect the process of opinion formation in subtle ways. This provides the theoretical basis for the algorithmic characterisation of interactional justice in self-organising multi-agent systems in Sec. 9.6, and experiments described in Sec. 9.7. Section 9.8 concludes with some remarks, looking back at the implications of knowledge aggregation (via interactional justice) for Ostrom's institutional design principles, and forwards to the final chapter on knowledge management and 'good' self-governance.

9.2 Example: The Kitchen Aggravation

Imagine yourself back in the shared house that has cropped up at the start of every chapter. Suppose that you have amicably negotiated a housemate agreement. Suppose in addition it stipulates the rule that "if the cooker and the fridge are dirty, then the housemates shall clean the kitchen".

What could possibly go wrong?

Well, suppose there are three housemates, Inara, Jayne and Kayleigh. Inara thinks that the cooker is dirty but the fridge is clean. Jayne thinks that the cooker is clean but the fridge is dirty. Kayleigh, though, thinks that both the cooker and the fridge are dirty.

The question is: does this trigger the rule, and the housemates should clean the kitchen?

So applying the ideas of Chapter 4, the flatmates could use voting in order to resolve the dilemma in the social situation. The problem stems partly from the fact that there are two *judgements* that need to be made, rather than preferences that need to be ranked. These judgements are rather subjective: the three housemates may have very different standards of cleanliness. However, the greater part of the problem stems from the final decision depending on whether they take votes on the separate judgements, or whether they take a vote on the conjunction of the judgements.

If the housemates take a vote on whether or not the cooker is dirty, they will vote 2:1 and conclude "yes". If the housemates take a vote on whether or not the fridge is dirty, they will again vote 2:1 and conclude "yes". Logically, then, they should conclude "cooker is dirty" *and* "fridge is dirty" is true, and so trigger the cleaning rule. However, if they only take a vote on the individual conjunction of the two judgements, they will now vote 2:1 the other way, and conclude "cooker is dirty" *and* "fridge is dirty" is actually false, and so the cleaning rule is *not* triggered:

	Cooker is dirty	Fridge is dirty	Both are dirty
Inara	true	false	false
Jayne	false	true	false
Kayleigh	true	true	true
Majority	true	true	false

This is not necessarily the only problem in this kind of social situation. Suppose the housemates have to play the Biscuit Game of Sec. 7.2, and the packet of biscuits has 12 left. The three housemates submit a vector of demands $\langle d_{\text{Inara}}, d_{\text{Jayne}}, d_{\text{Kayleigh}} \rangle = \langle 6, 6, 6 \rangle$. Suppose the pairwise vector of allocations $\langle r_{\text{Inara}}, r_{\text{Jayne}}, r_{\text{Kayleigh}} \rangle = \langle 6, 5, 1 \rangle$. Now, without an external controller or oracle to advise them otherwise, and instead of applying the methods of Chapter 7, imagine that the housemates *take a majority vote* on whether or not they think the distribution is 'fair'.

If the three of them were utility-maximising self-interested agents with an 'event horizon' containing just this one social situation, the vote would split 2:1 in favour of the distribution being 'fair': two of the housemates got, or nearly got, what they wanted. If Kayleigh complained, the other two could say "We had a vote. You lost. That's democracy. Shut up".

Of course, this is not democracy at all: this is *majoritarian tyranny*, a completely different political regime altogether. We will return to this issue in Chapter 10, but the concern of this chapter is how to resolve social situations that involve subjective, qualitative judgements of this kind, without recourse to centralisation, and without throwing away the concepts of social choice and justice, as well as our computational formalisations of them.

9.3 Judgement Aggregation

In this section, we generalise preference selection of Chapter 4 to judgement aggregation. We start again with a result of Condorcet, this time the *Jury Theorem* (Pacuit, 2019); consider a kind of 'classic' problem referred to as the *Doctrinal Paradox* or the *Discursive Dilemma* (List, 2013); and finally consider the issues of deliberation and influence, which leads on to a discussion of opinion formation in Sec. 9.4.

9.3.1 *The Condorcet Jury Theorem*

Condorcet's Jury Theorem is an 'early' result in social choice theory, and concerns the *relative probability* of some group of individuals, i.e. a jury reaching the correct decision on some proposition. (For a more 'recent' treatment, see Suzuki (2015).)

The theorem revolves around whether it is better or worse to have more or fewer jurors. This, perhaps unsurprisingly, depends on how good or bad they are at reaching the correct decision independently. Perhaps surprisingly, though, if they are better than average, the majority is more likely to be better than any one individual; if they are worse than average, the majority is likely to be worse as well. Condorcet's Jury Theorem proves that this is the case.

We give a sketch of the proof. To begin with, it is assumed that the outcome of the proposition is binary, and that one of the outcomes is correct, and the other one incorrect. It is further assumed that the jury will reach their decision by taking a majority vote, and that each member of the jury has an independent probability of voting for the correct decision.

Therefore, we form a jury to make a judgement on some proposition, and assume that each member of the jury has an equal and independent chance, better than random ($p > \frac{1}{2}$) but worse than perfect ($p < 1.0$) of making a correct judgement. Then the Condorcet Jury Theorem says that:

- The majority of jurors is more likely to be correct than any one individual juror; and
- The probability of a correct judgement approaches 1 as the jury size increases.

To see this, suppose there is only one juror j. Then the probability of making a correct decision is p, and of making an incorrect decision, $1 - p$. Obviously, if ($p > \frac{1}{2}$), then $p > (1 - p)$. Now if we add two more jurors:

- If j voted incorrectly, then the probability of changing an incorrect (majority) vote to a correct vote is $(1 - p)p^2$.
- If j voted correctly, then the probability of changing a correct (majority) vote to an incorrect vote is $p(1 - p)^2$.

If $p > \frac{1}{2}$, then $(1 - p)p^2 > p(1 - p)^2$. So the probability of getting a correct vote has increased accordingly. (Of course, with independent probabilities, these are technically different 'p's, but if they are both greater than $\frac{1}{2}$, the maths works out the same, so we won't distinguish between them.)

More generally, if we assume an odd number of jurors n, and that $(n-1)/2$ jurors make the correct decision, and $(n-1)/2$ jurors make the incorrect one, then the probability of a correct/incorrect decision is already determined, and again we are concerned only with the decision of the nth juror. But the nth juror, like all the jurors before and including the first, has a probability of making a correct decision if $p > \frac{1}{2}$, so the probability of getting a correct vote has increased accordingly.

What happens if we add more jurors after the nth juror? Rewind a little, and decisions of the nth, $n+1$th and $n+2$th jurors can be:

nth	$n+1$th	$n+2$th	Probability correct decision
no	no	no	$p1$
no	yes	no	$p2$
no	no	yes	$p3$
no	yes	yes	$p4 = (1-p)*p*p$
yes	no	no	$p5 = p*(1-p)*(1-p)$
yes	no	yes	$p6$
yes	yes	no	$p7$
yes	yes	yes	$p8$

By adding two new jurors after the nth, we see that:

- $p1, p2$ and $p3$ are unchanged; and $p6, p7$ and $p8$ are unchanged, but
- $p4 > p5$ iff $p > 1/2$.

Therefore, $p4+p6+p7+p8$ (i.e. the probability of a correct decision) is greater than $p5+p1+p2+p3$. Moreover, since $p_n = p5+p6+p7+p8$ and $(1-p_n) = p1+p2+p3+p4$, and $p4 > p5$, then $p_{n+2} = p4+p6+p7+p8 > p_n$.

In other words, the majority of jurors is more likely to be correct than any single juror (unless there is only one juror); and as more jurors are added, the probability that the majority decision is correct increases (and indeed approaches 1.0).

This works both ways: if each juror is *less* likely to vote correctly, i.e. $p < \frac{1}{2}$, then adding more jurors only increases the probability of voting for the incorrect outcome, and the "least worst" jury size is just one juror.

9.3.2 The Doctrinal Paradox

As in Sec. 4.3.3, one might conclude from the Condorcet Jury Theorem that throwing enough jurors with majority voting at a problem is "job done"; conveniently overlooking that if the jurors are not very good at reaching a decision, then by adding more jurors the probability of reaching the *correct* decision is turned into small chunk chutney.

This also overlooks the problem outlined in the previous section: that majority voting on the premises of a conjunction could lead to a contradictory conclusion to a majority vote on the conjunction itself. That is, we saw that a majority vote for p = "the cooker is dirty" was true, a majority vote for q = "the fridge is dirty" was true, but a majority vote on the conjunction $p \wedge q$ was false. But we can construct such contradictions for any logical connective, for example, with the following implication:

	p	q	$p \to q$
Inara	true	false	false
Jayne	false	false	true
Kayleigh	true	true	true
Majority	true	false	true

The individual premises and implications are each consistent, but the set of majority-accepted propositions ($\{p, \neg q, p \to q, \}$) is logically inconsistent.

It is straightforward to construct an example for the or-connective as well. Moreover, the problem persists in modal propositions as well. For example, three judges stand in judgement of the following propositions:

- Obligation: p = Flatmate A was contractually obliged to clean the kitchen (**obl**(A, c)).
- Action: q = Flatmate A did not clean the kitchen ($\neg c$).
- Liability: r = Flatmate A is liable for breach of contract **obl**$(A, c) \wedge \neg c \to sanction(A)$.

This can also lead to majoritarian inconsistency called the Doctrinal Paradox (or the Discursive Dilemma). Suppose that each of the judges makes a judgement on each of the propositions as shown in what follows. The three judges are individually consistent. The first judge believes that A was obliged to clean the kitchen and did not, so is liable to sanction. The second judge believes that A was obliged to clean the kitchen and did, so is not liable to sanction. The third judge believes that A was not obliged to clean the kitchen but cleaned it anyway, so she is not liable to sanction:

	p (obligation)	q (action)	r (liability)
Judge 1	**true**	**true**	**true**
Judge 2	**true**	**false**	**false**
Judge 3	**false**	**true**	**false**
Majority	**true**	**true**	**false**

Again, we see that the set of individual judgements are each consistent, but the set of majority-accepted propositions is logically inconsistent. In logic, there is the notion of the *minimally inconsistent set*: a set all of whose proper subsets are consistent, but which itself is inconsistent. Technically, proposition-wise majority voting may generate inconsistent collective judgements if the set of judgements has a minimally inconsistent subset.

In social systems, like organisations and institutions, there are many decision-making bodies: juries, legislatures, committees, etc. All of them are concerned with *aggregenda*, the need to aggregate individual judgements on multiple logically connected propositions into collective sets of judgements. The dilemma here is that the outcome of collective decision-making by majority voting depends on one of the following approaches:

- *Premise-based approach, issue by issue*: Majority judgements on the premises; or
- *Conclusion-based approach, case by case*: Majority judgement on the conclusion.

The two approaches may lead to opposite outcomes.

It turns out Arrovian preference aggregation (see Sec. 4.5.3) is a special case of judgement aggregation, and much effort in social choice theory has been invested in the search for non-dictatorial judgement aggregation rules which overcome Arrow's Impossibility Theorem, for example, by relaxing the conditions on universal domain, collective rationality or independence.

However, this begs another question: What about *deliberation* and *influence* — if one or other juror/expert/flatmate tries to persuade the others to change their judgement, or if one seeks out the advice and guidance of another? This takes us into the domain of *opinion formation*.

9.4 Opinion Formation

Anecdotally, there are two ways to get something done: either do it yourself, or get someone else to do it for you. We have already seen one example of this maxim in action, in the trust framework of Sec. 8.3, where the agents could either make a trust-decision on the basis of their own personal experiences, or on the basis of the recommendations made by others.

In the previous section, the jurors in the Condorcet Jury Theorem made their judgements independently. So the question is, what if reaching a judgement-decision was — as it really is — like making a trust-decision, and the jurors could engage in processes of inquiry and deliberation (such as those seen in Chapter 5), or indeed attempts to influence or manipulate them (such as those seen in Chapter 4).

By relaxing the independence assumption, we are introducing the idea of *opinion formation* into the issue of *knowledge aggregation*.

The dissemination of information is a ubiquitous process between people, and between computers, and so between agents. It plays a fundamental role in numerous analogue and digital settings, including the penetration of technological innovation, word-of-mouth (gossip) and the spread of rumours, propagation of news, and distributed problem-solving.

Consequently, opinion formation has been widely studied in law, economics, sociology, philosophy (especially rhetoric), psychology, physics and computer science. In terms of modelling opinion formation as observed in social systems , the general problem can be expressed as: specify the 'rules' for the mathematical description of the dynamic development of opinions, and test if the model mirrors the patterns observed in reality.

Many such models have been developed, including for example:

- Sznajd model (Sznajd-Weron and Sznajd, 2000);
- Hegselmann–Krause (HK) model (Hegselmann and Krause, 2002);
- Deffuant–Weisbuch (DW) model (Deffuant *et al.*, 2000); and
- Ramirez-Cano–Pitt (RCP) model (Ramirez-Cano and Pitt, 2006).

An exhaustive survey is presented in Mastroeni *et al.* (2019): here we skip past the Sznajd model (because it is based on ferromagnetic spin system in statistical mechanics) and briefly survey the HK model, as it was the source model for many subsequent variations, including the DW and RCP models. The latter is the one implemented in the framework for interactional justice (Sec. 9.6).

9.4.1   Hegselmann–Krause Model

In the Hegselmann–Krause (HK) model (Hegselmann and Krause, 2002), assume that we have n-agent system, and at time t:

- x_i represents the opinion of agent i in an interval on $\mathbb{R}$ at time t.
- An agent's opinion changes according to interaction with, and distance from, other agents' opinions $x_j, j \neq i$.
- The degree of change is determined by an interaction coefficient $a_{i,j}$ accounting for the weight given by i to the opinion of j.

Then it can be seen how the opinion of agent i evolves in discrete time:

$$x_i(t+1) = a_{i,1}x_1(t) + a_{i,2}x_2(t) + \cdots a_{i,|N|}x_{|N|}(t)$$

The Deffuant–Weisbuch (DW) model of opinion formation (Deffuant *et al.*, 2000) is a continuous-time extension of HK model. In particular, it introduces the notion of *bounded confidence*. This means that interaction influence is zero for mutual distances above a certain threshold. This is based on the idea that it unlikely for one agent to be influenced by another one whose opinion is too far from its own (although it does not account for an agent being more strongly influenced by an agent whose opinion is close to its own, i.e. *confirmation bias* (Tavris and Aronson, 2015). Consequently, opinions are not guaranteed to converge to a single value, but may eventually diverge.

9.4.2   Ramirez-Cano–Pitt Model

In the Ramirez-Cano–Pitt (RCP) model (Ramirez-Cano and Pitt, 2006), which also extends the HK model, there are three key features: mindset, confidence and affinity.

It is assumed that there are a number of issues (factual propositions) under discussion at time t. On any one issue, an agent has a *mindset* $\mu \in [0,1]$, and communicates this as its *expressed opinion* on the issue $o_i \in [0,1]$.

Each agent has a *confidence*, in itself and in others. Confidence weights the relation between an agent and each of its acquaintances, i.e.:

$$w_i : N \times T \to [0,1]$$

so that $w_{i,j}(t) \in [0,1]$ expresses the confidence (function) that agent i assigns to agent j at time t. When $i = j$, this is a measure of *self-confidence*. Note that confidence is normalised to 1, i.e.:

$$\sum_{j=1}^{n} w_{i,j}(t) = 1$$

The *affinity* between agents represents the closeness of the match between one agent's mindset and another agent's expressed opinion, i.e.:

$$a_i : N \times T \to [0,1]$$

Equations for calculating and updating opinions, confidence and affinities are specified in the framework for interactional justice (Sec. 9.6). Prior to that, we consider an important parameter for any opinion formation model: the underlying (social) network, as the properties of the network may substantially affect the outcomes of information dissemination.

9.5 Social Networks

A social network is a social structure made up of three components:

- A set of social actors (individuals or organisations);
- Sets of dyadic ties; representing; and
- Any social relationship between actors.

Questions of interest include defining the structure of the whole, identifying the patterns observed in those structures, and explaining behaviour with respect to those structures and patterns.

For example, given a random organisation, one might draw up two graphs: one based on a 'reports to' relation, which might produce a typical organisational hierarchy with the CEO at the top, and another based on 'actually talks to' which might produce a random-looking graph with some well-connected nodes and most less well-connected. It might be assumed that the CEO is one of the well-connected nodes, but that would be wrong: it is the mailman in the postroom. The implication is: if there is a piece of information that one wants to disseminate throughout the organisation, the most effective person to tell is not the node at the top of the organisational hierarchy, but the most-connected node in the social network. Another example is described in Gladwell (2000), where to popularise a computer game, the marketers went to a school and asked children to point out the coolest kid they knew. Once someone pointed to themselves, they gave them a free copy of the game, then sat back while social imitation drove up sales.

Therefore, a key issue in social networks is the network topology, and how topology effects these patterns, for example, in social selection (how groups form), and social influence (how opinions form). We have already seen examples of both, in the network effect and the depreciation of values discussed in Sec. 8.6.1. For some recent work on social influence, see (Nowak *et al.*, 2020), but next we require some formal definitions and metrics in order to study network topologies.

9.5.1 *Networks: Some Definitions and Metrics*

Formally, a network is defined as a graph $G = \langle N, E, R \rangle$ where N is the set of nodes (in our case, agents), E is the set of edges, and R is the incidence relation such that $(i, e, j) \in R$ means that there is an edge or link e between nodes i and j. Intuitively, any 3-tuple in R means that the two nodes i and j can communicate directly with each other over some communication channel represented by e. However, since for our purposes here we do not distinguish between edges and all edges are assumed to be bidirectional, we will work with a set N and R as a binary relation on N (i.e. $R \subseteq N \times N$). Any 2-tuple in R means the two nodes can communicate directly (somehow) with each other.

If $(i, j) \in R$, then i is said to be a *neighbour* of (adjacent to) j, and vice versa. The *social network* of a node/agent i is defined as the set of nodes $SN_i = \{j \mid ((i,j) \in R) \lor ((j,i) \in R)\}$. (Note $(i,j) \in R \to \neg((j,i) \in R)$, but not vice versa.)

The *degree* k of a node i is the number of edges between and other nodes in the graph, i.e. $\mid SN_i \mid$ or the cardinality of the set SN_i. Degree distribution refers to the probability $p(n)$ that an arbitrarily selected node has a degree of n.

A network is *fully connected* if for every node $i \in N$ there is a *path* (i.e. some sequence of edges) to every other node $j \in N - \{i\}$.

The *path length* or *geodesic* distance $d_{i,j}$ is the shortest number of edges that must be traversed to get from i to j. Given a fully-connected network and defining $d_{i,j} = 0$ when $i = j$ defines the average path length L as:

$$L = \frac{2}{N(N-1)} \sum^{i \in N} \sum^{j \in N - \{i\}} d_{i,j}$$

The average path length is a useful metric because it scales with the size of the network differently for different network topologies.

The *clustering coefficient* is a probabilistic measure of whether any node j in the social network SN_i of a node i is also in the social network of other nodes in SN_i. However, unlike path length, there are several alternative methods for measuring clustering coefficient, the first of which was the *open triangles* method, whereby clustering the coefficient C is given by:

$$C = \frac{3 \times \text{number of connected triangles}}{\text{number of connected triples}}$$

where:

- Connected triangle: three nodes i, j, k whereby $\{(i,j), (j,k), (i,k)\} \subseteq R$ (i.e. three nodes all connected), and
- Connected triple: three nodes i, j, k whereby $\{(i,j), (j,k)\} \subseteq R$ (i.e. an open triangle).

Note that $0 \leqslant C \leqslant 1$. The clustering coefficient is a useful metric because clustering or transitivity ("friend of a friend is a friend") is a frequently observed phenomenon in many large-scale naturally-occurring networks.

Finally, *centrality* is a node-related rather than graph-related metric, and tries to identify the relative 'importance' of a node's position in a network. There are various different measures of centrality, including: *degree centrality*, which measures a node's importance relative to its connectivity to other nodes, given by:

$$C(i)_{degree} = \frac{k_i}{(n-1)}$$

closeness centrality, which measures the average distance of a node to any other node, given by:

$$C(i)_{closeness} = \frac{(n-1)}{\sum^{j \in N-\{i\}} d_{i,j}}$$

and *betweenness centrality*, which measures a node's importance with respect to the number of paths that go through it.

For a detailed survey of network metrics and a discussion of their relative usefulness in 'measuring' networks, see Prettejohn *et al.* (2011).

9.5.2 Ring and All-to-All Networks

In a ring network, every agent is connected to two neighbouring agents in an unbroken chain ($a \leftrightarrow b \leftrightarrow c \leftrightarrow \cdots \leftrightarrow a$). In an all-to-all network, every agent in the set of all agents A is connected to every other: $\forall a \in A. \forall b \in A - \{a\}. a \leftrightarrow b$.

Qu-Prolog code for generating a ring network is shown in Fig. 9.1 and for generating an all-to-all network in Fig. 9.2. The outputs for 20 agents are shown in Figs. 9.3 and 9.4, respectively. (The latter is not included for any particular educational reasons; it is just quite trippy).

The ring network and all-to-all network are at the 'limits' of fully-connected network topologies. Therefore, while they do not

```
init_socnet( ring, Agents, Edges ) :-
      Agents = [First|_],
      link_neighbours( Agents, First, [], Edges ).

link_neighbours( [Last], First, SoFar, [(Last,First)|SoFar] ) :-
      !.
link_neighbours( [This,Next|Rest], First, SoFar, Edges ) :-
      link_neighbours( [Next|Rest], First, [(This,Next)|SoFar], Edges ).
```

Fig. 9.1. Partial Specification/Implementation of Ring Network Generation

290   *Self-Organising Multi-Agent Systems*

```
init_socnet( all2all, Agents, Edges ) :-
    link_all2all( Agents, [], Edges ).

link_all2all( [], Edges, Edges ).
link_all2all( [H|T], SoFar, Edges ) :-
    link_one2rest( H, T, [], Hedges ),
    append( Hedges, SoFar, Further ),
    link_all2all( T, Further, Edges ).

link_one2rest( _, [], Edges, Edges ).
link_one2rest( N, [H|T], SoFar, Edges ) :-
    link_one2rest( N, T, [(N,H)|SoFar], Edges ).
```

Fig. 9.2.   Partial Specification/Implementation of All-to-All Network Generation

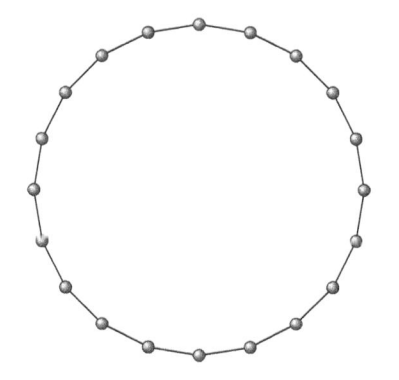

Fig. 9.3.   Example of a Ring Network

Fig. 9.4.   All-to-All Connected Network

appear often in real networks (although all-to-all networks are common with small groups), they are useful as boundary conditions for experiments.

9.5.3 Random Graphs (Erdös–Rényi) Networks

An Erdös–Rényi (ER) network, or random graph, is defined by $G = \langle A, p \rangle$ where A is the set of all agents and p is the probability of a connection between the agents (i.e. $a \leftrightarrow b$ with probability p).

Qu-Prolog code for generating an ER network is shown in Fig. 9.5. The algorithm is straightforward: generate an all-to-all network and then visit each link in turn, retaining it with probability p.

The output for 20 agents with $p = 0.16$ and for $p = 0.33$ is shown in Figs. 9.6 and 9.7, respectively. Clearly, the number of connections increases as p increases. An ER network with $p = 1.0$ generates an all-to-all network.

Although all-to-all networks are a feature of 'small' communities, as populations grow the connectivity gets more fragmented, giving rise to different types of networks. Random networks, or ER networks, satisfy the condition that generally the distribution of connection degrees can be approximated by a Poisson distribution. Therefore, ER-networks generally have small geodesic distances, but they also generally have small clustering coefficients; moreover, nodes with 'large' and 'small' degree distributions are unlikely. However, both of these features are exhibited by real-world networks. Therefore, for modelling and simulating social networks, we need algorithms which generate networks with these features.

```
init_socnet( random(P), Agents, SomeEdges ) :-
    link_all2all( Agents, [], AllEdges ),
    select_edges( P, AllEdges, [], SomeEdges ).

select_edges( _, [], Edges, Edges ).
select_edges( P, [H|T], SoFar, Edges ) :-
    random( R ),
    R =< P, !,
    select_edges( P, T, [H|SoFar], Edges ).
select_edges( P, [_|T], SoFar, Edges ) :-
    select_edges( P, T, SoFar, Edges ).
```

Fig. 9.5. Partial Specification/Implementation of ER Network Generation

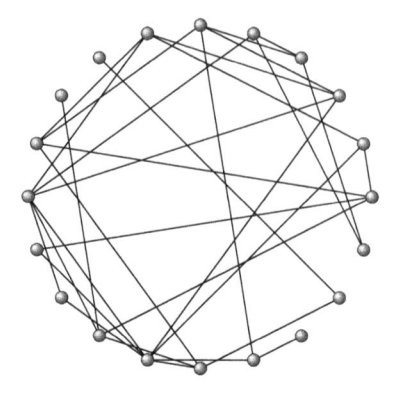

Fig. 9.6. ER Network with $p = 0.16$

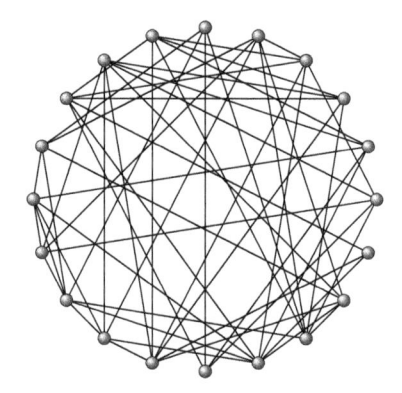

Fig. 9.7. ER Network with $p = 0.33$

9.5.4 Small-World (Watts–Strogatz) Networks

A small-world (Watts–Strogatz, WS) network is defined by $G = \langle A, k_N, p_w \rangle$ where A is the set of all agents, each with k_N neighbour connections, and p_w is a probability of each connection being randomly *re-wired*, being detached from one agent and attached to another.

Qu-Prolog code for generating a small-world network is shown in Fig. 9.8. There are essentially two steps: firstly, link each node to k neighbours. Then visit each of these edges in turn: with a probability p_w re-assign the edge to another random agent, provided the edge does not already exist.

```
init_socnet( watts_strogatz(K,B), Agents, Edges ) :-
     link_k_neighbours( K, Agents, Agents, [], SomeEdges ),
     reassign_some_edges( B, SomeEdges, Agents, SomeEdges, Edges ).

link_k_neighbours( _, [], _, Edges, Edges ).
link_k_neighbours( K, [H|T], [_|Neighbours], SoFar, Edges ) :-
     link_k( K, H, Neighbours, [], SomeEdges ),
     append( SoFar, SomeEdges, Further ),
     append( Neighbours, [H], Agents ),
     link_k_neighbours( K, T, Agents, Further, Edges ).

link_k( 0, _, _, Edges, Edges) :- !.
link_k( K1, H, [N|Rest], SoFar, Edges ) :-
     K is K1 - 1,
     link_k( K, H, Rest, [(H,N)|SoFar], Edges ).

reassign_some_edges( _, [], _, Edges, Edges ).
reassign_some_edges( B, [(X,Y)|Rest], Agents, [(X,Y)|SoFar], Edges ) :-
     random( R ),
     R =< B, !,
     random_agent( Agents, [(X,Y)|SoFar], A ),
     append( SoFar, [(X,A)], Further ),
     reassign_some_edges( B, Rest, Agents, Further, Edges ).
reassign_some_edges( B, [_|Rest], Agents, [(X,Y)|SoFar], Edges ) :-
     append( SoFar, [(X,Y)], Further ),
     reassign_some_edges( B, Rest, Agents, Further, Edges ).
```

Fig. 9.8. Partial Specification/Implementation of WS Network Generation

The output for 30 agents with $k = 3$ and for $p_w = 0.25$ is shown in Fig. 9.10. Note how most of the connections are around the 'rim' of the network, with a few connections 'bridging' the network.

Therefore, the WS networks generally do have a small geodesic distance and a high clustering coefficient. However, many 'large' real-world networks exhibit some features which are not (generally) produced by WS networks, in particular a very large distribution of node connectivities. In many real-world networks, the degree distribution tends to follow a power-law, so another network-generation algorithm is needed.

9.5.5 Scale-Free (Barabási–Albert) Networks

In a scale-free (Barabási–Albert) network, the degree distribution follows a power-law $q_k \approx k^{-\gamma}$, where q_k is the probability q that a

```
init_socnet( barabesialbert(M0,M), Agents, Edges ) :-
    select_m0_agents( M0, Agents, [], M0Agents, Rest ),
    link_all2all( M0Agents, [], M0Edges ),
    length( M0Edges, SumE ),
    DecM0 is M0 - 1,
    m0_agent_n_links( M0Agents, DecM0, [], LinksM0 ),
    each_agent_m_links( Rest, M, SumE, LinksM0, [], RestEdges ),
    append( M0Edges, RestEdges, Edges ).
```

Fig. 9.9. Partial Specification/Implementation of Barabási–Albert Network Generation

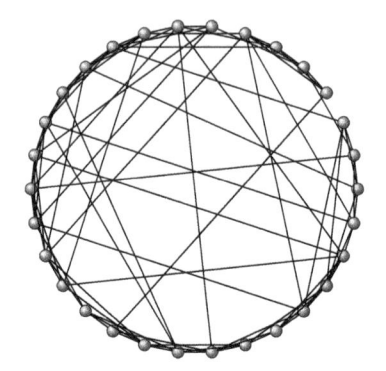

Fig. 9.10. WS Network with $k = 3, q_k = 0.25$

node has degree k, k is the degree of a node, and γ is the degree exponent.

The power-law derives from the development of 'real' networks, which often start with a small number of nodes which are all fully connected, and grow from there. The large degree distribution is then a function of network formation through *preferential attachment*, where the probability of a new node making a connection to an existing node is proportional to the degree of the existing node.

Partial Qu-Prolog code for generating a scale-free network is shown in Fig. 9.9. The algorithm requires keeping track of the current number of links for each node currently, and the total number of links currently in the network. It starts by selecting m_0 agents and making an all-to-all connected network between them. Each of these nodes then starts with $(m_0 - 1)$ links, and the total number of links is $\sum_{i=1}^{m_0-1} i$. Each of the other $\mid A \mid - m_0$ nodes is then successively added with m links each. To choose a link, one already-added node is selected at random, and is linked with a probability of its degree

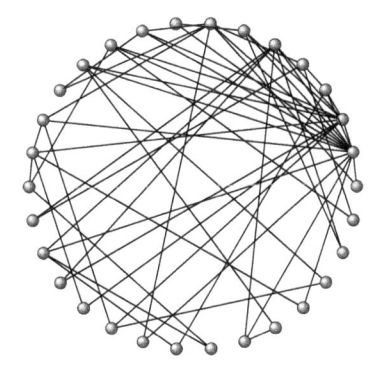

Fig. 9.11. Barabási–Albert Network with $m_0 = 3, m = 2$

divided by the total number of links in the network. This is repeated until m connections are made.

The output for 30 agents with $m_0 = 3$ and $m = 2$ is shown in Fig. 9.11. The original cluster of m_0 agents can be identified in the north-eastern corner, while the nodes added last generally have only 2 or 3 connections. Note also that in contrast to the WS-network, except around the 'hub' of m_0-nodes, nodes are generally not interconnected with each other.

Completing the code is, in the dreaded phrase, left as "an exercise for the reader".

9.6 A Framework for Interactional Justice

This section specifies a framework for interactional justice, based first on agents making an individual self-assessment (of how 'fairly' they believe that they have been treated by the enactment of the institution's procedures), and then communicating this to other agents in their social network form an overall collective assessment of their treatment.

9.6.1 *Individual Self-Assessment*

Agents use several metrics to assess their treatment by the rules of an institution. Here, we use utility, satisfaction and legitimate claims, from an individual and a 'neighbourhood' perspective.

Firstly, each agent i computes the utility U_i of its appropriation in each round in which it participates by:

$$U_i = \begin{cases} \alpha_i q_i + \beta_i(r_i - q_i) & \text{if } r_i \geq q_i \\ \alpha_i r_i - \gamma_i(q_i - r_i) & \text{otherwise} \end{cases} \quad (9.1)$$

where α_i, β_i and γ_i are agent-specific coefficients with $\alpha_i > \gamma_i > \beta_i$. Therefore, there are diminishing returns (any excess is of less utility), and a loss of utility for any shortfall. The average utility is given by dividing the sum of all utilities by the number of rounds in which the agent participates. The 'ideal' utility is given by $\alpha_i q_i$, i.e. assuming everything demanded is supplied, so relative utility is given by $\sum U_i / \sum IU_i$.

Secondly, each agent computes its personal 'satisfaction' σ_i with its allocation and the outcome of its appropriation:

$$\sigma_i = \begin{cases} \sigma_i + \varphi_i(1 - \sigma_i) & \text{if } r_i \geq q_i \\ \sigma_i - \psi_i \sigma_i & \text{otherwise} \end{cases} \quad (9.2)$$

where φ_i and ψ_i are also agent-specific coefficients that influence positive and negative reinforcement, respectively.

Finally, each agent measures the fairness F_i of the allocations with respect to its legitimate claims, given by:

$$F_i = \sum_{l \in LC_i} w_l \, accuracy(l) \quad (9.3)$$

where the *accuracy* of a legitimate claim is the (weighted) average *distance* that the agent 'observes' between what the legitimate claim specifies that the allocation should be and the actual allocation produced by the selected distribution method.

The distance between the two allocations is computed as follows. Let $pw(\vec{v})$ be the set of pairwise comparisons between ordered elements of $\vec{v}$ (i.e. if $\vec{v} = \langle x, y, z \rangle$, then $pw(\vec{v}) = \{(x,y), (x,z), (y,z)\}$). Then the distance between two vectors (allocations) is given by:

$$distance(\vec{v}_1, \vec{v}_2) = \frac{|\, pw(\vec{v}_1) \cap pw(\vec{v}_2)\,|}{|\, pw(\vec{v}_1)\,|} \quad (9.4)$$

Each agent communicates its computed assessments (U_i, σ_i and F_i) to the agents in its social network ($\forall j . j \in SN_i$), and receives their self-assessments in return. Each agent then computes the Gini index (*cf.* Equation (7.3)) of their own and the received self-assessments for each metric M_* (where $\mathcal{A}_i = SN_i \cup \{i\}$, μ is the mean, and ϕ_x is the computed assessment for each $x \in \mathcal{A}_i$):

$$gini(M_*) = 1 - \frac{1}{2}\frac{1}{\mu}\frac{1}{|\mathcal{A}_i|^2}\sum_{i=1}^{|\mathcal{A}_i|}\sum_{j=1}^{|\mathcal{A}_i|}|\phi_i - \phi_j| \qquad (9.5)$$

Finally, each agent computes μ_i by a sum of individual measures and Gini indices (weighted s.t. $\sum_{x=1}^{6} w_x = 1.0$):

$$\mu_i = w_1 gini(M_U) + w_2 gini(M_\sigma) + w_3 gini(M_F)$$
$$+ w_4(U_i/IU_i) + w_5\sigma_i + w_6 F_i \qquad (9.6)$$

where μ_i is the agent's self-assessment of the institution's fairness, (i.e. an institutional value, as defined later), and represents the agent's *mindset*, used in the computation of the collective assessment.

9.6.2 Collective Assessment

Collective assessment is implemented using a model of 'leading' and 'following' behaviours in multi-agent systems (Ramirez-Cano and Pitt, 2006), based on studies of influence in social networks (Friedkin and Johnsen, 1990; Hegselmann and Krause, 2002).

In this model, each agent i possesses a (constant) *mindset* μ_i and, at time t, an *opinion* $o_i(t)$ on a topic. Initially, an agent's opinion is equal to their own mindset, i.e. $o_i(0) = \mu_i$, but is influenced by a process of opinion exchange with agents in their social network. Therefore, each agent maintains: a list of opinions $o_{i,j}(t)$ as expressed to them (note this is the opinion of j ($o_j(t)$) as expressed to i, different from $o_i(t)$); an *affinity* to these other agents $aff_{i,j}(t)$, which is a measure of how closely their expressed opinions match the agent's own opinion and mindset; and a *confidence* $w_{i,j}(t)$ in other agents and itself (self-confidence). All these values are real numbers in the range [0, 1].

Letting t denote the current value and t' the next computed value, and as before $\mathcal{A}_i = SN_i(t) \cup \{i\}$, then the equations used to update opinions, values and weights are as follows. An agent i's new opinion is computed from the weighted sum of all opinions expressed by all agents in i's social network (including its own opinion):

$$o_i(t') = \sum_j^{j \in \mathcal{A}_i} w_{i,j}(t) o_{i,j}(t) \tag{9.7}$$

The affinity function evaluates the linear similarity between an expressed opinion and the mindset:

$$\mathit{aff}_{i,j}(t') = \frac{\mid o_{i,j}(t) - \mu_i \mid}{\mathbf{max}(\mu_i, 1 - \mu_i)} \tag{9.8}$$

One agent's confidence in another changes over time differently for each agent, based on the affinity between the two agents. Agents increase the confidence in those agents whose opinions fit their mindset. Thus, the confidence in other agents is (re-)calculated according to the following equation, and normalised so that the sum of all confidence, in other agents and itself, is 1.0:

$$w_{i,j}(t') = \frac{w_{i,j}(t) + w_{i,j}(t) \mathit{aff}_{i,j}(t)}{\sum_k^{k \in SN_i(t)} (w_{i,k}(t) + w_{i,k}(t) \mathit{aff}_{i,k}(t))} \tag{9.9}$$

9.6.3 *Implementation*

As before, the simulator for interactional justice is a Prolog program with modules for: simulating an institution, simulated agents, resource allocation, opinion formation, winner determination, social networking and inter-agent communication.

In this simulation, an institution $\mathcal{I}$ time t is defined by a 6-tuple:

$$\mathcal{I}_t = \langle A, \mathcal{L}, P, \epsilon, \mathcal{G}, \mathcal{V} \rangle_t$$

where as before A is the set of agents, $\mathcal{L}$ is the specification instance, P the 'game' protocol, ϵ the environment, $\mathcal{G}$ is a graph whose nodes specify a social network on node A, and $\mathcal{V}$ is the set of institutional values.

An agent $i \in A$, $A \in \mathcal{I}$ is a set of competencies with associated attributes, defined by:

$$i = \langle \mathit{attr}, \mathit{raf}, \mathit{ije}, \mathit{SN}, \rho, \mathcal{J} \rangle$$

where:

- *attr* is a set of attributes, including behavioural parameters, weights and other coefficients;
- *raf* defines its participation in the operational-choice resource allocation game;
- *ije* defines its participation in the evaluation of the institution by interactional justice;
- *SN* is i's social network (a sub-graph of $G \in \mathcal{I}$);
- ρ is the set of roles occupied by i in $\mathcal{I}$; and
- $\mathcal{J}$ is i's set of value-judgements, for evaluating elements of $\mathcal{V}$ in $\mathcal{I}$.

Institutions and agents are implemented as opaque global data structures which are inspected by customised access procedures (like an object), or by message passing, i.e., each agent implements a message queue which, although it can be accessed in various ways, enables the protocols used, for example, in resource allocation and interactional justice, to be implemented by synchronised communication.

The DoF of the rules in $\mathcal{L}$ and the corresponding range are shown in Table 9.1. In particular, six different methods are defined for performing resource allocation, and two different methods are defined for performing role assignment to two designated roles (the *head* and the *gatekeeper*).

Only one value is specified in $\mathcal{V}$: *fairness*. This means that agents should be able to evaluate their treatment by the institutional processes and decisions made by other agents occupying institutional roles.

Algorithm 2 specifies the cyclic process used to play the LPG' game over m rounds (m initially 0), to expose the effects of different resource allocation methods.

Algorithm 3 computes the individual self-assessments. Algorithm 4 specifies the cyclic process converging on the collective assessment over n rounds (n initially 0).

Table 9.1. Degrees of Freedom for Resource Allocation Method

DoF	Range
resource allocation method	{smallest_first, largest_first, ration, by_turn, roles_first, random}
role assignment method	{voting, random}
role of *head*	A
role of *gatekeeper*	A

ALGORITHM 2: Playing the LPG' Game

1 **repeat**
2   players $\leftarrow \emptyset$;
3   **for** *each agent* $i \in A$ **do**
4   **if** $rnd(1) > p(i, play)$ **then**
5   players $\leftarrow$ players $\cup \{i\}$;
6   play LPG' (players) ;
7   **for** *each agent* $i \in$ players **do**
8   update utility U_i (equation 9.1) ;
9   update satisfaction σ_i (equation 9.2) ;
10   update $\{accuracy(l) \mid l \in LC_i\}$ (equation 9.4) ;
11     $inc(m)$;
12 **until** m rounds;

ALGORITHM 3: Computing Individual Self-Assessment

1 **for** *each agent* $i \in$ players **do**
2   compute F_i (equation 9.3) ;
3   **for** *each agent* $j \in SN(i)$ **do**
4   send(i, j, inform(U_I, σ_i, F_i) ;
5   compute metrics $gini(U_i)$, $gini(\sigma_i)$, $gini(F_i)$ (equation 9.5) ;
6   compute mindset μ_i (equation 9.6) ;

9.7 Experiments with Interactional Justice

In this section, we report some experimental results testing the effectiveness of interactional justice. The experimental method is to set up some initial conditions with few dependent variables (so allowing limited agent variation given the relatively small population size), and, under these conditions, we report what is observed. Simulation runs are repeated to take randomness into account: a simulation run comprises m rounds of Algorithm 2, one pass of Algorithm 3, and n rounds of Algorithm 4.

ALGORITHM 4: Computing Collective Assessment
---
1 **repeat**
2   **for** *each agent $i \in A$* **do**
3   **for** *each agent $j \in SN(i)$* **do**
4 | send$(i, j, \text{inform}(\text{opinion}(o_i)))$;
5   process opinions $o_{i,j}$;
6   update opinion o_i (equation 9.7) ;
7   update affinities $\textit{aff}_{i,j}$ (equation 9.8) ;
8   update weights $w_{i,j}$ (equation 9.9) ;
9     $inc(n)$;
10 **until** *n rounds*;

9.7.1 *Economy of Scarcity*

The first experiment concerns an economy of scarcity and different resource allocation methods. The randomly generated initial conditions are as follows:

- 30 agents: Self-confidence $(w_{i,i})$ in random(1) and $lc_i \subseteq LC$;
- Social network: Random graph $G = \langle A, 0.15 \rangle$;
- $\mathcal{L}$ includes rules as per Table 9.1;
- Main loop: $m = 100$ rounds Algorithm 2, $n = 100$ rounds Algorithm 4; and
- $\mathcal{J} = \langle \sigma, U, F, gini_{M_\sigma}, gini_{M_U}, gini_{M_F} \rangle$.

The results, averaged over 11 runs for each of the six resource allocation methods, are shown in Fig. 9.12, displaying the (average) minimum, average and maximum of self-confidence $(w_{i,i})$, mindset (μ_i) and opinion (o_i) (after execution of Algorithm 4), and also the average satisfaction (σ_i), evaluation of the resource allocation by legitimate claims (F), and ratio of actual utility to ideal utility (U/IU).

There are three observations to be made. Firstly, this is an economy of scarcity, so *none* of the resource allocation methods is going to 'work', and the average agent satisfaction and legitimate-claim evaluation are both less than 0.5. On their personal metrics, in previous work (Pitt *et al.*, 2014), the agents would have left the institution as

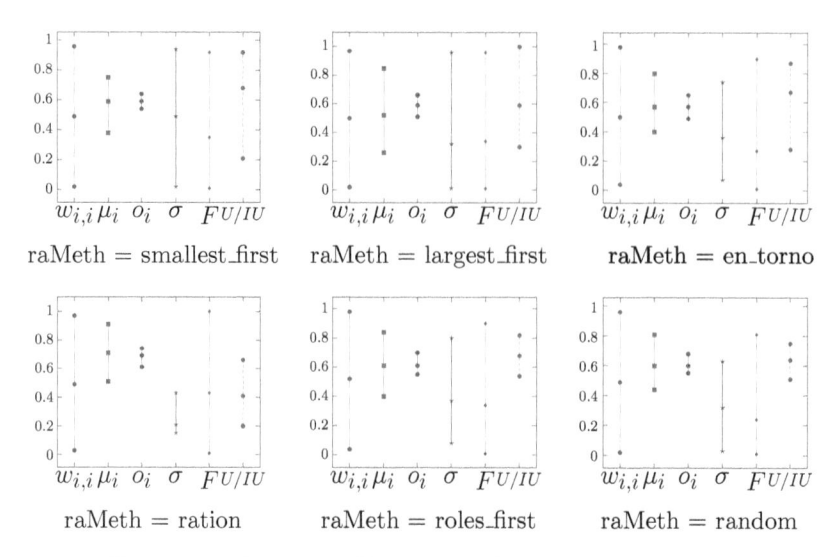

Fig. 9.12. Economy of Scarcity and Interactional Justice

'unfair'. Consequently, although the asserted value was fairness, an institution with interactional justice may be more sustainable than without.

Secondly, communication can make agents more satisfied with their situations, since it is evaluated relative to the situation of other agents. When they are able to compare their situation, firstly with the neighbours (agents in their social network) and secondly by opinion formation over the social network, the tendency converges towards an average opinion that is greater than 0.5 — note that average individual satisfaction (σ) is less than 0.5.

Finally, this convergence can be considered as a display of the *wisdom of crowds* (Surowiecki, 2004), as the opinions converge on the average (note that mindsets are independently formed, and use metrics, not opinions, of neighbours). We would suggest that this wisdom, represented by a single value emerging from a heterogenous group of agents, is a product of knowledge aggregation (Ober, 2008).

9.7.2 *'Clique' Detection and Protection*

In this experiment, we investigate the behaviour of the system if the resource allocation method is being corrupted by the *head* to favour a 'clique'.

To simulate this, we select the agent with the highest number of neighbours and make it the 'hub' of the clique. With $p = 0.15$, clique size was about 6–10 agents, so there is a ratio of 3–4:1 between the clique and the outgroup. Nevertheless, when it comes to role assignment, all of its neighbours vote for the hub, ensuring it is elected no matter what other agents do. Then, irrespective of the stated institutional resource allocation method, the head/hub allocates resources first to any members of the clique that are playing in this round, then resources are allocated at random to non-members.

With all other parameters set as before, the spread of final opinion (least, average, greatest) for this 'clique first' resource allocation method is $0.45 - 0.53 - 0.60$. The corrupt method is indistinguishable from the six allocation methods used in Sec. 9.7.1: the opinion spread has no special characteristics of its own.

However, the effect of favouring a clique, and the convergence of the collective opinion, are illustrated by comparing Figs. 9.13(a) and 9.13(b). Both plots show utility against mindset (left) and opinion (right) for each of 50 runs, where a blue square is the average of the agents in the clique (Fig. 9.13(a)) or, the agents in the social network of the most-connected agent (Fig. 9.13(b)); and a red triangle is the average of the outgroup. The clique is clustered with high utility and high mindset (i.e. their opinion is that the institution is treating them fairly), while the outgroup are clustered with low(er) utility and low(er) mindset. However, the opinion formation process drags them all towards the average opinion in the range 0.5–0.6. In comparison, Fig. 9.13(b) shows the average of 50 runs with the random resource allocation method. Each blue triangle is an agent in the social network of the hub, but without favouritism. As can be seen, their utilities are randomly distributed, but the opinion formation converges on a value in the same range, between 0.5 and 0.6.

This highlights a general problem of "automating visualisation". To a human observer, Fig. 9.13(b) displays a 'suspicious' pattern; but it is harder for an agent to detect that a clique is being favoured by a corrupt head. However, it may be possible to use interactional justice to provide some *protection* against clique formation. One approach is to base the self-confidence on an initial starting value of 0.5 and update it according to its *experience*. If an agent's experience was 'good' (resources were allocated) or 'bad' (resources not allocated), and a majority of playing agents in its social network

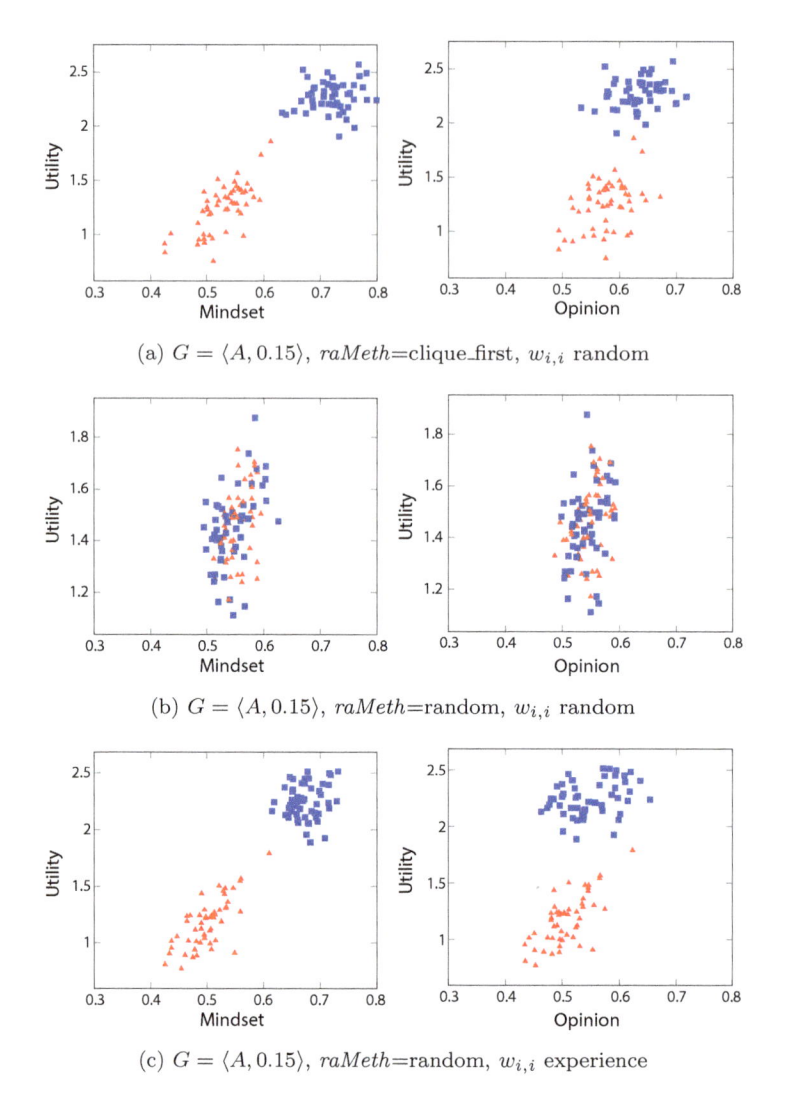

(a) $G = \langle A, 0.15 \rangle$, $raMeth$=clique_first, $w_{i,i}$ random

(b) $G = \langle A, 0.15 \rangle$, $raMeth$=random, $w_{i,i}$ random

(c) $G = \langle A, 0.15 \rangle$, $raMeth$=random, $w_{i,i}$ experience

Fig. 9.13. Utility vs. Mindset/Opinion, Various Configurations

had the *same* experience, then it should increase its self-confidence; otherwise, decrease it.

The results are shown in Fig. 9.13(c). The clique still persists, obviously, but because of the stronger self-confidence of the outgroup, more runs stay in the range 0.4–0.5.

9.7.3 Network Variations

The results of the previous experiment still assume a random network. A 'real' clique would most likely be fully connected, and would have a high self-confidence (so less likely to shift opinion) as a consequence.

In a third set of experiments, various network configurations were examined in the context of a corrupt *head* implementing clique-first resource allocation. Fixed conditions were $G = \langle A, 0.15 \rangle$, self-confidence based on experience, and the clique fully connected. Then three variations were examined: $r = d$ with 'outgroup' connected randomly; $r = 1.0$ with outgroup connected randomly; and $r = 1.0$ with outgroup fully connected. The results are shown in Fig. 9.14, for 50 runs: with average mindset after 100 rounds of LPG' of the clique (blue squares) and outgroup (red triangle) vs. average utility on the left, and average opinion after 100 rounds of opinion formation of the clique/outgroup vs. average utility on the right.

Overall, the polarisation of both utility and opinion between the clique and the outgroup can be observed (Fig. 9.14(a)). The clique has slightly higher average utility with $r = 1.0$ as they appropriate more than is demanded, as coefficient $b = 1.0$ only. The effect of over-appropriation is to lower the average mindset and opinion of the out-group (Fig. 9.14(b)); the effect of a fully connected out-group, as experiences worsen and mindsets get stronger (as a result of interactional justice), is to lower those averages even further (Fig. 9.14(c)), and in some cases to lower the clique opinions, even to the extent that they recognise that the institution is indeed unfair — reformation would (surely) follow.

These results would suggest exactly why it is in the interests of an oligarchy to operate an 'establishment' (a fully connected network of the elite), to offer 'bread and circuses' to the outgroup (i.e. don't appropriate everything), limit social mobility (i.e. limit network connections between the clique and the outgroup), and practise 'divide and conquer', (i.e. the clique pits one subset of the outgroup against another, and ensure the outgroup does not unite, organise and cooperate (as advocated by Marx)).

The significance of this shift is that, although it has not been implemented in these experiments, an institution falling below some threshold τ (although a judicious selection of τ would be important: it

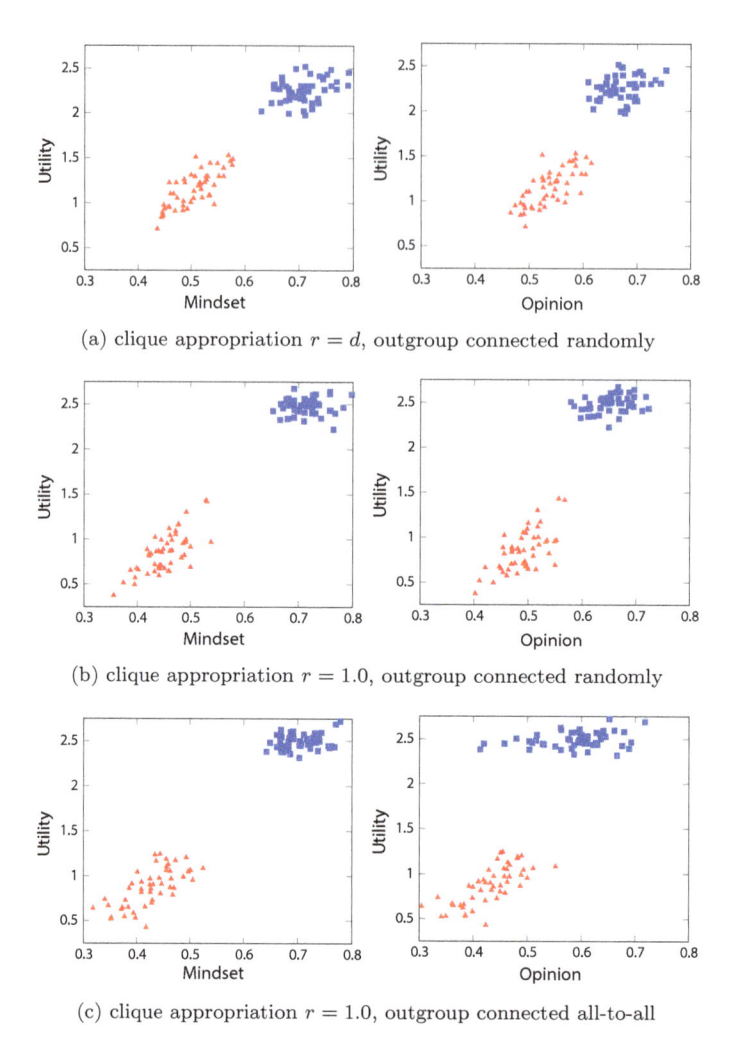

(a) clique appropriation $r = d$, outgroup connected randomly

(b) clique appropriation $r = 1.0$, outgroup connected randomly

(c) clique appropriation $r = 1.0$, outgroup connected all-to-all

Fig. 9.14. Utility vs. Mindset and Opinion, Network Variations

would need to be congruent itself) could be a trigger for *institutional reformation*, or role re-assignment (Burth Kurka *et al.*, 2018).

The experiments all used a single type of network. In recent work, it has been shown that the emergence of expertise using a simple formulation of RTSI (Nowak *et al.*, 2020) is independent of the underlying social network (Pitt *et al.*, 2020b). Further work is being undertaken to converge the opinion formation of interactional justice with the social influence of RTSI.

9.8 Summary

Self-organising multi-agent systems face a dilemma. The rules of the system have to be mutable, otherwise the system is insufficiently flexible, robust or resilient to adjust successfully to changing environments, or to satisfice the values of the agents. This essential characteristic exposes a vulnerability though: the system can be arranged not just to meet changed circumstances, but also so that it serves the interests of a few, not the collective.

We have seen how self-governing institutions offer an effective approach to fair, inclusive and sustainable common-pool resource management for both social systems (Ostrom, 1990) and open computer systems (Pitt *et al.*, 2012a, 2014). Nevertheless, collective choice arrangements which allow unrestricted self-modification of the institutional rules (Suber, 1990) present three problems.

Firstly, ensuring *congruence*: the institutional rules should be fit-for-purpose with respect to the prevailing environment (Ostrom institutional design principle 2 (Ostrom, 1990)), given the 'large' space of possible rule configurations and the 'large' range of rates of environmental change.

Secondly, ensuring *acceptability*: the outcomes produced by the rules should be acceptable to the participants, given that even if the participants share the same *values*, they may apply different metrics for assessing the achievement of those values.

Thirdly, minimising *risk*: the potential downside of self-organisation is exposure to the *iron law of oligarchy* (Michels, 1962 [1911]), which states that no matter how 'democratically' an institution is constituted, it will inevitably be taken over by a clique who run the institution in pursuit of their own self-interest and not the common interest or collective well-being.

In the absence of an all-knowing centralised controller, or some external authority, the knowledge of 'what is going on' and 'where things are going' rests with the agents themselves. Therefore, dealing with congruence, acceptability and risk are essentially tied into issues of knowledge management and self-governance.

Accordingly, this chapter has involved an overview of opinion formation and judgement aggregation over a social network leading to an algorithmic characterisation of *interactional justice*. Informally, interactional justice is a user-centric aspect of justice required for realising values of fairness and inclusivity in organisations and communities, and is concerned with how people feel they are being treated by the processes, deliberations and decision-making in an institution. Algorithmically, in an open multi-agent system, it is; with specifying three processes: firstly, how an 'agent' individually 'feels' it is being 'treated' by the outcomes of deliberation; secondly, how an 'agent' communicates how it 'feels' it is being 'treated' by the outcomes of deliberation; and thirdly, how a group of 'agents' collectively determines how it 'feels' its members are being 'treated' by the outcomes of deliberation (Pitt, 2017).

The simulator that we developed here has exposed some of relationship between, on the one hand, the individual and collective treatment of agents with respect to their set of shared and congruent values offered by an institution's judicial procedures (e.g. in distributive justice), and, on the other, the concerns of congruence, acceptability and resistance to oligarchy. In one experiment, we showed how an awareness of 'situational similarity' resulted in agents tolerating an economy of scarcity; without interactional justice, agents would have left the institution or the rules would have 'thrashed' in the search for a fairer set (there being no fair set in an economy of scarcity). In two subsequent experiments, we saw how interactional justice could provide some detection of, and protection from, corrupt behaviour that primarily benefits the interests (values) of a clique.

We would therefore conclude that by addressing congruence, acceptability and risk, interactional justice makes three contributions to 'good' self-governance. Firstly, in *transforming knowledge*: from knowledge based on personal sensory experience or derived from comparison or exchange with others, to knowledge arrived at by consensus or majority agreement. This transformation is critical to knowledge aggregation and knowledge alignment (Ober, 2008). Secondly, it *increases stability*, satisfying the concept of the well-ordered society (Rawls, 1971). Finally, this collective agreement also implies and produces *reduced conflict*, contributing indirectly to the realisation of Ostrom's sixth institutional design principle (access to fast and efficient conflict resolution) (Ostrom, 1990).

However, our ultimate aim is to use this characterisation of interactional justice to satisfice a shared set of congruent values, to confront the (supposedly inevitable) asymmetric distribution of power and the iron law of oligarchy (Michels, 1962 [1911]), *and* provide the foundations of a well-ordered institution. But, in a well-ordered institution, if the collective feeling of the agents is that they have been treated "badly", how do they reform the institution rather than quitting it? This is the contribution of knowledge aggregation to knowledge management, and in turn effective knowledge management is critical to the exercise of 'good' or 'democratic' self-governance. This is the subject of Chapter 10.

Chapter 10

Algorithmic Self-Governance

10.1 Introduction

This chapter examines social interaction through the lens of *comparative politics*, a sub-field of *political science*. Comparative politics involves the study of national politics through an analysis of the political institutions within a country, and of international politics through an analysis of the treaties and conflicts between countries. Such analysis can involve both comparisons at one time between organisations and states, or comparisons over time by observing the trajectory of a single organisation or state.

The reason for turning to comparative politics is that many of the unresolved or recurring problems highlighted in the preceding chapters are a feature of socio-political systems, and have therefore been addressed by sociologists and political scientists. In particular, there are four interrelated issues we need to address.

Firstly, there is the issue of *knowledge management*. The previous chapter examined the process of knowledge aggregation, which is one process in the scope of knowledge management (Ober, 2008).

Knowledge management is predicated on dealing with both symbols — symbolic representation (data), symbolic meaning (information) and symbolic reasoning (knowledge) — and the processing of such symbols, i.e. the creation, storage, transmission, interpretation, assimilation and application of data, information and knowledge. The key concern is how to use knowledge for socially productive purposes, enabling a diverse collective to make 'correct' decisions and act upon those decisions effectively (Ober, 2008).

Secondly, there is the recurring issue of *majoritarianism*. The simplicity of majority rule gives it an intuitive appeal, but it is not, as we have seen, the ultimate unproblematic solution. In particular, there is a concern about how to balance majority preference against expert judgement: for example, in those situations where the popular opinion is in favour of one alternative, but those well-informed on the matter recommend the other.

Thirdly, there is the issue concerning the *tolerance of dissent*: how does a group enable critics to expose inconsistencies between core values and current practices (Ober, 2008), without labelling them as "disruptive" or accusing them of being "an enemy of the people".

Finally, there is the issue of constitutional choice and the 'dilemma of the rules', which itself has two dimensions:

- The rules have to be sufficiently unrestricted to allow freedom of (collective) action; but equally, rules have to be sufficiently restricted to resist the *iron law of oligarchy* (Michels, 1962 [1911]); and
- At least in social systems, rules provide the material conditions for human flourishing, promote free exercise of constitutive human capacities, and sustain the desirable conditions of social existence (Ober, 2017).

Therefore, the objectives of this chapter are as follows:

- To discuss the roles of knowledge management, relevant expertise aggregation and dissent-tolerance in self-organising systems;
- To demonstrate how a theory of political science, Ober's Basic Democracy (Ober, 2017), can be implemented and animated; and
- To discuss *algorithmic comparative politics* as a source of insight into political regimes and design principles for self-organising systems (*cf. democracy by design* (Pitt and Ober, 2018)).

The chapter is organised as follows. The final example from the SmartHouse, in Sec. 10.2, takes note of trying to self-organise at scale. We then examine the issues raised earlier: knowledge management in Sec. 10.3, relevant expertise aggregation in Sec. 10.4, and disobedience in Sec. 10.5. Section 10.6 reviews the theory of Basic Democracy, the thought experiment Demopolis, and the simulator SimDemopolis. Experiments with SimDemopolis described in Sec. 10.7 show how Basic Democracy can avoid tyranny, in the form of oligarchy, autocracy and majoritarianism. This leads to a discussion of the inter-disciplinary potential of "algorithmic comparative politics" in Sec. 10.8. We conclude in Sec. 10.9: that understanding political processes in self-organisation through algorithmic design, analysis and animation is critical, if we want to better understand how "we" can live together, better, both "in real life" and online, and moreover how "we" can do that at scale.

10.2 Example: The Ministry of Culinary Affairs

Let us imagine that the housemates, after the collapse of the autocracy established in Chapter 6, now wish to restore democracy and establish the People's Republic of Absurdistan.

One of the housemates has been appointed as the Minister in the Ministry of Culinary Affairs, which has responsibility for all aspects of kitchen cleanliness, biscuit distribution and so forth. The Minister brings a proposal for new legislation before the House of Parliament, which includes the following clauses:

- *A Minister may by regulations make such provision as the Minister considers appropriate if the Minister considers that such provision should be in force.*
- *Regulations under this section may not*:
  ○ *impose or increase taxation,*
  ○ *make retrospective provision, or*
  ○ *create a relevant criminal offence.*
- *Regulations under this section may make any provision that could be made by an Act of Parliament (including modifying this Act).*

So, the first clause states that the Minister can do what he likes: the minister may make a provision if the minister considers it "appropriate" that a provision should be a provision. The second clause says that there are constraints on this provision. But the third clause states that the provision can modify this act; so presumably, it can modify the second clause to *remove* the constraints on the provision.

Only, as they say, in Absurdistan...

Except, this is in fact an extract from an Act put before a real Parliament. Before looking at Fig. 10.1, make a guess which country it is... Were you right? Recall the *Game of Nomic*, the Paradox of

Fig. 10.1. Excerpt from the UK's European Union (Withdrawal) Bill 2018 (The section was repealed in 2020. Any modifications made according to its provisions are unknown)

Self-Amendment, and the unrestricted modification of rules discussed in Sec. 6.7.3: not so abstract any more, is it?

Only, as they say, in Absurdistan...[1]

It could be argued that, in the real Act, the Ministerial powers granted by the Act were time-limited by sunset clauses; but since the sunset clauses were also part of the act, the Minster could have

---

[1]There is a so-called "stan stigma", whereby a negative perception is associated with those countries whose name ends in "-stan". We use the term here in its non-associative literal meaning as "place of" (i.e. place of the absurd). No disrespect to any real countries is implied or intended. For the country that the example does refer to, it is left to the reader to decide, based on knowing that 'Eng' is derived from the Indo-European word for "absurdly incompetent public school-educated narcissist".

modified these clauses and extended the power without duration, or parliamentary scrutiny. A better argument is that in any system admitting potentially unrestricted self-modification, and by unrestricted we mean a lack of scrutiny, transparency, accountability and responsibility, it is essential that the issues of governance are addressed.

10.3 Knowledge Management

10.3.1 *Knowledge Management in Classical Athens*

It has been shown that Athenian democracy, on a number of independent metrics, massively outperformed its rival city states, economically, architecturally, militarily and diplomatically; despite a relative parity in territorial size, population density, cultural development and availability of mineral resources (Ober, 2008). The exceptional success of Athenian democracy was attributed to the greater social benefits derived from higher levels of cooperation. This in turn was based on the Athenians' superior capacity for resolving public collective action problems, which itself was a product of special features of their participatory and deliberation model of self-governance. One of the most important of these special features was the distinctive Athenian system for *organising useful knowledge.*

Suppose $\mathcal{I}$ is an institution attempting to solve some problem facing the set of individuals who are members of $\mathcal{I}$. $\mathcal{I}$ itself is an abstraction, and does not exist as an entity capable of 'physical' action (although it may be capable of 'legal' action). Therefore, solving the problem may rely on the abstract $\mathcal{I}$ institutionally coordinating the collective physical actions of the concrete set of individuals — $\mathcal{I}ans$ say. Then there are, essentially, three epistemic issues relating $\mathcal{I}$ and $\mathcal{I}ans$:

(1) **Collective decision-making:** How does $\mathcal{I}$ know what $\mathcal{I}ans$ know?
(2) **Collective coordination:** How do $\mathcal{I}ans$ do what $\mathcal{I}$ decides (or intends) to do?
(3) **Collective 'memory':** How does $\mathcal{I}$ record or remember what $\mathcal{I}ans$ did (successfully)?

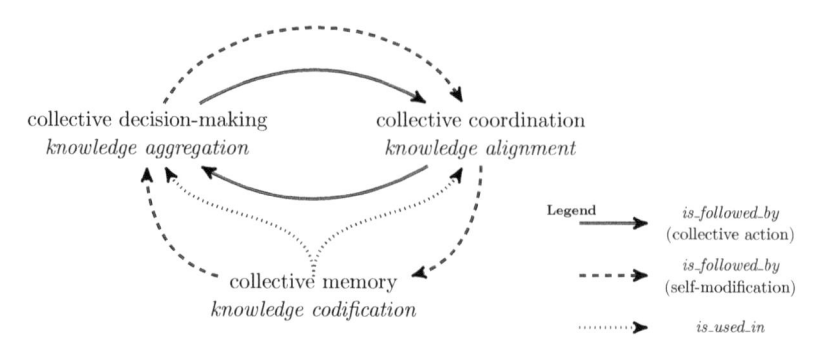

Fig. 10.2. Athenian Knowledge Management Processes (Based on Ober (2008))

The analysis in Ober (2008) determines that the Athenians developed highly effective, transparent and interdependent epistemic processes, including: *knowledge aggregation*, by which dynamic knowledge, created by and between citizens, delivered the 'right' course of action that 'best' represented or served their shared values; *knowledge alignment*, which used mutual knowledge to coordinate individuals in successfully satisfying that course of action; and *knowledge codification*, which standardised institutional structures and procedures, increasing openness and effectiveness and supporting inclusiveness, verification and accountability. The relationship between these processes is illustrated in Fig. 10.2. Note the arrows represent sequencing rather than dataflows. There are two sequences: in the inner sequence (solid arrows), knowledge aggregation precedes knowledge alignment and both processes are supported by codified knowledge (dotted arrows) to solve collective action problems (e.g. the distribution of common-pool resources (CPRs)). However, codified knowledge itself can be modified by a "knowledge aggregation — knowledge alignment" sequence, as represented by the outer sequence (dashed arrows), used for selecting and modifying the rules for the distribution of CPRs.

Processes of knowledge aggregation proved to be highly effective in enabling a group of otherwise disparate and heterogenous individuals, when acting as (or in the context of) $\mathcal{I}$, to get the 'right' answer to a given question, in three ways: firstly, by providing incentives for knowledgeable individuals to pool their knowledge for the benefit of the group (these incentives did not have to be financial, but could be in the form of social capital (reputation) in an economy of esteem

(Brennan and Pettit, 2005)); secondly, by ensuring that the cost of communication was sufficiently low to overcome the imposition of getting information from "where it was" to "where it needed to be"; and thirdly, sorting processes sifted not only false information from the true but also sifted information useful in a given context from the irrelevant.

Having reached the 'right' decision by aggregating knowledge, processes of knowledge alignment ensured that this same group of individuals with a common interest in coordinating their actions could do so effectively. Athens/Athenians then achieved high levels of coordination between individuals and institutions by intermixing four epistemic mechanisms for accurate collective coordination. These are first choice, where one agent acts and the others follow in an alignment cascade; informed leader, where one agent deemed 'more informed' is designated the leader and the others follow his/her direction; rule-following, where each agent believes there is a rule, expects others' actions to conform to that rule, and so follows the rule itself; and commitment-following, where credible pre-commitments from each are required to ensure that all will act in unison (e.g. turning up for a battle with a weapon and armour is a credible pre-commitment to join in the coming fight as opposed to turning up empty-handed).

Having achieved a successful coordination by aligning common knowledge, the outcomes of both collective decision-making and collective coordination yield even greater benefit through processes of knowledge codification. This effectively creates an institutional 'memory' which can inform future behaviour of institutional members. In Athens, dynamic forms of knowledge used in the aggregation and alignment processes were codified in written laws or decrees. However, the Athenians managed to ensure that such codified knowledge was sufficiently stable to allow for confident planning, political engagement and civic education, but also sufficiently fluid to avoid ossification and allow introspective improvement by amendment.

10.3.2 *Facts, Policies and Values*

These knowledge management processes have, to a greater or lesser extent, been undermined in contemporary liberal democracies. In a relatively short time, we have travelled a long way from Fukuyama's *"End of History"* (Fukuyama, 1992) (predicting, after the Cold War ended, the lasting hegemony of liberal democracy as the dominant political regime) to the *"End of Democracy"* (e.g. Runciman, 2018).

For example, the process of knowledge aggregation has been undermined by control, doubt and deception. In terms of control, both information sources and communication channels are often owned by the same parent organisation, while the sources and channels appear independent. In terms of doubt, there has been the fomenting of distrust in traditional reputable sources and expertise, in particular the judiciary, academia and the education system. This has been complemented by the systematic (mis)use of doubt (Oreskes and Conway, 2010), for example by setting up an apparently independent 'thinktank' with a grandiose title, and publishing a 'paper' doubting some phenomenon (e.g. anthropogenic climate change). This is duly reported in the popular press. A proper scientist duly debunks the claim, but this is *not* reported by the press. As before, both thinktank and press are covertly owned or funded by the same parent organisation. Finally, in terms of deception, online social media are being distorted by "troll armies", whose role it is to inject biased information into a national consciousness and giving it specious credibility by apparent preponderance.

Ober (2008) suggests that while effective knowledge aggregation needs a diversity of knowledge, for effective knowledge alignment there needs to be *common knowledge*. Online social media has witnessed the exploitation of confirmation bias (Tavris and Aronson, 2015), which has led to the creation of filter bubbles (Pariser, 2011) and the elimination of common knowledge through polarisation and fragmentation. The lack of common knowledge has provided data analytics and machine learning algorithms with opportunities for targeted micro-advertising, which didn't stop at pushing products but pushed political messaging as well. There is evidence of external interference and manipulation of national elections as a result. Moreover, the splintering of knowledge can have deleterious effects on collective action and public health initiatives: for example, the anti-vax campaign has led to the loss of "herd immunity" and outbreaks of diseases like measles and mumps, while the wearing of masks as a means of limiting the spread of COVID-19 has been equally contentious.

Polarisation undermines knowledge codification, too. Beyond the loss of shared values, perhaps the most significant loss is the loss of a shared narrative. This has led to different sections of society facing off against each other in mutual incomprehension and suspicion: rich vs. poor, young vs. old, and so on. Divide and conquer is not exactly an original technique, but it remains remarkably effective (especially if the electoral system is gerrymandered so that 43% of the votes give 56% of the parliamentary seats; see also Daley, 2016).

This matters. It may be that "peak liberal democracy" occurred in the 30 years following the Second World War, characterised by significant international achievements such as, for example, the European Convention on Human Rights (1953), the civil rights movement, and the welfare state, combined with mass participation in political parties, which reached their largest membership in this period. Widespread participation ensured that political representatives were proportional to opinions of the membership, whose critical mass tended to the centre, not the extremes.

This period was also characterised by two other features. Firstly, there was a broad agreement across the spectrum of opinion on a set of facts, i.e. an established core of socially constructed knowledge that was generally (if not universally) accepted as *intersubjective agreement* (if not 'objective truth'). Even if one could construct a different narrative or interpretation from the facts, the facts themselves were the same. Both educational institutions (under the responsibility of the state) and media organisations (under the remit of private corporations) respected this set of facts.

Secondly, there was a mutual agreement across the spectrum of opinions on a shared set of congruent values. This being liberal democracy, we suppose that 'Western' democracies in the post-war period were implicitly or explicitly concerned with preserving and promoting the 'national interest', as well as maintaining and expanding civil rights, achieving fairness in distributive justice, and the collective provision of health, education and infrastructure. Liberal democrats tended to take for granted the fundamental capacity of basic democracy to achieve three ends, namely security, prosperity and the avoidance of tyranny (although basic democracy is neither committed to, nor opposed to, value neutrality).

This, then, characterised the essence of politics in this era: political power was a dashboard for social change, not an instrument for it; and so the primary objective of political parties, whether to the left or to the right of centre, was to devise and enact a set of evidence-based (fact-driven) policies to maintain, achieve or maximise the shared set of congruent values. The objective was at once both moral and prudent, because liberal democracy functioned better (and certainly better than the authoritarian/planned political/economic alternative) for aligning bounded-rational political choices and decisions with moral preferences and outcomes (Ober, 2017). Politics itself was essentially nuanced: it required dialogue, deliberation, negotiation and compromise, in particular with those who might have a different narrative with respect to the facts, different priorities with respect to the values, or different beliefs about the benefits of social change.

The trajectory of democratic deficit and decline since the 1970s is charted in Pitt (2019b): from the prioritisation of the interests of a clique, through the polarisation of political discourse, on to the undermining of civic dignity. The essence of this corruption has been an abasement of knowledge management processes that disrupts the intersubjective agreement on the "facts" that underpin the legitimacy of democratic governance. The design of self-governance mechanisms for cyber-physical and socio-technical systems need to take this into account.

10.4 Relevant Expertise Aggregation

Relevant expertise aggregation (REA) is proposed as a decision-making method aimed to address the tension between majority preference and expert judgement (Ober, 2013). REA is a process of decision-making that is both 'democratic' (in the sense that it takes into account the expressed preferences of the majority) and 'epistemic' (in the sense that it takes into account the knowledge and judgement of experts). The deliberative process involves expert groups making policy recommendations based on domain expertise and citizen groups making policy choices based on those recommendations.

A procedure is informally described in Ober (2013). A governing institution is faced with a set of problems that need to be addressed. For each problem, it identifies a limited number of domains: each domain is ranked in $[0, 1]$ and weighted (with the sum of weights on the domains normalised to 1) according to its perceived relevance to the issue. A group of experts in each domain is consulted: it is supposed that these experts are reliable, i.e. they have good reasons to disclose their true opinion, and have a probability better than random of reaching the 'correct' decision (appealing to the Condorcet Jury Theorem, as per Sec. 9.3.1). The group of domain experts is offered a limited number of policy options, each option being understood as a potential solution to the issue. Each option is given a final score as a proportion of the expert votes multiplied by the weight of the domain, and summed over all domains. The final scores are used by the governing/decision-making body to determine policy selection. This can be done in a number of different ways, depending on the political regime.

Suppose a community has to make a decision about a bridge crossing a river. The decision about the bridge might take into account, *inter alia*, financial, architectural, environmental and social considerations. There might be several options: leave the bridge as it is, repair the bridge, rebuilding (repurpose) the bridge, remove the bridge altogether.

The process is as illustrated in Fig. 10.3. To address the given issue (labelled "?"), the relevant factors are divided into domains, the domains are weighted, and expert testimony sought on each domain. The number of expert votes for each option in each domain is multiplied by its weight, and summed across all domains. The final scores are input into a decision procedure which either determines the final choice (in non-democratic regimes) or helps guide the final choice (in democratic ones).

There are several issues to be taken into consideration: for example, determining the domains, their weighting, and the policy options. Some of these might require (meta) deliberation as well. For full details of REA, see Ober (2013).

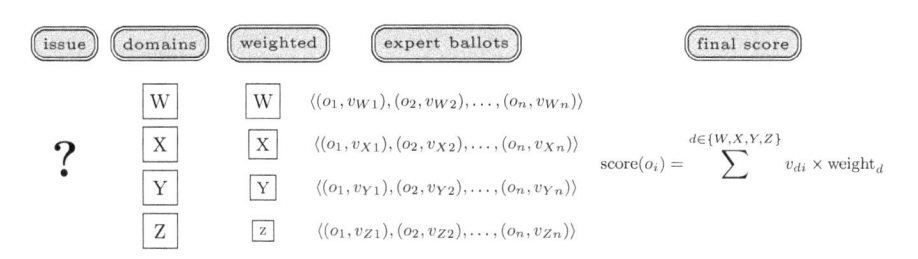

$$\text{score}(o_i) = \sum_{d \in \{W,X,Y,Z\}} v_{di} \times \text{weight}_d$$

Fig. 10.3. Relevant Expertise Aggregation (Following Ober (2013, p.146f))

A formal algorithmic specification, and its implementation using multi-agent systems, has been used to select policies for regulating community energy systems (Pitt *et al.*, 2018b) (e.g. given uncertainty in renewable energy generation, how much energy to import, export, generate, store, etc.). In this simulation, there are a set of criteria for evaluating policies, and for each criterion there is a set of metrics evaluating it. Each agent 'knows' a subset of criteria, and a subset of the related metrics. At regular intervals, a number of 'expert' groups, comprising a subset of the agents, were formed. Given a starting policy (which could either be an initial policy or some random policy), each group of agents used machine learning algorithms to produce a recommendation for the 'best' policy option under the existing and expected operational conditions. There were two approaches to policy optimisation: off-line evolution, which used genetic programming (GP) to discover an optimal policy *a priori*; and on-line evolution, which used GP and reinforcement learning to select different operating policies at run-time.

10.5 The Tolerance of Dissent

We have said before that open norm-governed systems have to deal with the expectation of error: this allows for the divergence between actuality, i.e. what is the case, and ideality, i.e. what ought to be the case, as we saw in the rooms scenario of Sec. 2.6.2. Dealing with this divergence, as we saw with the processes of alternative dispute resolution in Chapter 5, is essentially a corrective procedure.

However, we have to be sure what we are correcting. A recurring feature of organisational and social relations is that a behaviour may be proscribed, but specific episodes are tolerated and 'common-sense' reasoning is applied instead ("under normal circumstance . . . but these circumstances aren't normal"). For example, an organisation's expenses policy may state that normally taking taxis is prohibited; but 'reasonable' taxi receipts are paid and the rule "no taxis" is conveniently waived (not normal), 'unreasonable' receipts are denied and the rule "no taxis" is applied. The same feature can be seen in the floor access protocol of Sec. 5.5: an agent could retain the resource beyond its allotted time if no other agent requested it.

Differentiating between reasonable and unreasonable cases is what has been referred to as the principled violation of policy (Burth Kurka and Pitt, 2017). A new degree-of-freedom is introduced to the norm-governed game, giving agents the decision to pardon (or not) non-compliant events. A case can be made that flexibility in norm application can be beneficial from several perspectives: for example, cost, efficiency, acceptability, mutability and fairness.

Lewis and Ekárt (2017) also explore this violation concept, but in the learning context. By considering the behaviour of agents playing a resource allocation game as they adjusted to new conditions, they showed that disobedience to norms can be seen as a form of exploratory behaviour, the latter being a crucial ingredient for learning. They further show that pardoning has a key role in enabling diversity of behaviour in the system, in order that the institution permits, rather than inhibits, learning of preferable solutions.

Furthermore, another feature of organisational and social systems is that the rule may be 'correct', but those empowered with enforcing it may be applying it incorrectly. For example, in a resource allocation scenario with a common-pool resource, the rule might be a queue, but a corrupt allocator might allocate resources to its clique first. Yet another possibility, though, is that the agent empowered with enforcing the rule may be doing it correctly, but that the rule itself is 'incorrect': for example, if it is not congruent with its environment (in fact violating another one of Ostrom's institutional design principles).

There are at least three possibilities for errors in norm-governed systems:

(1) The norm is right, those violating it are wrong (the conventional view); or
(2) The norm is right, those applying it are wrong (*cf.* Sec. 10.7.2); or
(3) The norm itself is wrong.

Using the idea of interactional justice, as discussed in Sec. 9.6, agents form a subjective assessment of their treatment, communicate their opinions to each other, and form a collective assessment of their treatment. This treatment could be exposed to be (in some sense) 'unfair': however, it stopped short of achieving a restoration of justice through institutional reformation, and it did not identify whether or not it was the rule or the rulers that were at fault.

As it turns out, *disobedience* has been used historically as a form of resistance and call for change in unfair regimes, and is considered as a human right in some constitutions. Moreover, if it is a critical factor in systemic improvement: "Democratic tolerance for political dissent allows critics to expose inconsistencies between core values and current practices" (Ober, 2008, p. 4). Moreover, Ober points out that a primary objective of political criticism has been to expose the operation of institutionalised authority on the ideological dispositions of individuals subject to that authority (and especially its influence on choice, a point made in socio-political theories developed from Marx (Ober, 2008, p. 272)).

Therefore, we need to allow for criticism, perhaps as an element of reflection, but also for dissent and disobedience in self-organising systems. A systematic investigation of collective disobedience, both for bringing about rule-change or ruler-change, and for the exploration of the trajectories of political regimes, can be found in Burth Kurka *et al.* (2018).

10.6 Basic Democracy and Demopolis

In Ober (2017), *basic* democracy has been proposed as a means of collective self-governance distinct from *liberal* democracy, i.e. it is a conventional rule-based system of empowerment, decision-making and public action that is both prior to and separate from concerns such as justice, morality and rights. The aim in Ober (2017) is to construct a 'first principles' theory of democracy, itself construed as collective self-governance by citizens. It is grounded in the study of classical Athenian democracy, and therefore assumes that it precedes liberalism (e.g. Rawls, 1971), and is defined by both self-determination (citizens' capacity for making, selecting, modifying, applying and enforcing rules), and systematic constraints on that process.

Ober's analysis of basic democracy (Ober, 2017) is predicated on a thought experiment, Demopolis, which provides a platform to specify the conditions for its founding and maintenance, to examine its consequences, and to identify its benefits (*vis-á-vis* other regime types). Demopolis starts with the assumption of an extensive and diverse group of people who share a preference for non-tyranny, can find a geographical space to co-locate, and can defend that space from rivalrous claims. They establish basic rules on participation, legislation and entrenchment, with which they will govern themselves as residents of a masterless (non-tyrannical) state. Only subsequently do they address more complex policy issues, such as (*inter alia*) the choice and prioritisation of 'liberal' values.

This thought experiment demonstrates that basic democracy is available as a *theoretical* regime type for a *hypothetical* community in search of a social order that is without tyranny but neutral with respect to prioritising liberal values. Whether it is a *practical* option for an *actual* community depends on the limitations of any thought experiment, i.e. whether it is feasible, desirable, or ethical to perform it.

However, in the context of open computer systems and networks, we *can* assume that the preconditions for the thought experiment do hold: that we start from a *tabula rasa* with a group of heterogenous agents which are unconstrained by space but are coded with a preference for non-tyranny. The question becomes: to what extent can the principles of basic democracy be automated, to afford the self-organisation of tyranny-avoiding collective governance in open systems *ab initio*. The answer to this question can provide significant insight firstly, into establishing stable foundations for the supply of sustainable institutions (Ostrom, 1990) or achieving fairness in resource allocation (distributive justice (Pitt *et al.*, 2014)), and secondly, into the potential use of basic democracy as a theory for informing the development and management of socio-technical systems.

10.6.1 *Basic Democracy*

In contrast to the self-governing institutions for common-pool resource management studies by Ostrom, classical Athenian democracy and 18th century post-revolution America focused first on the question of designing institutions to prevent the occurrence (or recurrence) of tyranny, and only subsequently addressed the question of how to create a fully just, virtuous or otherwise benevolent social order. Establishing the political framework to answer the former is, according to Ober (2017), the essence of *basic* democracy; as opposed to the admixture of concerns for morality, autonomy, rights, justice and values that characterises *liberal* democracy, which can be seen as a political framework for addressing the latter question.

The theory developed in Ober (2017) seeks to demonstrate the validity of three claims, that basic democracy:

- Is a reasonably stable form of collective self-government by a diverse group of citizens;
- Can be both legitimate and effective; and
- Demonstrates the importance of civic education.

Ober argues that stability requires rules, which themselves must restrict the absolutist tendencies of the collective rulers and degeneration into different political regimes (*cf.* the ancient Greek theory of anacyclosis (Walbank, 1957)). In other words, the rules themselves must resist entropic tendencies like the iron law of oligarchy (Michels, 1962 [1911]) (which (again) asserts that any organisation, no matter how democratically it is founded, is inevitably usurped by a minority group that endeavours to maximise their own, and not the collective, benefit).

Ober also discriminates between basic democracy and majoritarian tyranny, distinguishing between the functional and normative meanings of democracy (i.e. capable of collective action and self-governance, and *ought to be* capable of collective action and self-governance) and the potentially brutal and arbitrary outcomes of unconstrained domination of 'the many' over 'the few'. This distinction also acknowledges that 'capability' includes limitations: with abilities are attached responsibilities.

Legitimacy and effectiveness of basic democracy are derived from its benefits for citizens: Ober argues that it provides the material condition for human flourishing (e.g. security and prosperity); promotes free exercise of constitutive human capacities (e.g. reasoning and communication) and sustains desirable conditions of social existence (e.g. political equality and civic dignity (Waldron, 2012)).

The importance of civic education is related to maintaining stability: how can 'new' citizens (e.g. by birth or immigration) recognise the benefits of basic democracy and participate voluntarily in its political processes.

Finally, the critical essence of basic democracy is that it is "neither morally committed nor opposed to value neutrality, universal human rights, or egalitarian principles of distribution" (Ober, 2017, p. 14).

Instead, basic democracy is a political framework for social coordination which provides stable foundations for such liberal ideas and values.

10.6.2 *Demopolis*

Ober offers two exemplars of basic democracy: the first being classical Athenian democracy (Ober, 2008), and the second being the thought experiment Demopolis itself (Ober, 2017).

Demopolis addresses a question about social order, namely, how a human community can reliably realise the benefits deriving from social coordination and cooperation — without submitting to a ruling oligarchy or an autocratic monarchy. Demopolis is a state founded on the principles and practice of basic democracy.

The founding of Demopolis begins with a normal distribution of the human population, sorting that population according to their preference for governance by autocracy, and then separating out that group which has low tolerance for autocracy (although in other respects, social, economic, value preference, etc., they are diverse).

Suppose (it is a thought experiment) this group inherits a defined territory and agrees to address the question of how to establish a state with the capacity to achieve three goals: security, prosperity and non-tyranny. Although the ends cannot be traded-off, the key stipulation is non-tyranny.

This general agreement between the group, called the Founders, is the first stage in a three-stage constitutional process. The second stage is to agree on the basic rules on participation, legislation and entrenchment. The rule on participation states that all have a duty to share in the process of making and enforcing rules. The rule on legislation will specify how to make future (stage three) rules. The rule on entrenchment ensures that all future stage three rules must meet a constitutional standard with respect to the stage one agreement and stage two foundational rules.

Stage three concerns the making and enforcing of post-foundation rules, including certain self-imposed constraints. Ober observes that in classical Athens these constraints came in two forms: first, formally distinguishing day-to-day policy made by a simple majority vote in a legislative citizen assembly, from fundamental constitutional law, made by a more cumbersome, multi-stage quasi-judicial process; and second, formally subordinating the decrees made in the first to laws made in the second.

Our goal is to investigate the specification, implementation and experimental animation of the first three stages of founding Demopolis, to determine the extent to which the principles of basic democracy can be automated as the basis for self-organisation of tyranny-avoiding collective governance.

10.6.3 *SimDemopolis*

As another application of the sociologically inspired computing methodology, this section briefly describes the specification and implementation, in Prolog, of an experimental testbed, SimDemopolis. This version of SimDemopolis, and its citizens/agents, borrows some of its data structures and algorithms from Pitt (2017), and more details are given there. Open source code is available from http://sourceforge.net/p/simdemopolis.

The specification of SimDemopolis consists of three sections: facts, rule overview, and knowledge codification. The facts identify the 'brute' facts, i.e. those facts true by virtue of physical reality. The 'institutional' facts, those facts which are true by conventional agreement between the agents in SimDemopolis, are coded in the knowledge codification section.

The rule overview section specifies the names of the rules currently in force, and the knowledge codification specifies the implementation of each rule (this can be thought of, in object-oriented programming terms, as the interface and the methods).

The rule overview is itself divided into two sections: the mutable rules and immutable rules. Mutable rules can be changed, immutable rules have to be transformed into mutable rules before they can be changed. This distinction between mutable and immutable rules is drawn from Suber's *Game of Nomic* (Suber, 1990) (see Sec. 6.7.3) and the purpose is threefold. Firstly, to distinguish between rules for conducting 'day-to-day' business, which can be changed quickly; and the 'quasi-judicial process', concerning higher-level policy-making and constitutional matters, which take longer to change. Secondly, to allow entrenchment, which limits the agents' collective ability to make rules in stage three of SimDemopolis (used in Sec. 10.7.3); and thirdly, to implement the *bright lines* feature (Schelling, 1960), giving citizens/agents clear information and instructions concerning what constitutes a violation of a rule, and how to respond to it. So, for example, trying to transmute an immutable rule about citizen exclusion into a mutable one should be clearly done for a very good reason (and not to disenfranchise or discriminate against a minority).

SimDemopolis has immutable rules for its constitution, including *enactment, amendment, repeal* and *transmutation* of rules, rules about admission to or exclusion from citizenship, and the sanctioning system. It has five mutable rules for *participation, role assignment, access control, resource allocation* and *minor claims*. Each of these mutable rules has a major role assigned, respectively identified as the *chair, director, controller, allocator* and *adjudicator*. These roles are all assumed to require some exceptional 'effort' to perform, and there are some minor roles which all perform or require relatively little 'effort'.

Each of these rules is further elaborated in the knowledge codification section. This elaboration consists of four parts: the *call*, which will invoke a protocol implementing that rule, the *roles* in that protocol; the (institutionalised) *powers* (Jones and Sergot, 1996) associated with that protocol (so that it can be checked that an agent which performs an action is empowered and permitted to do so; and that agents perform actions which they are obliged to do (Artikis, 2012)), and the *degrees of freedom*, i.e. the changeable parameters of the rule, which *de facto* includes the roles.

So, for example, the pre-initialisation specification of the participation rule looks as follows (note that ^^ is a self-defined Prolog operator meaning 'points to'):

```
knowcode^^[
     participation^^[
        call^^particip_check,
        roles^^[
            chair^^_, franchised^^[]
        ],
        powers^^[
            chair^^[cfv, declare, resign],
            monitors^^[vote]
        ],
        dof^^[
            who^^all, extent^^equal
        ]
     ],
```

The whole SimDemopolis ruleset is stored as a single global variable. This facilitates the enactment and revocation of rules, as it involves (in Prolog) inserting or deleting the name of the rule and its 4-tuple specification, and then consulting a module which contains the specification of the *call* (in order to enact some legislation), or to unload a module (in order to revoke it).

10.7 Experiments with SimDemopolis

This section describes the use of SimDemopolis in a series of experiments to *animate* the specification. The three animations demonstrate how participation, legislative and entrenchment rules can mitigate the risk of, respectively, oligarchy, autocracy and majoritarian tyranny.

10.7.1 *Civic Participation*

The first experimental animation is to test a civic participation rule that "all citizens have a duty to share, in one way or another, in making, adjudicating and enforcing the rules" (Ober, 2017, p. 49). Here, we will interpret "in one way or another" as "equally". This animation has three variations: firstly, a baseline test for equal sharing of roles; secondly, to detect 'power grabs' and 'free riding'; and thirdly, to detect bias in the role assignment protocol.

10.7.1.1 *Variation 1: Base Case*

This first experimental animation is to test a civic participation rule that *all should share equally* in the selection, modification and application of Demopolis' rules. It is implemented by leveraging the ideas of a metric-based analysis of power in procedures (Pitt *et al.*, 2013) (Sec. 7.6) and opinion formation to transform subjective assessments into collective assessments (Pitt, 2017). Initially, some agents volunteer (or are volunteered, or are chosen at random) and are appointed to the roles of Demopolis with institutionalised power (Jones and Sergot, 1996). At certain intervals, a participation check is done, each agent checks in its social network to see how much 'work' its neighbours have done. Using the Gini index, which is a commonly used metric for measurement of inequality, it makes a local self-assessment of the 'even-ness' of the distribution of the workload in its neighbourhood. These self-assessments are exchanged using an opinion formation process (Ramirez-Cano and Pitt, 2006). The franchised take a vote, and if the majority vote (collective assessment) is that the distribution is unequal, then the role-assignment protocol is called.

The results are shown in Fig. 10.4, for each of 20 separate runs for a population of 30 agents A and a random graph $G = \langle A, p \rangle$, where p is the probability of a link between any two members of A: (a) fully connected $G = \langle A, 1.00 \rangle$, (b) $G = \langle A, 0.25 \rangle$, and (c) $G = \langle A, 0.15 \rangle$. Each run (on the y-axis) is a separate horizontal strip. Each square in a run indicates a call to the participation rule at that timepoint (time on the x-axis): a blue square indicates that a vote for role re-assignment did not take place, a yellow square indicates that it did.

There are two observations. Firstly, above a certain threshold, $p \approx 0.25$, the system works in distributing the load equally. It appears though to be quasi-stable (Leibenstein, 1957), in the sense that if the role assignments are taken as the control variables, then the system goes through a period of stability until the agents' opinions on the (in)equality exceeds the threshold and they vote to change; followed by a period of instability while the re-assignment takes place until a configuration is found that satisfies opinions, and so on. However, as p decreases, the periods of alternating re-assignment and stability are more fragmented, because below $p = 0.15$, the connectivity between agents is insufficiently dense for opinions to filter through the network. Indeed, at $p = 0.05$ or for a ring network, the image is entirely blue: role re-assignment does not occur.

Secondly, this connectivity result vindicates the practices of democratic federalism, subdivisions of the demos, and subsidiarity, whereby decisions are taken as close to the point of impact as possible. For example, much of the business of the Athenian state was carried out at the level of the deme or the tribe, or by representatives chosen (by lottery) from the demes, and grouped according to tribe (Ober, 2008). What this meant in practice was that social knowledge (e.g. who was cheating) was embedded in local networks (at the deme level, say — at which something like $p = 0.25$ could be reasonably assured), became available at the tribe level, and was transmitted up to the city-state level. Two other aspects of 'cheating' are investigated next.

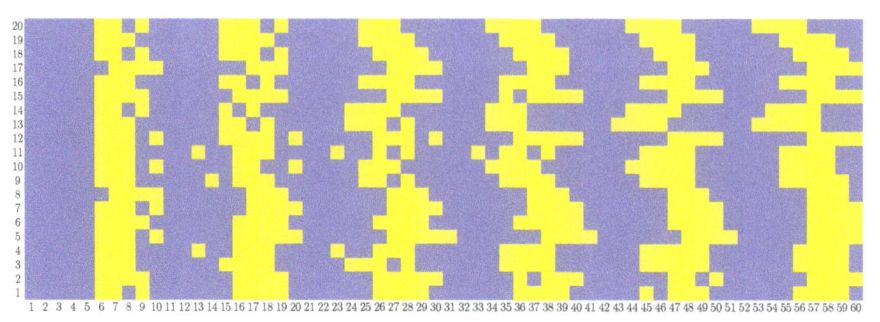

$G = \langle A, 1.00 \rangle$ (x-axis: time; y-axis: run number)

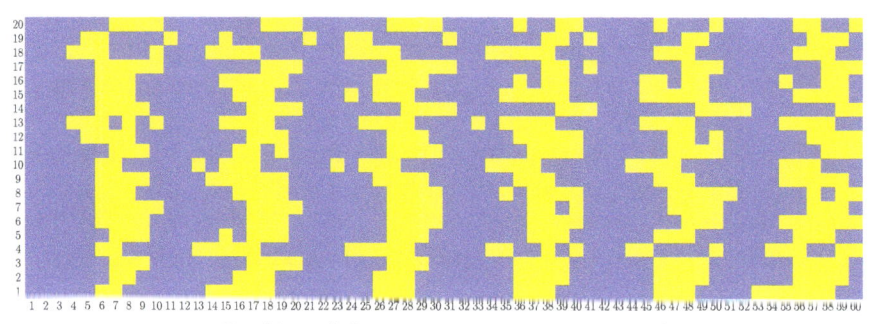

$G = \langle A, 0.25 \rangle$ (x-axis: time; y-axis: run number)

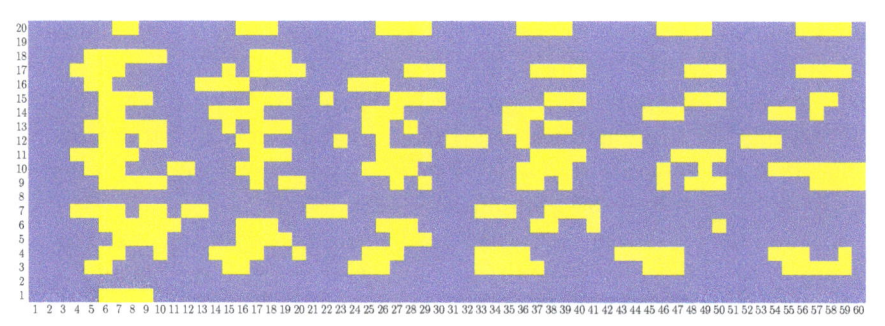

$G = \langle A, 0.15 \rangle$ (x-axis: time; y-axis: run number)

Fig. 10.4. Role Re-Assignment with the Participation Rule

10.7.1.2 *Variation 2: 'Power Grabs' and 'Free Riding'*

The second variation examines the possibility of gaming the participation rule, either by shirking one's duties and refusing to accept a role assignment, or by discharging one's civic duties with 'excess zeal' and refusing to resign from a role. Either approach has potentially serious consequences: for example, abnegation of responsibility to participate in civic activity through free riding can lead to the emergence of oligarchic tyranny by default; while the reinforcement of benefits of positions of power or authority can lead to the emergence of oligarchic tyranny by intention ('power grab').

In this experimental variation, a couple of 'citizenship' ratings are associated with each agent: one denoting its propensity to free ride; the other its propensity to grab power. If a random variable exceeds this propensity, the agent either free rides or power grabs. All but two of the agents are assigned the value 1.0 for both ratings; of the remaining two, for one the free-riding rating is set to 0.0, for the other, the power-grabbing rating is set to 0.0. Then, when the free-riding agent is assigned a role, it refuses; when the power-grabbing agent should resign from a role, it refuses. The behaviour of all other agents is unaffected.

To address this problem, the *director* refers it to the agent occupying the *adjudicator* role of the *minor claims* protocol. The *adjudicator* performs the following computation: if an agent refuses to resign and is in the top quartile of role occupancy, then it is compelled to resign (it is deemed to be power grabbing), otherwise it is excused; or, if an agent refuses to accept and is in the bottom quartile of role occupancy, then it is coerced to accept (it is deemed to be free riding), otherwise it is excused.

The results are shown in Fig. 10.5, for 10 separate runs of 30 agents for 100 rounds. The box plot shows the distribution of number of rounds in a role, and any outliers.

Without the minor claims protocol (Fig. 10.5(a)) the power-grabbing agents are clearly identified (as the separate symbols to the right of the box plot), except in run number 9. In run 9, the power-grabbing agent was also loosely connected, so it never received enough votes to be appointed to a role, therefore it never had the opportunity to exercise its characteristic. (This hints at another network issue: increased connectivity means an increased likelihood of a chance for misbehaviour, but also an increased likelihood of being outed when misbehaviour occurs.) With the minor claims protocol (Fig. 10.5(b)), power-grabbing agents are compelled to resign. However, in neither case is it possible to identify free riders by the values alone, in only 100 rounds, because as with power grabbing, it is also

(a) Without Minor Claims Protocol

(b) With Minor Claims Protocol

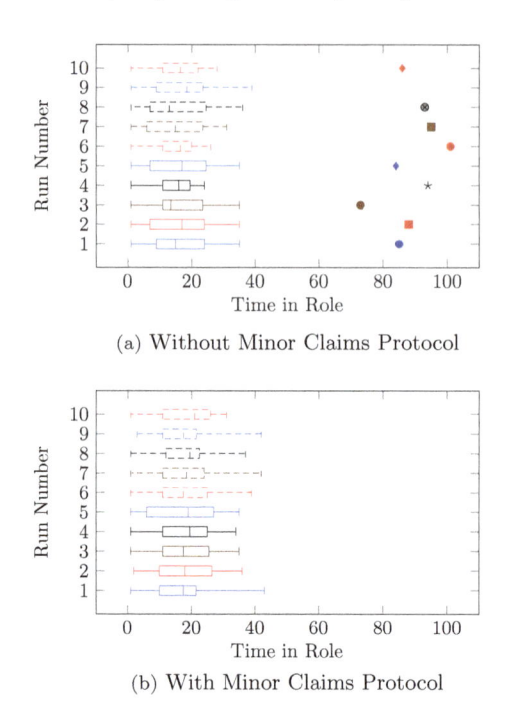

Fig. 10.5. Free-Riding and Power-Grabbing Detection

possible to have low/no opportunity through 'unpopularity'. However, if the number of times an agent refused to resign or participate was counted, the *adjudicator* could use this information in its judgement in the minor claims protocol.

Besides demonstrating that the participation rule can include checks to ensure that "all participate equally", there are two general comments to make about this experiment. Firstly, it highlights a couple of limitations of the Gini index. This metric indicates relative inequality: some might have done too much or some might have not done enough, but it is not possible to tell which is which. Furthermore, a massive increase in an outlier value makes little discernible difference to the index value: for example, it is possible to double or triple the value of an outlier and make only 0.05 difference to the Gini index, i.e. it can be misleading as a measure of *change* in a distribution over time.

Secondly, it demonstrates the coarseness of using metrics for assessing behaviour or accomplishment. Any one metric can only be taken as an indicator, not as definitive. What is actually needed is a basket of metrics which indicate both qualitative and quantitative values, and in the case of quantitative metrics, understanding what is being measured. This is important with respect to apparently 'redundant' democratic accountability and transparency rules: no one rule will expose all relevant forms of violation.

10.7.1.3 Variation 3: Role Assignment Bias

In a third variation dealing with another manifestation of an entropic tendency towards oligarchy, we examine the effect of a 'biased' agent. The agent with the most outgoing arcs in its social network has its behaviour in the role-assignment *director* role fixed. Firstly, it always re-assigns itself to the *director* role, and secondly, it ignores the popular vote and assigns some member of its social network to each other role; i.e. the 'clique' centred on the corrupt agent forms an oligarchy with a monopoly on 'executive power'.

The results are shown in Fig. 10.6. Each horizontal strip is a separate run, of 100 rounds, $G = \langle A, 0.25 \rangle$, $|A| = 30$. As before, at each consecutive timepoints, blue squares indicate no role-assignment and yellow squares indicate a vote for role re-assignment. The black square denotes the first occasion when the biased agent is appointed to the *director* role. As the most popular agent, this can happen early (in runs 19 and 20, Fig. 10.6 (top two rows), at the start). After that, the bias in role assignment is revealed as the other agents keep voting against the 'oligarchy' and the system is no longer quasi-stable.

However, faced with this behaviour, the participation rule only provides a basis for detection and offers neither prevention nor cure, although one possible 'cure' could be the classical Athenian practice of ostracism, which allowed for a time-limited expulsion of one prominent individual (but not disenfranchisement) each year, based

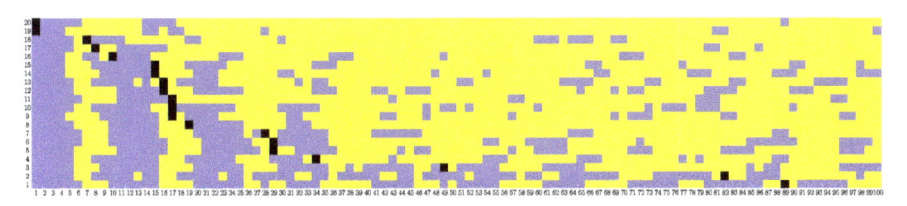

Fig. 10.6. Role Assignment with Biased *Director*

on a complex double-vote (Ober, 2008). Other mechanisms can also be encoded in the legislative process, as discussed in what follows.

10.7.2 Legislation

The second area of agreement in the second stage of founding Demopolis is in the specification of the legislative framework, i.e. the enactment and repeal of procedures, transmuting rules between mutable and immutable, and in another dimension, dealing with the systematic delegation of political authority from the demos to its representatives, i.e. the transition between direct participation and representation. However, the key issue is that representatives do not violate the terms and conditions under which administrative jurisdiction is delegated to them. The risk is that a representative might, unchecked, seek to satisfy its partial interests rather than the common interests. If this happens, malpractice in governance can degenerate into autocracy.

This issue is explored in SimDemopolis using a variation of the delegation game described in Ober (2017, p. 133ff). In this game, there are two players, the demos (D) and their representative (R). We assume that the demos is capable of governing itself, but has chosen to enact a piece of legislation which gives authority to a representative (e.g. in a negotiation with some external third party). The three possible outcomes of the game are the status quo of representative democracy, autocracy (elite capture), and direct democracy (the fourth, no violation by R but revocation by D, is mutually destructive). The game form and the payoffs are shown in Fig. 10.7.

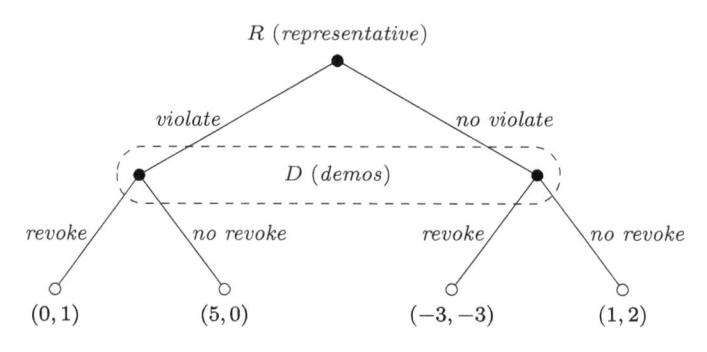

Fig. 10.7. Delegation Game — Game Tree

The representative R has a choice whether to violate or not violate its delegated authority, while the demos D has a choice of whether to revoke or not revoke that authority. The preferred outcome for R is autocracy, i.e. to make decisions or rule on its own, unencumbered by constraints: this requires that R violates and D does not revoke, the preferred outcome for D is representative democracy: R does not violate and there is no need to revoke. Otherwise, if R violates and D revokes, then direct democracy is restored; similarly if R does not violate and yet D still revokes, then the political regime reverts to direct democracy but in diminished form, as the 'social contract' is undermined by the demos itself.

Using Algorithm 5 and 30 agents, we 'play' an *iterated* delegation game with a limit of 100 rounds. To begin with, the agents enact a rule that appoints one of their number, R, as their representative. Thereafter, in each round, R has a probability to violate, which is increased by a factor α if it violates and gets away with it (demos does not revoke); and by a factor β if it does not violate (the demos gets more utility than it does). R makes its choice, and then D decides whether or not to revoke. This decision is based on the same algorithms for opinion formation and voting as used before, except the agents exchange opinions on whether to revoke or not, rather than interactional justice (demonstrating the genericity of the opinion formation algorithms). The agents base their opinions by calculating the Gini index of their own and their neighbours utility.

ALGORITHM 5: Computing Collective Assessment

1   $n \leftarrow 0$; $\mathcal{A} \leftarrow$ agents ;
2   $R \leftarrow enact(\mathcal{A})$; $D \leftarrow \mathcal{A} - R$; R.pviolate $\leftarrow 0$;
3   **repeat**
4   update R.pviolate ;
5   violate $\leftarrow$ choose-action(R) ;
6   opinion-formation(D, topic = revoke) ;
7   revoke $\leftarrow$ choose-action(D) ;
8   assign pay-offs(violate, revoke) ;
9       $inc(n)$;
10 **until** *until D choose revocation* $|| \; n = 100$;

A prototypical result is illustrated in Fig. 10.8. This shows (as a percentage, against time): the increasing probability of R violating

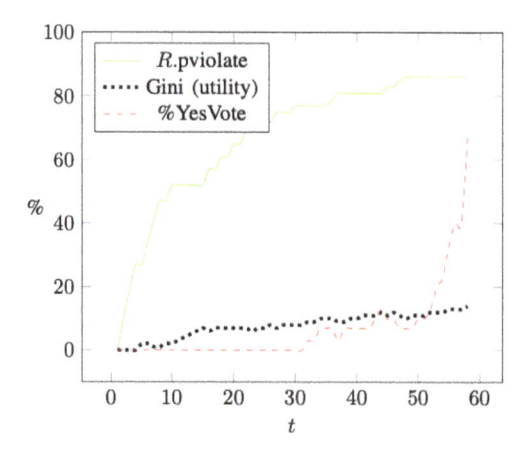

Fig. 10.8. Detecting Autocratic Misrepresentation

the increasing Gini index, and the subset of D that vote for revocation. The latter percentage remains approximately zero for some time, until a threshold is reached and some agents start to perceive misuse of the representative's authority, after which the opinion formation 'kicks in', a majority vote to revoke the representative's authority, and direct democracy is restored.

There are three general comments about this animation. Firstly, the process of local monitoring and opinion formation with respect to a global property can be applied to multiple 'topics'. Secondly, the use of immutable rules for the enactment and repeal of mutable rules acts as a significant restraint on autocratic power. Thirdly, the reconfiguration of rules at run-time is an essential feature of what might be called *plug-and-play governance*. This approach to collective self-governance is particularly important for socio-technical systems — *cf.* the example of the computer game Minecraft, where people hosting servers can configure governance rules through the use of plug-ins (Frey and Sumner, 2018).

10.7.3 *Entrenchment*

To demonstrate the need for, and benefit of, entrenchment and the 'bright lines' feature (Schelling, 1960), we run a simple game in 'mal-Demopolis'. We assume that all agents, as required, have a preference for non-tyranny. However, we now also assume that there is another

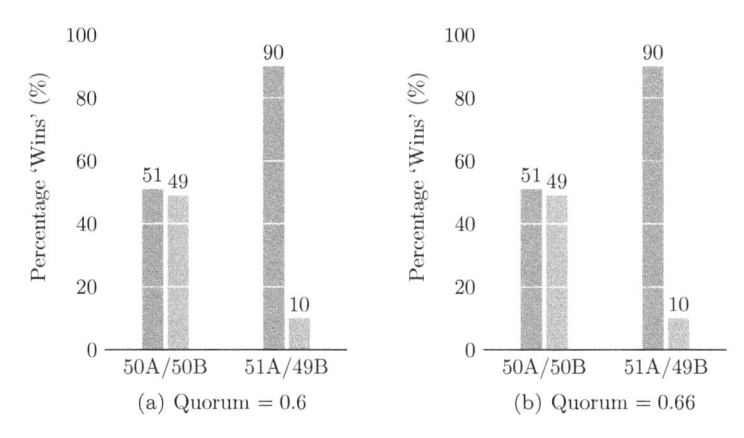

Fig. 10.9. Majoritarian Tyranny

polarised preference: we identify one group as *TypeA* agents and the other group as *TypeB* agents. At each round, citizens of mal-Demopolis are either present or absent with a fixed probability p. These are the players, in each round, of some partial public goods question such as the distribution of some resources. At the end of each round, the players take a vote to eliminate an agent that is deemed to be underperforming in its citizenship duties or undermining the principle of "equal participation". *TypeA* agents will vote to remove a *TypeB* agent, and vice versa. The rule specifies that there has to be majority, Q, in favour of elimination either way, otherwise nothing happens.

The result is shown in Fig. 10.9. With 100 agents equally split between *TypeA* and *TypeB*, $p = 0.5$, and $Q = 0.6$, within a few hundred rounds, a 'pure' majority has been established: either the *TypeA* agents eliminate *TypeB*, or vice versa, with equal probability. However, even a minimal shift in the initial distribution is enough to significantly increase the likelihood that the majority eliminates the minority: with 51 *TypeA* and 49 *TypeB* agents, the *TypeA* agents eliminate the others 90% of the time. Moreover, increasing the quorum necessary to eliminate an agent to a two-thirds majority $Q = 0.66$ doesn't alter the situation beyond taking longer to happen. With an equal distribution of agents, one type still eliminates the other; with the 51–49 split, the outcome can be predicted with even greater (95%) confidence, both generally (one type will eliminate the other) and specifically (the majority type will eliminate the minority).

What is seen here is that the rules have provided an opportunity for *majoritarian tyranny*, even though all the agents supposedly had an initial preference for non-tyranny.

This is not the behaviour observed in SimDemopolis: indeed it *cannot* be observed because the organisation of the rules prevents it, for two reasons related to entrenchment.

Firstly, the specification of the rules has followed one of the knowledge management process design principles analysed in Burth Kurka *et al.* (2019), which recommends: *Clear line between common interest questions and factional or partial goods questions. Appropriate procedural rules for decision-making in each domain.* In mal-Demopolis, the common interest question, i.e. who should or should not have citizenship rights, was (deliberately) conflated with the partial goods question, i.e. who should or should not be allocated resources. The players in each round decided not only the partial goods but also the common interest questions. In SimDemopolis, the citizenship rule is 'clearly' separated from the partial goods rule. Therefore, to apply the rule it is not enough to consult those who are present for the partial goods question; all agents who have citizenship rights have to be consulted for the common interest question.

Secondly, the citizenship rule is safeguarded in Demopolis by its specification as an immutable rule. Therefore, to change the rule requires firstly following the quasi-judicial protocol that is used to transfer immutable rules to mutable ones, or vice versa. If a majority wanted to change (decrease) the size of the quorum needed to eliminate an agent, it is clearly delineated by the bright lines feature. This also emphasises the need for, and benefits of, *review* to prevent oppression of minorities by majoritarian tyranny.

Note this would not necessarily provide protection in a population where differences over polarised preferences are much greater than the quorum needed for a decision to exclude citizenship rights. In these cases, other provisions for guaranteeing minority rights are required, but this becomes a matter for extending basic democracy to liberal democracy. This issue, and other open questions, are discussed further in the next section.

10.8 Algorithmic Comparative Politics

The simulation of Demopolis is not, perhaps, the way software engineers design systems; it is not either, perhaps, the way political scientists use data and computers to study comparative politics (there is much more concern with, for example, sentiment analysis (Pang and Lee, 2008)). However, we might consider this an inter-disciplinary study of *algorithmic comparative politics*. If comparative politics is the analysis of political institutions, then algorithmic comparative politics is the animation of political institutions using self-organising multi-agent systems. As well as implications for the design of socio-technical systems, there are implications for modelling, historicism and the public understanding of democracy.

On the design of socio-technical systems, we have proposed eight principles of *Democracy by Design* (DbyD) (Pitt and Ober, 2018). Following Cavoukian (2012), whose *privacy by design* (itself an instance of value-sensitive design (Friedman *et al.*, 2008)) proposes that privacy be taken into account throughout system development as a primary requirement (value), we advocate a corresponding instantiation of value-sensitive design through Democracy by Design. This takes the principles of basic democracy into account throughout the systems design, engineering and operational lifecycles. Democracy embedded in design ensures that procedural rules for democratic deliberation and decision-making are entrenched from the beginning, rather than trying to graft them on later; moreover, it ensures that the delegation of political authority can also be revoked. (Note that this conception of democracy by design is intended for engineering socio-technical systems, not as a framework for a broad reformist agenda to promote citizen engagement (Thomas, 2014).) The eight foundational principles of democracy by design are as follows:

DbyD Principle 1. *Prevention rather than re-invention.* The Bright Lines feature anticipates corrosion or corruption of democratic procedures, and can prevent it from becoming a problem in the first place. This is because it is not just a matter of changing the rules, but also attitudes, and education: people have to learn how to participate effectively in self-governance. Procedures should not be so arcane that their practice can only be conducted by an initiated elite.

DbyD Principle 2. *Democracy is not an end-state, nor the default.* Given the observed entropic tendencies towards oligarchy, autocracy or majoritarian tyranny, users have to put some effort into monitoring and protecting democracy. The cost of this effort is compensated by greater gains from productive outcomes of engagement, which are not uniquely limited to avoiding tyranny.

DbyD Principle 3. *Seamless transfer of power.* No outgoing elected authority should attempt to transfer its executive powers to another body, nor to encumber the incoming elected authority with policies or personnel designed to frustrate. Relinquishing power should be done gracefully in order to avoid de-legitimising the democratic process.

DbyD Principle 4. *Visibility, inclusivity, transparency, accountability and review.* The codification of knowledge should be visible and accessible; inclusivity should be maximised, ideally lowering transaction costs of engagement; the beneficiaries of decisions should be transparent; and the takers of decisions should be traceable, accountable and redeemable by review. Accountability and review are essential for systemic improvement.

DbyD Principle 5. *No compromises on democratic processes.* Trade-offs should not be accommodated with efficiency or functionality taking precedence over democracy. All legitimate stakeholders and possibly competing interests should be accommodated, e.g. through polycentric governance mechanisms, in order to deliver positive-sum 'win–win' outcomes.

DbyD Principle 6. *Inter-dependence of diversity.* Like a suspension bridge, democracy is composed of multiple diverse and seemingly opposing forces acting against each other, but can produce a quasi-stable system with the appropriate checks and balances; eliminating diversity or removing a counter-balancing force produces instability.

DbyD Principle 7. *Education in the recognition of prosocial benefits.* Recognise the fluidity of the user population: ensure that newcomers can learn the unique benefits of participation, accept the legitimacy of political authority, and recognise that such authority can be changed, challenged and granted to them as well.

DbyD Principle 8. *Procedural evaluation.* Be judicious in the selection, application and interpretation of metrics used to evaluate the legitimacy and effectiveness of the rules; and know how to accommodate plurality of, and reconcile conflict between, different metrics.

The implications for modelling are that in the past political theories would make predictions, and these theories could only be tested in laboratory experiments, yet often their predictions were not necessarily observed 'in the wild'. However, with SimDemopolis, we have shown that it is possible to construct a precise and testable model of a theory of politics, and investigate the behaviours and trajectories of political systems.

This work also has three implications for historical political science. Firstly, as indicated earlier, implementation of an algorithm for Relevant Expertise Aggregation shows how the documentation of classical processes in Ober (2013) was sufficiently complete and accurate for specification of an algorithm used in the modern setting of SmartGrid policy selection (Pitt *et al.*, 2018b). Secondly, the SimDemoplis experiment enables analysis through simulation rather than the posing of counterfactuals. Thirdly, it provides confirmation for conjectures about classical Athens: for example that learning and innovation were endogenous, that there was no external authority telling the Athenians what to do, and that the role of the oracle was limited (*cf.* Poblet *et al.*, 2020). The experiments in SimDemopolis were self-contained, and once they were set running, *il n'y a pas de hors-simulation*, there is no outside simulation, as Derrida might have said if he had not been so busy trying to deconstruct sovereignty and democracy.

One of the demands often imposed on academics from departments of engineering and the natural sciences is to engage in the public understanding of science. Social and political scientists are not imposed upon quite so much to engage in the public understanding of democracy. If anything, quite the opposite, at least in the UK: citizenship studies are made so grindingly dull, it is not perhaps surprising that so many schoolchildren are put off engaging with local government and national politics.

However, simulation environments such as this, if developed into exploratory tools, could provide schoolchildren with the insight into democratic theory and practice and the knowledge to resist the slide from populism into extremism. It might also inspire academia to try to restore collegiate and knowledge-based self-organisation of science and technology, and resist the slide into centralised, metric-based bureaucratic managerialism.

Fundamentally, the increased public understanding of science and democracy would stress:

- The importance of responsible knowledge management;
- The importance of civic education and critical thinking;
- The importance of civic dignity;
- The distinction between democracy and majoritarian tyranny; and
- The blatant arrogation of political power and influence.

A bit of civil disobedience regarding these matters would not go amiss either, if only to make the oligarchy realise that burning the tower down so they can keep the top-floor apartments generally tends to be counter-productive.

At root, this is the essence of democracy: (at least) the confluence of multiple transparent and inclusive knowledge management processes that enable a diverse and heterogenous collective of individuals to satisfice a shared set of congruent values, and to avoid tyranny.

It might be noted that in the Brexit referendum and its aftermath, the UK experienced almost a total breakdown of its knowledge management, bright lines and tyranny avoidance processes. We have already seen the example of the EU Withdrawal Bill, but to this chargesheet can be added the usurpation of power by an oligarchy; the denigration of expertise; the reduction of civic dignity (civic dignity is undermined when a demos is not presented with the facts and tricked into voting for a proposition that is not in their best interests); majoritarian tyranny masquerading as democracy; the referendum result being presented as timeless, infallible, an unquestionable decision; the data manipulation and illegality of the campaign; the denigration of its judiciary, journalists and national broadcaster; and the treatment of dissent as treachery and sabotage.

It might be concluded, that as of 2020, the UK is a failing state.

10.9 Summary: Why This Stuff Matters

This chapter has studied algorithmic self-governance and comparative politics in general, and in particular the algorithmic specification and operationalisation of principles and processes of Ober's Basic Democracy. In particular, it was shown how Basic Democracy can guard against the entropic tendency to tyranny, in its various forms: oligarchy, autocracy and majoritarian tyranny.

Ober (2017, p. 176) contends that basic democracy "answers a central question about political philosophy, before and after liberalism: How might we, whoever we are, better live our lives, together?" We believe that in the Digital Transformation, we will increasingly encounter socio-technical systems of the kind exemplified, at its best, perhaps, by the community energy systems described in Sec. 1.2.1 (and at its worst, perhaps, by those platforms that seek to provide a meagre service in return for treating its users as a commodifiable data and revenue stream). In the sense that the work presented here could lead to more of the former, it represents a contribution to answering a central question about the digital transformation: How might we, whoever we are, better live our *digital* lives, together?

As a personal conclusion, to extend Binmore: I believe that we evolved the intellectual capacity to engage with social construction because it offered our species an effective, efficient and mutually satisfiable way to solve collective action problems that inevitably arise when a group of individuals with different preferences and priorities tries to live together. I further believe we evolved the intellectual capacity to engage with socially constructed *politics* because it offered our species etc. etc. *tries to live together at scale*.

That we also developed the technology to do this on a planetary scale, but then handed it over to a bunch of tax-dodging state-denying yatch-substituting neoliberals, while at the same time voting for a neo-colonial klepto-kakocracy, is for a study on Self-Harming Systems, not Self-Organising ones.

But this leaves the last comment for democracy: it is said that you do not miss what you never had; it is perhaps equally true you would miss what you did have. What is not clear is whether you would miss something that gradually morphs into something else, and yet you are told "this is democracy". It is not easy to define 'democracy', but in one final paradox: some things, like some people, are better defined by their absence, not their presence. You will regret it if it's gone.

Bibliography

Acemoglu, D. (2005). Politics and economics in weak and strong states, *Journal of Monetary Economics* **52**, 7, pp. 1199–1226.

Alwateer, M. and Seng, L. (2020). Emerging drone services: Concept, challenges and societal issues, *IEEE Technology & Society Magazine* **39**, 3, pp. 1–100.

Andrews, P., Polack, F., Sampson, A., Stepney, S., and Timmis, J. (2010). The CoSMoS process, version 0.1: A process for the modelling and simulation of complex systems, Technical Report YCS-2010-453, University of York.

Anshelevich, E., Dasgupta, A., Kleinberg, J., Tardos, E., Wexler, T., and Roughgarden, T. (2004). The price of stability for network design with fair cost allocation, in *Proceedings of the 45th FOCS*, pp. 295–304.

Arrow, K. (1951). *Social Choice and Individual Values* (New York, NY: Wiley).

Arthur, W. (1994). Inductive reasoning and bounded rationality, *American Economic Review: Papers and Proceedings* **84**, pp. 406–411.

Artikis, A. (2012). Dynamic specification of open agent systems, *Journal of Logic and Computation* **22**, 6, pp. 1301–1334.

Artikis, A. and Sergot, M. (2010). Executable specification of open multi-agent systems, *Logic Journal of the IGPL* **18**, 1, pp. 31–65.

Artikis, A., Pitt, J., and Sergot, M. (2002). Animated specifications of computational societies, in C. Castelfranchi and L. Johnson (eds.), *Proceedings AAMAS'02* (New York, NY: ACM), pp. 1053–1062.

Artikis, A., Sergot, M., and Paliouras, G. (2015). An event calculus for event recognition, *IEEE Trans. Knowl. Data Eng.* **27**, 4, pp. 895–908.

Artikis, A., Sergot, M., and Pitt, J. (2009). Specifying norm-governed computational societies, *ACM Transactions on Computational Logic* **10**, 1, pp. 1–42.

Artikis, A., Sergot, M., and Pitt, J. (2007). An executable specification of a formal argumentation protocol, *Artificial Intelligence* **171**, 10–15, pp. 776–804.

Artikis, A., Kamara, L., Pitt, J., and Sergot, M. (2004). A protocol for resource sharing in norm-governed ad hoc networks, in J. Leite, A. Omicini, P. Torroni, and P. Yolum (eds.), *Declarative Agent Languages and Technologies II (DALT), LNCS*, Vol. 3476 (Berlin, Heidelberg: Springer), pp. 221–238.

Asaro, P. (2019). AI ethics and predictive policing: From models of threat to an ethics of care, *IEEE Technological Society Magazine* **38**, 2, pp. 40–53.

Ashby, W. Ross. (1952). *Design for a Brain* (London: Chapman-Hall).

Atkinson, A. (1970). On the measurement of inequality, *Journal of Economic Theory* **2**, 3, pp. 244–263.

Axelred, R. (1986). An evolutionary approach to norms, *The American Political Science Review* **80**, 4, pp. 1095–1111.

Baker, K. (1975). *Condorcet: From Natural Philosophy to Social Mathematics* (Chicago, IL: Chicago University Press).

Balke, T., de Vos, M., and Padget, J. (2013). I-ABM: Combining institutional frameworks and agent-based modelling for the design of enforcement policies, *Artificial Intelligence and Law* **21**, 4, pp. 371–398.

Bartlett, R. and Collins, S. (2011). *Nicomachean Ethics (translation): Book V* (Chicago, IL: Chicago University Press).

Beer, S. (1959). *Cybernetics and Management* (London: The English Universities Press).

Beer, S. (1981). *Brain of the Firm, (2nd edn.)* (Chichester: Wiley).

Bellman, K., Tomforde, S., and Würtz, R. (2014). Interwoven systems: Self-improving systems integration, in *Eighth IEEE International Conference SASO Workshops (SASOW)*, pp. 123–127.

Bellman, K. L., Botev, J., Hildmann, H., Lewis, P. R., Marsh, S., Pitt, J., Scholtes, I., and Tomforde, S. (2017). Socially-sensitive systems design: Exploring social potential, *IEEE Technological Society Magazine* **36**, 3, pp. 72–80.

Bentham, J. (1948 [1789]). *An Introduction to the Principles of Morals and Legislation* (New York NY: Hafner Publishing Co.).

Berger, P. and Luckmann, T. (1966). *The Social Construction of Reality* (Garden City, NY: First Anchor Books).

Bhuta, N., Rotolo, A., and Sartor, G. (2014). Awareness and responsibility in autonomous weapons systems, in J. Pitt (ed.), *The Computer After Me* (London: ICPress), pp. 253–266.

Binmore, K. (2005). *Natural Justice* (Oxford: Oxford University Press).
Binmore, K. (2010). Game theory and institutions, *Journal of Comparative Economics* **38**, 3, pp. 245–252.
Blader, A. and Tyler, T. (2003). A four-component model of procedural justice: Defining the meaning of a "fair" process, *Personality and Social Psychology Bulletin* **29**, 6, pp. 747–758.
Bonabeau, E., Dorigo, M., and Theraulaz, G. (1999). *Swarm intelligence: From natural to artificial systems* (Oxford: Oxford University Press).
Boseley, S. (2020). 'Absolutely wrong': How UK's coronavirus test strategy unravelled, *The Guardian*, 1 April.
Bourazeri, A., Pitt, J., and Arnab, S. (2016). Social mPower: An educational game for energy efficiency, in *Serious Games, Interaction and Simulation — 6th International Conference (SGAMES)*, pp. 133–140.
Bowles, S. and Gintis, H. (2002). Social capital and community governance, *The Economic Journal* **112**, 483, pp. F419–F436.
Braess, D., Nagurney, A., and Wakolbinger, T. (2005). On a paradox of traffic planning, *Transportation Science* **39**, 4, pp. 446–450.
Bragaglia, S., Chesani, F., Mello, P., and Sottara, D. (2012). A rule-based calculus and processing of complex events, in A. Bikakis and A. Giurca (eds.), *Rules on the Web: Research and Applications (RuleML)*, LNCS, Vol. 7438 (Berlin, Heidelberg: Springer), pp. 151–166.
Brams, S. and Taylor, A. (1996). *Fair Division: From Cake-Cutting to Dispute Resolution* (Cambridge: Cambridge University Press).
Brennan, G. and Pettit, P. (2005). *The Economy of Esteem* (Oxford: Oxford University Press).
Bretier, P. and Sadek, D. (1996). A rational agent as the kernel of a cooperative spoken dialogue system: Implementing a logical theory of interaction, in J.-P. Müller *et al.* (eds.), *Intelligent Agents III: Agent Theories, Architectures, and Languages (ATAL)*, No. 1193 in LNAI (Berlin, Heidelberg: Springer), pp. 189–203.
Bryant, V. (1985). *Metric Spaces* (Cambridge: Cambridge University Press).
Buckingham Shum, S., Aberer, K., Schmidt, A., Bishop, S., Lukowicz, P., Anderson, S., Charalabidis, Y., Domingue, J., de Freitas, S., Dunwell, I., Edmonds, B., Grey, F., Haklay, M., Jelasity, M., Karpistenko, A., Kohlhammer, J., Lewis, J., Pitt, J., Sumner, R., and Helbing, D. (2012). Towards a global participatory platform: Democratising open data, complexity science and collective intelligence, *European Physical Journal: Special Topics* **214**, 1, pp. 109–152.

Burns, J. and Hart, H. L. A. (eds.) (1977). *The Collected Works of Jeremy Bentham: A Comment on the Commentaries and a Fragment on Government* (London: The Athlone Press).

Burth Kurka, D. and Pitt, J. (2017). The principled violation of policy: Norm flexibilization in open self-organising systems, in *2nd IEEE International Workshops on Foundations and Applications of Self* Systems, FAS*W@SASO/ICCAC*, pp. 33–38.

Burth Kurka, D., Pitt, J., and Ober, J. (2019). Knowledge management for self-organised resource allocation, *ACM TAAS* **14**, 1, pp. 1:1–1:41.

Burth Kurka, D., Pitt, J., Lewis, P., Patelli, A., and Ekárt, A. (2018). Disobedience as a mechanism of change, in *12th IEEE International Conference SASO*, pp. 1–10.

Butler, S. and Demiris, Y. (2008). Predicting the movements of robot teams using generative models, in *Distributed Autonomous Robotic Systems 8 (DARS)*, pp. 533–542.

Cao, Z. and Zegura, E. (1999). Utility max-min: an application-oriented bandwidth allocation scheme, in *18th Annual Joint Conference of the IEEE Computer and Communications Societies (INFOCOM)*, Vol. 2, pp. 793–801.

Carr, H. and Pitt, J. (2009). Voting rules in agent societies, in G. Vouros (ed.), *First International Workshop OAMAS, LNAI*, Vol. 5368, pp. 36–53.

Cardoso, R. P., Hart, E., and Pitt, J. V. (2019). Evolving robust policies for community energy system management, in A. Auger and T. Stützle (eds.), *Proceedings of the Genetic and Evolutionary Computation Conference, GECCO*, ACM, pp. 1120–1128.

Carr, H., Artikis, A., and Pitt, J. (2009). PreSage-MS: Metric spaces in PreSage, in H. Aldewereld, V. Dignum, and G. Picard (eds.), *Engineering Societies in the Agents World X (ESAW), LNCS*, Vol. 5881 (Berlin, Heidelberg: Springer), pp. 243–246.

Carver, T. and Vondra, A. (1994). Alternative dispute resolution: Why it doesn't work and why it does, *Harvard Business Review* **May–June**, pp. 1–11.

Castelfranchi, C. (1999). Affective appraisal versus cognitive evaluation in social emotions and interactions, in *Affective Interactions, Towards a New Generation of Computer Interfaces*, pp. 76–106.

Castelfranchi, C. and Falcone, R. (2002). Trust is much more than subjective probability: Mental components and sources of trust, in *Hawaii International Conference on System Sciences (HICSS) 33*, pp. 1–10.

Cavoukian, A. (2012). Privacy by design, *IEEE Technological Society Magazine* **31**, 4, pp. 18–19.

Cevenini, C. (2003). Legal considerations on the use of software agents in virtual enterprises, in J. Bing and G. Sartor (eds.), *The Law of Electronic Agents* (Oslo: Unipubskriftserier), pp. 133–146.

Chapman, P. (2002). Life universal computer, http://www.igblan.free-online.co.uk/igblan/ca/.

Chevaleyre, Y., Endriss, U., Lang, J., and Maudet, N. (2007). A short introduction to computational social choice, in *Proceedings of the 33rd Conference on Current Trends in Theory and Practice of Computer Science (SOFSEM)*, no. 4362 in LNCS (Berlin, Heidelberg: Springer), pp. 51–69.

Cho, J.-H., Swami, A., and Chen, I.-R. (2010). A survey on trust management for mobile ad hoc networks, *IEEE Communications Surveys & Tutorials* **13**, 4, pp. 562–583.

Christoforou, A. (2012). On the identity of social capital and the social capital of identity, *Cambridge Journal of Economics* **37**, pp. 719–736.

Clark, K. and Robinson, P. (2015). Robotic agent programming in teleor, in *Proceedings of the IEEE International Conference on Robotics and Automation (ICRA)*, pp. 5040–5047.

Cox, M., Arnold, G., and Villamayor Tomás, S. (2010). A review of design principles for community-based natural resource management, *Ecology and Society* **15**, 4, p. 38.

Cranefield, S., Oren, N., and Vasconcelos, W. (2018). Accountability for practical reasoning agents, in *6th International Conference on Agreement Technologies (AT)*, pp. 33–48.

Craven, R. and Sergot, M. J. (2008). Agent strands in the action language nC+, *Journal of Applied Logistics* **6**, 2, pp. 172–191.

Crawford, S. and Ostrom, E. (1995). A grammar of institutions, *The American Political Science Review* **89**, 3, pp. 582–600.

Daley, D. (2016). *Ratf**ked: How the Democrats Won the Presidency But Lost America* (New York, NY: W. W. Norton & Co.).

Daly, H. (1994). Operationalizing sustainable development by investing in natural capital, in A. Jansson, M. Hammer, C. Folke, and R. Costanza (eds.), *Investing in Natural Capital: The Ecological Economics Approach to Sustainability* (Washington, DC: Island Press), pp. 22–37.

Dastani, M., Dignum, V., and Dignum, F. (2003). Role-assignment in open agent societies, in *Proceedings of Conference on Autonomous Agents and Multi-Agent Systems* (ACM), pp. 489–496.

Davenport, T. and Prusak, L. (1998). *Working Knowledge: How Organizations Manage What They Know* (Harvard, MA: Harvard Business School Press).

Deffuant, G., Neau, D., Amblard, F., and Weisbuch, G. (2000). Mixing beliefs among interacting agents, *Advances Complex System* **3**, 1, pp. 87–98.

Demiris, Y. and Khadhouri, B. (2006). Hierarchical attentive multiple models for execution and recognition of actions, *Robotics Autonomatics System* **54**, 5, pp. 361–369.

Dennett, D. (1987). *The Intentional Stance* (Cambridge, MA: MIT Press).

Dommel, H.-P. and Garcia-Luna-Aceves, J. (1997). Floor control for multimedia conferencing and collaboration, *Multimedia Systems* **5**, 1, pp. 23–38.

Dorigo, M. (1997). Ant colony system: A cooperative learning approach to the traveling salesman problem, *IEEE Transactions on Evolutionary Computation* **1**, 1, pp. 53–66.

Dorigo, M. and Stützle, T. (2004). *Ant Colony Optimization* (Cambridge, MA: MIT Press).

Doursat, R., Sayama, H., and Michel, O. (eds.) (2012). *Morphogenetic Engineering: Toward Programmable Complex Systems* (Berlin, Heidelberg: Springer).

Dryzek, J. and Pickering, J. (2017). Deliberation as a catalyst for reflexive environmental governance, *Ecological Economics* **131**, pp. 353–360.

Easwaran, A. and Pitt, J. (2002). Supply chain formation in open, market-based multi-agent systems, *International Journal of Computational Intelligence and Applications* **2**, 3, pp. 349–363.

Edmonds, B., Gilbert, N., Gustafson, S., Hales, D., and Krasnogor, N. (eds.) (2005). *Socially Inspired Computing. Proceedings of the Joint Symposium on Socially Inspired Computing* (AISB).

Elster, J. (1992). *Local Justice: How Institutions Allocate Scarce Goods and Necessary Burdens* (New York, NY: Russell Sage Foundation).

Fakhar Manesh, M., Pellegrini, M. M., Marzi, G., and Dabic, M. (2020). Knowledge management in the fourth industrial revolution: Mapping the literature and scoping future avenues, *IEEE Transactions on Engineering Management* **68**, 1, pp. 289–300.

Falcone, R. and Castelfranchi, C. (2001). Social trust: A cognitive approach, in C. Castelfranchi and Y. Tan (eds.), *Trust and Deception in Virtual Societies* (Dordrecht: Springer), pp. 55–90.

Ferscha, A., Davies, N., Schmidt, A., and Streitz, N. (2011). Pervasive socio-technical fabric, *Procedia Computer Science* **7**, pp. 88–91.

Finin, T., Fritzson, R., McKay, D., and McEntire, R. (1994). KQML as an agent communication language, in *Proceedings of the Third International Conference on Information and Knowledge Management (CIKM)* (New York, NY: ACM), pp. 456–463.

Fishburn, P. (1974). Paradoxes of voting, *American Political Science Review* **68**, pp. 537–546.

Forgy, C. (1982). Rete: A fast algorithm for the many pattern/many object pattern match problem, *Artificial Intelligence* **19**, 3597, pp. 17–37.

Frey, S. and Sumner, R. (2018). Emergence of complex institutions in a large population of self-governing communities, *CoRR* abs/1804.10312.

Friedkin, N. and Johnsen, E. (1990). Social influence and opinions, *Journal of Mathematical Sociology* **15**, pp. 193–205.

Friedman, B., Kahn, P., and Borning, A. (2008). Value sensitive design and information systems, in K. Himma and H. Tavani (eds.), *The Handbook of Information and Computer Ethics* (Hoboken, NJ: Wiley-Interscience), pp. 69–101.

Fukuyama, F. (1992). *The End of History and The Last Man* (New York, NY: The Free Press).

Gächter, S. (2007). Conditional cooperation: Behavioral regularities from the lab and the field and their policy implications, in B. Frey and A. Stutzer (eds.), *Economics and Psychology: A Promising New Cross-Disciplinary Field* (Cambridge, MA: MIT Press), pp. 19–50.

Gallup, G. (1970). Chimpanzees: Self recognition, *Science* **167**, 3914, pp. 86–87.

Gardner, M. (1970). Mathematical games – the fantastic combinations of John Conway's new solitaire game 'life', *Scientific American* **223**, pp. 120–123.

Giddens, A. (1984). *The Constitution of Society: Outline of the Theory of Structuration* (Cambridge: Polity Press).

Gillet, S. and Leite, I. (2020). A robot mediated music mixing activity for promoting collaboration among children, in *Companion of the 2020 ACM/IEEE International Conference on Human-Robot Interaction HRI)*, pp. 212–214.

Gini, C. (1912). *Variabilità e mutabilità* (Bologna: C. Cuppini).

Gladwell, M. (2000). *The Tipping Point: How Little Things Can Make a Big Difference* (New York, NY: Little, Brown).

Glance, N. S. and Huberman, B. A. (1994). The dynamics of social dilemmas, *Scientific American* **270**, 3, pp. 76–81.

Goel, A., Hulett, R., and Krishnaswamy, A. (2018). Relating metric distortion and fairness of social choice rules, in *Proceedings of the 13th Workshop on Economics of Networks, Systems and Computation (NetEcon)*, p. 1.

Goldman, B. and Cropanzano, R. (2014). "justice" and "fairness" are not the same thing, *Journal of Organizational Behaviour* **36**, 2, pp. 313–318.

Graeber, D. (2011). *Debt: The First 5,000 Years* (Brooklyn, NY: Melville House).

Graeber, D. (2015). *The Utopia of Rules: On Technology, Stupidity, and the Secret Joys of Bureaucracy* (Brooklyn, NY: Melville House).

Greenberg, J. (1993). The social side of fairness: Interpersonal and informational classes of organizational justice, in R. Cropanzano (ed.), *Justice in the Workplace: Approaching Fairness in Human Resource Management* (Hillsdale, NJ: Lawrence Erlbaum), pp. 79–103.

Grosz, B., Kraus, S., Talman, S., Stossel, B., and Havlin, M. (2004). The influence of social dependencies on decision-making: Initial investigations with a new game, in *Proceedings of the 3rd Conference on Autonomous Agents and Multi-Agent Systems (AAMAS)*, pp. 782–789.

Harari, Y. (2014). *Sapiens: A Brief History of Humankind* (London: Harvill Secker).

Hardin, G. (1968). The tragedy of the commons, *Science* **162**, 3859, pp. 1243–1248.

Hart, J. and Scassellati, B. (2014). Robotic self-modeling, in J. Pitt (ed.), *The Computer After Me*, Chapter 14 (London: ICPress), pp. 207–218.

Hegselmann, R. and Krause, U. (2002). Opinion dynamics and bounded confidence: Models, analysis and simulation, *Journal of Artificial Societies and Social Simulation* **5**, 3, pp. 1–33.

Heller, M. (1998). The tragedy of the anticommons, *Harvard Law Review* **111**, 3, pp. 621–688.

Hess, C. and Ostrom, E. (eds.) (2006). *Understanding Knowledge as a Commons: From Theory to Practice* (Cambridge, MA: MIT Press).

Hewitt, C. (1986). Offices are open systems, *ACM Transactions on Information Systems* **4**, 3, pp. 271–287.

Holland, S., Pitt, J., Sanderson, D., and Busquets, D. (2013). Reasoning and reflection in the game of nomic: Self-organising self-aware agents with mutable rule-sets, in *7th IEEE International Conference SASO Workshops*, pp. 101–106.

Huebscher, M. and McCann, J. (2008). A survey of autonomic computing — Degrees, models and applications, *ACM Computing Surveys* **40**, 3, p. 7.

Hussain, A., Ali, S., Ahmed, M., and Hussain, S. (2019). The anti-vaccination movement: A regression in modern medicine, *Cureus* **10**, 7, p. e2919.

Jain, R., Chiu., D., and Hawe, W. (1984). Quantitative measure of fairness and discrimination for resource allocation in shared computer systems, Technical Report, Research Report TR-30, DEC.

Jasso, G. (1978). On the justice of earnings: A new specification of the justice evaluation function, *American Journal of Sociology* **83**, 6, pp. 1398–1419.

Jones, A. (2002). On the concept of trust, *Decision Support Systems* **33**, 3, pp. 225–232.
Jones, A. and Sergot, M. (1993). On the characterisation of law and computer systems: The normative systems perspective, in J.-J. Meyer and R. Wieringa (eds.), *Deontic Logic in Computer Science: Normative System Specification* (Chihester: Wiley), pp. 275–307.
Jones, A. and Sergot, M. (1996). A formal characterisation of institutionalised power, *Journal of the IGPL* **4**, 3, pp. 427–443.
Jones, A., Artikis, A., and Pitt, J. (2013). The design of intelligent sociotechnical systems, *Artificial Intelligence Review* **39**, 1, pp. 5–20.
Jong, S. and Tuyls, K. (2011). Human-inspired computational fairness, *Autonomous Agents and Multi-Agent Systems* **22**, pp. 103–126.
Kahneman, D. (2011). *Thinking, Fast and Slow* (New York, NY: Farrar, Straus and Giroux).
Kass, N. (2001). An ethics framework for public health, *American Journal of Public Health* **91**, 11, pp. 1776–1782.
Kay, J. (1993). *Foundations of Corporate Success: How Business Strategies Add Value* (Oxford: Oxford University Press).
Kelly, F., Maulloo, A., and Tan, D. K. H. (1998). Rate control for communication networks: Shadow prices, proportional fairness and stability, *The Journal of the Operational Research Society* **49**, 3, pp. 237–252.
Klejnowski, L., Niemann, S., Bernard, Y., and Müller-Schloer, C. (2013). Using trusted communities to improve the speedup of agents in a desktop grid system, in *Proceedings of the 7th International Symposium on Intelligent Distributed Computing (IDC)*, pp. 189–198.
König, P. (2020). Dissecting the algorithmic leviathan: On the sociopolitical anatomy of algorithmic governance, *Philosophy & Technology* **33**, pp. 467–485.
Konow, J. (2003). Which Is the Fairest One of All? A Positive Analysis of Justice Theories, *Journal of Economic Literature* **41**, 4, pp. 1188–1239.
Koutsoupias, E. and Papadimitriou, C. (2009). Worst-case equilibria, *Computer Science Review* **3**, 2, pp. 65–69.
Kowalchyk, A. (2006). Resolving intellectual property disputes outside of court: Using ADR to take control of your case, *Dispute Resolution Journal* **61**, 2, pp. 28–37.
Kowalski, R. (1988). Logic-based open systems, in *Representation and Reasoning*, (Tübingen: Max Niemeyer, pp. 125–134).
Kowalski, R. and Sergot, M. (1986). A logic-based calculus of events, *New Generation Computing* **4**, pp. 67–95.
Kropotkin, P. (1902). *Mutual Aid: A Factor of Evolution* (London: Heinemann).

Lamport, L. (1998). The part-time parliament, *ACM Transactions of Computing Systems* **16**, 2, pp. 133–169.

Lan, T., Kao, D., Chiang, M., and Sabharwal, A. (2010). An axiomatic theory of fairness in network resource allocation, in *INFOCOM*, pp. 1343–1351.

Landauer, C. and Bellman, K. L. (2003). Meta-analysis and reflection as system development strategies, in D. L. Hicks (ed.), *International Symposium on Metainformatics MIS, Lecture Notes in Computer Science*, Vol. 3002 (Springer), pp. 178–196.

Landauer, C. and Bellman, K. (2016). Reflective systems need models at run time, in *Proceedings of the 11th International Workshop on Models@run.time*, pp. 52–59.

Lansing, J. and Kremer, J. (1993). Emergent properties of Balinese water temple network, *American Anthropologist* **95**, pp. 97–114.

Leibenstein, H. (1957). *Economic Backwardness and Economic Growth* (New. York, NY: Wiley).

Lewis, M. (2010). *The Big Short: Inside the Doomsday Machine* (New York, NY: W. W. Norton & Co.).

Lewis, P., Platzner, M., Rinner, B., Tørresen, J., and Yao, X. (eds.) (2016). *Self-aware Computing Systems — An Engineering Approach*, Natural Computing Series (Berlin, Heidelberg: Springer).

Lewis, P. R. and Ekárt, A. (2017). Social and asocial learning in collective action problems: The rise and fall of socially-beneficial behaviour, in *2nd IEEE International Workshops on Foundations and Applications of Self* Systems, FAS*W@SASO/ICCAC 2017*, pp. 91–96.

List, C. (2013). Social choice theory, in E. Zalta (ed.), *The Stanford Encyclopedia of Philosophy (Winter 2013 Edition)* (Stanford University), pp. https://plato.stanford.edu/archives/win2013/entries/social-choice/.

List, C. and Goodin, R. (2001). Epistemic democracy: Generalizing the condorcet jury theorem, *Journal of Political Philosophy* **9**, 3, pp. 277–306.

Liu, C.-C., McArthur, S., and Lee, S.-J. (eds.) (2016). *Smart Grid Handbook, 3 Volume Set* (Chichester: Wiley).

Lofgren, M. (2012). The revolt of the rich, *The American Conservative*, August 27.

Lopes, J., Marrone, P., Pereira, S., and Dias, E. (2019). Health 4.0: Challenges for an orderly and inclusive innovation, *IEEE Technology & Society Magazine* **38**, 3, pp. 17–19.

Luke, S., Cioffi-Revilla, C., Panait, L., and Sullivan, K. (2005). MASON: A New Multi-Agent Simulation Toolkit, *Simulation: Transactions of the society for Modeling and Simulation International* **82**, 7, pp. 517–527.

Macbeth, S., Busquets, D., and Pitt, J. (2014). System modeling: Principled operationalization of social systems using PreSage-2, in D. Gianni,

A. D'Ambrogio, and A. Tolk (eds.), *Modeling and Simulation-Based Systems Engineering Handbook* (Boca Raton, FL: CRC Press), pp. 43–66.

Macbeth, S. and Pitt, J. (2015). Self-organising management of user-generated data and knowledge, *Knowledge Engineering Review* **30**, 3, pp. 237–264.

Malinowski, B. (1920). Kula: The circulating exchange of valuables in the archipelagoes of eastern new guinea, *Man* **20**, pp. 97–105.

Marsh, S. (1994). *Formalising trust as a computational concept*, Ph.D. thesis, University of Stirling.

Marsh, S., Atele-Williams, T., Basu, A., Dwyer, N., Lewis, P., Miller-Bakewell, H., and Pitt, J. (2020). Thinking about trust: People, process, and place, *Patterns* **1**, 3, pp. 1–8.

Maslow, A. (1943). A theory of human motivation, *Psychological Review* **50**, 4, pp. 370–396.

Mastroeni, L., Vellucci, P., and Naldi, M. (2019). Agent-based models for opinion formation: A bibliographic survey, *IEEE Access* **7**, pp. 58836–58848.

May, K. (1952). A set of independent, necessary and sufficient conditions for simple majority decision, *Econometrica* **20**, pp. 680–684.

Maynard Smith, J. (1982). *Evolution and the Theory of Games* (Cambridge: Cambridge University Press).

Mazumdar, R., Mason, L., and Douligeris, C. (1991). Fairness in network optimal flow control: Optimality of product forms, *IEEE Transactions on Communications* **39**, 5, pp. 775–782.

McCullough, M. E. (2001). Forgiveness: Who does it and how do they do it? *Current Directions in Psychological Science* **10**, 6, pp. 194–197.

McKenna, P. (2008). Vote of no confidence, *New Scientist* **198**, 2651, pp. 30–33.

Michaal, D. and Chen, S. (2005). *Serious Games: Games That Educate, Train, and Inform* (Muska & Lipman/Premier-Trade).

Michalak, T., Rahwan, T., Moretti, S., Narayanam, R., Skibski, O., Szczepański, P., and Wooldridge, M. (2015). A new approach to measure social capital using game-theoretic techniques, *ACM SIGecom Exchanges* **14**, 1, pp. 95–100.

Michels, R. (1962 [1911]). *Political Parties: A Sociological Study of the Oligarchical Tendencies of Modern Democracy* (New York, NY: The Free Press).

Milanovic, K. and Pitt, J. (2018). The social construction of "shared reality" in socio-technical systems, in *Trust Management XII. (IFIPTM). IFIP Advances in Information and Communication Technology*, Vol. 528 (Berlin, Heidelberg: Springer), pp. 149–159.

Mitchell Waldrop, M. (2015). Autonomous vehicles: No drivers required, *Nature* **518**, 7537, p. 20.
Mo, J. and Walrand, J. (2000). Fair end-to-end window-based congestion control, *IEEE/ACM Transactions on Networking* **8**, 5, pp. 556–567.
Monbiot, G. (2017). *Out of the Wreckage* (London: Verso).
Moulin, H. (1988). Condorcet's principle implies the no show paradox, *Journal of Economic Theory* **45**, pp. 53–64.
Moulin, H. (2003). *Fair Division and Collective Welfare* (Cambridge, MA: MIT Press).
Muller, J. (2019). *The Tyranny of Metrics* (Princeton, NJ: Princeton University Press).
Murillo, J., Busquets, D., Dalmau, J., López, B., Munoz, V., and Rodríguez-Roda, I. (2011). Improving urban wastewater management through an auction-based management of discharges, *Environ. Modelling & Software* **26**, pp. 689–696.
Nafz, F., Seebach, H., Steghöfer, J.-P., Anders, G., and Reif, W. (2013). Constraining self-organisation through corridors of correct behaviour: The restore invariant approach, in C. Müller-Schloer, H. Schmeck, and T. Ungerer (eds.), *Organic Computing – A Paradigm Shift for Complex Systems. Autonomic Systems, vol 1* (Berlin, Heidelberg: Springer), pp. 79–93.
Nagle, J. (1987). On packet switches with infinite storage, *IEEE Transactions on Communications* **35**, 4, pp. 435–438.
Nash, J. (1950). Equilibrium points in n-person games, *Proceedings of the National Academy of Sciences of the United States of America* **36**, 1, pp. 48–49.
Neville, B. and Pitt, J. (2003). A computational framework for social agents in agent mediated e-commerce, in A. Omicini, P. Petta, and J. Pitt (eds.), *Engineering Societies in the Agents World (ESAW) IV*, no. 3071 in LNAI (Berlin, Heidelberg: Springer), pp. 376–391.
Neville, B. and Pitt, J. (2004). A simulation study of social agents in agent mediated e-commerce, in R. Falcone (ed.), *AAMAS Trust Workshop*, pp. 83–91.
Neville, B. and Pitt, J. (2009). PreSage: A programming environment for the simulation of agent societies, in K. Hindriks, A. Pokahr, and S. Sardina (eds.), *Programming Multi-Agent Systems, LNCS*, Vol. 5442 (Berlin, Heidelberg: Springer), pp. 88–103.
Nielsen, J. (1994). Heuristic evaluation, in J. Nielsen and R. Mack (eds.), *Usability Inspection Methods* (Hoboken, NJ: Wiley), pp. 25–64.
Nilsson, N. J. (1994). Teleo-reactive programs for agent control, *Journal of Artificial Intelligence Research* **1**, pp. 139–158.

Nigussie, Z., Tsunekawa, A., Haregeweyn, N., Adgo, E., Cochrane, L., Floquet, A., and Abele, S. (2018). Applying Ostrom's institutional analysis and development framework to soil and water conservation activities in north-western Ethiopia, *Land Use Policy* **71**, pp. 1–10.

Nikolai, C. and Madey, G. (2009). Tools of the trade: A survey of various agent based modeling platforms, *Journal of Artificial Societies and Social Simulation* **12**.

Norman, D. (1988). *The Design of Everyday Things* (New York, NY: Basic Books).

North, M. J., Collier, N. T., and Vos, J. R. (2006). Experiences creating three implementations of the Repast agent modeling toolkit, *ACM Transactions on Modeling and Computer Simulation (TOMACS)* **16**, 1, pp. 1–25.

Nowak, A., Vallacher, R., Rychwalska, A., Roszczyńska-Kurasińska, M., Ziembowicz, K., Biesaga, M., and Kacprzyk-Murawska, M. (2020). *Target in Control: Social Influence as Distributed Information Processing* (Berlin, Heidelberg: Springer).

Nozick, R. (1974). *Anarchy, State, and Utopia* (New York, NY: Basic Books).

Ober, J. (2008). *Democracy and Knowledge* (Princeton, NJ: Princeton University Press).

Ober, J. (2013). Democracy's wisdom: An aristotelian middle way for collective judgement, *American Political Science Review* **107**, 1, pp. 104–122.

Ober, J. (2017). *Demopolis: Democracy Before Liberalism in Theory and Practice* (Cambridge: Cambridge University Press).

Odell, J. (1999). Objects and agents: How do they differ? http://www.jamesodell.com/Agents_and_Objects.pdf.

Olson, M. (1965). *The Logic of Collective Action* (Harvard, MA: Harvard University Press).

Oreskes, N. and Conway, E. (2010). *Merchants of Doubt: How a Handful of Scientists Obscured the Truth on Issues from Tobacco Smoke to Global Warming* (London: Bloomsbury Press).

Ostrom, E. (1990). *Governing the commons: The Evolution of Institutions for Collective Action* (Cambridge: Cambridge University Press).

Ostrom, E. (2005). *Understanding Institutional Diversity* (Princeton, NJ: Princeton University Press).

Ostrom, E. (2010). Beyond markets and states: Polycentric governance of complex economic systems, in K. Grandin (ed.), *Les Prix Nobel. The Nobel Prizes 2009* (Nobel Foundation), pp. 408–444.

Ostrom, E. and Ahn, T. (2003). *Foundations of Social Capital* (Cheltenham: Edward Elgar Pub.).

Ostrom, V. (1972). Polycentricity, Digital Library of the Commons, https://dlc.dlib.indiana.edu/dlc/handle/10535/3763.
Pacuit, E. (2019). Voting methods, in E. Zalta (ed.), *The Stanford Encyclopedia of Philosophy (Fall 2019 Edition)* (Stanford University), pp. https://plato.stanford.edu/archives/fall2019/entries/voting-methods/.
Pang, B. and Lee, L. (2008). Opinion mining and sentiment analysis, *Foundations and Trends in Information Retrieval* **2**, 1–2, pp. 1–135.
Papadimitriou, C. H. and Roughgarden, T. (2005). Computing equilibria in multi-player games, in *Proc. 16th Annual ACM-SIAM Symposium on Discrete Algorithms (SODA)*, pp. 82–91.
Pariser, E. (2011). *The Filter Bubble: What the Internet Is Hiding from You,* (New York, NY: The Penguin Press).
Petruzzi, P., Busquets, D., and Pitt, J. (2013). Self-organising flexible demand for smart grid, in *7th IEEE International Conference SASO*, pp. 21–22.
Petruzzi, P., Busquets, D., and Pitt, J. (2014). Social capital as a complexity reduction mechanism for decision making in large scale open systems, in *8th IEEE International Conference SASO*, pp. 145–150.
Petruzzi, P., Busquets, D., and Pitt, J. (2015). A generic social capital framework for optimising self-organised collective action, in *9th IEEE International Conference SASO*, pp. 21–30.
Peyton Young, H. (2008). Social norms, in S. Durlauf and L. Blume. (eds.), *The New Palgrave Dictionary of Economics*, 2nd edn. (London: Palgrave Macmillan), pp. 1–7.
Piketty, T. (2014). *Capital in the Twenty-First Century* (Harvard MA: Harvard University Press).
Pinyol, I. and Sabater-Mir, J. (2013). Computational trust and reputation models for open multi-agent systems: A review, *Artificial Intelligence Review* **40**, 1, pp. 1–25.
Pitsikalis, M., Artikis, A., Dreo, R., Ray, C., Camossi, E., and Jousselme, A. (2019). Composite event recognition for maritime monitoring, in *Proceedings of the 13th ACM International Conference on Distributed and Event-based Systems (DEBS)*, pp. 163–174.
Pitt, J. (2003). Constitutive rules for agent communication languages, in *IJCAI-03, Proceedings of the Eighteenth International Joint Conference on Artificial Intelligence (IJCAI)*, pp. 691–698.
Pitt, J. (2004). Digital blush: Towards shame and embarrassment in multi-agent information trading applications, *Cognition, Technology & Work* **6**, 1, pp. 23–36.
Pitt, J. (2005). The open agent society as a platform for the user-friendly information society, *AI Society* **19**, 2, pp. 123–158.

Pitt, J. (ed.) (2014). *The Computer After Me* (London: ICPress).

Pitt, J. (2017). Interactional justice and self-governance of open self-organising systems, in *11th IEEE International Conference SASO*, pp. 31–40.

Pitt, J. (2019a). Deepfake videos and DDOS attacks (Deliberate Denial of Satire), *IEEE Technology & Society Magazine* **38**, 4, pp. 5–8.

Pitt, J. (2019b). Facts, policies, and values — the democratic triad: Technology for restoring civil discourse and civic dignity, *IEEE Technology & Society Magazine* **38**, 1, pp. 5–8.

Pitt, J. (2019c). Transparent ownership of mobility-as-a-service, *IEEE Technology & Society Magazine* **38**, 2, pp. 5–8.

Pitt, J. (2020a). Apologies for the inconvenience (but please use it wisely), *IEEE Technology & Society Magazine* **39**, 2, pp. 5–10.

Pitt, J. (2020b). From trust and loyalty to lock-in and digital dependence, *IEEE Technology & Society Magazine* **39**, 1, pp. 5–8.

Pitt, J. and Artikis, A. (2015). The open agent society: Retrospective and prospective views, *Artificial Intelligence and Law* **23**, 3, pp. 241–270.

Pitt, J. and Mamdani, A. (1999a). A protocol-based semantics for an agent communication language, in *Proceedings of the Sixteenth International Joint Conference on Artificial Intelligence, (IJCAI)*, pp. 486–491.

Pitt, J. and Mamdani, A. (1999b). Some remarks on the semantics of FIPA's agent communication language, *Autonomous Agents and Multi-Agent Systems* **2**, 4, pp. 333–356.

Pitt, J. and Nowak, A. (2014a). Collective awareness and the new institution science, in J. Pitt (ed.), *The Computer After Me*, Chapter 12 (London: ICPress), pp. 207–218.

Pitt, J. and Nowak, A. (2014b). The reinvention of social capital for socio-technical systems, *IEEE Technology & Society Magazine* **33**, 1, pp. 27–33.

Pitt, J. and Ober, J. (2018). Democracy by design: Basic democracy and the self-organisation of collective governance, in *12th IEEE International Conference SASO*, pp. 20–29.

Pitt, J. and Schaumeier, J. (2012). Provision and appropriation of common-pool resources without full disclosure, in I. Rahwan, W. Wobcke, S. Sen, and T. Sugawara (eds.), *Principles and Practice of Multi-Agent Systems (PRIMA)*, *LNCS*, Vol. 7455 (Berlin, Heidelberg: Springer), pp. 199–213.

Pitt, J., Busquets, D., and Macbeth, A. (2014). Distributive justice for self-organised common-pool resource management, *ACM TAAS* **9**, 3, pp. 14:1–14:39.

Pitt, J., Busquets, D., and Riveret, R. (2013). Procedural justice and 'fitness for purpose' of self-organising electronic institutions, in G. Boella, E. Elkind, T. Savarimuthu, F. Dignum, and M. Purvis (eds.), *Principles and Practice of Multi-Agent Systems (PRIMA), LNCS*, Vol. 8291 (Berlin, Heidelberg: Springer), pp. 260–275.

Pitt, J., Busquets, D., and Riveret, R. (2015). The pursuit of computational justice in open systems, *AI Society* **30**, 3, pp. 359–378.

Pitt, J., Clippinger, H., and Sørensen, C. (2018a). Values, axial currencies and computational axiology, *IEEE Technology and Society Magazine* **37**, 3, pp. 56–63.

Pitt, J., Dryzek, J., and Ober, J. (2020a). Algorithmic reflexive governance for socio-techno-ecological systems, *IEEE Technology & Society Magazine* **39**, 2, pp. 52–59.

Pitt, J., Mamdani, A., and Charlton, P. (2001). The open agent society and its enemies: A position statement and research programme, *Telematics and Informatics* **18**, 1, pp. 67–87.

Pitt, J., Schaumeier, J., and Artikis, A. (2011a). The axiomatisation of socio-economic principles for self-organising systems, in *Fifth IEEE International Conference SASO*, pp. 138–147.

Pitt, J., Schaumeier, J., and Artikis, A. (2011b). Coordination, conventions and the self-organisation of sustainable institutions, in D. Kinny, J. Hsu, G. Governatori, and A. Ghose (eds.), *Agents in Principle, Agents in Practice (PRIMA), LNCS*, Vol. 7047 (Berlin, Heidelberg: Springer), pp. 202–217.

Pitt, J., Schaumeier, J., and Artikis, A. (2011c). Role assignment in institutional clouds for rule-based enterprise management, in F. Olken, M. Palmirani, and D. Sottara (eds.), *Rule-Based Modeling and Computing on the Semantic Web (RuleML), LNCS*, Vol. 7018 (Berlin, Heidelberg: Springer), pp. 237–251.

Pitt, J., Schaumeier, J., and Artikis, A. (2012a). Axiomatisation of socio-economic principles for self-organising institutions: Concepts, experiments and challenges, *ACM TAAS* **7**, 4, pp. 39:1–39:39.

Pitt, J., Busquets, D., Bourazeri, A., and Petruzzi, P. (2014a). Collective intelligence and algorithmic governance of socio-technical systems, in D. Miorandi, V. Maltese, M. Rovatsos, A. Nijholt, and J. Stewart (eds.), *Social Collective Intelligence: Combining the Powers of Humans and Machines to Build a Smarter Society* (Berlin, Heidelberg: Springer), pp. 31–50.

Pitt, J., Kamara, L., Sergot, M., and Artikis, A. (2006). Voting in multi-agent systems, *The Computer Journal* **49**, 2, pp. 156–170.

Pitt, J., Peixoto Cardoso, R., Hart, E., and Ober, J. (2018b). Relevant expertise aggregation for policy selection in CAS, in *2018 IEEE SASO Workshops (SASOW)*, pp. 136–141.

Pitt, J., Ramirez-Cano, D., Kamara, L., and Neville, B. (2007). Alternative dispute resolution in virtual organizations, in A. Artikis, G. O'Hare, K. Stathis, and G. Vouros (eds.), *Engineering Societies in the Agents World VIII (ESAW), LNCS*, Vol. 4995 (Berlin, Heidelberg: Springer), pp. 72–89.

Pitt, J., Nowak, A., Michalak, T., Borkowski, W., and Vallacher, R. (2020b). Knowing what the bits know: Social influence as the source of collective knowledge, in *2nd International Workshop on Agent-Based Modelling of Human Behaviour (ABMHub)*, pp. 1–7.

Pitt, J., Schaumeier, J., Busquets, D., and Macbeth, S. (2012b). Self-organising common-pool resource allocation and canons of distributive justice, in *Sixth IEEE International Conference SASO*, pp. 119–128.

Poblet, M., Allen, D., Konashevych, O., Lane, A., and Diaz Valdivia, C. (2020). From Athens to the blockchain: Oracles for digital democracy, *Frontiers in Blockchain* **3**. doi: 10.3389/fbloc.2020.575662.

Portugal, S., Hubel, T., Fritz, J., Heese, S., Trobe, D., Voelkl, B., Hailes, S., Wilson, A., and Usherwood, J. (2014). Upwash exploitation and downwash avoidance by flap phasing in ibis formation flight, *Nature* **505**, pp. 399–402.

Prasad Koirala, B., Koliou, E., Friege, J., Hakvoort, R., and Herder, P. (2016). Energetic communities for community energy: A review of key issues and trends shaping integrated community energy systems, *Renewable and Sustainable Energy Reviews* **56**, pp. 722–744.

Prettejohn, B., Berryman, M., and McDonnell, M. (2011). Methods for generating complex networks with selected structural properties for simulations: A review and tutorial for neuroscientists, *Front. Comput. Neurosci* **5**, pp. 1–11.

Prouskas, K. and Pitt, J. (2004). A real-time architecture for time-aware agents, *IEEE Transactions on Systems, Man, and Cybernetics, Part B* **34**, 3, pp. 1553–1568.

Putnam, R. (1993). The prosperous community: Social capital and public life, *The American Prospect* **13**, pp. 35–42.

Putnam, R. (2000). *Bowling Alone: The Collapse and Revival of American Community* (New York, NY: Simon & Schuster).

Ramirez-Cano, D. and Pitt, J. (2006). Follow the leader: Profiling agents in an opinion formation model of dynamic confidence and individual mind-set, in *Intelligent Agent Technology (IAT)*, pp. 660–667.

Rao, A. and Georgeff, M. (1998). Decision procedures for BDI logics, *Logic and Computation* **8**, 3, pp. 293–343.

Rawls, J. (1971). *A Theory of Justice* (Harvard MA: Harvard University Press).
Regenwetter, M. and Grofman, B. (1998). Approval voting, borda winners, and condorcet winners: Evidence from seven elections, *Management Science* **44**, 4, pp. 520–533.
Regner, T., Barria, J., Pitt, J., and Neville, B. (2010). Governance of digital content in the era of mass participation, *Electronic Commerce Research* **10**, 1, pp. 99–110.
Rescher, N. (1966). *Distributive Justice* (Indianapolis, IN: Bobbs-Merrill Company, Inc.).
Reynolds, C. (1987). Flocks, herds and schools: A distributed behavioral model, in *Proceedings of the 14th Annual Conference on Computer Graphics and Interactive Techniques (SIGGRAPH)*, pp. 25–34.
Reynolds, C. and Picard, R. (2004). Affective sensors, privacy, and ethical contracts, in *Proceedings CHI 2004 extended abstracts on Human Factors in computing systems*, pp. 1103–1106.
Richard Scott, W. and Davis, G. (2016). *Organizations and Organizing: Rational, Natural, and Open System Perspectives* (London and New York: Routledge).
Riker, W. (1986). *The Art of Political Manipulation* (Yale, CT: Yale University Press).
Riveret, R., Contissa, G., Rotolo, A., and Pitt, J. (2013). Law enforcement in norm-governed learning agents, in M. L. Gini, O. Shehory, T. Ito, and C. M. Jonker (eds.), *International conference on Autonomous Agents and Multi-Agent Systems, AAMAS '13* (IFAAMAS), pp. 1151–1152.
Robbins, J. (2019). If technology is a parasite masquerading as a symbiont — are we the host? *IEEE Technology & Society Magazine* **38**, 3, pp. 24–33.
Robert, S., Robert, H., Evans, W., Honemann, D., and Balch, T. (2000). *Robert's Rules of Order, Newly Revised, 10th edn.* (New York, NY: Perseus Publishing).
Rosenschein, J. and Zlotkin, G. (1998). *Rules of Encounter: Designing Conventions for Automated Negotiation among Computers* (Cambridge, MA: MIT Press).
Rosenzweig, M. (1971). Paradox of enrichment: destabilization of exploitation ecosystems in ecological time, *Science* **171**, 3969, pp. 385–387.
Roy, S. and Chattopadhyay, J. (2007). The stability of ecosystems: A brief overview of the paradox of enrichment, *Journal of Biosciences* **32**, 2, pp. 421–428.
Runciman, D. (2018). *How Democracy Ends* (New York, NY: Basic Books).
Russell, S. and Norvig, P. (2016). *Artificial Intelligence: A Modern Approach* (Englewood Cliffs, NJ: Prentice-Hall).

Sandel, M. (2013). *What Money Can't Buy: The Moral Limits of Markets* (London: Penguin Books).

Sanderson, D. and Pitt, J. (2011). An affective anticipatory agent architecture, in *Proceedings of the 2011 IEEE/WIC/ACM International Conference on Intelligent Agent Technology (IAT)*, pp. 93–96.

Sara Santos, M. and Pitt, J. (2013). Emotions and norms in shared spaces, in T. Balke, F. Dignum, B. van Riemsdijk, and A. Chopra (eds.), *Coordination, Organizations, Institutions, and Norms in Agent Systems IX, LNAI*, Vol. 8366 (Berlin, Heidelberg: Springer), pp. 157–176.

Schelling, T. (1960). *The strategy of conflict* (Harvard MA: Harvard University Press).

Schermerhorn, J. R., Uhl-Bien, M., and Osborn, R. (2011). *Organizational Behavior, 12th edn.* (Hoboken, NJ: Wiley).

Schmickl, T. and Crailsheim, K. (2008). Trophallaxis within a robotic swarm: Bio-inspired communication among robots in a swarm, *Autonomous Robots* **25**, 1–2, pp. 171–188.

Schwartz, S. (1992). Universals in the content and structure of values: Theoretical advances and empirical tests in 20 countries, *Advances in Experimental Psychology* **25**, pp. 1–65.

Schweik, C. M. (2007). Free/open-source software as a framework for establishing commons in science, in C. Hess and E. Ostrom (eds.), *Understanding Knowledge as a Commons: From Theory to Practice* (Cambridge, MA: MIT Press), pp. 277–310.

Searle, J. (1969). *Speech Acts* (Cambridge: Cambridge University Press).

Searle, J. (1997). *The Construction of Social Reality* (New York, NY: The Free Press).

Sergot, M. (2001). A computational theory of normative positions, *ACM Trans. Comput. Log.* **2**, 4, pp. 581–622.

Sergot, M. (2007). Action and agency in norm-governed multi-agent systems, in A. Artikis, G. O'Hare, K. Stathis, and G. Vouros (eds.), *Engineering Societies in the Agents World (ESAW VIII), LNCS*, Vol. 4995 (Berlin, Heidelberg: Springer), pp. 1–54.

Shapley, L. (1953). A value for n-person games, in H. Kuhn and A. Tucker (eds.), *Contributions to the Theory of Games II*, Annals of Mathematics Studies (Princeton, NJ: Princeton University Press), pp. 307–317.

Sieloff, C. (1999). "If only HP knew what HP knows": The roots of knowledge management at HewlettPackard, *Journal of Knowledge Management* **3**, 1, pp. 47–53.

Simon, H. (1956). Rational choice and the structure of the environment, *Psychological Review* **63**, 2, pp. 129–138.

Singh, R., Ravindra Bodhe, A., Kanuparthi, P., Ananthakrishnan, A., and Pitt, J. (2019). From classification to definition: The changing nature of human adjudication, *IEEE Technology & Society Magazine* **38**, 4, pp. 55–62.

Skyrms, B. (2004). *The Stag Hunt and the Evolution of Social Structure* (Cambridge: Cambridge University Press).

Smith, R. (1980). The contract net protocol: High-level communication and control in a distributed problem solver, *IEEE Transactions on Computers* **C-29**, 12, pp. 1104–1113.

Soltan, K. (1981). Jasso on distributive justice, *American Sociological Review* **46**, 3, pp. 348–352.

Solum, L. (2004). Procedural justice, *Southern California Law Review* **78**, 181, pp. 275–289.

Special Report (2018). The story of the Internet is all about layers, The Economist.

Steels, L. and Brooks, R. (1994). *The Artificial Life Route to Artificial Intelligence: Building Situated Embodied Agents* (New Haven: Lawrence Erlbaum Assoc.).

Stewart, I. (1999, May). Mathematical recreations: A puzzle for pirates, *Scientific American*, pp. 98–99.

Stockdale, K. (2015). Police understandings of restorative justice — the impact of rank and role, *Restorative Justice* **3**, 2, pp. 212–232.

Suber, P. (1990). *The Paradox of Self-Amendment: A Study of Law, Logic, Omnipotence, and Change* (Oxford: Peter Lang Publishing).

Surowiecki, J. (2004). *The Wisdom of Crowds* (New York, NY: Little, Brown).

Sutton, R. (2008). *The No Asshole Rule: Building a Civilized Workplace and Surviving One That Isn't* (New York: Grand Central Publishing).

Suzuki, J. (2015). *Constitutional Calculus: The Math of Justice and the Myth of Common Sense* (Baltimore, MD: J. H. University Press).

Sznajd-Weron, K. and Sznajd, J. (2000). Opinion evolution in closed community, *International Journal of Modern Physics C* **11**, 6, pp. 1157–1165.

Tavris, C. and Aronson, E. (2015). *Mistakes were Made (But Not By Me) revised edn.* (Boston and New York: Mariner Books).

Tesler, L. (1981). The smalltalk environment, *Byte* **6**, 8, p. 90.

Thomas, N. (2014). Democracy by design, *Journal of Public Deliberation* **10**, 1, p. Art.17.

Thompson, D. (1980). Moral responsibility and public officials: The problem of many hands, *American Political Science Review* **74**, 4, pp. 905–916.

Tideman, N. (2006). *Collective Decisions and Voting: The Potential for Public Choice* (London and New York: Routledge).

Uphsur, R. (2002). Principles for the justification of public health intervention, *Canadian Journal of Public Health* **93**, pp. 101–103.

Uslaner, E. (2002). *The Moral Foundations of Trust* (Cambridge: Cambridge University Press).

Vasalou, A., Hopfensitz, A., and Pitt, J. (2008). In praise of forgiveness: Ways for repairing trust breakdowns in one-off online interactions, *International Journal of Humanities-Computer Studies* **66**, 6, pp. 466–480.

Vasalou, A., Pitt, J., and Piolle, G. (2006). From theory to practice: Forgiveness as a mechanism to repair conflicts in CMC, in K. Stolen, W. Winsborough, F. Martinelli, and F. Massacci (eds.), *Trust Management. iTrust*, *LNCS*, Vol. 3986 (Berlin, Heidelberg: Springer), pp. 397–411.

von Neumann, J. (1959). On the theory of games of strategy, in A. Tucker and R. Luce (eds.), *Contributions to the Theory of Games IV*, Annals of Mathematics Studies (Princeton, NJ: Princeton University Press), pp. 13–42.

Walbank, F. (1957). *A Historical Commentary on Polybius* (Oxford: Oxford University Press).

Waldron, J. (2012). *Dignity, Rank, and Rights* (Oxford: Oxford University Press).

Walen, A. (2020). Retributive justice, in E. Zalta (ed.), *The Stanford Encyclopedia of Philosophy* (Fall 2020 Edition), (Stanford University), https://plato.stanford.edu/archives/fall2020/entries/justice-retributive/.

Wall, D. (2014). *The Sustainable Economics of Elinor Ostrom: Commons, Contestation and Draft* (Oxford & New York: Routledge).

Weber, M. (1965). *Politics as a Vocation* (Philadelphia, PA: Fortress Press).

Weisberg, H. (2014). *Willful Ignorance: The Mismeasure of Uncertainty* (Hoboken, NJ: Wiley).

Wilensky, U. and Rand, W. (2015). *An Introduction to Agent-Based Modeling: Modeling Natural, Social and Engineered Complex Systems with NetLogo* (Cambridge, MA: MIT Press).

Winfield, A., Michael, K., Pitt, J., and Evers, V. (2019). Machine ethics: The design and governance of ethical AI and autonomous systems, *Proceedings of the IEEE* **107**, 3, pp. 509–517.

WIPO Arbitration and Mediation Center (2007). Dispute resolution for the 21st century, http://arbiter.wipo.int.

Wittgenstein, L. (1922). *Tractatus Logico-Philosophicus* (translated by F. Ramsey and C. K. Ogden) (London: Kegan Paul).

Wooldridge, M. (2009). *An Introduction to MultiAgent Systems*, 2nd edn. (Chichester: Wiley).

Zolotas, M. and Pitt, J. (2016). Self-organising error detection and correction in open multi-agent systems, in S. Elnikety, P. Lewis, and C. Müller-Schloer (eds.), *1st International Workshops on Foundations and Applications of Self-* Systems (FAS*W)* (Piscataway, NJ: IEEE), pp. 180–185.

Index

A

acceptability, 307
accountability, 239
affinity, 286, 298
agent, 51, 61, 189, 218, 221, 251, 261, 296, 328
   autonomous, 16, 99, 164, 214, 265
   BDI, 19
   communication, 23–28
   society, 13–14
   software, 4
   teleo-reactive, 20
agent unified modelling language (AUML), 24
ALFEBIITE, 28
anacyclosis, 326
animation, 35, 224, 328
anthropogenic climate change, 6, 164, 168, 177, 268, 318
appropriation, 7, 164, 181, 208, 305
architecture
   BDI agent, 19
   HAMMER, 21
   MAPE-K, 21
ARCOL, 26
argumentation, 136, 182
arm's length relationship, 12
artificial social constructionism, 271–272
assessment
   collective, 297
   individual, 295
asymmetric supermajority, 106
asynchrony, 17
Athens, 315
autocracy, 312, 330
Autonomic Computing, 21
autonomic mechanism, 221
axiology, 268

B

ballot, 104
Big Data, 137
Bingo, 200
Binmore, Ken, 98, 243, 345
boids, 45–46
bright lines, 328

C

cake cutting, 95
Camus, 39
cellular automata, 46, 48
chess, 17, 60
citizen, 326, 328
civic participation, 330, 336
clique, 302, 320
clustering coefficient, 288
co-dependence, 11, 249
coalition, 55, 96

collective action, 4, 9, 58, 163, 167, 173–174, 260, 326
Colored Trails, 138
Coloured Trials, 139
common-pool resource (CPR), 7, 9, 139, 163, 169, 172, 240, 265, 323
community, 263
community energy system, 259, 264
comparative politics, 311
   algorithmic, 341, 344
compliance, 217
computer-mediated communication, 258
computing
   cloud, 41, 168
   grid, 213, 249
Condorcet, 109
   jury theorem, 279, 321
   loser, 108
   other paradox, 118
   paradox, 117
   winner, 108
confidence, 251, 286, 298
   bounded, 285
confirmation bias, 318
congruence, 176, 184, 241, 307
content creation, 136
contract-net protocol, 23
coordination, 168
citizen, 164
counts as, 27, 246
credible pre-commitments, 163, 317
cybernetics, 48
   management, 55

D

Daly Rules, 58
Deep Blue, 17
democracy, 191, 196, 233, 238, 279, 317–318, 320, 324, 345
   Athenian, 315, 325
   basic, 324, 327
   liberal, 319, 324
   representative, 180
Demopolis, 191, 327–328

depletion, 164
desert theory, 211
design contractualism, 138
dialectical materialism, 136
dictatorship, 105
Digital Society, 3
Digital Transformation, 3
dignity
   civic, 320, 326, 344
   zone of, 191
disobedience, 132, 323–324
dissent, 132, 312, 322
distance
   between allocations, 296
   geodesic, 288
distributive justice
   Rescher's canons, 216
diversity, 60, 323
Drools, 38
due process, 13

E

economy
   digital, 26
   gift, 196, 269
   information trading, 28
   market, 13
   of esteem, 269, 316
   of scarcity, 12, 171, 217, 301
   relational, 265
   rentier, 133
   sharing, 269
education, 246, 266, 272, 317
efficiency, 81, 121, 211
El Farol Bar, 94, 163
emergence, 45, 48
   planned, 50
engineering, 343
   morphogenetic, 42
   software, 159
entrenchment, 338, 340
entropy, 56
error
   ex post, 148, 152
   handling, 132

recovery, 152, 159
toleration, 141, 148
European Union (Withdrawal) Bill, 312
Event Calculus (EC), 32, 35
   monitoring, 229
   operational choice, 187
   protocol
      access control, 141, 143
      dispute resolution, 154
      regulatory compliance, 148
      voting, 124
evolutionary game theory, 96
exclusivity, 169
existential crisis, 39
expectation, 249, 254, 263
expertise, 60, 267, 318
extensive form, 76
externalities, 247

F

facts, 317
   institutional, 27, 57, 172, 184, 228, 328
fairness, 57, 121, 205, 212, 215, 296
favour, 259
financial crash, 200
FIPA Agent Communication Language (FIPA ACL), 25
Firefly, 166
first past the post, 110
flocking, 45
forgiveness, 253, 258
Foundation for Intelligent Physical Agents (FIPA), 25
free riding, 164, 174
full disclosure, 12, 171, 227
fuzzy inference, 257

G

game
   n-player, 94
   battle of the sexes, 91
   coordination, 90
   delegation, 337

focal point, 93
Hawk–Dove, 83
kitchen stand-off, 73, 81
linear public good (LPG), 170–171, 217
LPG', 171
of chess, 71
of chicken, 83
of life, 47
of nomic, 198, 314, 328
pirate, 95
prisoners' dilemma, 85
   iterated, 87
serious, 43
stag hunt, 91
ultimatum, 93
unscrupulous diners' dilemma, 264
glider, 48
governance
   algorithmic, 132
   democratic, 320
   self-, 172, 307–308, 315, 326
Green New Deal, 8
guardrail, 191, 195

H

Health 4.0, 3
hierarchy of needs, 52
human rights, 319

I

independent guess aggregation, 59
index
   Banzhaf power, 239
   democratic participation, 238
   Gini, 216, 225, 236, 297, 337
   Jain, 216
indivisible goods, 12
Industry 4.0, 4
institution, 27, 57, 183, 219, 246, 261, 265, 299, 315
   electronic, 179, 184
   self-governing, 177
   well-ordered, 309

Institutional Analysis and
 Development (IAD), 177
institutional design principles,
 176–177, 241, 265
 number 1–8, 182, 191, 193
institutionalised power, 27, 34, 50,
 124, 180
institutions
 self-governing, 172
intellectual property, 136
intelligence, 17
intentional stance, 19
Internet, 267
 application layer, 195
interoception, 276
intersubjective agreement, 319
iron law of oligarchy, 194, 307, 312,
 326

J

joint enterprise, 167
judgement aggregation, 279, 284
justice, 135, 205
 computational, 205, 244
  framework, 241–242
 distributive, 210, 212, 217,
  225
 fast-track, 269
 interactional, 295, 306
 procedural, 232, 241
 restorative, 194
 retributive, 226, 232

K

kakocracy, 345
knowledge
 aggregation, 275, 309
 alignment, 316
 codification, 57, 316
 common, 318
 diversity, 318
 gap, 55
 management, 311, 315, 320
KQML, 26

L

language
 action, 29, 239
 agent communication, 26
law, 25, 52, 134, 246, 317, 327
 Goodhart's, 266
 of thermodynamics, second, 48
 rule of, 13
legislation, 336, 338
legitimate claims, 216, 219–220, 296

M

majoritarian tyranny, 60, 279, 312,
 326, 330
majority, 190
 absolute, 105
 relative, 105
Marx, Karl, 13, 52, 94, 109, 136, 193,
 210, 224, 267, 305, 324
MASON, 35
matrix form, 76
mechanism design, 174
methodology
 biologically-inspired, 14–15, 42
 sociologically-inspired, 14–15, 182,
  251, 328
mirror test, 52
modeless, 160
morphogenesis, 42

N

neo-colonialism, 267
Netlogo, 35
network
 ad hoc, 60, 168, 249, 251
 centrality, 288
 effect, 194, 267, 287
 fully connected, 289
 random graph (Erdös-Rényi),
  291, 331
 ring, 289
 scale-free (Barabási-Albert), 293
 small-world (Watts-Strogatz), 292
 social, 286, 295

Nobel Prize for Economic Science, 200
norm, 28, 54, 147, 183, 254, 260, 271, 323
  fairness, 93
norm-governed multi-agent system (NG-MAS), 28

O

obligation, 28, 35, 126, 145
oligarchy, 312, 330
open society, 13
opinion, 286, 298
opinion formation, 284, 286, 330
optimisation, 185
organisation, 53, 55
Ostrom, Elinor, 98, 199, 202, 227
ownership, 17, 137, 185

P

paradox
  Anscombe's, 120
  Braess, 95
  no show, 119
  of enrichment, 96
  of self-amendment, 197, 314
  Simpson's, 120
permission, 28, 35, 126, 145
personhood, 52, 246
planned emergence, 87
Plato, 13
plurality, 105, 216
policy, 8, 58, 317
political meta-game, 98
political science, 311
polycentricity, 8, 193
Popper, Karl, 13, 32, 193
power law, 293
preference relation, 76
preferential attachment, 294
PreSage-2, 35, 38, 140, 199, 225, 264
price of anarchy, 81
price of stability, 81
principle
  balancing, 238
  difference, 211
  efficiency, 211
  equal opportunity, 211
  greatest equal liberty, 211
  no asshole, 207
  participation, 234
  transparency, 238
principled
  operationalisation, 16
  violation of policy, 323
Prisoners' Dilemma, 85
profile, 104
Prolog, 35, 183, 197, 224, 298, 328
provision, 7, 164, 181, 208

Q

Q-learning, 62
Qu-Prolog, 18, 45, 289, 294
quantum theory
  feminist, 201
quasi-stable, 48, 331

R

rapid prototyping, 224
rationality, 89
Rebel Without a Cause, 83
reflection, 31, 53, 55, 62, 129, 241, 324
regimentation, 132, 147
reinforcement, 190
relevant expertise aggregation, 320, 322, 324
Repast, 35
resources
  common-pool, 168
  conceptual, 246, 261, 268
  endogenous, 12, 58, 216
Rete, 38
retributivism, 226
rights, 29
  exogenous, 211
  human, 319
  minimal recognition of, 191

Robert's Rules of Order, 123, 128, 154, 232
Roman Senate, 110
rule
  aggregation, 104
  conventional, 5, 51, 128, 131, 180, 242, 260, 324
  Coombs, 115
  Hare, 114
rules
  collective choice, 175
  constitutional choice, 175
  dilemma of, 312
  mutable/immutable, 328
  operational choice, 175
Run-Time Event Calculus (RTEC), 35

S

sanction, 34, 125, 146, 182, 189, 230, 283
sanctions
  graduated, 227
satisfaction, 61, 217–218, 296
self, 52–53
self-*, 42
self-awareness, 53
self-determination, 12
self-organisation, 48, 51, 265
  dimensions of, 56
  parameter, 60, 62
  policy, 62, 66
Shapley value, 96
SimDemopolis, 328
simulation, 35, 253, 264
SmartHouse, 6, 43, 259
SmartMeter, 7, 43
social
  construction, 245
social capital, 196, 259, 265
social decision, 104
social influence, 287
social welfare maximisation, 80
solution concept, 78
stages of action, 160

stigmergy, 23, 42
strategy
  dominant, 78
  mixed, 79
  Nash equilibrium, 78
  Pareto optimal, 79
  pure, 79
structuration, 51
subtractability, 169
superrationaliy, 89
supply chain, 249
sustainability, 58, 163
swarms, 45
system
  autonomic, 135
  community energy, 6, 8, 58, 259, 345
  cyber-physical, 3, 10, 160, 320
  multi-agent, 22–23, 264
  open, 10, 13
  self-harming, 345
  situated, 17
  socio-technical, 3, 10, 160, 168, 320
system of systems, 193

T

taxation, 192
teleology, 39
theorem
  Arrow's impossibility, 120, 128
  Condorcet jury, 279, 321
  folk, 89
  Gödel's incompleteness, 129
  Gibbard–Satterthwaite, 121
  recursive system, 55
The Big Bang Theory, 166
The Seventh Seal, 71
theory
  Game, 71, 99
  of distributive justice, Rescher's, 215, 217
  Ostrom institution, 163, 202
  Social Choice, 101, 129
  social construction, 245
  Speech Act, 26

thesis
  Suber's, 198
  zero contribution, 173
tragedy of the anti-commons, 208
tragedy of the commons, 173
trust, 11, 248, 253
  socio-cognitive, 251
Turing machine, 47
tyranny, 312, 330, 345
  majoritarian, 344

U

uncertainty, 249–250
usability heuristics, 159
utilitarianism, 75, 211, 226
utility, 57, 74, 170, 208, 243, 251, 296
  cardinal, 75
  ordinal, 75

V

values, 265, 271–272, 317
viable systems model, 55

voting
  Borda count, 219
  protocol, 123
voting procedure, 104
  approval, 116
  Borda count, 113
  Copeland Scoring, 116
  D'Hondt method, 116
  instant runoff, 114
  plurality, 112
  runoff, 113

W

welfare economics, 211
wicked problem, 10
wisdom of crowds, 60
Wittgenstein, L., 27